Remembering the First World War

Remembering the First World War brings together a group of international scholars to understand how and why the past quarter of a century has witnessed such an extraordinary increase in global popular and academic interest in the First World War, both as an event and in the ways it is remembered.

The book discusses this phenomenon across three key areas. The first section looks at family history, genealogy and the First World War, seeking to understand the power of family history in shaping and reshaping remembrance of the war at the smallest levels, as well as popular media and the continuing role of the state and its agencies. The second part discusses practices of remembering and the more public forms of representation and negotiation through film, literature, museums, monuments and heritage sites, focusing on agency in representing and remembering war. The third section covers the persistence and return of the war to contemporary politics. A series of case studies examine the re-emergence of the war in different national contexts, probing the relationship between private engagement, changing political circumstances, and the prerogatives of the state in remembrance of the war.

Placing remembrance of the First World War in its longer historical and broader transnational context and including illustrations and an afterword by Professor David Reynolds, this is the ideal book for all those interested in the history of the Great War and its aftermath.

Bart Ziino is a lecturer in history at Deakin University, Australia. His publications include *A Distant Grief: Australians, War Graves and the Great War* (2007) and the co-edited volume *The Heritage of War* (Routledge, 2012).

Remembering the Modern World
Series Editors: David Lowe and Tony Joel

The *Remembering the Modern World* series throws new light on the major themes in the field of history and memory in a global context. The series investigates relationships between state-centred practices and other forms of collective and individual memory; looks at the phenomenon of anniversaries and national days in the context of global and national identities; shows how some cities and sites play active roles in generating acts of remembrance; and asks why some phenomena and events are remembered more widely and easily than others.

Titles in the series:

Remembering the Cold War
David Lowe and Tony Joel

Remembering Genocide
Nigel Eltringham and Pam Maclean

Forthcoming titles in the series:

Remembering the Second World War
Patrick Finney and Stephan Petzold

Remembering Women's Activism
Sharon Crozier-de Rosa and Vera Mackie

Remembering the First World War

Edited by
Bart Ziino

Routledge
Taylor & Francis Group
LONDON AND NEW YORK

First published 2015
by Routledge
2 Park Square, Milton Park, Abingdon, Oxon OX14 4RN

and by Routledge
711 Third Avenue, New York, NY 10017

Routledge is an imprint of the Taylor & Francis Group, an informa business

© 2015 Bart Ziino

The right of the editor to be identified as the author of the editorial material, and of the authors for their individual chapters, has been asserted in accordance with sections 77 and 78 of the Copyright, Designs and Patents Act 1988.

All rights reserved. No part of this book may be reprinted or reproduced or utilised in any form or by any electronic, mechanical, or other means, now known or hereafter invented, including photocopying and recording, or in any information storage or retrieval system, without permission in writing from the publishers.

Trademark notice: Product or corporate names may be trademarks or registered trademarks, and are used only for identification and explanation without intent to infringe.

British Library Cataloguing in Publication Data
A catalogue record for this book is available from the British Library

Library of Congress Cataloging-in-Publication Data
A catalog record for this title has been requested

ISBN: 978-0-415-85628-7 (hbk)
ISBN: 978-0-415-85632-4 (pbk)
ISBN: 978-1-315-73843-7 (ebk)

Typeset in Bembo
by Cenveo Publisher Services

Printed and bound by CPI Group (UK) Ltd, Croydon, CR0 4YY

Contents

List of figures   vii
List of contributors   ix
Series editors' foreword   xiii
Acknowledgements   xv

Introduction: Remembering the First World War today   1
BART ZIINO

PART 1
Family history, genealogy and the First World War   19

1. **'Great-grandfather, what did *you* do in the Great War?': The phenomenon of conducting First World War family history research**   21
JAMES WALLIS

2. **Family history and the Great War in Australia**   39
CAROLYN HOLBROOK AND BART ZIINO

PART 2
Practices of remembering   57

3. **Framing the Great War in Britain: Modern mediated memories**   59
ROSS WILSON

4. **Teaching and remembrance in English secondary schools**   74
ANN-MARIE EINHAUS AND CATRIONA PENNELL

5. Museums, architects and artists on the Western Front: New commemoration for a new history? 90
ANNETTE BECKER

6. Music and remembrance: Britain and the First World War 110
PETER GRANT AND EMMA HANNA

PART 3
The return of the war 127

7. 'Now Russia returns its history to itself': Russia celebrates the centenary of the First World War 129
KAREN PETRONE

8. Çanakkale's children: The politics of remembering the Gallipoli campaign in contemporary Turkey 146
VEDICA KANT

9. Commemoration and the hazards of Irish politics 165
KEITH JEFFERY

10. Little Flemish Heroes' Tombstones: The Great War and twenty-first century Belgian politics 186
KAREN SHELBY

11. Between the topos of a 'forgotten war' and the current memory boom: Remembering the First World War in Austria 207
SABINE A. HARING

Afterword 223

Remembering the First World War: An international perspective
DAVID REYNOLDS

Index 239

Figures

1.1	'Heirlooms 4 Heroes' leaflet.	22
1.2	A photographic tribute on the Western Front.	31
5.1	Haïm Kern, 'Ils n'ont pas choisi leur sépulture' (They did not choose their tomb), Chemin des Dames, 1998.	93
5.2	Detail, Haïm Kern, 'Ils n'ont pas choisi leur sépulture' (They did not choose their tomb), Chemin des Dames, 1998.	94
5.3	Peter Corlett, 'Cobbers', Fromelles Memorial Park, 1998.	101
5.4	Detail, Peter Corlett, 'Cobbers', Fromelles Memorial Park, 1998.	102
5.5	Ernest Pignon-Ernest, Bois de Soyécourt, Somme.	105
5.6	Kingsley Baird, 'Tomb', 2013.	107
6.1	Bolt Thrower in performance.	122
6.2	Bolt Thrower, publicity shot for *Those Once Loyal*. Taken at the Royal Artillery Monument, London.	122
7.1	Winning design in the First World War monument contest held by the Russian Military History Society.	141
8.1	'Dur Yolcu!' Verse carved into the landscape visible to every visitor crossing the Dardanelles.	146
8.2	Atatürk memorial on Çanakkale battlefields. Atatürk quotes and statues dot the peninsula and serve as a reminder of how his personality is intertwined with Çanakkale's history.	152
8.3	Statue of Hüseyin Kaçmaz, the last Turkish veteran of the campaign, who also fought in the Turkish War of Independence.	154
8.4	Glass tombstones at the symbolic cemetery, opened in 2007. The tombstones create a strong sense of loss and challenge the notion that the victory was Atatürk's single-handed accomplishment.	158
9.1	Island of Ireland Peace Tower at Mesen/Messines, dedicated 11 November 1998.	172
9.2	Killarney First World War memorial (dedicated 2009). The Irish inscription reads 'Light them to eternal paradise'.	174
9.3	Cork City war memorial as restored in 2008, reproducing the original 1925 inscription, and subsequent addition of 1939–45.	177
9.4	Orange banner commemorating the 36th (Ulster Division) on the first day of the Battle of the Somme, 12 July 2012.	181

10.1 *Heldenhuldezerken* possibly in Oeren. 187
10.2 A damaged *heldenhuldezerk* in the Oeren–Alveringem cemetery, 1918. 191
10.3 The IJzertoren, 23 August 1936. 193
10.4 The 1930 poster for the IJzer Pilgrimage. 197
10.5 The *heldenhuldezerk* erected behind the ruins of the first IJzertoren. 199
10.6 The 2003 poster for the IJzerwake. 203

Contributors

Annette Becker is a Professor at the University of Paris-Ouest Nanterre la Defense and a senior member of the Institut Universitaire de France. In 2013, she was a Visiting Fellow at the United States Holocaust Memorial Museum in Washington, DC. After focusing mostly on the trauma, commemoration and humanitarian aspects of the Great War (she is a member of the board of the *Review of the International Committee of the Red Cross*), Annette Becker is currently working on the links between the two world wars, especially the many aspects of occupation, the forms of violence bequeathed by the First World War to the Second, and the Second World War's own extraordinary innovations in that field. She has published two books on occupations of the Great War: *Oubliés de la Grande Guerre; Humanitaire et culture de guerre, populations occupées, déportés civils, prisonniers de guerre* (Noêsis, 1998 and 2003), and *Les cicatrices rouges, 1914–1918, France et Belgique occupées* (Fayard, 2010). She is coordinator of the French edition (Fayard) of the *Cambridge History of the Great War* (directed by Jay Winter) while working with the International Research Centre of the Historial de la Grande Guerre on the English edition.

Ann-Marie Einhaus is a Lecturer in Modern and Contemporary Literature in the Department of Humanities at Northumbria University. Her research interests lie in First World War fiction, particularly the short story and contemporary writing about the war, and her first monograph, *The Short Story and the First World War*, was published by Cambridge University Press in 2013. With a background in history as well as literary studies, she is also interested in the relationship between literature, history and memory more generally, particularly with regard to modernist as compared to mainstream writing.

Peter Grant is Senior Fellow in Grantmaking, Philanthropy and Social Investment at Cass Business School, City University. His latest book *Philanthropy and Voluntary Action in the First World War* was published by Routledge/Taylor & Francis in 2014. Forthcoming chapters include 'Popular Music Since 1960' in Ann-Marie Einhaus and Isobel Baxter (eds), *The Edinburgh Companion to the First World War and the Arts*. Peter is a trustee of the DHL Foundation and of the Amy Winehouse Foundation and former Chair of the Voluntary Action History Society.

x Contributors

Emma Hanna completed her PhD at the University of Kent in 2005 and joined the University of Greenwich where she is now a Senior Lecturer in History. Her first monograph, *The Great War on the Small Screen: Representing the First World War in Contemporary Britain*, was published by Edinburgh University Press in 2009. Emma's current research interests are focused on entertainment and morale on the home and fighting fronts in the First World War. Emma is a Co-Investigator on the Arts and Humanities Research Council/Heritage Lottery Fund sponsored 'Gateways to the First World War' (2014–2016), one of five national UK-based centres working to enhance engagement with the centenary of the First World War.

Sabine A. Haring is Assistant Professor at the Institute of Sociology at the Karl-Franzens-University Graz, having received her PhD in social and economic sciences studies at the University of Graz. Her main research fields are historical and political sociology, history of the nineteenth and twentieth centuries, sociological theory, sociology of emotions, and First World War studies. Recent publications include (with Helmut Kuzmics): *Emotion, Habitus und Erster Weltkrieg. Soziologische Studien zum militärischen Untergang der Habsburger Monarchie* (Göttingen: V & R Unipress, 2013); 'K. u. k. Soldaten an der Ostfront im Sommer und Herbst 1914. Eine emotionssoziologische Analyse' in *Jenseits des Schützengrabens. Der Erste Weltkrieg im Osten: Erfahrung – Wahrnehmung – Kontext*, eds Bernhard Bachinger and Wolfram Dornik (Innsbruck – Wien – Bozen: Studienverlag).

Carolyn Holbrook is a Research Fellow in the School of Social Sciences at Monash University. Her book, *Anzac: The Unauthorised Biography*, about the history of the Great War in Australian memory, was published in 2014. Her main areas of academic research are war and memory and twentieth century Australian political and cultural history. Her current project traces the history of Australian policy-making in the 1940s and 1980s, and compares historical processes with how contemporary policy is made. Carolyn has previously worked as a policy adviser in the Department of the Prime Minister and Cabinet, Canberra, and as a food and wine journalist.

Keith Jeffery is Professor of British History at Queen's University Belfast and a Member of the Royal Irish Academy. Among his books are *Ireland and the Great War* (2000), *The GPO and the Easter Rising* (2006), and the prize-winning *Field Marshal Sir Henry Wilson: A Political Soldier* (2006). His groundbreaking history, *MI6: The History of the Secret Intelligence Service 1909–1949*, was published in 2010.

Vedica Kant holds an MPhil in Modern Middle Eastern Studies from the University of Oxford, where she focused on the history of the Turkish Republic. Her thesis focused on pan-Islamic movements in the Middle East and South Asia during the Cold War. She also has a BSc in Economics and Political Science from Singapore Management University. She has written widely on Turkish and South Asian history, politics and culture including for *The Turkish Review*, *The Majalla*, *Asharq Al-Awsat*, *Live Mint*, *The Sunday Guardian* and *The National Geographic Traveller*. Vedica is currently also working on a book about the Indian involvement in the First World War to be published by Roli Books.

Catriona Pennell is a Senior Lecturer at the University of Exeter. She is a historian of nineteenth and twentieth century British and Irish history, with a particular focus on the social and cultural history of the First World War and British imperial activity in the Middle East since the 1880s. Catriona's research focuses on the experiences of ordinary people and communities in global war as well as the relationship between war, experience and memory. Her first book, *A Kingdom United: Popular Responses to the Outbreak of the First World War in Britain and Ireland* (Oxford University Press, 2012), was nominated for the RHS Whitfield Prize 2012 and the Economic History Society First Monograph Prize 2013.

Karen Petrone is Professor of History and Chair of the Department of History at the University of Kentucky. She is the author of *Life Has Become More Joyous, Comrades: Celebrations in the Time of Stalin* (2000) and *The Great War in Russian Memory* (2011), and has co-edited three books: *The New Muscovite Cultural History* (2009), *Gender Politics and Mass Dictatorship* (2011) and *Everyday Life in Russia Past and Present* (2014). She is currently working on a book-length project on late-Soviet and early post-Soviet war memory.

David Reynolds is Professor of International History and a Fellow of Christ's College, Cambridge. He is the author of eleven books, and three edited or co-edited volumes. His most recent book, *The Long Shadow: The Great War and the Twentieth Century* (2014), examines the legacies of the Great War for the twentieth century, and was awarded the 2014 Hessell–Tiltman Prize. He has also written and presented nine historical documentaries for BBC TV, ranging across the international history of the twentieth century, as well as the award-winning BBC Radio 4 series *America, Empire of Liberty*.

Karen Shelby is an Assistant Professor of Art History at Baruch College, City College of New York. Her research focuses on the visual culture of the Great War with an emphasis on the memory of the conflict in Belgium, specifically Flemish nationalism. In her publications she addresses the cultural politics of exhibition narratives of the war in museums along the Western Front; memorials and cemetery design; and the role of pilgrimage in First World War mourning practice.

James Wallis is currently completing his doctoral research at the University of Exeter, as part of an Arts and Humanities Research Council funded collaborative partnership with Imperial War Museums London. His project examines key permanent and temporary exhibitions of the First World War held within the museum over a fifty-year timeframe. It includes an ethnographic documentation that investigates the exhibition-making process behind the new permanent First World War galleries that opened in July 2014. His research interests include the cultural memory of this conflict and its commemoration within battlefield landscapes.

Ross Wilson is a Senior Lecturer in Modern History and Public Heritage at the University of Chichester. He has written on the experience, representation and memory of the First World War in Britain and the United States. His wider research focuses on issues of museum, media and heritage representations in the modern era. This work has been published in the books *Representing Enslavement and Abolition in Museums* (2011), *Landscapes of the Western Front* (2012) and *Cultural Heritage of the Great War in Britain* (2013).

Bart Ziino is a Lecturer in History in the School of Humanities and Social Sciences at Deakin University. He is the author of *A Distant Grief: Australians, War Graves and the Great War* (2007), *The Heritage of War* (co-edited, 2012) and several studies of Australian remembering of the Great War, both by those who experienced it and by their descendants. He is currently engaged in several projects, including a history of private sentiment and experience in Australia during the Great War, and a collaborative study of Australian extraterritorial war heritage.

Series editors' foreword

Organized thematically, this ambitious new series takes a broad view of what constitutes remembering great historical events and phenomena in the late modern period (i.e. since 1789). Volumes in the series draw on such things as: ceremonies associated with anniversaries and national days; episodes of memorialization and commemoration including museum exhibitions; filmic representations and popular culture; public discourse and debate as shaped and reflected by speeches of political and civic leaders; and school curricula *et cetera*. *Remembering the Modern World* makes a fresh contribution to memory studies by placing much emphasis on narrative (with substantive introductory chapters addressing the main theoretical and methodological issues), and by drawing on the strengths of complementary disciplines including History, Cultural Heritage, Anthropology, Journalism Studies, Sociology, International Relations and Law. To complement the text, wherever appropriate volumes are encouraged to make widespread use of maps, timelines, illustrations, and especially photographs taken by contributing authors during field research.

The series offers a comparative glance across the contemporary world in a manner that explores both the reach of globalization and the insistence of localizing forces. As for themes projected for examination throughout the series, these include *inter alia* war and peace, genocide, political and social emancipation, imperialism, decolonization, terrorism, sporting triumphs, tragedies and rivalries, heroes and villains, political revolutions and constitutional crises, and feminism.

Each book in the series will start with an overview of the most significant theoretical and methodological approaches historians and other scholars have deployed in relation to the kind of material being explored within the volume. The aim is to sketch the theoretical and methodological landscape, enabling interested readers to follow key references to what has become a well-theorized field. The substantive chapters/sections thereafter might be theoretically suggestive, but primarily focus on presenting narrative constructed around whatever case studies are being remembered.

Remembering the Modern World throws new light on key themes for students, scholars, and general readers of contemporary history. The series aims to: provide greater understanding of relationships between state-centred practices and other forms of shared or common memories; examine the phenomenon of anniversaries and national days in the contexts of global and national identities; explore the 'transition zones' between narrative histories and explorations of history's significance in contemporary societies; and ponder why some phenomena and events are remembered more widely and easily than others. In its ambitious geographical and topical reach, the series suggests connections and invites new research questions that inform further historical inquiry.

David Lowe
Tony Joel

Acknowledgements

Thanks are due firstly to Tony Joel and David Lowe, series editors, for their invitation to propose and edit a collection on this theme. It has been a rewarding opportunity, and I am grateful for their faith and advice.

At Routledge, I have been grateful for the support of Senior Editor Eve Setch, and particularly for Amy Welmers' diligent and good-humoured shepherding of this book through its production.

At its best, editing a volume is a process of making friends, and being intellectually challenged by contributors who not only work to the principles of the project, but probe and extend them. I thank the contributors to this book for doing just this, for seeing the potential of the work, and for entrusting their own efforts to it. I thank them too for their forbearance, especially those who tolerated my repeated probing of their work, and requests that some new eventuation be considered. I hope they feel suitably repaid for their efforts.

A number of colleagues and friends at Deakin University have provided the intellectual and collegial support necessary for all academic pursuits. In the making of this volume, they have been a catalogue of friendly ears to occasional moans of complaint and – echoing those who emerged from the war itself – cries of 'never again'. In particular I would like to thank Greg Burgess, Helen Gardner, Tiffany Shellam, Matthew Richards and Chris Waters.

The Alfred Deakin Research Institute provided funding for translation of Annette Becker's work, and I am grateful to Helen McPhail for her highly competent work in this task.

My greatest debt is to my family for their love and support. Thank you, Jenny, Thea and Ted. For you, a book is not suitable recompense, but I hope you like it.

Introduction
Remembering the First World War today

Bart Ziino

'Remembering the First World War' is an expansive topic, and one that has already produced an extraordinary and diverse array of scholarly inquiry. The centenary of the First World War has naturally been a source of considerable debate and stimulus – at least among academics and politicians, and in cultural institutions – for a long time before its realization in 2014 and beyond. That debate has been premised on the obligations, opportunities and not infrequently the anxieties that are entailed in the determination to mark the centenary of the first of the twentieth century's two catastrophic global conflicts. The politics of the centenary divide between those who see opportunities to remind their (usually national) communities of the significance of their wartime past, and invoke their obligation to remember in that vein; those concerned to complicate that past, to challenge older conceptions of events, to rework contemporary relationships with the First World War; and those who prefer either to oppose or ignore the event altogether. This volume takes its cue from that contemporary debate, recognizing that we are now beyond living memory of the war, and yet to all appearances still fascinated by it, and by our own links to its events. That persistent fascination with the war has been rendered by key scholars as a form of resistance to the loss of its living links, and an effort to re-imagine and reassert our connections to the conflict.[1] The politics of that effort remain insistent: what meanings do individuals and societies engaged in remembering the war attribute to the events and experiences of a century ago? In responding to this question, *Remembering the First World War* focuses on contemporary practices of remembering the war; it seeks to expose the processes by which the war is being remembered today, by whom, and for what purposes.

The tools for this inquiry are familiar: government agencies are managing key commemorative events surrounding the outbreak of the war, major battles and the armistice; new memorials are being constructed on and away from the battlefields; historians are emerging from a plethora of academic conferences and entering the mainstream media with invocations to join in a debate over the complexity of the war and its legacies; museum curators tread a fine line between the expectations of both in their efforts to engage their various publics without antagonizing any one section of them. Film-makers and novelists seek for truths beyond the historian's constraints of evidence. For those historians who observe, there will be continuing opportunities to investigate the production and reception of official and unofficial narratives of war, an opportunity that historians in this volume are taking on the very cusp of the centenary.

At the point of the centenary of the First World War, one could easily detect a wide spectrum of attitudes in public forums. The Canadian historian Jack Granatstein, for instance, insisted that not only did Canadians 'need to remember' the war but, rather prescriptively, that 'We really must remember the Great War properly.'[2] Eminent British historian Hew Strachan looked forward to a more open public and academic engagement with the centenary, such that 'If we do not emerge at the end of the process in 2018 with fresh perspectives, we shall have failed.'[3] Others turned their back on the centenary altogether, fearing that its marking would be nothing more than a parochial and narrowly nationalist celebration. In *The Guardian* in January 2014, journalist and broadcaster Simon Jenkins had already apologized to Germans for an anticipated 'avalanche of often sickening Great War memorabilia, largely at their expense. ... The horror, the mistakes, the cruelty, the crassness of war will be revived over and over again, "lest we forget".' Finally, he asked, 'Can we really not do history without war?'[4]

This kind of debate – conducted here within newspaper columns – certainly has its analogue in the broader public, though there remain fundamental questions to be asked about the nature of public engagement with the First World War more generally. Leading into the centenary a number of surveys of popular knowledge of the war suggested that for those engaged in remembering the First World War, there was something to worry about in terms of public receptiveness. In Australia, where war commemoration enjoys a privileged relationship with ideas about national identity, focus group investigation in 2010 revealed that 'There is almost no awareness or anticipation of the impending 100th World War I anniversaries, including the Gallipoli landings and Anzac Day.'[5] Knowledge of Australia's war history, the report found, was 'generally poor', and declined across age cohorts, though even older Australians 'often have only sketchy or incorrect knowledge'.[6] Not quite half of the Canadians questioned in 2014 could identify Vimy Ridge as a significant battle of the First World War, and war knowledge very quickly diminished from there.[7]

In Britain too, the research think tank British Future found that despite politicians' claims about the centrality of the war to national consciousness, 'what is in fact evident is how little most people know about a conflict that now seems extremely distant and which is often either supplanted by, or conflated with, the second world war'.[8] The even more expansive polling – in seven countries – commissioned by the UK's British Council, showed similar levels of ignorance, though with local variations.[9] On the other side of the coin, interestingly, polling in Germany suggested broad interest in the First World War, especially among those aged 14–29.[10] All this should not necessarily incline us to the view that ignorance necessarily means apathy: the more significant finding is that despite lapses in discrete knowledge, individuals across age cohorts tended to express a belief – whether sincerely held or socially expected – that the centenary *ought* to be marked in a significant way.[11] And indeed, in Australia at least, social researchers found that 'People do not want detailed historical information', so much as a knowledge of key events and attitudes. There were, however, 'quite strong opinions about how ... commemorations should (and should not) feel'.[12]

That emphasis on feeling is important, especially as none of the combatants of that war remain now to speak directly of their experiences or their conception of the event. Yet the past quarter of a century has witnessed an extraordinary increase in popular and academic interest in the Great War as an event, and in the ways it is represented. Since the 1990s, in several victor nations at least, we have seen increases in attendance at and participation in the anniversaries of the war, burgeoning output of popular histories, novels and films, and increasing political attention to the war in school curricula and commemorative events. Even in potentially less fertile fields, such as Germany, there are those ready to insist on the state's obligation to confront the past, though based on a leftist concern to perpetuate the message 'No more war!'[13] How do we explain this phenomenon? Part of the answer must be, as David Reynolds points out, that the end of the Cold War decoupled the First World War from the Second, and the persistence with which 'the twentieth century kept reshaping the Great War in its own light', thus encouraging an effort to again understand the First World War in its own terms. For Reynolds, the passing of the remaining veterans of the First World War has rendered the task at the centenary 'not so much remembrance as understanding'.[14] And yet people are taking part in forms of remembrance, on a series of levels, to which strong emotions are attached and felt. We must then remain sensitive to the ways in which remembering the war occurs, what meanings are being transmitted, and how understanding of the war is received in the early twenty-first century.

The production of war memory

Several important scholars have in recent years made significant efforts at theorizing our contemporary relationships with the First World War. In doing this they are building on academic endeavours centred on recovering the experiences of those who, during and after the war, conducted their own forms of commemoration, in their own historically specific conditions. This project has led to a much more nuanced understanding of the dynamism of commemoration of an event that engaged entire populations not only in the passions of war, but in the desolation of loss and bereavement. The discourse on 'memory' – variously configured – has helped to drive this work, and its key features require some elaboration here, in order to understand the current practices of First World War remembrance being conducted around the world. Jay Winter's scholarship has been critical. One of the more helpful contributions to memory studies in the last decade and more is his observation that among its practitioners few use the term 'memory' in the same way. This is helpful, because one of the more fundamental problems has been a disassociation between individuals who remember events that they experienced, and the social forces that in their turn shape and reshape private memories over time. The relationship between private memory and the loosely-defined 'collective memory' is mutually constitutive: private memories are not perfect recordings of the past, but are shaped by subjective attitudes and social mores that encourage the articulation of some memories, while making others less publicly acceptable. Just as those social contexts can change over time, then, memory itself can change over time. Hiving off the public signs and symbols of 'collective memory' from the production of that memory – in the actions of individuals and communities as much as the state – threatens to hollow out the value of memory as a category of analysis.

For this reason Winter has advocated investing the term 'memory' with a greater sense of agency, and indeed to prefer 'remembrance' as a better descriptor of the processes of memory-making. One can more profitably refer to the acts of 'remembering' and 'forgetting', rather than to the simple existence of 'memory', especially 'collective memory', in understanding the dynamism and the politics of memory. This distaste for the passive voice has insisted on a much more responsible examination of how memory is shaped and transmitted in its social and political contexts. As Joanna Bourke has observed, 'individuals "remember", "repress", "forget" and "are traumatized", not societies ... The collective does not possess a memory, only barren sites upon which individuals inscribe shared narratives, infused with power relations'.[15] Thus does Winter make his preference for 'remembrance' over passive terms:

> To privilege 'remembrance' is to insist on specifying agency, on answering the question who remembers, when, where, and how? And on being aware of the transience of remembrance, so dependent on the frailties and commitments of the men and women who take the time and effort to engage in it.[16]

In this concern, Winter was enriching the work of other scholars who were insisting that what was required was closer attention to the processes of memory-making, especially the relationship between private and public memory, and the reception of the narratives so produced. Alon Confino observed that the study of memory had bifurcated, and concerned itself separately with personal testimonies on one hand, and the representation of the past and shared cultural knowledge by succeeding generations on the other. This ignored the problem of why 'some pasts triumph while others fail ... Why do people prefer one image of the past over another?'[17] Similarly, Jan Assmann was concerned with the processes of transmitting particular conceptions of the past to subsequent generations when he developed a working definition of 'cultural memory'. In this conception, cultural memory reflected a process that sought to fix the meanings and significance of particular events beyond the lifetimes of those who experienced them. Here, wrote Assmann, was 'a collective concept for all knowledge that directs behaviour and experience in the interactive framework of a society and one that obtains through generations in repeated societal practice and initiation'.[18] Where private memory shapes identity, so too does cultural memory, though on much broader scales, through the cultural channels available to mass society, including memorials, ceremonies, museums, film and literature.

The selectivity involved in this process is important; it demands recognition of the politics of memory and, by extension, the agency of those who work to have their particular memories of war recognized in public. Further, acknowledging the existence of agents of remembrance does not presuppose equal power in shaping popular understandings of the meaning of events. T. G. Ashplant, Graham Dawson and Michael Roper, in particular, have elaborated on the nature of the contest conducted between the state, communities and individuals in shaping the wartime past. The politics of war memory, they contend, refers to an unequal power struggle, in which memory is installed at the centre of a cultural world, through that variety of cultural channels:

> The politics of war memory and commemoration is precisely the struggle of different groups to give public articulation to, and hence gain recognition for, certain memories and the narratives within which they are structured. The history of war memory and commemoration involves tracing the outcomes of particular struggles, as represented both by those memories which are publicly articulated, and by those which have been privatized, fragmented or repressed.[19]

The struggles over war memory remind us that the narratives attached to the First World War are not static, or agreed, but are subject to constant contestation, and change over time. This is in the nature of cultural memory, and in recognizing this, we can see the life histories of remembering, at a series of levels – public, private, institutional – and the cultures of remembrance that those processes have bequeathed to the present. In other words, remembering and giving meaning to the past has a history of its own, which can be tracked over time, both for individuals, and for broader social formations.[20] Thus our relationship with the First World War is not simply a relationship between now and the events of 1914–18, but one informed by the processes of transmission of familial and cultural memory in the intervening years.

How do we understand 'remembering' beyond living memory?

Acknowledging the importance of generational transmission of war memory allows us to look more closely at those who continue to 'make' remembrance today, especially as we are now all but entirely disconnected from those with a living memory of the war itself. In one sense, we should expect that as witnesses to the First World War pass away, the cultural memory of the war that remains should become more and more ossified and fixed. The survival of particular narratives of the past is dependent on their engaging with individual memories, which are in turn shaped by those broader narratives.[21] Dan Todman has sensitively charted the rarefying of remembering the war over several generations in Britain, in which the links to direct experience of the war and all its personal complexities have drawn away. In their place, private and detailed understanding of the war has been increasingly populated with national myths developed and redeveloped over the decades following the war. In this, the war becomes 'more of a symbol – easily shared and commonly understood – than a multi-faceted, personally remembered event'.[22] In a similar way, Harald Wydra refers to the initiation of new generations into cultural memory, in which 'Societies, like individuals, "learn" habitual acts of performance by forgetting the exact circumstances' in which such acts are historically and personally located.[23] Such habits of commemoration can be fostered by official ceremonies and memorials, which take on a semblance of concretizing what it is that is not to be forgotten, and so can facilitate a process of disengaging from actual events, while maintaining a sense of dedication to their ostensible meaning.[24] The process here is one of gradual consolidation of complex past realities into a broadly accepted symbolic currency, that yet retains a sensibility that it reflects events worthy of remembrance.

And yet that process – inevitable as it may ultimately be – has not proceeded as relentlessly as we might expect. With the deaths of the last veterans, we are not seeing a transition 'from memory to history', so much as between different forms of remembering. The question that has come to occupy historians, given the persistent interest in the First World War, is this: if there are no participants or witnesses left, how do we explain what we describe as 'remembering'? The short answer is that those who engage in remembrance simply cannot be remembering a war in which they had no part. On the other hand, they are certainly remembering something, and in this they are again remaking the narratives attached to the war. The loss of the last veterans thus becomes a catalyst for the production of new memories of the past, with new modes of production. Stéphane Audoin-Rouzeau and Annette Becker describe the critical moment in which access to witness testimonies suddenly diminished: 'Then the 1970s and 1980s swept away that version of the war for good. Like it or not, the umbilical cord was severed.'[25] In its place is something requiring more precise terminology than 'memory' alone can muster. Rejecting the idea that individual experiences of war can be transmitted to subsequent generations, Dan Todman argued that 'historians need to pay particular attention to *who* is remembering *what*, to traditions in remembrance and the means by which these are communicated and transmitted, rather than how later generations might inherit ancestral experience'.[26] That is, we need to understand the processes by which we reconstruct the past in the present, rather than how participants' memories might somehow be perfectly transmitted and received by succeeding generations. In this sense, Todman insists that we must make key distinctions between the 'experienced and unexperienced past', and this has led him – and others – to question the utility of the term 'remembering' for those born after the events at hand.[27] These are, indeed, processes of a different order and quality to the acts of remembrance conducted by those who themselves participated in the war.

Here, recourse to Winter's distinction between memory and remembrance becomes more useful again, in that where memory is the preserve of those with direct experience of the war, remembrance allows for the act of remembering – the construction and reconstruction of the past – to be conducted both by those with and those without that experience. To meet the current situation, in which we are actively making meaning of the wartime past without any direct connection to it, Winter has proposed the term 'historical remembrance'. 'Historical remembrance', he explains,

> is a way of interpreting the past which draws on both history and memory, on documented narratives about the past and on the statements of those who lived through them. Many people are active in this field. Historians are by no means in the majority.[28]

The agents of historical remembrance, as Winter says, can be historians, though they share the field with film-makers, novelists, architects, curators and others involved in cultural production. These latter do not necessarily share historians' obligations to produce evidence, and this may be one factor that gives historical remembrance such vitality and persistence. As Graeme Davison has observed, the myths of the war 'might flourish even more luxuriantly when ... freed from the limitations of historical fact and the human frailties of its surviving representatives. Feeling connected to the past, after all, is not at all the same as being connected with history'.[29]

As Davison shows, having defined the issue, the task is to explain it. Why has remembrance persisted so powerfully? To this end Winter has labelled the popular fascination with the past and its actors the 'memory boom'. He tracks two such 'booms', the latest of which emerged in the 1970s, and has been intense and enduring. Taking its cue from the Second World War and the Holocaust, its preoccupations are with remembering the victims of the violent twentieth century. An increasing recognition and acceptance of the traumatizing effects of war on individuals, and of their traumatic memories, has brought these people – witnesses – to the centre of how remembering the past has been conducted in the late twentieth and early twenty-first centuries. Their testimonies are valued for their access to traumas that must be acknowledged and, as Winter observes, 'their stories and their telling of them in public are historical events in their own right'.[30] In terms of the First World War, we remain obsessed with 'the soldier's story', though as a witness the soldier has increasingly taken on the persona of the victim – of the generals, of the guns, of societies that failed to appreciate them. Understood this way, Winter has characterized the current memory boom as an act of resistance to that drawing away of direct experience of the past that is all too apparent to those who remain. Morbid count-downs to the last veterans of the First World War were only one, if very obvious, sign of that awareness.[31] While Winter too could predict the ultimate if gradual emptying of meaning from sites of memory created after the war, he suggested that the memory boom of the late twentieth century 'may be understood as an act of defiance, an attempt to keep alive at least the names and the images of the millions whose lives have been truncated or disfigured by war'.[32] Thus would sites of memory created in the urgent need to find meaning and comfort immediately after the war 'inevitably become sites of second-order memory, that is, they are places where people remember the memories of others, those who survived the events marked there'.[33]

That effort at prolongation is not simply a mimicry of the memories of others; it is an effort at remaking the past in ways that preserve the affective power of participants' memories. Marianne Hirsch's theory of postmemory speaks to those who resist the homogenization of cultural memory, especially the children of witnesses to the past, who 'remember' those same events only through the stories and images with which they grew up, and their own observations of the continuing effects of past events on parents. Hirsch willingly concedes that postmemory is not the same as memory – it is constituted not by recall, but by 'imaginative investment' – but insists that it shares the emotional force of participants' memories, and so needs to be taken seriously as a form of remembering the past.[34] The widespread practice of family history might also be understood as a mode of 'imaginative investment' in the past, with the potential for such emotive connections. Its extraordinary escalation has prompted Dan Todman to suggest that remembering the war as a significant event will be prolonged through those processes of family history: family memory, and the preservation apparatus that supports it – in the form of state archives, personal papers, photographs and memorabilia – helps facilitate a sense of individual engagement with the war, even beyond the capacity of families to do so from their own resources. It is those supports to family history research, he suggests, which may well become the ultimate markers of First World War remembrance in Britain, as they attempt to compensate for the loss of living links to the conflict.[35]

Conceiving of continuing popular interest in the First World War as defiance of the ossification of memory helps us to begin to understand the activities of the agents of remembrance today. There is no sense of condescension here, nor doubting that genuine feelings of connection to the past exist, though as the children of the war generation – the generation so critical in shaping the myths of the war that continue to resonate today – are themselves passing away, we are now obliged to grapple with the ways in which generations without direct connection to those who fought are reconstructing their relationship with the war. This is the concern of *Remembering the First World War*. The book is organized around three key themes, each providing scope to interrogate contemporary production and reception of narratives about the war, at a series of levels and in different international contexts. Part 1 reduces the focus immediately to individuals and their endeavours to engage the wartime past through the practices of family history. Part 2 is concerned with a series of cultural media through which individuals and the agents of cultural production – including the state, novelists, artists, curators and musicians – come into contact and negotiate their efforts at meaning-making in the twenty-first century. Part 3 takes a broader perspective still as it investigates the formulation and reformulation of national narratives relating to the war, especially where those narratives have been in contest or repressed. Taking long perspectives on the histories of remembrance in several different contexts, this section of the book exposes keenly how very much alive are the politics of memory surrounding the global conflict of a century ago.

Part 1: Family history, genealogy and the First World War

The great problem for historians today, as I have suggested above, is to understand the persistence of interest and the genuine sense of connection individuals still feel to the wartime past. Perhaps in no other way is the intensity of that interest in the First World War more evident than in the boom in family history, and the emphasis on individual stories of war that pervades the war's public representations. While the reasons for the explosion in genealogy are of course much broader than an interest in the war itself, the First World War is a critical node around which family history comes into contact with national and international narratives of the past. In Britain, surveys in 2013 found that, despite patchy knowledge of the war, significant numbers of people (almost half) were aware of a family connection to the First World War, while the greater part of the remainder simply did not know if such a connection existed.[36] What this suggests is not just the potential but the reality that families remain key sites at which the past and present converge, and reshape each other. As Jay Winter has observed:

> the richest texture of remembrance was always within family life. This intersection of the public and the private, the macro-historical and the micro-historical, is what has given commemoration in the twentieth century its power and its rich repertoire of forms.[37]

It is also the case that personal memories – even simply an awareness – of family members who encountered the war give affective power to remembering in the present, as the resonances of the war that were visible in ancestors' lives become the substance of remembrance. Winter is rightly insistent on the importance of family transmission of stories about the past to the sustenance of broader narratives. Without such engagement with the past on these levels, public ceremonies can do little to prevent the atrophy of remembrance.[38]

There are two key themes to observe in this section, both revolving around the relationship between family historians and broader public narratives of the war. The first is the impact of a broad recognition in government and cultural institutions of the public appetite for family history as a means of engaging the past, and the subsequent provision of family history resources in ever greater quantities, and with ever greater ease of access. This is a truly international phenomenon that one might trace through the series of local and national archives that have been busily digitizing individual service records, to the efforts to collect and present private records of the war for a mass audience, a theme that has so marked the extraordinary efforts of the 'Europeana 14–18' European database project.[39] This feeds into the second theme, which is the collaboration between family historians and more powerful cultural agents in making meaning of the past, a process that is becoming clearer in the forums established by cultural institutions that allow users to articulate their responses to family history in concert and comparison with others. The rehearsing of family narratives of the First World War thus proceeds much more openly, though not without a level of guidance from the institutions that facilitate it.

In pursuing this analysis, chapters in this section pick up not only Winter's point above, but Ashplant, Dawson and Roper's observation that it is the interaction between different agencies of remembering, rather than individual remembering per se, that will become the matter for analysis beyond living memory of the war.[40] James Wallis thus considers the ways in which amateur family history can reshape the contours of modern First World War remembrance, through a study that combines an emphasis on the post-living-memory generation and its capacities to 'know' the wartime past, with the work of those who frame First World War history through making particular resources available in particular ways. This includes the Imperial War Museum's 'Lives of the First World War' project, which has substantial aims in seeking 'to engage everyone in remembering' through family history.[41] Carolyn Holbrook and Bart Ziino's concerns are similar, in seeing a mutually constitutive relationship between the conduct of family history in Australia, and the powerful public narratives of the war that offer broader contexts for that research. They nevertheless argue for a recognition of the significant agency of family historians, even those without direct knowledge of ancestors, in shaping war knowledge in the present.

Part 2: Practices of remembering

If family history is one key process of remembrance, then more public forms of representation and negotiation also require investigation. In Part 2, the focus is much more squarely on those involved in cultural production in public: not the faceless 'state', but a whole series of professionals and artists who engage in transmitting and, often, questioning versions of the past, including teachers, politicians, historians, curators, artists, architects and musicians. Such people are centrally placed in the struggle over war memory, by choice or otherwise. Indeed they are central to Winter's conception of 'historical remembrance', as they provide some key shared opportunities for conceptions of the past to be reflected, contrasted and reshaped as part of communal, national and transnational groups.

Authors in this section take a broad approach to understanding the war's more recent cultural products, and the national and transnational histories from which they have emerged. In what ways are public representations of the First World War serving national and international audiences? New memorials, new exhibitions, amended education curricula, as well as new books, films, music and television documentaries and dramatizations are some of the hallmarks of centenary activity around the world, as people mobilize their resources to engage in what they expect will be a potent and focused period of opportunities for remembrance of the war and its participants. Already some of the themes of that mobilization can be seen in particular quarters, especially in Europe, where the centenary has provoked a rhetoric of fraternity and unity, while some of the tensions of the war, its origins and outcomes, remain difficult to paper over. This is particularly evident in the plethora of exhibitions opened in readiness for August 2014. An exhibition in Brussels entitled *14–18, It's Our History!* focused on both the Belgian and European dimensions of the struggle, claiming that 'The entirety of Europe's history emerged from the First World War.'[42] In Germany and Austria, exhibitions have promoted a sense of common experience across borders. An exhibition at the Austrian National Library speaks to the 'common past' of the countries of the former empire; a joint French/German exhibition seeks to examine not only the differences between the combatants that sustained the conflict, but 'also how similar the experiences of the soldiers and the artists who served actually were'.[43] Even the Archive of Serbia's exhibition of key documents, including the Austro-Hungarian ultimatum, drew similar sentiments, as the failure of dialogue and negotiations in 1914, and the ensuing hostilities between neighbours, framed a contemporary 'obligation to foster trust and understanding'.[44]

Still, tensions were never far below the surface. In 2013 the Serbian Prime Minister expressed fears that centenary commemorations would 'lead again to Serbian people being accused of triggering the biggest armed conflict in the history of humanity', and the European Commission abstained from organizing any commemorative events itself, as a way of avoiding immersion in potential dispute over the past.[45] French officials were sensitive to the difficulties of engaging with Germany to mark what was ultimately a German defeat and French victory, while engagement with Turkey was made even more problematic by severe diplomatic strain over recognition of the Armenian genocide. Criticisms of a low-key German approach to the centenary prompted officials at the German embassy in London to reassert that questions of guilt 'should be left more or less to historians and shouldn't feature dominantly in politicians' speeches', and that the focus of commemoration should be those who died, and on the unity of Europe fostered by the European Union.[46] And again in Serbia, a statue to Gavrilo Princip, assassin of Archduke Franz Ferdinand, was erected on the centenary of the event as a tribute to a patriot and 'freedom fighter'.

Ross Wilson's provocative chapter opens this section, turning on its head the common criticism that British remembrance of the war is too much defined by cultural products emphasizing mud and futility. He argues that such representations of war are actively selected and redeployed in contemporary British society for a series of ends, not only as a well-accepted shorthand form, but as a way of rejuvenating and reasserting a genuine sense of the trauma that accompanied the First World War as a significant event in British history and identity. Thus does Wilson assert that reference to various cultural media should be understood as framing memory, rather than reflecting the very act of remembering. Ann-Marie Einhaus and Catriona Pennell usefully broaden the scope of mediation of the war, by insisting that more people will come into contact with the First World War through school than they will through family, therefore necessitating an understanding of how knowledge of the war is transmitted through education systems. Their chapter shows the surprising complexity in English school teaching about the war, and asks how the classroom affects the transmission of 'memory' and in what ways, noting the variety of responses among teachers, and the tensions that can emerge between disciplinary approaches. As elsewhere, the First World War in the classroom is subject to the same tensions between feeling connected to the past, and being connected to history, that are seen elsewhere in the volume.

Annette Becker's contemplation of new museums and installations on the former Western Front elaborates her ongoing concerns with the representation and obscuring of violence in public art and exhibition, and the dangers of feeling and empathy overwhelming the obligations of historians.[47] Reading the Western Front as a site for the international assertion and negotiation of remembrance narratives, she is encouraged by efforts at representing the war's totality, the breadth of its impacts and the persistence of its legacies. Finally, in this section, Peter Grant and Emma Hanna interrogate the efforts to shape the aural dimensions of remembrance over time, arguing that at times music has been central to debate over war commemoration, and that it remains a potent vehicle for discussing the nature of remembrance today, through its engagement with, and occasional subversion of, changing mythologies of war in Britain. The chapter's long historical sweep allows us to see the installation of a canon of musical remembrance, as much as we might detect the same in literature and film, and its reproduction in the present through performance in private and public. Yet music promises, as much as any other medium, continued contestation and reflection on the war and contemporary relationships with it. Together these chapters offer ways of understanding not only how debate over the war is carried on, but how the experiential and emotive force of the past – even in the history classroom – is integral to popular engagement with the wartime past today.

Part 3: The return of the war

Today the war is emerging again even in political climates in which remembrance of 1914–18 previously struggled to thrive. In this final section of the book, the lens opens wider again, to examine the reconfiguration of national narratives relating to the war, in the context of long histories of contestation, dominance and repression of the narratives of war nurtured in families, communities and alternative political formulations of the nation. It aims particularly to expose how the processes of remembrance discussed in previous sections of the book have their place in defining national – and in some cases international – relationships to the war over time. The politics of memory surrounding the war in these places, as we will see, are very much alive.

In its material outcomes, the war destroyed empires and created new nations, demanding a search and a contest for new narratives of nationhood. It intervened in and aggravated domestic political divides in ways that remain palpable today; authors in this section all acknowledge this presence of the war in contemporary politics in a series of case studies that allow them to tease out the roles that efforts to acknowledge the First World War can play. Current practices must be seen in the context of long histories of remembrance, state sanctioned and not. The case studies included here are hardly exhaustive, so much as they showcase the ways in which participation in commemoration of the First World War remains a political act, as much as it also tends to private sentiment. In doing so, they speak not only to the presence of the war a generation beyond those who fought it, but its likely uses beyond its own centenary.

Karen Petrone's study of Russian efforts to reintegrate the First World War with Russian history is perhaps the most extreme example of the recuperation of a 'lost history', though she notes well that the process of recuperation is necessarily contested. Petrone's analysis of centenary projects is sensitive to the efforts of Russian elites to rehabilitate the war as a time – outside the Soviet era – when Russia was a major international power, and to the level of purchase these conceptions might gain in Russian society generally. Attention to current memorial-building projects helps to define the kind of memory the Russian state is seeking to construct, and Petrone warns that the new history of the First World War projected in public in Russia may turn out to be as partial as the one projected under the Soviets.

Vedica Kant investigates a struggle in Turkey between two narratives of the Çanakkale/Gallipoli campaign, that reflects a contemporary contest over the nature of the Turkish republic itself. Kant catalogues the long dominance of a secular narrative that sees Çanakkale as the point to which the origins of the republic, and its key figure Mustafa Kemal, can be traced. The challenge to that narrative emerges through the soft Islamism of a long-entrenched government, which is intent on highlighting the republic's religious foundations, as a way of reconciling it with a much longer Ottoman history. The public rhetoric and new memorial-making that underpin that narrative, Kant argues, have not gone uncontested, and indeed, the stakes in debate over the past remain high in Turkey.

In Ireland too, the stakes are high, and here too the war was integral to the processes of founding the Irish republic and Northern Ireland, though in the republic the war did not feature in its founding narratives. Keith Jeffery traces the several factors that made remembrance of the First World War so difficult in Ireland, while arguing that there was never total amnesia or total commitment to forgetting the war and those who participated in it. Here, the links between local agents and national myths are teased out to show the circumstances in which Irish service in the First World War can eventually find a place in the civic culture of the Irish republic. The centenaries of the war and 1916 might provide opportunities, but they are loaded too with challenges.

The politics of divided communities also inform Karen Shelby's examination of the war in Belgian politics, in which she examines Flemish commemoration of the war as an expression of dissent from incorporation in the broader Belgian state. In particular, her chapter analyses the political symbolism of a tombstone, writ large in the memorial tower erected as a symbol of Flemish sacrifice, and harnessed to demands for Flemish independence. In a Belgian state without a dominant culture of remembrance, that symbol remains today a point around which the politics of division can coalesce.

Finally, Sabine A. Haring's examination of several generations of Austrian reconstruction of the First World War returns us to the difficulties of understanding the war beyond the events that succeeded it. The National Socialist era necessarily made difficult not only reference to the Second World War, but to the First, and the 1950s saw reversion to a nostalgic vision of the Habsburg Empire. Though historians led an increasing awareness of the First World War from the 1980s, the war remained, Haring argues, confined to the margins of national narratives. Even in the midst of the centenary, the war that gave shape to modern Austria continues to be formulated anew.

Conclusion

The centenary of the First World War has several potentialities, and indeed its only certainty – as this volume attests – is that the purposes to which remembrance is put will vary widely in relation to historical and current political contexts. Where remembrance of the war has historically been persistent, we should certainly expect to see the perpetuation of existing narratives of the war, and the performance of a 'habit of commemoration', in which participants are not necessarily encouraged to look beyond what they already 'know' about the significance of the First World War. That process will be assisted, no doubt, by the emotional connections people are still making to the war, through its personalization in their own family histories, or the cultural products of the war that emphasize individual experiences as the key avenue to the wartime past. Historians might be genuinely suspicious of the capacity of personal feeling to provide the foundation for an enduring and intelligent connection to a complex past. On the other hand, the persistence of powerful emotional responses to the war and those who fought it does not immediately shut down the possibilities for the fresh perspectives that so many historians are now demanding. Rather can they provide the impetus to seek broader, more complex comprehension of the war, where it is made publicly available. In Winter's schema of historical remembrance, historians are only one group among numerous active agents; our unease about the limited space we occupy should push us to embrace our own role as makers of the past in an attempt to rework popular narratives of the war, in ways responsible to the evidence and to the people of the past. One does not want to forego the potential for directing the affective connections people are insistently making with the past, awaiting a time when the last flourishing of popular remembrance of the First World War has exhausted itself, and the field is abandoned to us. Perhaps that time is not too far away: the experiential factor may, indeed, be most telling in a remembrance event set to last more than four years. Still, those who emerge in 2018 may yet be more inclined to seek a more complex understanding of what had propelled their forebears through that original trial, and what produced the perspectives on the world that would shape the century that followed.

Notes

1 Jay Winter, *Remembering War: The Great War Between Memory and History in the Twentieth Century* (New Haven and London: Yale University Press, 2006). Dan Todman has produced an excellent synthesis of the literature; see Dan Todman, 'The Ninetieth Anniversary of the Battle of the Somme' in *War Memory and Popular Culture: Essays on Modes of Remembrance and Commemoration*, eds M. Keren and H. Herwig (North Carolina and London: McFarland & Company Inc., 2009), 23–40.
2 J. L. Granatstein, 'Why is Canada botching the Great War centenary?', *The Globe and Mail*, 21 April 2014. Online. Available HTTP: <www.theglobeandmail.com/globe-debate/why-is-canada-botching-the-great-war-centenary/article18056398> (accessed 23 June 2014).
3 Hew Strachan, 'First World War anniversary: we must do more than remember', *Daily Telegraph*, 17 January 2013. Online. Available HTTP: <www.telegraph.co.uk/history/9795881/First-World-War-anniversary-we-must-do-more-than-remember.html> (accessed 23 June 2014).
4 Simon Jenkins, 'Germany, I apologise for this sickening avalanche of first world war worship', *Guardian*, 31 January 2014. Online. Available HTTP: <www.theguardian.com/commentisfree/2014/jan/30/first-world-war-worship-sickening-avalanche?commentpage=1> (accessed 23 June 2014).
5 National Commission on the Commemoration of the Anzac Centenary, *How Australia May Commemorate the Anzac Centenary*, May 2011, 67. Online. Available HTTP: <www.anzaccentenary.gov.au/documents/anzac_centenary_report.pdf> (accessed 23 June 2014).
6 Ibid., 70.
7 'Vimy Ridge: "The birth of a nation" – but how much do Canadians know about the battle?', *Centenary News*, 8 April 2014. Online. Available HTTP: <www.centenarynews.com/article?id=1578> (accessed 23 June 2014).
8 Dan Todman, 'Did they really die for us', in *Do Mention the War: Will 1914 Matter in 2014?*, ed. Jo Tanner (London: British Future, 2013), 16. Online. Available HTTP: <www.britishfuture.org/publication/do-mention-the-war> (accessed 23 June 2014).
9 Anne Bostanci and John Dubber, *Remember the World as Well as the War* (Manchester: British Council, 2014). Online. Available HTTP: <www.britishcouncil.org/organisation/publications/remember-the-world> (accessed 23 June 2014).
10 'Young Germans are eager to learn more about WWI', Deutsche Welle, 20 January 2014. Online. Available HTTP: <www.dw.de/young-germans-are-eager-to-learn-more-about-wwi/a-17373053> (accessed 23 June 2014).
11 Strachan, 'First World War anniversary'.
12 *How Australia May Commemorate the Anzac Centenary*, 70, 67.
13 'German MP calls lack of plans to mark the First World War centenary a "scandal"', *Centenary News*, 3 March 2014. Online. Available HTTP: <www.centenarynews.com/article?id=1502> (accessed 23 June 2014).
14 David Reynolds, *The Long Shadow: The Great War and the Twentieth Century* (London: Simon & Schuster, 2013), 420.
15 Joanna Bourke, 'Introduction. "Remembering" War', *Journal of Contemporary History* 39:4 (2004), 473–4.
16 Jay Winter, *Remembering War: The Great War Between Memory and History in the Twentieth Century* (New Haven and London: Yale University Press, 2006), 3.

17 Alon Confino, 'Collective Memory and Cultural History: Problems of Method,' *American Historical Review* 102:5 (December 1997), 1390.
18 Jan Assmann, 'Collective Memory and Cultural Identity', *New German Critique* 65 (1995), 126.
19 T. G. Ashplant, Graham Dawson and Michael Roper, 'The politics of war memory and commemoration: contexts, structures and dynamic', in *The Politics of War Memory and Commemoration*, eds T. G. Ashplant, Graham Dawson and Michael Roper (London: Routledge, 2000), 16.
20 See especially Alistair Thomson, *Anzac Memories: Living with the Legend*, 2nd edn (Melbourne: Monash University Publishing, 2013).
21 Ashplant, Dawson and Roper, 18.
22 Dan Todman, *The Great War: Myth and Memory* (London: Hambledon and London, 2005), 186.
23 Harald Wydra, 'Dynamics of generational memory: understanding the east and west divide', in *Dynamics of Memory and Identity in Contemporary Europe*, eds Eric Langenbacker, Bill Niven and Ruth Wittlinger (New York: Berghahn, 2013), 15.
24 See Ashplant, Dawson and Roper, 45.
25 Stéphane Audoin-Rouzeau and Annette Becker, *14–18: Understanding the Great War*, trans. Catherine Temerson (New York: Hill and Wang, 2002), 11.
26 Todman, 'The Ninetieth Anniversary', 23.
27 Ibid., 24.
28 Winter, *Remembering War*, 9.
29 Graeme Davison, 'The habit of commemoration and the revival of Anzac Day', *ACH: Australian Cultural History* 23 (2003): 81.
30 Winter, *Remembering War*, 6.
31 Wikipedia, 'List of last surviving World War I veterans by country'. Online. Available: <http://en.wikipedia.org/wiki/List_of_last_surviving_World_War_I_veterans_by_country> (accessed 23 June 2014).
32 Winter, *Remembering War*, 12.
33 Jay Winter, 'Sites of memory and the shadow of war', in *A Companion to Cultural Memory Studies*, eds Astrid Erll and Ansgar Nüning (Berlin: De Gruyter, 2010), 62.
34 Marianne Hirsch, 'The generation of postmemory', *Poetics Today* 29:1 (2008), 106–7, 109.
35 Todman, *Great War*, 229.
36 'Polling data', in *Do Mention the War*, 33; Bostanci and Dubber, 7.
37 Winter, 'Sites of memory and the shadow of war', 65.
38 Ibid., 72.
39 See, for example 'Library and Archives Canada to digitise 640,000 First World War service files', *Centenary News*, 6 February 2014. Online. Available HTTP: <www.centenarynews.com/article?id=1430> (accessed 23 June 2014); 'Commemorations in 2014 of two World Wars', *French News Online*, 25 November 2013. Online. Available HTTP: <www.french-news-online.com/wordpress/?p=32051#axzz31THcR4bR> (accessed 23 June 2014); Europeana 1914–18. Online. Available HTTP: <www.europeana1914–18.eu/en> (accessed 23 June 2014).
40 Ashplant, Dawson and Roper, 12.
41 'Lives of the First World War remembered forever in Centenary online memorial', *Centenary News*, 21 May 2014. Online. Available HTTP: <www.centenarynews.com/article?id=1642> (accessed 23 June 2014).
42 'Major First World War Centenary exhibition opens in Belgium', *Centenary News*, 27 February 2014. Online. Available HTTP: <www.centenarynews.com/article?id=1493> (accessed 23 June 2014).
43 'Three presidents visit the Austrian National Library's First World War exhibition', *Centenary News*, 26 March 2014. Online. Available HTTP: <www.centenarynews.com/article?id=1546> (accessed 23 June 2014); 'French and German museums collaborate for

First World War exhibition', *Centenary News*, 15 April 2014. Online. Available HTTP: <www.centenarynews.com/article?id=1584> (accessed 23 June 2014).
44 'Archive of Serbia opens new exhibition to mark First World War Centenary', *Centenary News*, 9 March 2014. Online. Available HTTP: <www.centenarynews.com/article?id=1513> (accessed 23 June 2014).
45 'Centenary of Great War stirs bad memories for fractured continent', *EurActiv.com*, 2 January 2014. Online. Available HTTP: <www.euractiv.com/general/centenary-great-war-stirs-bad-me-news-532574> (accessed 23 June 2014).
46 'Germany shuns 1914 centenary', *Mail Online*, 30 December 2013. Online. Available HTTP: <www.dailymail.co.uk/news/article-2530907/Germany-shuns-1914-First-World-War-centenary-Academics-say-country-adopted-stupid-inappropriate-reluctance-commemorate-start-war.html> (accessed 23 June 2014).
47 See Audoin-Rouzeau and Becker, especially part 1. Also Christina Twomey, 'Trauma and the reinvigoration of Anzac: an argument', *History Australia* 10:3 (December 2013), 85–108.

Part 1

Family history, genealogy and the First World War

1 'Great-grandfather, what did *you* do in the Great War?'
The phenomenon of conducting First World War family history research

James Wallis

> There will soon be men and women, to whom the war is not even a memory – nothing but a great adventure just missed through an unlucky accident of birth. They'd like to know, they say; and their children's children rise in vision plying our ears with questions easy to be answered now, but unanswerable when the moss is thick on our graves.[1]

Max Plowman's 1928 forecast is coming true. The generation that fought the First World War is now gone, and yet the great-grandchildren of those who fought it would still ply the ears of their ancestors. This chapter considers how amateur family history, as a contemporary grass-roots commemorative practice, is reshaping the landscape of modern First World War remembrance. Though this conflict no longer resides within living memory, it has retained a high level of interest within academic circles, public debate and popular concern. In particular, the increasingly widespread practice of family history is transforming both public understanding and continued commemoration of the war. The availability of digitized war records online, coupled with the material remnants of wartime, offer researchers unique and highly personal understandings of the war. Furthermore, the chapter explores how such individual interpretations of the past do not always fit within wider national narratives. It contemplates how the process of enacting family history contributes towards an individual's sense of identity and ontological security through a social performance of narrative practices. This will be brought together through a discussion about the 'Lives of the First World War' digital commemoration project, which will enable the general public to uncover and share their family history research. Thus by unpacking these discourses of duty and memory, this chapter critically engages with a form of remembrance that will increasingly feature in public and private life over the course of the war's centenary.

At first glance, the leaflet shown in Figure 1.1 is perhaps an unusual place to begin an examination of the phenomenon of amateur family history and the First World War. The motifs are all fairly familiar: the sun setting on a field of crimson poppies, the abbreviated title strikingly similar to the successful British charity 'Help for Heroes', and in the centre, a slate medallion with the engraved outline

22 James Wallis

Figure 1.1 'Heirlooms 4 Heroes' leaflet. Courtesy of Allison Kesterton (www.fasttrackengraving. wix.co.uk/heroes!facilities/c66t)

of an advancing (at what looks like walking pace) British Tommy. The reverse of the leaflet reveals that these medallions can be purchased, in order to commemorate 'YOUR family member who Fought or died in WWI'. Purchasers may include personalized information about any relatives who fought, and the medallions will thus act as individually designed memorials which 'will last for generations to come'. The assertion that the object will retain a sufficient level of significance for it to resonate with families is reinforced by the somewhat insistent instructions of the twice appearing sentence, 'Don't let them Fade Away', and the more forceful invocation to 'Tell the next generation'. Admittedly, it is something of an easy target to critique the incoming – indeed already materializing – wave of commercialization in connection with the conflict's centenary which begins in the summer of 2014. But can we draw something out from this example of a highly sanitized and heroic commemorative narrative? We have reached a point where the notion of 'family heirloom' carries such value within society that it can be purchased – that even with temporal distance from the event depicted, these physical pieces of meaningful remembrance can be, quite literally, forged on demand.

The chances are that, if you are reading this chapter, you already have an impression or understanding of what your relatives did during the First World War. Discussing familial involvement may have been one of your first encounters with the conflict. Many writers and academic historians who have gone on to write about the war can trace their interest back to the process of uncovering what their relatives had done, sparking a long-burning interest in the subject. Awareness of family involvement represents a clear and evidence-based marker of one's dedication to the subject; such investigation is recognized as a symbol of status, because it culminates in knowledge that has high value within contemporary British society. It is thus commonplace for authors to dedicate their works to wartime relatives. Some provide detailed historical accounts about an individual's wartime contribution;[2] others record how the war impacted family life after 1918, as well as the more commonplace personalized textual memorials to those who did not return. For this latter category, the healing effects of time have quelled what had originally been heartfelt grief, and over the years, morphed it into intrigue. This notion has developed to such an extent that the historian David Reynolds hints at an unsaid pressure to conform, writing: 'It seems customary for historians of my generation to dedicate books about the Great War to the memory of soldierly grandparents.' In his case, Reynolds applies the trope for a particular purpose, by informing the reader that both of his grandfathers were in reserved occupations, and so 'for a book that aspires to shift our view of the Great War out of the trenches, these two men seem rather apt dedicatees'.[3] The wider point he makes is symptomatic of a desire to understand the First World War as a multi-dimensional and global event.[4] To a greater or lesser extent, members of the public are becoming more receptive to this idea. With increased interest being generated by the centenary, they are able to witness established historians expounding their views on the latest historical debates in the popular media, and in their historical works, which with High Street bookshops' requirement for high sales volumes, are now targeted as much at the public as they are towards fellow academics.

There seems little doubt that the general public's keenness to get to grips with the latest historical thinking, and learn about this subject for themselves, is unprecedented. This signals a narrowing of the gap between historians and the public – which becomes more apparent when one considers how far removed the staunch revisionist movement, led by military historians principally during the 1990s and early 2000s, was from the widespread and commonly held popular understanding of the war.[5] The more recent assertion within academic environs has been to re-adjust emphasis from the national to the global, back to its 'original 1914–18 definition … as a "world" war'.[6] This desire to move the conflict away from popular stereotypes of the Western Front, and thus expand public understanding of the war's global nature, is slowly trickling through to the grass-roots level. This has largely been due to the fact that this academic learning has been able to capitalize on the public's enthusiasm for accessing the conflict through the individual stories of those who experienced it firsthand. In response, historians have adapted a combination of these approaches to conduct research that sheds new light on previously held understandings. Catriona Pennell's research on the 1914 British public's response to the outbreak of war consciously sought to 'reconstruct the feelings, emotions and actions of the British and Irish people faced with the outbreak of war', because 'an entire population's feelings cannot be adequately described by the monolithic label of war enthusiasm'.[7] Exposing the diversity of individual experiences of the conflict in this way not only serves academic innovation, but also offers modes of engagement favoured by more general readers.

In returning to Reynolds' 'dedicatees', and the fact that their endeavours contributed towards the war effort in very different, and perhaps unexpected, ways, it is clear that the four-year centenary represents a chance to re-appraise understanding of the conflict. There is an aspiration that a more nuanced knowledge might aid overturning of some previously held conceptions. However, even if the public appear receptive to these efforts, will academics match this spirit by engaging with the concept of investigating personal stories of the war through the cultural practice of family history? This method is expected to play a fundamental role in promoting public engagement with the First World War over the course of the centenary. Initial impressions hint at a gradual acceptance amongst some historians that this will inevitably be one of the ways through which members of the public can attain a degree of personal relevance to the events of 1914–18. This is in rather stark contrast to the more traditional view taken by the historical discipline; that family history should be taken at arm's length, because it lacks methodological rigour, objectivity and credibility. Any integration would be somewhat contested, because as Tanya Evans put it, family history was considered 'misty-eyed and syrupy', a hobby conducted by self-absorbing narcissists that could not reveal any insight of interest to any 'proper' historian.[8] Now, with this aforementioned degree of re-alignment and increased interaction between both parties, things have the potential to be different – even if only in a temporary four-year truce. Within Britain, the monumental change occurred in July 2009, with the passing of Private Harry Patch in Somerset, the last veteran of the trenches. At this point, the final tantalizing piece of direct living memory of the First World War was extinguished. There was duly much fanfare over the occurrence of this highly anticipated moment, as Britain stood to acknowledge the symbolic status of this 111-year-old man as the last of the 'Tommies'.[9] A few months later, the 'Service to Mark the Passing of the World War One Generation' at Westminster Abbey on Armistice Day brought about a conscious and acute sense of loss – an awareness that the final human tie to the conflict had been cut. Patch's portrayal in the media highlighted his 'everydayness' as an 'ordinary' individual, who could be related to through some unspecified personal connection. Through this, an onus was placed on the post 'living memory' generation to go and (re)discover their familial connections to the conflict.[10] That juncture represented the point when family history took on a heightened and significant burden as a discourse of commemoration. For the sociologist Anthony King, this was a 'significant re-invention' that aligned it with current memorial practices. In contrast to the more collective-focused, traditional forms of national commemoration, soldiers from the conflict were now being 'personalized and re-situated in a network of existing familial relations'.[11]

This sensibility was being embedded well in advance of the war's centenary: over the traditional period of remembrance within the British calendar, a *Daily Mail* supplement informed its readers that 'it couldn't be a better – or more fitting – time to find out more' about their wartime family history. Here was a phenomenon with the potential to provide intimate links to the war: 'it seems we can all tell of a great-great uncle who made the ultimate sacrifice or a great-grandfather who miraculously survived the Somme'.[12] The risk is that such generalizations establish a false understanding amongst those embarking on their family history; that they will uncover tales of heroism, sacrifice and bravery amongst the horrors of the battlefield. Unacknowledged was the fact that family history could be engaged to overturn these preconceptions by showing that not every fighting soldier fought on the Western Front. Descendants might trace relatives to the fighting fronts of Palestine, Mesopotamia and Italy, amongst others. Additionally, uncovering other roles that contributed towards the war effort, including clerks, stretcher bearers, chaplains, logistics troops and nurses could further illustrate a more complex war experience. To fulfil this potential, what was required by the time of the centenary were the resources to be in place that would allow the public to conduct their family history research, and thus be able to establish relevant and meaningful connections to their wartime relatives.

The post 'living memory' generation is not, however, a blank canvas. It is vital to consider their prior understanding of the First World War, and its meaning. For the vast majority, understanding is derived from a fusion of inherited family tales, powerful cultural representations and adaptations on the screen and stage, poignant yet potent pieces of literature and fiction, and the commemorative rituals of Remembrance Sunday.[13] This proves a powerful concoction, 'internalised by the imagination as if part of our own experience'.[14] Certainly the presence of the conflict within British national culture has led to it becoming a nigh-on sacred event – an understanding which can be traced back to its initiation in the early 1920s.[15] As Britain, amongst other nations, began to come to terms with the war's unprecedented impact, veterans' families established a respectful silence towards those not wanting to share their experiences. As Robertshaw and Kenyon have observed, this 'drew a veil over the subject'.[16] The commemoration of 'The Glorious Dead' was completed through the production of official national memorials, which contained strong symbolic evocations of sacrifice in the national cause. As such, 'individual death was subsumed into a wider national and imperial narrative, where distinctions of rank, occupation and position are ameliorated to promote the idea of collective endeavour'.[17] Tying the citizen to the nation, the state was able to exert social unity through this commemorative process, by providing a necessary vehicle for families to situate and project their grief. It took until 1928 with the tenth anniversary of the Armistice, for the nation and its people to re-consider what the war had meant, and whether it had been worth the effort. Much debate revolved around how it could be represented or documented truthfully, and Watson observes that the power of the many literary works published during this period came from their proximity to the event, with the credentials of authors who had been there.[18] Further mass readership publications during the inter-war years were designed to introduce the conflict to the generation of children who had since grown up and wanted to learn about the event that had shaped their upbringing.[19] In many respects, the outbreak of the Second World War made the inherent difficulty of attempting to translate the experiences of the First World War to those who had not fought in it even harder. Nevertheless, the earlier conflict retained its haunting impact that left subsequent generations trying to comprehend it, and it would both haunt and fascinate one generation in particular. On the back of commemorative efforts for the war's fiftieth anniversaries, a wide popular interest in the subject began to lift that 'veil'.

Over the course of the 1960s, tussles followed over how the conflict should best be remembered and understood. Three highly influential works produced during this period were Alan Clark's *The Donkeys* (1961), A.J.P. Taylor's *The First World War – An Illustrated History* (1963) and the staged version of *Oh! What a Lovely War!* (1963). The legacy of these largely satirical and sardonic portrayals of the conflict, promoting a view that blamed the British leadership for overseeing a needless and futile conflict, has been well documented elsewhere.[20] What is important to draw out here is the impact of the televized BBC series, *The Great War* (1964). This quickly achieved epic status as a visually and emotionally powerful account of the conflict because the 26-part series introduced the concept of speaking directly to the now aged veterans about their wartime experiences. As Hanna has argued, it led to an understanding of the war 'marked by the faces' of individual participants.[21] Viewers were able to hear and see veterans telling the war 'how it really was' in raw, sensational and emotional terms. One might note, of course, that these testimonies were themselves shaped by the time and the act of their recording.[22]

Such frankly spoken responses formed the basis of a new recognition of the value of veterans' accounts of warfare, with authors such as Lyn Macdonald and Martin Middlebrook capitalizing on interest in oral histories of the conflict in the early 1970s. Their emphasis on the 'warts-and-all reality' highlighted the importance of the individual eyewitness as a means through which the public could now access the conflict – turning what had previously been viewed as a highly impersonal event into something meaningful to those who had not experienced it.[23] This mentality coincided with the flourishing of amateur family history on the back of the highly successful televized series *Roots* in 1977.[24] As veterans began to pass in large numbers, by the early 1990s, the war was depicted principally through emotive novels that emphasized its psychological impact on individual combatants. Such representations relied upon 'a limited set of images to present the Great War to the wider public', which meant that it would be understood in a particular way. Remembering is pursued for a purpose, and the war, as a shared cultural heritage, could be used as 'a means of illustrating and motivating issues in the present, to comprehend and explain notions of identity, place and politics'.[25] Within this contemporary context, individuals asked to bear witness to the conflict were required to testify to the torment of the soldiers and to empathize with their suffering. The war was framed through these accepted tropes, as pushed largely by the media, because this understanding 'held social and political resonance within contemporary Britain'.[26] Perceiving the war as a trauma fulfilled a function of serving as a basis for identity and 'claims for validity and recognition'.[27]

This process coincided with the gradual release of national archival records, and it became socially acceptable for families to begin investigating the endeavours of their wartime relatives. Doing such research involved trips to local archives and the Public Record Office – scouring through the records of lived experiences and deciphering their occasionally illegible handwriting. It was a privilege of those with both time and money, until the technological development of the internet in the late 1990s, when the digitization of wartime records removed some of these spatial and temporal constraints.[28] This made what had been unknown or forgotten now knowable, and the records were formatted so as to be accessible to those beginning family history research. With data now recoverable, transmittable and conservable, the amateur family history movement found its feet.[29] With the passing of living memory, the rhetoric of inspiring greater numbers to connect with and access this global conflict on the personal level, as enabled by family history, increased. The appeal of being able to discover and establish an in-depth, individual and 'real' narrative within a defining moment of the nation's recent history remains highly alluring for prospective family historians.

Conducting this research consists of a methodological set of practices that enable researchers to make detective-like connections between sets of archival information, and then record them in a suitably scholarly way. This post 'living memory' period has seen the development of comprehensive publications and numerous websites dedicated to aiding research into known or unknown relatives' wartime stories in an approachable manner and at a leisurely pace.[30] Beginners often start with passed-down inter-generational anecdotes from senior family members, or draw inspiration from the tangible material traces of the past. These are the revered and treasured objects preserved or largely forgotten in attics. As Saunders and Cornish have noted, such materials can appear as 'worthless trash, cherished heirloom, historical artefact, memory item or commercially valuable souvenir depending on those who own or observe them'. Certainly they have retained a capacity to hold a 'fragile connection across temporal distance', or preserve 'a material presence in the face of embodied absence'. Schofield, moreover, has advanced the idea of 'social commemoration', through which 'the object stands for a family member I never met'.[31] These fragments of the past in the present – photographs, medals, diaries, letters and other ephemera – can provide vital clues, and it then becomes a case of following the paper trail from the military archival records.[32]

Searching for First World War relatives fits within, and has been heavily influenced by, the broader phenomenon of family history. This popular and fashionable pastime has captivated audiences around the world.[33] Equally it has led to the establishing of a successful commercial sector – featuring genetics and mitochondrial DNA testing – an impact from the influential flagship television series *Who Do You Think You Are?*.[34] The motives of those conducting family history are derived, some contend, from a need to fill a perceived void in values, fostered by the development of a consumerist society, and increasingly mobile lifestyles that have eroded the traditional values of family, church and community.[35] Current generations understand their depersonalized and fragmented existence as lacking the cohesiveness of traditional society. The threat of these 'senses of dislocation, rootlessness and personal meaninglessness' leads to a nostalgic yearning for an imagined stable past, and socio-cultural methods, such as family history, are deployed to counter such feelings.[36] Such manifestations of the past construct a tangible legacy that extends beyond the lifetime of the researcher, and through this process, they construct an ontologically secure recognizable identity.[37] Academics have termed this 'a practice of self-definition and self-making', with Bishop and Saar arguing that family historians are fascinated more by this form of self-exploration and self-understanding than they are by any research findings. Issues of identity politics, performance and individuality are hence entwined in this process, and it must be considered for whom family history and its outcomes are pursued.[38]

If much academic attention has focused on the role of family history as a practice of self-making, let us contemplate its popular appeal by examining what Kramer has termed the 'genealogical imaginary'. These 'pleasures of creativity, fantasy and speculation' entice family historians by enabling them to put themselves in the shoes of another, and to interact with and understand their life experiences.[39] These imaginative engagements equate to researchers 'consciously and knowingly embed[ding] themselves in their social, geographical and temporal context[s]'.[40] This locating of the self forms the primary act of family history, because it fosters distinguishable individual and family identities expressible through historical evidence. This is articulated orally through the format of a prepared recital of events deemed appropriate for an audience.[41] This social act of rehearsal is accordingly susceptible to manipulation, with Bishop observing that researchers can choose to craft narratives with 'only a tenuous connection to reality ... [with] a fictional quality, not necessarily accurate'.[42] Facts can be given either elevated status, or discarded at the narrator's discretion, and are therefore vulnerable to accusations of 'cherry picking'. This is particularly significant, given that First World War family historians now form part of a generation who do not themselves have any direct personal experience of the conflict. However, by drawing upon Hirsch's concept of 'postmemory' and Landsberg's idea of 'prosthetic memory', one can see that generations who did not experience particular historical events can still formulate compelling understandings of them.[43] Whilst the emphasis of these theories lies in the trauma of the Holocaust and upon passing on survivor memory directly between generations, it is nevertheless apparent that indirect understandings of historical events are able to forge powerful inter-generational bonds through narratives of family history, particularly those of loss. Out of this rises a conviction that family historians must pass on their understandings of these events to subsequent generations.

In the case of First World War narratives, their potency lies in their potential to be moulded to fit within the established frameworks of contemporary First World War understanding within Britain. These consist of the widely held and established public perceptions of the conflict. Winter has observed that 'the richest texture of remembrance is always within family life'.[44] Accordingly, any coupling between this, the 'material and ethereal artefacts that stem from the conflict' and the war's cultural memory can be mobilized to afford individuals the basis of a powerful belief in being able to define what the war was like as an experience, and what it achieved.[45] Historians have expressed concern that the strengths of such beliefs form 'a major barrier to a more historical understanding, one based on the critical assessment of evidence'. The matter was not whether family historians could convey an accurate account of their forebears' experiences, but that their portrayals were being aligned to fit with existing popular representations of the conflict, what Todman termed the war's 'cultural baggage'.[46]

In this way, family history is a constructible resource that can be tailored by individuals so that it reaffirms what they believe the First World War to have been like, by drawing on the dominant popular memory to frame their stories.[47] Here the motifs of heroism, death and suffering are particularly important. Relating back to the concept of identity, family historians often desire – both collectively and individually – to 'identify with historical tragedy ... to gain a sense of moral entitlement from fashionable victimological identities'.[48] The researcher is able to frame their findings as a bona fide moral act; 'if, in the future, [my] children or grandchildren wanted to know what happened, they might not be able to do so ... I acknowledged that I had a duty to fulfil towards them, as well as a debt of gratitude to pay.'[49] Family historians perceive this sense of duty as echoing the notions of duty and responsibility that were displayed through the conflict. Bottero's research has illustrated how family historians often discuss 'how hard people's lives were in the *past* (and the much greater resilience – and moral worth – required to endure them) compared to *now*'.[50] This is particularly important within a First World War context, where references to the values of 'duty' and 'sacrifice' frequently occur, in contrast to their perceived absence within contemporary society. Despite the complicated structure of the British Army and lack of distinction between volunteering and conscription, such understandings are adapted and simplified so as to fit with the notion of individual soldiers 'just doing their duty' by fighting for their country, which is valued by many family historians.[51]

Renewed public interest has allowed the post 'living memory' generation to know 'more about what their great-uncles or great-grandfathers did in the First World War than their immediate families ever did'.[52] However, even with increased access to new outlets of knowledge, family history has a real 'lottery' element which features unfamiliar occupations and locations. Consequently, many desire the reassurances of having a relative's war story compiled comprehensively by a professional researcher or historian. Chris Baker is one of the pioneers of this field, with his company 'fourteeneighteen' offering 'professional research and advisory services for anyone wishing to know more about the men, events and battlefields of the First World War'.[53] A typical week involves him investigating an average of twenty soldiers, primarily from the British Army, which adds to the 5,000 stories he has already accumulated. He recognized the demand from people 'who, for whatever reason, find it [family history research] hard to do themselves or who have tried and struggled'.[54] He discerned three driving factors behind this: that not everyone could travel to the various archives, know what they were looking for, or be able to understand what they might find. The real value of this company lies in the latter: that even with access to the digitized archival records, being able to decipher understanding from the jargon-filled content is quite another. Converting technical information from the military data into a personal narrative is what Baker's clients value most of all. Reports accordingly place emphasis on building up a picture of the client's relative: facts typically found on the enlistment attestation forms, such as a man's height, build and eye colour, are highly valued by descendants because they can draw perceived links between generations.

Furthermore, the service has 'developed techniques and efficiencies in searching and in building an unparalleled library of knowledge'.[55] For Baker, clients may run the risk of narrowing their understanding of the war through the lens of one individual story if the facts found are not placed within their broader historical context. Examples include consulting the trends that might have influenced an individual's enlistment, the educational standards of the time, what the British Army did for its training, and why an individual's unit was sent into a particular battle at a particular time. Thus a professional researcher can illuminate a relative's war story through their expertise of knowing the British Army's 'structures, regulations and ways of working' alongside their awareness of historical context.[56] The marrying up of records with historical expertise, when presented to the client in an accessible and clear format, allows them to obtain a deeper understanding of their relative's war. Baker does not shield his clients in any way: delivering reports is not always straightforward, especially when findings do not align with the oral tales kept within families, or when research establishes details of a relative who was killed. Essentially, the reports induce surprise in their unpredictability, as evidenced by the website's testimonials,[57] and Baker thus fosters a particular understanding of the war for his clients.

This is furthered when clients undertake individually tailored battlefield tours in northern France and Belgium that trace the story of their relative – allowing them to 'walk in their footsteps' or journey to the location where they were killed or buried. The historian is able to engage the client's imagination by depicting the events that took place in that location, and meaning is gained through being able to interpret this landscape through a prior detailed knowledge derived from report findings. Acting as testament to their relatives' experiences, these trips allow clients to 'physically enact a sense of historical connection with a place associated with an imagined collective past'.[58] Again, Baker prioritizes the importance of contextual information to describe the detailed aspects of trench life, such as revealing the daily routine within them, which shows that 'fourteeneighteen' operates with the understanding that its work comes with an obligation to overturn possible client preconceptions. In this way, visiting the symbolic battlefield landscape (Figure 1.2) enables the sensory experience of being situated in the same location as one's relatives, and crafting an identity there through a social performance of commemoration.[59] Baker referred to clients stating that this allowed them to re-exert tangible family bonds that had become increasingly stretched in the globalized world.[60] Furthermore the sense of meaning uncovered within the battlefields is perceived by clients to be 'untarnished by the values of contemporary society'.[61]

Increasingly, we are seeing the combination of commemoration with the potency of family history from a commercial perspective. One such project capitalizing on the rising public interest in this subject is a long-term partnership between Imperial War Museums (IWM) and DC Thompson Family History. Launched in May 2014, 'Lives of the First World War' ('Lives') seeks to frame public memory of the conflict through personal stories.[62] It will become a unique online database that employs crowd-sourcing in order to realize its aspiration of piecing together 'the Life Stories of more than eight million men and women who made a contribution during the First World War' who served from across Britain and the Commonwealth. It will do this by collating and

Figure 1.2 A photographic tribute on the Western Front. © James Wallis

sharing a vast collection of material from family historians and direct descendants who can contribute (and simultaneously digitally preserve) their own family heirlooms such as scans of photographs, diaries and letters.[63] This approach of documenting stories within an online repository builds upon the foundation laid by several similar projects over recent years, including the University of Oxford led project 'The Great War Archive'.[64] Its existence relies upon public interaction, enabled through social media, by allowing individuals to upload and share material online. A comparison can be drawn with Noakes' research into the BBC's interactive 'People's War' website, an endeavour designed to uncover Second World War family stories. This brought together 'separate acts of remembering' into 'new, shared sites of remembrance'. Furthermore, this revealed a diversity of experiences, even of the same historical event. For Noakes, the website was able to present a multiplicity of stories, which could challenge conventional historical focus, as it was able to 'feed into and reshape shared remembrance … enabling the inclusion of memories which were previously marginal to or excluded from collective remembrance'.[65] This unlocked new knowledge of the event, presented 'a less unified picture of the past', and thus altered public remembrance.

'Lives' will operate in a similar manner, as its format provides the necessary space – in its informality, as well as its formality and credibility linked to IWM – to make users feel confident in vocalizing their relatives' wartime stories. When completed, this act establishes a degree of genealogical exclusiveness and ownership for users, by virtue of the fact that they are 'claiming' their relatives through the distinguishing act of choosing to 'remember' them online. Additionally, the cumulative results of the project will be linked together by the collective identity of this virtual community. It allows various degrees of involvement, so that intrigued beginners can contribute information, such as passed-down colloquial family tales, whilst not restricting those wanting to share detailed historical research. This blending of personal archives with official military records – two sets of resources never before brought together on such a large scale – forms the crux of the project.

The intentions of 'Lives' are attractive in their ambition to be comprehensive and through the innovative use of digital technology to enrich understanding of the past. What is more, the outcomes will reflect two core principles: education and memorialization. In time, 'Lives' will become a natural educational resource for future generations, who will be able to add to and enhance the content generated. The project's ongoing status and longevity gives the public an unprecedented opportunity to 'rescue, bring to light and maybe help verify a host of war stories'.[66] However, at the same time, its format is formulated and controlled by IWM as a state-funded organization. This represents an effort, on behalf of the 'agencies of civil society together with the state', to 'continue to transmit memory of the war, and the national narrative it underpins, but through the rather different channels of education and entertainment'.[67] This state-shaped channel ensures that the conflict's public commemoration will align with constructed narratives of the national past, and their values upheld by a new generation.[68] The negative connotations typically associated with the war's popular understanding are thus largely absent, in recognition of these links with official and national narratives. By enabling members of the public to become 'active witnesses' to these, family history is therefore implemented as a methodology to contribute to the purpose of the state, and is portrayed by IWM 'as a means of educating and informing the wider public for society's betterment'.[69] We see this through the rhetoric employed referring back to the original purpose of the Imperial War Museum when it was established in 1917.[70] Technological developments have enabled the vision of 'recording the toil and sacrifice of those who served in uniform and on the home fronts ... [and] asking the public to help it tell the story of the global conflict'[71] to be realized, delivered digitally, and rigorously quantified on an unprecedented scale. This makes IWM's remit contemporary and relevant to the post 'living memory' generation, whilst ensuring that it acquires custodial responsibility in maintaining future care over the project. It also reveals how seriously IWM is engaging with the practice of family history, over the centenary period. In acknowledgement of the efforts invested, the project has been identified as a key resource for the academic community; the chair of the 'Lives' Academic Advisory Group has outlined how findings will enable the compilation of new statistics.[72] In turn, this will allow the measuring of factors such as the nature of service in local areas to further historical understanding in under-studied aspects of the conflict.

The second principle is the project's commemorative role in forming a 'permanent digital memorial' to the wartime generation who both were killed in, and survived, the conflict. 'Lives' is promoted as an opportunity for today's generation to pay its respects to the efforts and sacrifice of that generation. Furthermore, this demonstrates the act of 'remembering' as one which develops a sense of self-identity. As discussed earlier, these contributors are able to 'cast themselves in the role of a storyteller ... willing to share information they have uncovered'.[73] As a performative practice of asserting identity, this act of sharing allows the contributor to 'carve out, through narrative, a place for one's family in the larger picture' – in this case, an individual's involvement within a national narrative – and thus 'confers meaning on the information and people' discovered.[74] This is brought together by Santos and Yan's idea that 'In the way that a nation needs its national cultural identity recognized in order to unite its citizens, a family needs its identity and emotional bonding.'[75]

In conclusion, it is clear that the value of family history as a practice, when inter-weaved with academic history, has the unique capability to shift common narratives of the war and question what had previously been largely accepted. This 'amateurization' of history, as shown within 'Lives', is effecting changes in the landscape of public remembrance and commemoration, with King suggesting, ' ... personality and family have become the primary spheres of definition, debate and action while others (the nation, state, class or trade unions) have receded'.[76] Family history has come to the fore, as Parker observes:

> If *le vice anglais* was once flagellation, it is now nostalgia, as we look back longingly to the world in which our great-grandparents lived. There may have been poverty and hardship, we tell ourselves, but there was more sense of community. People tended to get and stay married, [and] maintain close relationships with their extended families.[77]

Even so, it seems fitting to return to David Reynolds, and consider the challenge he attributes to First World War family history:

> the effect of this technological revolution is hard to gauge. Potentially the internet is a 'borderless reservoir of information': will it encourage people to surf the barriers of national memory cultures and gain a broader sense of the conflict? Or will the digital age serve mainly to deepen the conventional channels of British war remembrance, drawing new generations into engagement with the tragedies of individual soldiers?[78]

The answer perhaps lies somewhere in the middle. There is doubtless a risk that the generation taking part in the centenary commemorations will learn about the conflict solely by battlefield visitation that revolves around connecting to the 'tragedies of individual soldiers' that sit alongside the war's popular mythology. On the other hand, the centenary provides an unprecedented opportunity to develop collective knowledge of the conflict through the breadth of experiences that outlets such as 'fourteeneighteen' and 'Lives of the First World War' offer. In many respects, only time will tell.

Notes

1 M. Plowman, *A Subaltern on the Somme* (New York: Dutton, 1928), viii–ix.
2 See J. Schofield, 'Message and Materiality in Mesopotamia, 1916–17: My Grandfather's Diary, Social Commemoration and the Experience of War', in *Contested Objects: Material Memories of the Great War*, eds N. Saunders and P. Cornish (Oxford: Routledge, 2009), 203–19.
3 D. Reynolds, *The Long Shadow: The Great War and the Twentieth Century* (London: Simon & Schuster, 2013), xiv.
4 H. Jones, 'As the Centenary Approaches: The Regeneration of First World War Historiography', *The Historical Journal* 56:3 (2013), 878.
5 See Jones, 862–5. Gary Sheffield had warned that 'unless the problems caused by the cultural baggage associated with the First World War are overcome, revisionist historians run the risk of merely talking to each other'. G. Sheffield, 'Military Revisionism: The Case of the British Army on the Western Front', in *A Part of History: Aspects of the British Experience of the First World War* (London: Continuum, 2008), 7.
6 Jones, 876.
7 C. Pennell, *A Kingdom United: Popular Responses to the Outbreak of the First World War in Britain and Ireland* (Oxford: Oxford University Press), 1.

8 T. Evans, 'Secrets and Lies: The Radical Potential of Family History', *History Workshop Journal* 71:1 (2011), 49, 51. For a warmer reception in sociology and tourism research, see C. Santos and G. Yan, 'Genealogical Tourism: A Phenomenological Examination', *Journal of Travel Research* 49:1 (2010), 56–67; R. Bishop, '"The Essential Force of the Clan": Developing a Collecting-Inspired Ideology of Genealogy through Textual Analysis', *Journal of Popular Culture* 38:6 (2008), 990–1010.
9 P. Parker, *The Last Veteran: Harry Patch and the Legacy of War* (London: Fourth Estate, HarperCollins, 2009), 286–92.
10 Todman has suggested that it is this beguiling process of being able to 'discover' the First World War in new ways, as enabled by new platforms that decompress temporal distance to the event, 'that has made it so attractive to later generations'. D. Todman, 'Remembrance' in *A Part of History*, 215.
11 A. King, 'The Afghan War and "Postmodern" Memory: Commemoration and the Dead of Helmand', *The British Journal of Sociology* 61:1 (2010), 23.
12 G. Walters, 'Find the Hero in Your Family', *Daily Mail*, 8 November 2013, Weekend Supplement, 9.
13 J. Meyer, 'Introduction: Popular Culture and the First World War' in *British Popular Culture and the First World War*, ed. J. Meyer (Leiden: Brill, 2008), 1–17.
14 T. Benton and C. Cecil, 'Heritage and Public Memory', in *Understanding Heritage and Memory: Understanding Global Heritage*, ed. T. Benton (Manchester: Manchester University Press in association with the Open University, 2010), 23.
15 C. Moriarty, 'Private Grief and Public Remembrance: British First World War Memorials', in *War and Memory in the Twentieth Century*, eds M. Evans and K. Lunn (Oxford: Berg, 1997), 125–42.
16 A. Robertshaw and D. Kenyon, *Digging the Trenches: The Archaeology of the Western Front* (Barnsley: Pen & Sword Military, 2005), 14.
17 R. Wilson, 'It Still Goes On: Football and the Heritage of the Great War in Britain', *Journal of Heritage Tourism* 9:3 (2014), 197–211. Also see M. Heffernan, 'For Ever England: The Western Front and the Politics of Remembrance in Britain', *Ecumene*, 2 (1995), 293–323.
18 J. Watson, *Fighting Different Wars: Experience, Memory and the First World War in Britain* (Cambridge: Cambridge University Press, 2006), 204, 209, 210.
19 See J. Hammerton (ed.) *A Popular History of the Great War* (London: The Amalgamated Press, 1933–4).
20 See B. Bond, *The Unquiet Western Front* (Cambridge: Cambridge University Press, 2002), 51–4; D. Todman, *The Great War: Myth and Memory* (London: Hambledon Continuum, 2005), 102.
21 E. Hanna, 'A Small Screen Alternative to Stone and Bronze: *The Great War* Series and British Television', *European Journal of Cultural Studies* 10:1 (2007), 95.
22 For examples, see A. Thomson, *Anzac Memories: Living with the Legend* (Melbourne: Oxford University Press, 1994); L. Noakes, 'The BBC's "People's War" Website', in *War Memory and Popular Culture: Essays on Modes of Remembrance and Commemoration*, eds M. Keren and H. Herwig (North Carolina: McFarland & Company, 2009), 143, 145–6.
23 L. Macdonald, 'Oral History and the First World War', in *A Part of History*, 138.
24 R. Taylor and R. Crandall, *Generations and Change: Genealogical Perspectives in Social History* (Macon, Georgia: Mercer University Press, 1986).
25 R. Wilson, *Cultural Heritage of the Great War in Britain* (Aldershot: Ashgate, 2013), 11, 2.
26 Ibid., 59.
27 Ibid., 191.
28 N. Fabiansson, 'The Internet and the Great War: The Impact on the Making and Meaning of Great War History', in *Matters of Conflict: Material Culture, Memory and the First World War*, ed. N. Saunders (London: Routledge, 2004), 166–78.
29 K. Meethan, 'Remaking Time and Space: The Internet, Digital Archives and Genealogy', in *Genealogy and Geography: Locating Personal Pasts*, eds D. Timothy and J. Guelke (Aldershot: Ashgate, 2008), 107–8.

30 P. Reed, *Great War Lives: A Guide for Family Historians* (Barnsley: Pen & Sword, 2010); S. Fowler, *Tracing Your First World War Ancestors: A Guide for Family Historians* (Barnsley: Pen & Sword, 2013). See 'Trace a WW1 British Soldier'. Online. Available HTTP: <www.greatwar.co.uk/research/family-history/trace-ww1-british-soldier.htm> (accessed 15 May 2014); 'Tracing your World War Ancestors'. Online. Available HTTP: <www.allaboutgenealogy.co.uk/worldwarancestors.html> (accessed 15 May 2014).
31 Saunders and Cornish, 3; E. Hallam and J. Hockey, *Death, Memory and Material Culture* (Oxford: Berg, 2001), 18; Schofield, 203.
32 Space does not allow for a detailed guide to conducting this family history research. However, it is worth noting that key sources include the Commonwealth War Grave Commission's 'Debt of Honour' online database (www.cwgc.org), and the two, now digitized, data sets that comprise: the Medal Index Cards (extracted from WO 329). Online. Available HTTP: <www.nationalarchives.gov.uk/records/medal-index-cards-ww1.htm> (accessed 15 May 2014); and the 40 per cent of Service Records that survive today (WO 363). Online. Available HTTP: <www.nationalarchives.gov.uk/pathways/firstworldwar/service_records/sr_soldiers.htm> (accessed 15 May 2014). Genealogical source material such as Census Records and Death Certificates can also be useful. Post-war rolls of honour, local archives, memorials and regimental museums may provide further details. Contextual information can be gathered from the Battalion War Diaries (WO 95 and WO 154) which are being digitized in 2014 through a collaborative crowd-sourcing project known as 'Operation War Diary'. Online. Available HTTP: <www.operationwardiary.org> (accessed 15 May 2014).
33 D. Hey, *Journeys in Family History: Exploring Your Past, Finding Your Ancestors* (Richmond: National Archives, 2004).
34 C. Nash, 'Genome Geographies: Mapping National Ancestry and Diversity in Human Population Genetics', *Transactions of the Institute of British Geographers* 38 (2013), 193–206; A. Kramer, 'Mediatizing Memory: History, Affect and Identity in "Who Do You Think You Are?"', *European Journal of Cultural Studies* 14:4 (2011), 429–46.
35 A. Giddens, *Modernity and Self Identity: Self and Society in the Late Modern Age* (Cambridge: Polity Press, 1991); R. Baumeister, 'The Self and Society' in *Self and Identity: Fundamental Issues*, eds R. Ashmore and L. Jussim (Oxford: Oxford University Press, 1997), 199.
36 P. Basu, *Highland Homecomings: Genealogy and Heritage Tourism in the Scottish Diaspora* (London: Routledge, 2007), 48.
37 See Santos and Yan, 63; I. Robertson and T. Hall, 'Memory, Identity and the Memorialization of Conflict in the Scottish Highlands', in *Heritage, Memory and the Politics of Identity*, eds N. Moore and Y. Whelan (Aldershot: Ashgate, 2007), 19–36.
38 Bishop, 'Essential Force', 994–5, 1005; M. Saar, 'Genealogy and Subjectivity', *European Journal of Philosophy* 10:2 (2002), 231–45. Also see C. Nash, 'Genealogical Identities', *Environment and Planning D: Society and Space* 20:1 (2002), 27–52.
39 A. Kramer, 'Telling Multi-Dimensional Family Histories: Making the Past Meaningful', *Methodological Innovations Online* 6:3 (2011), 23–4.
40 Ibid., 22.
41 W. Bottero, 'Who Do You Think They Were? How Family Historians Make Sense of Social Position and Inequality in the Past', *The British Journal of Sociology* 63 (2012), 59; A. Kramer, 'Kinship, Affinity and Connectedness: Exploring the Role of Genealogy in Personal Lives', *Sociology* 45:3 (2011), 379–95.
42 Bishop, 'Essential Force', 1005; Saar, 232.
43 M. Hirsch, *Family Frames: Photography, Narrative and Postmemory* (Cambridge, Mass.: Harvard University Press, 1997); A. Landsberg, *Prosthetic Memory: The Transformation of American Remembrance in the Age of Mass Culture* (New York: Columbia University Press, 2004).
44 J. Winter, 'Sites of Memory', in *Memory: Histories, Theories, Debates*, eds S. Radstone and B. Schwarz (New York: Fordham University Press, 2010), 317.
45 Wilson, *Cultural Heritage*, 187.

46 D. Todman, 'The Ninetieth Anniversary of the Battle of the Somme' in Keren and Herwig, 32, 33.
47 Noakes, 146.
48 E. Hoffman, 'The Long Afterlife of Loss' in Radstone and Schwarz, 407; Bottero, 63; also P. Novick, *The Holocaust and Collective Memory: The American Experience* (London: Bloomsbury, 1999); Wilson, *Cultural Heritage*, 70, 85.
49 B. Murphy, 'Remembrance Remembered, Remembrance Observed. An Irishman's Daughter Visits His Grave', *Journal of Historical Sociology* 10:4 (1997), 354.
50 Bottero, 62. Emphasis in original.
51 It is worth re-iterating Bottero's (72) concern that family historians often fail to consider 'the bigger picture', or information which can contextualize their findings beyond the level of the individual.
52 T. Pollard, 'A View from the Trenches: An Introduction to the Archaeology of the Western Front', in *A Part of History*, 198.
53 'Fourteeneighteen. Soldier research'. Online. Available HTTP: <www.fourteeneighteen.co.uk/research-services> (accessed 20 May 2014).
54 Email interview conducted with the author (17 July 2011).
55 'Fourteeneighteen. Soldier research'. (accessed 20 May 2014).
56 Ibid.
57 'Fourteeneighteen. Testimonials'. Online. Available HTTP: <www.fourteeneighteen.co.uk/testimonials> (accessed 20 May 2014). Common themes include value for money, expressions of gratitude, the rescuing of an individual from memorial anonymity and incredulity at being able to piece together narratives, in spite of limited prior knowledge.
58 J. Iles, 'Encounters in the Fields: Tourism to the Battlefields of the Western Front', *Journal of Tourism and Cultural Change* 6:2 (2008); 150.
59 P. Brodwin, 'Genetics, Identity and the Anthropology of Essentialism', *Anthropological Quarterly* 75 (2002), 323; also C. Winter, 'Battlefield Visitor Motivations: Explorations in the Great War town of Ieper, Belgium', *International Journal of Tourism Research* 13:2 (2011), 164–76. The somewhat murky division between tourist and pilgrim has been documented by D. Lloyd, *Battlefield Tourism: Pilgrimage and the Commemoration of the Great War in Britain, Australia and Canada, 1919–1939* (Oxford: Berg, 1998).
60 Interview, 17 July 2011.
61 Iles, 150.
62 For coverage of the project launch, see BBC News UK, 'Lives of the First World War "digital memorial" goes live', 12 May 2014. Online. Available HTTP: <www.bbc.co.uk/news/uk-27369169> (accessed 20 May 2014). For details of its reception, see 'Here's what people have been saying about us … ' Online. Available: <http://blog.livesofthefirstworldwar.org/heres-what-people-have-been-saying-about-us> (accessed 20 May 2014); ww1geek, 'Lives of the First World War – First Impressions', 28 March 2014. Online. Available: <http://ww1geek.wordpress.com/2014/03/28/lives-of-the-fww-first-impressions> (accessed 20 May 2014).
63 'Lives of the First World War'. Online. Available <https://livesofthefirstworldwar.org> (accessed 20 May 2014). At its launch, the records of 4.5 million men and 40,000 women who served overseas with the British Army had been uploaded. On that day, the website was viewed 458,146 times, 12,488 members registered and approximately 3,000 images were uploaded.
64 See 'The Great War Archive'. Online. Available HTTP: <www.oucs.ox.ac.uk/ww1lit/gwa> (accessed 20 May 2014). The ongoing 'Europeana 1914–18' project has expanded this remit. Online. Available: <http://europeana1914–18.eu/en> (accessed 20 May 2014).
65 Noakes, 137.
66 The phrase used of 'piecing together' suggests that the information is awaiting a collative effort from the public to match the information from archival records to the individuals listed on the database. 'IWM needs YOU to help build Lives of the First World War',

12 May 2014. Online. Available: <https://livesofthefirstworldwar.org/press> (accessed 20 May 2014).
67 T. G. Ashplant, G. Dawson and M. Roper, 'The Politics of War Memory and Commemoration: Contexts, Structures and Dynamics', in *The Politics of War Memory and Commemoration*, eds T. G. Ashplant, G. Dawson and M. Roper (London: Routledge, 2000), 28.
68 Ibid., 16.
69 Wilson, *Cultural Heritage*, 162. In this instance, Wilson is referring to another, similar, IWM-led project on Flickr, 'Faces of the First World War', which ran in November 2011. Online. Available HTTP: <www.1914.org/faces> (accessed 20 May 2014).
70 See 'About Lives of the First World War'. Online. Available: <https://livesofthefirstworldwar.org/about> (accessed 20 May 2014).
71 Ibid.
72 Miranda Brennan, 'What's Different about Lives of the First World War?', 8 May 2014. Online. Available: <http://blog.livesofthefirstworldwar.org/whats-different-about-lives-of-ww1> (accessed 20 May 2014).
73 R. Bishop, 'In the Grand Scheme of Things: An Exploration of the Meaning of Genealogical Research', *Journal of Popular Culture* 41:3 (2008), 407.
74 Ibid., 403, 409.
75 Santos and Yan, 63.
76 King, 19.
77 P. Parker, 'How to Master the Art of Writing – In a Weekend', *Daily Telegraph* 7 September 2013, review section.
78 Reynolds, 433.

2 Family history and the Great War in Australia

Carolyn Holbrook and Bart Ziino

The boom in family history that is a hallmark of so much historical activity around the globe over the last three decades is one contributor to the resurgence of interest in the Great War itself. In Australia, as elsewhere in the western world, family history and the resources dedicated to it have been expanding rapidly. This chapter investigates recent practices of family history of the Great War in Australia. Our aim is to examine the role of family history in producing and reproducing knowledge of the Great War within Australian families, and the relationship between the conduct and transmission of family history on the one hand, and the contours of cultural memory on the other.

What is the relationship between the practice of family history and national narratives of the war? Today in Australia, an emphasis on the trauma of war and the suffering of individual soldiers co-exists – comfortably – with more familiar assertions, central to the Anzac legend, that a national character was shaped by the men who fought in the Great War. Family historians are certainly attuned to these interpretative frames, and fragmentary knowledge of the family past is easily enveloped by dominant public modes of recollection. But in their responses to their research in expanding digital archives, and similarly growing opportunities to share their knowledge with others online, family historians also show themselves to be increasingly interested in the lives and experiences of those beyond the frontlines, and those whose lives remained marked by the experience of war. In this, family history offers avenues by which to gain an appreciation of the Great War, that at once finds context and meaning in public myths, but which also has the potential to challenge and upset received wisdom about the war. The work of family historians shows that alternative histories of the war are not simply out there to be discovered in the archive, but are actively produced through an historical practice whose logic insists on expanding the cast of historical actors, and on connecting their experiences directly to the present.

Alistair Thomson has recently argued that family histories have the potential not only to challenge narratives of the Great War within families, but indeed that 'through family history, researched carefully and written with searing honesty and a critical eye, Australians can help create a different type of war history'.[1] Thomson made this argument in relation to his examination of the newly available repatriation files of Australian soldiers of the Great War. This massive and largely unexplored archive shines a light on the decades-long relationships between veterans and the government, as returned men sought pensions and other entitlements. Like the historian Bruce Scates, Thomson is confident that the repatriation files will allow family historians to 'complicate' the history of the Great War and resist its reduction to a simple tale of heroism and national birth.[2] Similarly, Tanya Evans sees the radical potential of the techniques of family history, in their capacity to 'throw into question the solidity not only of the history of family, class relationships and the power relations between men and women but also of the history of nation and empire'.[3]

Not all family historians will produce histories that subvert conventional understanding, but they are all operating in an environment of popular understanding of Australia's Great War that has shifted fundamentally over the past thirty years. The emergence of this psychological or empathic perspective owes much to what French historian Annette Wieviorka has called 'the era of the witness': the hearing and privileging of victims' testimonies, especially as they emerged from the Holocaust, in the construction of history and memory.[4] The shifts that have occurred through this phenomenon are apparent in Australians' relationship with the Great War. As Alistair Thomson observed of contemporary Anzac observance:

> Though young Australians may well take pride in their military forebears, they are more likely to pity the terrible experience of war than celebrate a warrior hero. The decline of its warrior elements is a striking change in the Anzac legend.[5]

Where once the radical potential of family history might have been to challenge the masculinist and heroic image of Australian servicemen propounded by the Anzac legend, today we find, as Christina Twomey argues, that 'war's traumatising effects have been a central trope in the post-1980s incarnation of Anzac'.[6] In this sense the methods of family history offer a way to connect with the wartime past, and gain access to a more intimate version of history. As in popular war memory, family historians find less a moral example from the past than a sympathetic conception of their forebears as fellow sufferers. Family historians naturally have much wider concerns than the Great War as an isolated event, but there are good reasons to accord the war some prominence in the current practice of family history. As we will see, the Great War is for some an entry point to further efforts in family history, while Bruce Scates has argued that identifying a soldier relative has achieved a level of cachet that comes from a broader embrace of Australia's military history, from politicians downwards, in recent years.[7]

Historians have not seen these shifts in popular engagement with the past entirely positively. Like historians elsewhere, Twomey expressed concern about the implications of the rise of the 'traumatised soldier' for popular understanding of the Great War.[8] She wondered whether emotional identification with service, sacrifice and especially soldiers' victimhood will 'provide ballast for a nationalist interpolation of Anzac' and limit the capacity for criticism, by rendering it disrespectful.[9] Thus, the emergence of the psychological reading of the Great War does not equate automatically with the production of newly complex interpretations. Rather, it has the capacity to be subsumed into existing representations as well as to produce new ones. Like Twomey, historian Joy Damousi sees family history as an important bearer of an emotional rendering of the past. She has detected a 'merging of military history and family history, in a way that encourages identification with our military past ... and a proud investment' in the nation-making version of Australian experience of the Great War.[10] With so many Australians approaching the war through the experience of grandfathers and great-grandfathers, Damousi has cautioned that 'sentimentality and nostalgia [rather than historical analysis] are perhaps now the prevailing modes of relating to Anzac Day'.[11] Soldiers – all of them someone's ancestor – may be on the couch, but they are still waving the national flag.

In the 1980s and 1990s a series of triggers, public, private and demographic, encouraged renewed interest in the Great War in Australia. By the 1970s, the Anzac tradition was widely believed to be in terminal decline. Attendances at the annual dawn service and Anzac Day march dwindled as veterans died away, and young people showed little interest in perpetuating the rituals. The hostility of many baby boomers towards what they perceived as the militaristic, imperial, chauvinistic and racist attitudes of the Great War generation was sharpened by the Vietnam War, which encouraged them to see war commemoration as indistinguishable from the glorification of war. The extraordinary revival of Anzac commemoration since the 1980s was thus unexpected, and owes much to a growing emphasis on personal experiences of war, especially as found in Bill Gammage's *The Broken Years* (1974), and Patsy Adam-Smith's even more widely read book, *The Anzacs* (1978). The phenomenal success of Peter Weir's film *Gallipoli* (1981), for which Gammage acted as an historical adviser, did much to promote a newly personal and sympathetic portrait of Australians in the Great War. The archetypal sacrifice of the young male, represented so memorably in the film, has become an enduring feature of Anzac commemoration in its revived form.

These new, individualized approaches to the First World War stimulated and complemented the pursuit of family history. So too did the increasing level of political patronage attached to commemoration in Australia, especially following Prime Minister Hawke's 'pilgrimage' to Gallipoli in 1990 for the campaign's seventy-fifth anniversary, during which he was accompanied by a group of elderly veterans. Hawke's declaration that a younger generation of Australians was remaking its relationship with the war marked the beginning of a new era of political commemoration of the Great War in Australia. The public seemed to be newly attuned to stories of soldiers who had been traumatized by their experience of war. Historian Mark McKenna has also suggested that the willingness of politicians to associate themselves with the Anzac tradition is due, in part, to the shortcomings of Australia Day as an occasion of national unity, laden as it is with the weight of debate over whether Australia was invaded or settled by Europeans.[12] The frail old soldiers, who had been born in the last decades of the nineteenth century, were bemused by their late celebrity and gracious about the morbid media 'death watch' to which they were subjected in their final years. The last veteran of the Gallipoli campaign, a trade union activist called Alec Campbell, was given a state funeral upon his death in 2002, at which he was eulogized by conservative Prime Minister John Howard as an embodiment of 'the Anzac spirit'.[13]

The emergence of politicians as significant patrons of Anzac commemoration was an important sign for Australian descendants of Great War soldiers. Renewed popular attention encouraged Australians to re-examine their family histories, perhaps especially where the details of a parent's war service were not well-known. For many, a silence had surrounded the war. David Nott remembered his father speaking in 1945 about the battle of the Somme, only to see that 'His memories overcame him then, and the conversation flew to the present, today's large snapper and my mother's way of cooking it.'[14] Margery Elmslie knew that her father had been in the war, 'but we didn't ever talk about it at home, and he barely ever went off to Anzac Day'. Elmslie's own – limited – impressions of the war came from school, 'and that was Simpson and the Donkey.'[15] Similarly, Jeff Pickerd always knew that his maternal grandfather, George Fuzzard, had fought in the Great War and survived the doomed charge at the Nek. But Pickerd still recalls the day when he saw the physical evidence of his grandfather's war service:

> [It was] one very hot summer's day when I was quite young, probably about seven or eight years old. My grandfather always wore a long-sleeved shirt [but] ... He came in this day and he had a white singlet and this was the first time I noticed this hole in his arm about the size of a ten cent piece. And it was both fascinating and horrendous. So I rushed off to my grandmother and said 'Grandpa's got a hole in his arm' and all she said to me was 'Shoosh, don't talk about it.' And that was the end of that.[16]

Notwithstanding reticence among returned men to speak, we see here that silence was a two-way street. On the one hand children might not feel comfortable enquiring into fathers' or grandfathers' personal lives. On the other, they were often little interested in doing so. Linley Hooper, born after the Second World War, baulked at discussions of the war. 'As children, we absolutely hated it when the dads sat around talking about the war ... so I often wonder if my parents felt that same about their parents and [did] not want to know about the war. I don't know, but certainly as a child ... I just closed my mind to it.'[17] Margery Elmslie rendered the situation rather more passively: she had known of her father's war service from an early age, 'But it wasn't interesting. No.' As historian Peter Read has observed, the transmission of history within families – largely *ad hoc* and contingent on circumstances – is predicated not only on an individual's desire to speak, but on the predisposition of others to listen.[18]

What then prompts the desire to engage with parents' experiences of the past, and especially the wartime past? Why do letters and diaries that have been left untouched underneath beds and in garages and wardrobes for decades suddenly come to be invested with historical significance? As we have suggested, there were public prompts that were important, even for those who had always been aware of the war and its resonance in their families. Monica Sinclair's father, Ron Sinclair, often spoke of his war experiences. The Great War, she writes, 'was part of the experience of growing up in our family. We were all aware that Dad had been "at the War" and that somehow this was a fact that affected his life, all our lives.' Despite her father's willingness to speak of the war, however, Sinclair would come to observe that 'Only in my later years have I become convinced that these effects were deep and far-reaching.' The specific prompt for her taking up her father's war letters, however, was seeing the film *Gallipoli*: returning from the cinema, she took out her father's letters, wondering 'what they might contain in the way of Dad's War memoirs. So much of the film had rung bells in me.'[19] Similarly, John Duffell had read some of his father's war letters as a child, but after moving house he believed them to be lost, until they re-emerged in his garage in 1990.[20] With the seventy-fifth anniversary of the Gallipoli landings approaching, he was struck by the wider public significance of the letters and had some of them published in the local press.

But the impetus to examine parents' war experiences has as much and more to do with the reader's own stage of life, as with the public appetite for the nation's war heritage, though the two are certainly connected. In the 1980s and 1990s the inter-war generation was itself approaching retirement age, which brought with it greater curiosity and opportunities to pursue family history. As a child, Elizabeth Whiteside had been aware of her father's letters, but did not look at them: 'we were always conscious of them, as children ... I suppose we just sort of got the feeling that they were important, you know, they were there.'[21] Even beyond her father's death, she did not have the time or inclination to read the letters. Still, she took them with her when she moved house in 1970, only to leave them again undisturbed for a further twenty years. When Margery Elmslie's widowed mother came to live with her, Margery made sure to collect her father's letters, a few of which she had read, though again 'all these things, the letters got put in that cupboard, in that drawer, and they were left there for 35 years'. In the early 1990s, Elizabeth Whiteside took the opportunity to travel after her retirement, visiting her father's early home in the United States. Only after her return did she turn her attention to his letters: 'I thought – and I had time, I had time I hadn't before – it's time perhaps to have a look at these letters, so that's the beginning.'[22] Margery Elmslie was aware of her own mortality when she decided to read her father's letters, and to circulate them among her extended family, which had been conducting a series of reunions. 'I was coming up to 80', she recalled, and 'I thought I'd better do something before I ... fall off the branch. ... I was getting old, and I felt that I had to do it.'[23] A sense of obligation, whether to one's parents, to oneself, or to subsequent generations, is consistently reported by family historians. Elizabeth

Whiteside combined prosaic realities with the same sensibility: 'It was partly a matter of tidying up, too, but something had to be done.'

The experiences of family historians such as Elizabeth Whiteside and Margery Elmslie illustrate that the conduct of family history of the Great War is not simply an act that is inspired (and captured) by the workings of powerful public narratives, though they are important. The interaction between the private and public making of the past that occurs through family history and public narratives of war is complex and nuanced. If we are to achieve a finer understanding of the knowledge that family historians produce, and its relationship to public myths of the war, we must examine more closely the process of making family history. We have each argued elsewhere that family historians reinterpret and draw new meaning from the testimonies of their ancestors. We have also shown how family historians are frequently drawn into a process of re-examining their own identities.[24] The creation of family history involves not merely an investigation of the identity of one's ancestors but a degree of self-examination and emotional introspection. Such a process is in the nature of family history more generally, which speaks, as Graeme Davison has observed, 'not to our sense of historical significance, but to our need for personal identity'.[25] The act of choosing a path through one's family history, Ashley Barnwell argued, is an exercise in affirming our desired identities: 'Family history research ... is a practice of self-authentication, but also a creative act of revisionist life-writing.'[26]

If family history is about seeking an identity with which one is comfortable, then it is surely connected with wider public narratives of a politically acceptable past. In this sense, the process of family history has the potential both to confirm and unsettle accepted versions of the family and national past. David Nott's experience of reading his father's letters was positive: 'I relived the war through his eyes and ears and by his words, and in a strange and rather wonderful way, seemed to be in contact with him.'[27] Others found new conceptions of their fathers in reading those letters. Though the war had loomed so large in her childhood, Monica Sinclair found that her father's letters 'told a story I had never known before ... helping me to understand him in a new light'.[28] Margery Elmslie, who enjoyed reading her father's letters, nevertheless described the experience as a 'family revelation': 'my father, as I knew him, was this silent man, kind man, who always had a cigarette in his mouth, never had an opinion of anything. But there, he is full of opinions'. In the letters, she explained, 'I see a different man altogether ... to what I knew.'[29]

Family historians often express regret as they read the war correspondence of uncles and fathers who have since died. As she read her uncle's letters, Eunice Laidler found herself wishing, 'as many of my generation wish, that I had asked more questions and been more attentive and retentive at the time. Now the people I could consult are dead and gone, and I have only my own memory to rely on.'[30] Without immediate reference to those who endured the war firsthand, descendants of former soldiers are left to reformulate and make sense of their ancestors' lives through the prism of their own times. In this they can hardly be unaffected by public narratives of the war, though we need also to recognize family historians' seeking of wider contexts in which to understand that past. Family historians' reactions to what they read, in other words, are guided not just by what they find in personal documents — or indeed official records — but by the fact that their reading occurs in an environment that has shifted significantly in its attitudes towards individual experiences in the Great War. The most significant shift is the wide acceptance of the traumatic effects of war service on soldiers, and the sympathy that flows from that acceptance. The trend is not restricted to wartime ancestors, though perhaps it finds its most compelling examples here. Graeme Davison has pointed out that modern family historians look to their ancestors 'less as moral exemplars than as fellow sufferers', and that 'While the old family history records achievements, the new commemorates suffering.'[31]

The tendency of family historians to see ancestors in the light of suffering and trauma corresponds with the remarkable transformation of the Anzac legend. A tradition that was once grounded in British race patriotism and the superior martial ability of the Australian soldiers has relinquished both these elements. Drained of its military connotations, the legend is more likely to evoke sympathy for the suffering of the soldiers than admiration for their manly fighting ability. What that transition makes possible, in terms of popular representation of the Great War, is an attitude that permits criticism of the war, while preserving the soldiers themselves as worthy of praise on the one hand, and deserving of sympathy as victims on the other. Thus, Bruce Scates found that respondents to his surveys of battlefield travellers derided the overstated nationalism that has so often defined the Anzac tradition, in favour of sympathy for the victims of war who remain on the battlefield.[32] Among our own subjects we find that psychological modes of understanding and explaining an ancestor's war experience have broad appeal. Informed by her own experiences as a nurse and midwife, Margery Elmslie was emphatic in her explanation of her father's low-key response to his war service:

> He didn't want to remember. He didn't want to remember. I'm sure. I mean, you know, your best friend being blown up, I mean nowadays you go off and have counselling and God alone knows what you get, and it was an everyday occurrence for him, he didn't want to remember that, those horrendous wounds.[33]

Elizabeth Whiteside found similar, psychological explanations for her father's behaviour after the war. She was engrossed in her father's letters when she read them in the early 1990s — 'it was a very emotional journey for me' — beginning to understand him as a young man, and becoming 'full of admiration for his spirit and his whole outlook on life'. While reading the letters, she reflected on a sometimes difficult relationship with her father. Whiteside found that she could better understand her relationship with her father in the light of the effects of his war service, the 'impossible things to cope with':

> Well actually I was reduced to tears many many times. Many many times. [Pauses] I suppose realizing what a fine young man he was. I still, as you see, get emotional about that. But I learnt so much from it. We were often at loggerheads. I didn't understand. I didn't understand. And I could have been a much better daughter. But he could have been a better father too in some ways. ... But in a way the publishing of this book was a healing process, both for me and particularly for my ... older brother, who struggled all his life, to try and find, I think, his own footing.[34]

Publishing her father's letters offered an opportunity for Whiteside to testify to suffering. She regretted not reading her father's letters while he was still alive – she felt that she could have developed a better understanding of him as a person. 'It may have been beneficial, perhaps even therapeutic for both of us, to have talked of those times.'[35]

The current generation of family historians – typically, though not always, over fifty years old – are not unaware of the factors that affect their interpretation of the past, having themselves seen and participated in the shifts that have occurred in war remembrance since the 1980s. It was this generation that experienced the Vietnam War, and to whom Peter Weir's *Gallipoli* was intended to speak. These family historians are part of the generation that has transformed the Anzac tradition and war memory more widely in Australia. Therefore, we should not be surprised at the insights of dedicated family historian Margaret Vines, a volunteer at the Genealogical Society of Victoria:

> I do think that recognition of post-traumatic stress has made a tremendous difference in the way people see war, so that when they look at the records of the First World War or any war relatives, they are seeing it now as part of that problem that 'oh he came back from the war and he could never settle down', you know, that sort of thing. Our own generation's experience with the Vietnam veterans, we can translate back to the First World War veterans, and see them much more clearly I think because of it, and see these psychological issues.[36]

The acknowledgement of war's trauma has encouraged an effort to understand those in the past through emotional connection, to 'experience' what the people in the past felt, by an act of empathetic historical imagining. In short, this entails an attempt to connect emotionally with an individual's achievements and traumas – in terms of war especially through tracing their journeys – in order to understand what the past was 'really like'. This mode of engaging with the past has the potential, on the one hand, for encouraging a broader understanding of the scale and violence of the war in which ancestors participated, and on the other for narrowing the modes of analysis of the past.

The power of public narratives of war in shaping private understanding of the wartime past might be seen more clearly by examining the responses of those who discover soldier-ancestors for the first time through family history. The records that these people consult (especially digitized ones) have the potential both to reinforce popular attitudes, and to expand the basis on which an understanding of the war, and new knowledge of it, might be produced. The National Archives of Australia's 'Mapping Our Anzacs' website, established following the full digitization in 2007 of more than 375,000 individual service records of the Great War, affords some insight into this issue. The site not only offers the public access to those records, but also provides 'three ways to commemorate the original Anzacs', including posting private materials in a separate 'scrapbook', and building a 'tribute' to ancestors who feature in the database.[37] Here, one might detect some encouragement to link family history to positive narratives of the military past, through the encouragement to 'commemorate' and pay 'tribute' to one's ancestors in a public forum. On the other hand, we might also see the emergence of a narrative of war that includes a much broader array of actors, and which is not necessarily focussed exclusively on a soldier and what he did at the battlefront.

Family historians who have come of age during or since the resurgence of Anzac commemoration – very often without direct memories of ancestors in the war – are much less ambivalent about the significance of their forebears' war experiences than the generation before can be. The transmission of knowledge within families can be sketchy, incorrect in detail, or entirely absent. For those without direct relationships with the war generation, we can certainly see the rarefaction of detailed knowledge and a greater embrace of public myths. Sometimes the private experience represented by the surviving records is simply enfolded into those dominant public narratives. In 2009, 'Woolwich' wrote of the great uncle, John Miller, whom s/he had never known, insisting now that 'I can only imagine the horrors he experienced.' 'Woolwich' thanked Miller and all the other soldiers 'who fought to ensure Australians have the wonderful lifestyle we enjoy today'.[38] Another contributor, 'stmarys' paid tribute to an ancestor with almost no other context in which to understand who they were, or what they had done:

> This is my great great great great uncle I thank him so much for fighting for Australia and my great great great great great uncle which is your father. ... you did so much for Australia ever if there was another 1 000 000 by your side without you i might not be alive today ... thankyou from your great great great great niece xoxoxo. ... [39]

Naturally, however, there is considerable variation in the level of knowledge that descendants of soldiers bring to family history research, and in how they respond. Carole Sach's engagement with family history was part of a personal quest to find out about her grandfather, whom she knew had died in the war, though the details of his experience remained obscure because her father 'was completely unapproachable about the subject'. Her eventual success, after a series of fruitless efforts at research, left her deeply relieved. Sach visited Gallipoli in 2010, and paid tribute to her grandfather online in 2014:

> Grandad, you have laid forgotten for many years, but not by me.
> Now I have found you and you are forgotten no more.[40]

The familiarity evidenced in addressing ancestors directly is common, and it belies the reality that so many family historians were only now discovering relatives of whom they had previously known nothing. In 2010 'TNottle' came across a great uncle who had died on the Somme in 1916. S/he was 'stunned to find this young man who none of my living relatives even knew existed'. 'TNottle' responded to the discovery in two ways: in the first instance, s/he explained the absence in terms of the traumatic effects of loss: 'it would have been too painful for my great grandmother to talk about, so the family forgot about him.' Armed with this new knowledge, and saddened at his/her great uncle's disappearance from family memory, 'TNottle' set out to rectify it, not only by posting a tribute, but by turning to sites of public history and commemoration. 'With ANZAC day 2010 almost upon us,' s/he wrote, 'for the first time, I will attend a dawn service. In May I will visit the National War Memorial in Canberra.'[41]

The experience of 'TNottle' demonstrates the degrees by which family history increasingly finds definition within broader public narratives. This does not mean, however, that all knowledge of ancestors will necessarily find meaning in this way. Other family historians are inspired to greater contextualization, and can insist – according to the logic of family history – on pushing the boundaries of that history laterally, to understand those other family members whose lives were contemporaneous with the Great War. This opens up the possibility of building more complex understandings of the past, and of the war. Marilyn Lourie admitted that she had been fascinated with history and in particular with the Anzac story since her school days, and in her retirement she planned an overseas trip with her sister that would take in the battlefields of the Western Front. Not knowing of any relatives who had served, she decided to 'adopt' several individuals, whose graves they might visit. Shortly before departure, however, Lourie discovered a cousin of her paternal grandmother who had died in 1918. 'What excitement', she reflected in 2014, 'that now we had our own family member to honour and pay homage to for his supreme sacrifice.'[42]

There are two key ways in which the interest and excitement that Marilyn Lourie shows can result in a broadening of understanding of the war, and of the circles of people involved. In the first place family historians are not necessarily averse to wider reading in the historical literature surrounding soldiers' experiences. In preparation for her trip, Lourie read a series of histories relating to Australians on the battlefront; David Nott also saw 'a job to do' in presenting his father's letters for publication, as he 'put the letters in context, relate[d] them to the chronology of the war, and annotate[d] them so that I could obtain a full understanding'.[43] Such tasks have become infinitely more productive with extensive digitization of newspapers.[44] Jeff Pickerd, a volunteer guide at Melbourne's Shrine of Remembrance, found digitized newspapers an invaluable resource in learning more about the battle in which his maternal grandfather participated: 'I am just finding more and more accounts of the charge at the Nek that probably haven't been seen in nearly 100 years.' He thinks that the old veterans 'would be quite impressed by what they could access'.[45] For some, like Charles Cameron, the modes of family history research can encourage a wider appreciation of the scale of the war itself. His enthusiasm for military history often takes him outside the boundaries of his own family, as he investigates the details of soldiers commemorated in the avenue of honour in his home town: 'I'll grab a name and research and understand what they did, where they died, how they died, how lonely they were.'[46] Through research into the stories of individual soldiers, the names aggregated on memorials – representing the scale of the war – become individualized again.

In the practice of family history, individualizing a soldier is not just about researching their personal story, but placing them in their family context. Thus it is not a substantial leap for family historians to begin contemplating the broader effects of the war, especially on soldiers' families. 'Lyndylulubelle' examined her grandfather's and great uncles' service records online, and was prompted to think not only of their experiences, but to 'wonder how their parents, my great grandparents ... felt farewelling 3 of their boys off to war in such a far off place'.[47] Marilyn Lourie was also drawn to consider the wider legacy of the war, on returning from her visit to the Western Front. She began

> to think about the families left behind and the impact of the war on them. On how they coped with the news of a loved one missing, wounded or killed. How did they keep going when each day could bring the news they were dreading. Also, what about the returning men? Many wounded, unable to work again, many shell shocked and unable to live a normal existence. What burden did this place on families?[48]

The responses of 'Lyndylulubelle' and Marilyn Lourie echo the empathic responses to which we have already referred. They also reflect the reality that family history does not start or end with the Great War. The logic of linking family members necessarily reveals, or at least points to, a range of experiences of war. This expands the horizons of understanding, and helps to resist the dominance of soldier-centric public myths.

The detail of those broader experiences of war is certainly available to family historians, and such stories do resonate with those descendants of the war generation. Oral transmission within families is an important avenue to experiences of loss and mourning. Writing in 2009, 'debbiecox' observed that while her own mother never knew an uncle who died at Gallipoli, she 'Just remembers that if he was mentioned grandma Janet got very upset and so did my great grandmother (his mother) and therefore he was not discussed.'[49]

Charles Cameron, born in 1971, grew up with an awareness of his family's involvement in the Great War. His grandfather, Malcolm, had been too young to enlist, but he kept a portrait of his oldest brother, Colin, who had been killed at Gallipoli, on the desk in his study. When his grandson enquired about the portrait, Malcolm told him: 'That was my brother Colin. He was killed by a machine gun in World War I.' Eventually, Cameron visited Gallipoli with his father and brother, and performed ceremonies in honour of their lost relative.

Beyond family memory, the traces of non-soldier experiences of war are also discernible in the government records that subsequent generations routinely consult. In service records one finds families' enquiries to military authorities, especially upon news of wounding and death. Circulars filled out by next of kin of men who died, as well as Red Cross reports of investigations into the fate of wounded and missing men, are also available. The repatriation files scheduled for digitization frequently feature families as bearers of the burden of care for physically and psychologically damaged men. Whether Bruce Scates's claim that the release of such records 'is set to change the way the Great War is remembered' is borne out, they will certainly facilitate more nuanced family histories, and more complex understanding of the war and its aftermath.[50] One descendant of a man who died in the war could see by these sources that 'His mother and sisters adored him and I ache to read the tormented letters his mother wrote when he was posted as missing and after he died.'[51] As she set about her further family research, Marilyn Lourie found similar letters 'heartbreaking to read' and a testament to the 'grief and trauma suffered by Charles's mother'. In digitized newspapers she discovered other family tragedies associated with the war at home, leading her to insist that a serviceman's widow was 'also ... a casualty of war, as are her children and parents'.[52] The story of the war might indeed be turned on its head through such research. After studying the repatriation records relating to his grandfather, Alistair Thomson was surprised and moved to find that 'my grandmother ... emerges as the tragic heroine of the tale. One man's war story becomes a family history that stretches across the decades and reverberates through the generations.'[53]

The forums in which family histories are encouraged and shared will affect the ways that they are presented and understood. Family historians are not working in isolation, and in the first instance genealogical societies, and the forums attached to family history websites, encourage that broader connection of the war to soldiers' families. Other forums are more likely to engage family history in the service of studying the war itself. Hence the 'Families and Friends of the First AIF', which was founded in 2002, merged a determination to '[Preserve] for future generations of Australians the sense of national identity and values that the First AIF created, beginning with the ANZAC tradition at Gallipoli' with an effort 'to bring together the families and friends of those who served in the Great War 1914–18'.[54] Government agencies are also well aware of the potential to engage Australians more closely with their (national) wartime history. With their own interests in shaping interpretation of the war, they are mobilizing family history as part of their centenary programmes. Since the

1990s, the Australian federal government has promoted the study of the nation's war history in schools, as well as the preservation and publication of private records and material culture of the war. Under the auspices of the 'Anzac centenary', it has made more than A$18,000,000 available via a community grants scheme, to encourage not only local commemorative events, but the preservation and display of artefacts relating to servicemen and women.[55] In its arrangements for the biggest event of the centenary – the Anzac Day service at Gallipoli in 2015 – the Government has privileged family connections to the war. Given the need to restrict the number of people attending Anzac Day at Gallipoli, priority has been given to 'Direct Descendants' of servicemen in the ballot for places. More than 42,000 people applied for the 8,000 places, some of them undoubtedly attracted by the beckoning of the National Archives of Australia. Its homepage asked visitors: 'Need proof that you are a descendant of a Gallipoli Anzac? Search our collection.'[56]

Even more explicitly than the Commonwealth (federal) government, the Government of Victoria has sought to build its Anzac centenary commemoration around the concept of family history. The state's Anzac Centenary Committee bears the hallmark of its chairperson, former conservative premier Ted Baillieu. In turn, Baillieu's distinctive commemorative philosophy has been shaped by his own family's experience of the Great War and what he calls 'the ricochets of war'. His maternal grandfather, William Knox, fought at Gallipoli and was later killed on the Western Front, leaving his mother without a father from the age of three. Such was her distress at losing her father at such a young age and being left an only child, that Diana Baillieu did not read the letters her father had sent to her mother during the war until she was in her eighties. When Ted Baillieu visited Gallipoli in 2008, he received news that his mother had suffered a stroke. At her insistence, he continued on to the site of his grandfather's grave at Vlamertinghe near Ypres in Belgium:

> From Vlamertinghe I rang my wife who happened to be in hospital with my mum. From her father's grave I spoke to her. It was a reverse symmetry to what happened to her and her father. Mum died two days after I got home. We held hands and she knew I was there and she knew I'd been to her father's grave. It was almost like some sort of force was at work.[57]

The confluence of Ted Baillieu's visit to his grandfather's grave with his mother's final illness left him with the conviction that war commemoration should be directed towards events that have personal significance. Baillieu believes that much greater meaning can be derived from this kind of personalized commemoration than from the large-scale events and nationalist incantations beloved of most contemporary politicians:

> I personally tend to try and avoid the clichés because they're like the exhibitions, the kids walk past them. They're like the sculptures you walk past in the park, and you didn't know they were there ... I don't think

there's much benefit in the grand occasions or the exhibitions or the sculptures, unless there are connections made.[58]

As proof of its aversion to ostentatious political acts of commemoration, the Victorian Anzac Centenary Committee has funded a series of projects that draw attention to lesser-known events of the Great War: 'for families and for local communities, these things are probably more important than the big events', says Baillieu. For instance, the Committee intends to commemorate the departure in August 1914 of seven men from Victoria as part of the Australian Naval and Military Expeditionary Force that took German New Guinea in 1914. Baillieu will invite descendants of these men to commemorate the centenary of their departure from Melbourne in August 2014: 'it won't be big, but it will be personal'.[59] In response to criticism that the making of such connections gives elevated status to descendants of Great War soldiers, Baillieu counters that there are many ways of making personal connections: 'it could be through a school or a house where a soldier lived. It doesn't have to be a family connection.' The Committee would like to see plaques placed on the former houses of significant Great War soldiers; it also intends for a relic of the Great War to be passed around Victorian schools: 'it will be put into the hands of every school child in Victoria ... they can touch something knowing that every other kid in Victoria has touched it. Hopefully kids will remember that for fifty years.'[60]

Conclusion

The imperatives of family history, in its focus on the lives of individuals, marry well with an approach to the Great War in Australia – indeed much more broadly than just in Australia – that emphasizes personal and emotional experiences of war as the principal avenue to connecting with the past. The dominance of personal stories as a means of engaging with the history of the war carries with it a number of possibilities for expanding knowledge and challenging received narratives of the war. It also carries with it the dangers of displacing historical and critical understanding with an emphasis on fellow feeling and victimhood. The continuing challenge is to understand the interaction between the private and public making of the past that occurs through family history and public narratives of war. Is war memory likely to ossify in a series of conventional, state-sanctioned symbols, or will it flourish and diversify amid the deluge of personal detail that is increasingly available to family historians? Given the financial and rhetorical resources that have been summoned by the nation-state for marking the centenary of Anzac, one might be doubtful of the prospects for the latter. But family historians are makers as much as they are consumers of history, and the knowledge that they produce and share has not only a potential but a logic that encourages interest in those beyond the frontlines, who were themselves engaged in and deeply affected by war. Family historians will tread this difficult line between analysis and sentiment, as they not only interpret the growing wealth of materials that can connect them to family pasts, but search for broader contexts in which to make sense of that past. Public centenary activities will propel that understanding in particular directions; they might also open space for less consensual histories to emerge from below.

Notes

1 Alistair Thomson, *Anzac Memories: Living with the Legend*, 2nd ed. (Melbourne: Monash University Publishing, 2013), 282.
2 Bruce Scates and Alistair Thomson, '"A Land Fit For Heroes?" – "Shattered Anzacs" and the Legacy of World War I', Making Public Histories Seminar Series, State Library of Victoria, Melbourne, 29 May 2014.
3 Tanya Evans, 'Secrets and lies: the radical potential of family history', *History Workshop Journal* 71 (2011), 51.
4 Annette Wieviorka, *The Era of the Witness*, translated by Jared Stark (Ithaca: Cornell University Press, 2006).
5 Thomson, 320.
6 Christina Twomey, 'Trauma and the reinvigoration of Anzac: an argument', *History Australia* 10:3 (December 2013), 88.
7 Bruce Scates, *Return to Gallipoli* (Melbourne: Cambridge, 2006), 101–2.
8 See especially Stéphane Audoin-Rouzeau and Annette Becker, *14–18: Understanding the Great War*, translated by Catherine Termerson (New York: Hill and Wang, 2002); Dan Todman, *The Great War: Myth and Memory* (London: Hambledon Continuum, 2005), 173.
9 Twomey, 107; also Bain Attwood, cited in Michelle Arrow, '"I just feel it's important to know exactly what he went through": *In Their Footsteps* and the role of emotions in Australian television history', *Historical Journal of Film, Radio and Television* 33:4 (2013), 600.
10 Joy Damousi, 'Why do we get so emotional about Anzac?', in Marilyn Lake and Henry Reynolds, with Joy Damousi, Mark McKenna and Carina Donaldson, *What's Wrong with Anzac? The Militarisation of Australian History* (Sydney: UNSW Press, 2010), 97.
11 Ibid., 96.
12 Mark McKenna, 'Anzac Day: How did it become Australia's national day?', in *What's Wrong with Anzac?*, 110–34.
13 John Howard, 'Address at State Funeral for Alec Campbell', Hobart, 6 May 2002. Online. Available: <http://australianpolitics.com/2002/05/24/john-howard-address-at-state-funeral-service-for-alec-campbell.html> (accessed 14 May 2014).
14 George Kirk, *Tales from Tangerine & World War I Diary of Pte. A. G. Kirk M.M.* (Maryborough: George Kirk, 2002), ix; David Nott (ed.), *Somewhere in France: The Collected Letters of Lewis Windermere Nott, January–December 1916* (Sydney: Harper Collins, 1996), viii.
15 Interview with Margery Elmslie, 4 February 2014.
16 Interview with Jeff Pickard, 22 March 2014.
17 Interview with Linley Hooper, 26 February 2014.
18 Peter Read, '"Before Rockets and Aeroplanes": Family History', *Australian Cultural History* 22 (2003), 132.
19 Monica Sinclair, *Dear Ad—Love Ron: the complete collection of the handwritten letters and diary entries of Ronald Augustine Sinclair, Australian Imperial Forces, Fifth Division Artillery, 14th Field Artillery Brigade, 114th Howitzer Battery on active service in Egypt, France and Belgium 1915–1919* (Neutral Bay, NSW: M. T. Sinclair, 1997).
20 Gilbert Mant, 'Introduction', in W. J. Duffell, *Soldier Boy: The Letters of Gunner W. J. Duffell, 1915–18* (Kenthurst: Kangaroo Press, 1992), 7.

21 Interview with Elizabeth Whiteside, 3 February 2014.
22 Whiteside interview, 3 February 2014.
23 Elmslie interview, 4 February 2014.
24 Bart Ziino, '"A Lasting Gift to His Descendants": Family Memory and the Great War in Australia', *History & Memory* 22:2 (2010), 125–46; Carolyn Holbrook, *Anzac, The Unauthorised Biography* (Sydney: New South, 2014).
25 Graeme Davison, *The Use and Abuse of Australian History* (Sydney: Allen & Unwin, 2000), 84.
26 Ashley Barnwell, 'The Genealogy Craze: Authoring an Authentic Identity through Family History Research', *Life Writing* 10:3 (2013), 263.
27 Nott, xiii, xv.
28 Sinclair, vii.
29 Elmslie interview, 4 February 2014.
30 Eunice Laidler, in Walter James McPherson, *Walter's War: Letters of Walter James McPherson, 59th Battalion, A.I.F. During World War 1, 1914–1918* (St Arnaud, Vic.: Rosewold Publications, 1998), 3.
31 Davison, 87, 101.
32 Scates, 109.
33 Elmslie interview, 4 February 2014.
34 Whiteside interview, 3 February 2014.
35 Elizabeth Whiteside, in Thomas Clair Whiteside, *A Valley in France*, 3rd ed. (Beaconsfield, Vic.: E. Whiteside, 2002), ix.
36 Interview with Margaret Vines, 26 February 2014.
37 Mapping Our Anzacs. Online. Available: <http://mappingouranzacs.naa.gov.au/about.aspx> (accessed 1 April 2014).
38 'My uncle'. Online. Available: <http://our-anzacs.tumblr.com/post/143434732/my-uncle> (accessed 1 April 2014).
39 'My great great great great uncle … thankyou'. Online. Available: <http://our-anzacs.tumblr.com/post/102095652/my-great-great-great-great-uncle-thankyou> (accessed 1 April 2014).
40 'My journey to Gallipoli'. Online. Available: <http://our-anzacs.tumblr.com/post/80713807831/my-journey-to-gallipoli> (accessed 1 April 2014).
41 'I remember you'. Online. Available: <http://our-anzacs.tumblr.com/post/537552589/i-remember-you> (accessed 1 April 2014).
42 Marilyn Lourie, 'Some family connections to World War 1', March 2014, 2. Unpublished ms. in possession of the authors.
43 Nott, xv.
44 For the range of Australian newspapers available, see the National Library of Australia's 'Trove' site. Online. Available: <http://trove.nla.gov.au/newspaper?q=%20> (accessed 30 May 2014).
45 Jeff Pickerd interview, 22 March 2014.
46 Interview with Charles Cameron, 13 February 2014.
47 'A little of Roys family history'. Online. Available: <http://our-anzacs.tumblr.com/post/145090719/a-little-of-roys-family-history> (accessed 1 April 2014).
48 Lourie, 'Some family connections', 2.
49 'Richard Williamson', Online. Available: <http://our-anzacs.tumblr.com/post/90612614/richard-williamson-was-my-great-uncle-his-sister> (accessed 1 April 2014).
50 Marina Larsson, *Shattered Anzacs: Living with the Scars of War* (Sydney: UNSW Press, 2009); Bruce Scates, 'Horrors of Anzac aftermath laid bare', *Age*, 7 November 2013.
51 'Vale "Billy"'. Online. Available: <http://our-anzacs.tumblr.com/post/348660077/vale-billy-beloved-brother-of-annie-winifred> (accessed 1 April 2014).
52 Lourie, 'Some family connections', 3.
53 Thomson, 259.

54 Families and Friends of the First AIF. Objectives and Constitution. Online. Available: <http://fffaif.org.au/?page_id=14> (accessed 1 April 2014).
55 Anzac Centenary Local Grants Program. Online. Available HTTP: <www.anzaccentenary.gov.au/documents/public.pdf> (accessed 1 April 2014)
56 National Archives of Australia. Online. Available: <http://naa.gov.au> (accessed 1 April 2014).
57 Interview with Ted Baillieu, 20 March 2014.
58 Ibid.
59 Ibid.
60 Ibid.

Part 2
Practices of remembering

3 Framing the Great War in Britain
Modern mediated memories

Ross Wilson

The conflict of 1914–18 casts a long shadow in former combatant countries. Even after the passing of the last veterans of the Great War, marking the end of 'living memory', the cultural remembrance of the first industrialized conflict fought on a global scale remains a powerful, emotive influence on societies whose forebears endured the conflict.[1] This popular memory of the Great War in Britain is frequently derided by revisionist historians as composed of 'myths' perpetuated by inaccurate media portrayals. Yet this conception relies upon the assumption that an audience passively consumes and reproduces 'myth' via cultural forms – film, literature, television, monuments – without a degree of agency or selection. To move beyond a debate that pits 'myth' against 'history' requires a more detailed study of the ways in which modern British audiences themselves draw upon and utilize cultural representations of war to make sense of contemporary economic, political and social concerns. Through such an analysis, this chapter argues that the media depiction of the 1914–18 war can be observed as providing a framework of *reference*, not a framework of *memory*. Representations of the war are actively engaged with and used to mobilize the memory of the war for varying political, social and cultural purposes in the present. This process can be traced through the allusions made within media, political and public discourse to such representations of war as the television series *Blackadder Goes Forth* (1989), the film *Oh! What a Lovely War* (1969) or Sebastian Faulks's novel *Birdsong* (1993). Studying the discourses that reference the war's cultural products reveals how individuals, groups and communities actively engage with and redeploy representations of the war, rather than merely reflecting the values and ideals of the representations themselves. This helps us to address the more fundamental question of why a war fought at the beginning of the twentieth century still bears relevance for contemporary British society. The war maintains value and meaning due to its perception as a historical trauma – a lesson in human suffering and loss – through which current concerns can be critiqued or justified. That trauma functions as a symbolic resource that can be drawn upon by groups to frame varying ideals and identities, to undermine authority or indeed to support the *status quo*. We see the active privileging of cultural representations of the Great War that enable the preservation of that trauma, thereby ensuring that a particular memory of the war endures.

The Great War and cultural memory in Britain

In Britain, remembering the Great War commonly evokes strong sentiments of pity; the mere mention of 'the Somme', 'Passchendaele' or 'the trenches' conjures images of soldiers suffering the maelstrom of industrialized war at the behest of their indifferent or incompetent commanding officers.[2] Revisionist scholars have sought to distinguish between this cultural memory and history, demonstrating the limited and at times inaccurate portrayal of the war by authors and artists.[3] These historians see the remembrance of war in Britain as being – unfortunately – derived from the war poetry of Siegfried Sassoon (1886–1967) and Wilfred Owen (1893–1918), the film adaptation of *Oh! What a Lovely War*, or the television series *Blackadder Goes Forth*, rather than a more 'realistic' appreciation of the events that took place on the battlefields and the home front during the four years of conflict that led to eventual victory.[4]

The critique levelled at these representations is that they perpetuate the cliché of the Great War as that of 'rats, gas, mud and blood', feeding a public memory of the war in Britain that focuses on disillusion, trauma and suffering.[5] Bond has also analyzed how specific tropes of atrocious battlefields where working class soldiers die as the result of official neglect have been replicated across a variety of media from the 1920s to the present day.[6] Therefore, from Robert Graves's autobiography *Good-bye to All That* (1929), to Pat Barker's novel *Regeneration* (1991), revisionist historians detect a common portrayal of the war that works to produce a distinct – and flawed – remembrance of the conflict in public consciousness.[7] Such assessments are politically loaded in contemporary Britain, where the struggle over war memory has, for many revisionist historians, resolved itself into a crusade to remove 'left-wing bias' from popular conceptions of the past.[8] This sort of struggle assumes a concerted effort at the reinforcement of 'myth', whether from government agencies, curriculum advisers, film makers or novelists. Yet attempts by scholars to portray the revision of the public perception of the war as 'neutral' and 'objective' equally obscures the subtle power relations inherent in this discourse. This makes the need to understand not only how the war is perceived, but the contexts and manner in which it is invoked in public, more pressing. Examining how and why the war is remembered through popular media reveals the ways in which the conflict constitutes a symbolic resource which is drawn upon as a means of promoting a range of ideological viewpoints.[9]

The assessment of the 'invention of tradition' with regard to the memory of the Great War in Britain has certainly demonstrated the way in which authors and artists have drawn upon a limited set of images to represent the conflict.[10] It has not, however, satisfactorily explained the relationship between this media representation and its wider public reception.[11] In essence, the argument for a media-manipulated remembrance of the past relies upon the assumption that cultural forms are vapidly consumed by a credulous public. The presumed facility of films, novels and television programmes to communicate directly encourages the belief that these visions of the war are those accepted as 'truthful' renditions. Such a standpoint neglects an assessment of why an 'interpretative community', group or society chooses to remember in particular ways.[12] Indeed, it negates the presence of an active decision to close off particular readings of the past in favour of others.[13] We need, then, to acknowledge a much greater level of agency in those reproducing and reinterpreting war memory: cultural memory of the war is not a product simply of media representations of the conflict, but a selection of materials to form a specific understanding of the Great War.[14]

J. V. Wertsch has assessed how cultural memory is formed through an interaction of individuals and cultural 'tools'.[15] Memory in this assessment is mediated, rather than simply transmitted. It is so done by agents who use monuments, memorials, commemorative practices, novels, film and theatre as vehicles or devices for expression, not as directives for comprehension.[16] Memory is, therefore, performed for a rationale; it serves the purposes of those who seek to maintain a particular version of the past. Whilst this takes place within a nexus of social, political and cultural concerns, it is, nevertheless, a demonstration that memory is not an inactive response to media representations. It is an engaged process that uses cultural forms to shape attitudes, identities and values in the present. It is in this respect that we can speak of the function of media in 'framing' perception, and the interaction of media and memory being revealed through 'frame analysis'. Frame analysis has been applied across a number of disciplines; its core concern is to reveal the perceptual structures embraced by individuals or communities in comprehending the world.[17] This approach is well-suited to an analysis of memory, as the process of remembering the past in the present can be regarded as an application of a framework, using references to the past as a means of placing oneself in the present.[18]

Therefore, it is not the contemporary issues which are framed by the popular memory of the Great War that are significant, nor are the politics that popular memory is presumed to represent; what is important is the manner in which contemporary Britons use these cultural representations to place those issues into context. In this, media depictions serve a variety of agendas and ideas, from dissenting politics to reinforcing norms.[19] This highlights the contested nature of the remembrance of the Great War, which can be understood not as a divide between popular perception and academic history, but one of meaning and value constantly harnessed and reinterpreted by individuals, groups and communities each seeking to further their own agenda.[20] Critics of popular memory need to acknowledge how the notion of the Great War as a trauma is widely shared, not due to an act of mass or self-delusion, but because it serves effective purposes across the political spectrum. Aligning one's own agenda within traumatic aspects of the past provides a means of political justification in the present.[21] Particular visions of the past, which are replicated in television, film and fiction, appeal because they enable the communication of shock, pain and distress in the contemporary era. As such, the cultural representations of the conflict are invoked to preserve this framework of understanding.

Framing the present with the past

This use of the cultural representations of the war is most clearly represented in *Blackadder Goes Forth*, so often the bête noir of historians seeking to revise popular memory and assert the 'history' of the Great War.[22] This television series, featuring suffering soldiers, incompetent officers, atrocious conditions and pointless military advances, serves as a reference for both public and political discourse and is applied in a wide variety of contexts. Its title, characters and plot are available to frame current issues in light of the traumatic past they represent. The object of this framing is opened up to ridicule or scorn as notions of incompetence and culpability are communicated through association with the trauma of the war. For example, within the popular media, the drama is evoked to discuss the necessity of remembrance or outrage at authority. This is most easily seen in critiques of current military engagements. In 2009, the conservative tabloid *The Sun* called for the remembrance of troops – not the politicians or generals – to be sustained during Remembrance Day, in the context of unpopular wars in Iraq and Afghanistan:

> All of the warring generals and most of the politicians from all sides welcomed war, any war, with open arms. They just couldn't wait to get stuck in. Think of Stephen Fry's brilliant portrayal of the fictitious mad General Melchett in *Blackadder Goes Forth* and you will get the picture.[23]

Similarly, the conservative *Daily Express* also drew upon *Blackadder Goes Forth* to express indignation at presumed government ineptitude in the provision of needless and unhelpful orders to troops in Afghanistan:

> For many troops the instruction is reminiscent of a scene in the comedy Blackadder, in which General Melchett orders Captain Darling to write a paper on 'military dress code' in the trenches while Blackadder is knee high in mud.[24]

In this manner, *Blackadder Goes Forth* becomes not a means by which memory is produced, but a frame through which memory can be expressed. Invoking characters, contexts and situations from the series enables a critical agenda to emerge which is applied not simply to the war itself, but to current political debate. This frame of reference, however, is not only applied to military issues; it can also be evoked in the wider operations of government to stress a dereliction of duty. For example, in 2013 the liberal *Independent* newspaper critically analyzed the British Government's economic strategy through reference to *Blackadder*:

> It is easy to mock, and to suggest that persisting with a failed economic policy and with a failed political message is the Lord Melchett strategy. He it was who, in *Blackadder Goes Forth*, said that going over the top and charging the German lines was precisely what had failed before and therefore what the enemy would be least expecting.[25]

In this regard, the popular memory of the war is used to place wider concerns into a context of official incompetence, blame and responsibility. The cultural representations of the war serve as a means to utilize the sense of trauma associated with the conflict. The result is its perpetuation. This process of framing present issues within past contexts suggests that popular memory of the Great War concerns the representation and use of power within contemporary society at least as much as it refers to the events of 1914–18. Referring to aspects of *Blackadder Goes Forth* becomes a means to portray, and to critique, the pursuit of tactics or strategy through allusion to the traumatic history of the Great War regardless of the object of opprobrium. This is evident in the extracts below which seek to undermine others through the employment of this framing device:

> What riles Tory MPs above all is the all-too-familiar picture of their leader playing the part of an aristocrat officer, barking unrealistic orders at his battle-scarred troops without a care for conditions in the trenches. 'It all comes across as a bit Melchett', says one disappointed Cameron MP, referring to Stephen Fry's portrayal of a pompous, dimwit First World War general in the *Blackadder* series. The Tory infantry see themselves as lions led by a donkey.[26]

> Does David perhaps think he is playing the role of General Melchett in *Blackadder Goes Forth*? He talks repeatedly of 'we know it's hard' and 'we may not succeed' and 'we have to do it' – but which 'we' is he referring to? Has the *Times* columnist suddenly joined up with the British army, which is losing so many of its brave young squaddies in the Afghan quagmire?[27]

Referencing this cultural product is, therefore, far more than a simple acquiescence in the reception of 'media-ted' visions of history, but a knowing application of the form to understand and frame the present in the context of a traumatic past.

Similarly, accusations of 'left-wing bias' in popular memories of the war tend to fragment when we recognize that there is no specific cause to which this referencing of the past is inherently attached: all parts of the political spectrum draw symbolic value from their association with it. The history of suffering is not the prerogative of a dissonant agenda; indeed it also serves as a means to remind society of the sacrifices undertaken for the nation. Contrary to the assertions of revisionist historians, the popular memory of the war in Britain is not dominated by a left-wing ideology. In the House of Commons in November 2001, Conservative Member of Parliament Michael Jack utilized those same tropes of suffering and death to reiterate the need for the current military operations in Afghanistan:

> We will remember the massive loss of life that occurred, for example, on the Somme. Faulks's book *Birdsong* reminded us that, on day one, 40,000

were killed. We will remember them, and we shall not forget their sacrifice. They were fighting for freedom, democracy and the things that we hold near and dear. That is why we have to engage, again, in military activity against terrorism – in this case, against al-Qaeda.[28]

In this manner, the referencing of media is not intended to support a radical, dissonant voice against authority, but one calling for action and a collective sense of effort. We also see this use of the poignant, piteous images prevalent within the representations of the conflict in support of traditional values, through the insistence on bearing witness to those who sacrificed their lives for their country. Writing in Newcastle's *Sunday Sun* in 2010, one commentator used the popular memory to enact this established mode of recognition:

The horror of war is only understood if you've been there. My great-grandfather's emotional and physical struggle is incomprehensible, though brilliant novels such as Sebastian Faulks' *Birdsong* give us a glimpse ... And that's why I'm wearing my poppy with pride, for my great grandfather and all those who perished before and after him.[29]

Framing debates within the context of the traumatic history of the Great War provides a means of utilizing literature, film and television for wider purposes rather than merely echoing the media representations themselves. The various portrayals of the conflict are used to demonstrate or illustrate wider social and political concerns. In this manner, television programmes such as the historical drama *Downton Abbey* (2010), set within a country estate and depicting both the conflict on the battlefields and its impact in Britain, were mobilized within the media and political discourse to evidence a continuing sense of traumatic loss in the war. One reviewer for the *Belfast Telegraph* noted:

With its sumptuous setting, exquisite costumes and the reassurance that everyone knew their place in those days, the series captured the last hurrah of a way of life which disappeared forever into the mud of the trenches of the First World War.[30]

Despite the series' overwhelming focus on the trials and tribulations of the landed gentry, in this rendering, the representation of the war as a tragic, 'lost past' serves as a means of reaffirming traditional bonds within society through a sense of a collective effort undertaken during wartime. In a House of Lords debate in 2010 to mark Remembrance Day, Conservative Peer Baron Astor of Hever drew upon the television series in the same manner, to remind members of this united action:

I believe that we still feel a connection to those who fought in the Great War, not because we watch episodes of *Downton Abbey*, but because every family in the land was affected by the conflict. It was truly the nation at war.[31]

The capacity to use *Downton Abbey* in this manner derives from its presumed representation of the 'truth' of the war. In its portrayal of battlefield scenes in the trenches it reiterates the truisms of the 'horror' and 'brutality' of the conflict. Newspaper reviewers regarded such depictions as truthful accounts of the 'squalor', 'mud' and 'death' of the battlefields.[32] Indeed, despite its critical reception within sections of the media, the insistence on portraying the danger and terror of the battlefields of the Western Front in *Downton Abbey* was still noted by commentators.[33] This focus demonstrates the significance of the battlefields within wider public life in Britain. The utility of this representation is in the opportunity to maintain the memory of the war as a traumatic event, in which profits are made at the expense of the masses. The present and the past are framed through cultural representations as a means of drawing upon the conflict as a symbolic resource to affirm issues of power, identity and politics.

Framing a sense of trauma

The reproduction of the trauma of the Great War through cultural forms such as *Downton Abbey* allows the war to retain a powerful social and political status for the purposes to which it is applied. Those who refer to the war are mobilizing its traumatic elements, not just to emphasize futility, but also a sense of collective trial, endurance and stoicism. Novels, film and television programmes are thereby used as frames; they are devices for proclaiming the relevance of the past for the present. This is perhaps best illustrated with the referencing of Barker's 1991 novel *Regeneration*. In the debates surrounding the issuing of pardons for executed soldiers in the British Army during the Great War, commentators mobilized Barker's emphasis on the 'horror' of war and the psychological damage of shell-shock to insist that it represented the 'truth' of the war.[34] Upon the announcement of the pardons in 2006, one commentator in *The Economist* placed great emphasis on Barker's work in detailing this 'truth':

> Meanwhile Pat Barker's successful *Regeneration* trilogy of novels accustomed people to the idea that trench warfare was not only hell but was also liable to drive soldiers mad.[35]

The campaign for the pardons demonstrates how representations of the conflict are activated to mobilize a sense of shock, horror and outrage within society. They are used by individuals, groups and communities to insist upon the traumatic status of the Great War as a means of pursuing further agendas. This maintenance is highly significant, as without returning to the event in this manner, in whatever mediated capacity, the conflict would lose its relevance for British society: memory would become history.[36] Cultural representations of the conflict provide a means to maintain and preserve the affecting and effecting trauma of the war. Indeed, as one commentator in *The Independent* newspaper noted during a tour of the battlefields, these cultural representations are the touchstones of memory:

> Forgetting the war is not an option here [on the former battlefields]; and in Britain, where it might be we aren't prepared to let go. As the last old soldiers fade away, the memory is kept alive by novels such as Sebastian Faulks's *Birdsong* and Pat Barker's *Regeneration* trilogy ... In recent years, the two minutes' silence on Armistice Day has been observed with renewed fervour[37]

The utility of these representations of the conflict is in their ability to evoke the presence and familiarity of the war. Indeed, this is the way in which all cultural media are used, from the work of the war poets and memoirists of the post-war era to the recent spate of films, novels and television programmes which concern the conflict of 1914–18.[38] Works such as Michael Morpurgo's *Private Peaceful* (2003) and *War Horse* (1982), or the latter's recent film adaptation (2012), are embraced for their preserving the war for contemporary society rather than their reimagining of it. This process can be witnessed in Remembrance Day sermons in churches in Britain, where these works are utilized to draw the congregation's attention to the place of the war in contemporary society. At Ipswich Unitarian Meeting House on Sunday 11 November 2012, the sermon directly evoked several representations of the war:

> The futility and madness of the 'Great War' were powerfully conveyed by its poets: Wilfred Owen, Siegfried Sassoon and Isaac Rosenberg. Their poems echoed through the 20th century, while plays and films like 'O what a lovely War' [sic], 'Private Peaceful', 'War Horse' and the novels of Pat Barker have continued to keep the terrifying lessons of that war fresh for each new generation.[39]

Similarly, in the Remembrance sermon delivered in 2012 at the Parish Church of St John-at-Hampstead, London, the Reverend Jan Rushton used the novels of the war to reassert the traumatic nature of the conflict:

> This horrific treatment was brought to our consciousness in Pat Barker's first set of novels about the Great War. Barker challenges us to look again at our own preconceived notions of what is right and acceptable in society.[40]

This referencing is significant as it evidences how cultural products can be assessed as tools used to facilitate 'memory work' within society. The objective of this use of novels, film and television programmes is not necessarily to argue that their content forms the 'truth' of the war – that is apparently self-evident – it is to ensure the conflict remains current across society so that it can be sustained as a symbolic resource. The truth is, therefore, following the pragmatic philosophy of William James, what is better for us to believe: the Great War is surviving its participants through the willing and active use of its representational tropes in public life.[41] This process of using media representations to relate the Great War to contemporary society and politics, then, exposes the centrality of an ongoing and widespread acceptance of the war's trauma.[42] The popular memory of the Great War of death, sorrow and pity is activated through these frames of reference, and serves some very popular purposes in British political and cultural life. For example, the 2012 television adaptation of Ford Maddox Ford's (1873–1939) novel *Parade's End* provided a means of emphasizing the traumatic experience of the conflict. The script for the dramatization explicitly draws attention to this suffering:

> Wide: pandemonium – heavy rain, shells exploding, flares bursting over No-Man's-Land … Broken trees, barbed wire, mud, flooded craters … A German soldier comes over the British parapet as if hurled, and hits the parados (the back wall of the trench). The German, however, has already been shot in the face, his eyes a mask of blood. A Very flare shows the state of the German, and also a dead infantryman … Christopher kneels by the German, feeling his neck artery.[43]

The potential for this representation of trauma to reflect contemporary concerns is affirmed in an interview with leading actor Benedict Cumberbatch:

> When I got into the trench created for *Parade's End* with one of those tin hats on, I realised you're standing basically in a grave … We're living through a time where we are fighting wars with equally tragic realities for our soldiers and their families. We are living in a time of political hypocrisy and there aren't that many really good people.[44]

This utility of cultural forms is also reflected in the way in which older representations of the war, theatre, film or television, are revived and made pertinent and illuminating with regard to modern events. In this manner, revivals of productions such as *Oh! What a Lovely War!*, first performed in 1963 and offering an indictment of the class structures that saw thousands of working class men killed at the behest of an incompetent upper class elite, are used as frames of reference, to place and to critically assess current issues within society. In the context of the beginnings of the Iraq War in 2003, a touring production of *Oh! What a Lovely War!* enabled a critique of the government's actions in leading a country to war and sending its citizens to their deaths in a war seemingly without meaning or any foreseeable end.[45] Such a critical use of the play can also be observed in newspaper articles which utilize the title *Oh! What a Lovely War!* to decry contemporary abuses of power or to highlight political failings. In the following examples, the title is used to assess the legacy, implications and profiteering from western military action in Iraq, Afghanistan and Libya:

> Oh what a lovely war in Afghanistan: we're staying till the job is done.[46]

> Oh! What a lovely war: Liam Fox and his lucky aides direct the conflict in Libya from a Spanish hotel – at the taxpayer's expense.[47]

> Oh what a lovely war on terror it's been for Halliburton.[48]

> Oh, what a lovely war for profits: Pharmaceutical firms, IBM, General Motors, even the cabbage growers – they've all benefited since 11 September.[49]

Referencing the media portrayals of the conflict enables their users and readers to activate the popular memory of the war as a trauma, and so quickly frame and understand and perceive current agendas. Rather than dismissing these allusions as journalistic clichés, they are more appropriately analyzed as evidence of how the conflict of 1914–18 is not over; it is a war which cannot be consigned to a passive historical rendering. Attempts to revise the popular memory of the war to ensure an 'accurate' reading of the conflict obscure the way in which the Great War functions within society as a symbolic resource drawn from a traumatic past. Indeed, revisionist history frequently attempts to deride popular memory despite relying upon the same historical trauma to support established ideals of honourable sacrifice and loyalty to the nation.[50] This is highly important for understanding the way in which cultural representations are used within society, as to maintain this sense of trauma, to remain symbolic, powerful and useful to individuals, communities and wider society, the war must be kept within mind. The popular memory of the Great War in Britain is not a misunderstood version of a historical event, it is not a misreading of the past nor a thoughtless act of consumption of apparently 'easier' media portrayals; it is an active engagement with cultural materials to preserve the trauma of the event. Attempts by historians to 'debunk' the 'myths' of the conflict thereby misunderstand the place of the remembrance of the war across Britain. It is not borne out of an inability to remember the correct version of history, but out of a desire not to consign it to history. As Žižek has observed:

> The point is not to remember the past trauma as exactly as possible: such 'documentation' is a priori false, it transforms the trauma into a neutral, objective fact, whereas the essence of the trauma is precisely that it is too horrible to be remembered, to be integrated into our symbolic universe.[51]

There is no inherent meaning of the war: what remains is a hegemonic struggle for the use of a past trauma. To be able to state association with this historical suffering provides justification for ideals and actions in the present. Notions of cultural trauma are particularly useful in this respect as they enable an alternative perspective on popular memory, not as a misapprehension of the past, but as a vital component of identity:

> Cultural trauma occurs when members of a collectivity feel they have been subjected to a horrendous event that leaves indelible marks upon their group consciousness, marking their memories forever and changing their future identity in fundamental ways.[52]

Following Breuer and Freud's diagnosis of the ability of trauma to form the individual, scholars have harnessed this approach to demonstrate the utility of 'trauma' as a mode of analysis.[53] In this fashion, trauma forms a means of communicating communal concepts of both an individual and a collective sense of self. This follows on from the work of Novick, who assessed the contemporary focus on 'victimhood' and trauma as a means of defining identity as opposed to a classical concern for the brave and victorious.[54] Cultural trauma can be regarded through a variety of media, from novels and films to monuments and commemorative practices. The significance of these representations or actions is their capacity to sustain a sense of shock, bereavement and suffering.[55] This is certainly evident in the range of British representations regarding the Great War, which, scholars have noted, bear marked resemblances to each other. The similarity within these depictions and the repeated motifs they contain demonstrates the existence of common perceptions about a historical episode and the desire to maintain and perpetuate this perception: to continue to frame the understanding of the war as a traumatic event. In effect, it reasserts what is already held to be self-evident by contemporary audiences, and then requires that audience serve as witnesses to this trauma; to bear the truth of the past into the present by testifying to its significance. Cultural forms act as a means to focus attention on this historic pain and distress. Indeed, media such as *Blackadder Goes Forth* or *Oh! What a Lovely War* that enable the communication of this trauma are valued above others because they provide a means of sustaining this understanding of the past. Such uses of trauma are not limited to one political ideology or another, rather the traumatic history of the war constitutes a symbolic resource that can be drawn upon by various groups for varying agendas.

Conclusion

The media representations of the Great War in Britain have become the object of a great deal of academic derision which regards these depictions as fuelling the 'inaccurate' popular memory of the conflict as one of 'rats, gas, mud and blood'. In this assessment, these media representations of the war are seemingly invested with a supreme power to shape the ideas of a public who are accorded little or no agency in the construction of memory.[56] The models used to understand the role of film, television and literature in remembering the Great War in Britain rely upon a simplistic understanding of consumption without reflection. Such assessments neglect how these portrayals of the conflict are used within society, as their intent is to debunk popular memory as 'myth'.[57] These studies focus on deconstruction through the methodological lens provided by the 'invention of tradition'.[58] In this manner, attempts at revising popular memory do no more than assert the merits of one competing vision of the past over another. This obscures the more central issue of why individuals, communities and wider society seemingly want to remember the conflict in a way that preserves a sense of trauma regarding the past.

By assessing the manner in which these cultural forms are evoked within political, public and media discourse, we can better understand the function of war memory. Representations of the war serve as 'tools', as frames: film, television and fiction such as *Blackadder Goes Forth* or *Birdsong* operate as touchstones, by which the popular memory of the war as traumatic event is brought to bear on contemporary matters. We can see the active role of memory in this process, which reveals a far more complex engagement with media representations than simple consumption. This dynamic memory work which takes place within society maintains the sense of trauma regarding the war. This is a highly significant aspect of the utility of cultural representations in remembering the past.[59] By the continual reassertion of the status of the conflict as a traumatic event, the Great War in Britain retains broad social significance; it serves as a means to assert issues of identity, power and politics. This sense of trauma is not limited to one political agenda; rather it provides a platform for individuals, groups and communities to frame current concerns in relation to the conflict. The analysis of the popular memory of the Great War in Britain has been overly concerned with what is remembered rather than how or even why society remembers in particular ways. Representations of the war are used to sustain a sense of trauma in the present, to mobilize the conflict for current concerns and to so ensure that the Great War retains meaning and value in Britain despite the cessation of hostilities nearly a century ago.

Notes

1 D. Todman, *The Great War: Myth and Memory* (London: Hambledon Continuum, 2007); P. Fussell, *The Great War and Modern Memory* (Oxford: Oxford University Press, 1975); A. Thomson, *Anzac Memories: Living with the Legend* (Oxford: Oxford University Press, 1994); J. F. Vance, *Death so Noble: Memory, Meaning and the First World War* (Vancouver: University of British Columbia Press, 1998).
2 R. Wilson, 'The Trenches in British Popular Memory', *InterCulture* 5:2 (2008): 109–18.
3 See B. Bond, *The Unquiet Western Front* (Cambridge: Cambridge University Press, 2002), 9; also S. Badsey, 'Blackadder Goes Forth and the "two Western Fronts" Debate', in *The Historian, Television and Television History*, eds G. Roberts and P. M. Taylor (Luton: University of Luton Press, 2001), 113–25; G. Sheffield, *Forgotten Victory, The First World War – Myths and Realities* (London: Review, 2002).
4 See Badsey, 'Blackadder'; S. Badsey, 'The Great War since the Great War', *Historical Journal of Film, Radio and Television* 22:1 (2002), 7–19; S. Badsey, *The British Army in Battle and Its Image 1914–1918* (London: Continuum, 2009).
5 G. Corrigan, *Mud, Blood and Poppycock* (London: Cassell, 2003).

6 Bond, 5.
7 B. Korte, 'The Grandfathers' War: Re-imagining World War One in British Novels and Films of the 1990s', in *Retrovisions: Reinventing the Past in Film and Fiction*, eds D. Cartmell, I. Q. Hunter and I. Whelhan (London and Sterling, VA: Pluto Press 2001), 120–31.
8 See N. Ferguson, *The Pity of War* (London: Penguin, 1998).
9 After W. Brown, *Politics Out of History* (Princeton: Princeton University Press, 2001).
10 After E. Hobsbawm and T. Ranger (eds), *The Invention of Tradition* (Cambridge: Cambridge University Press, 1983).
11 R. Williams, 'Culture Is Ordinary', in *Resources of Hope: Culture, Democracy, Socialism*, ed. R. Gable (London: Verso, 1989), 4–5.
12 S. Fish, *Is There a Text in This Class? The Authority of Interpretive Communities* (Cambridge, MA: Harvard University Press, 1980), 14.
13 J. V. Wertsch, *Voices of Collective Remembering* (Cambridge: Cambridge University Press, 2002), 12.
14 Wilson, 109–10.
15 Wertsch, 12.
16 Wertsch, 21.
17 See E. Goffman, *Frame Analysis: An Essay on the Organization of Experience* (New York: Harper and Row, 1974), 10–12.
18 After P. Connerton, *How Societies Remember* (Cambridge: Cambridge University Press, 1989); S. Radstone and K. Hodgkin, *Memory Cultures: Memory, Subjectivity, and Recognition* (New Brunswick, NJ: Transaction Publishers, 2005).
19 After A. Erll, 'Literature, Film, and the Mediality of Cultural Memory', in *Cultural Memory Studies: An International and Interdisciplinary Handbook*, eds A. Erll and A. Nunning (Berlin: Walter de Fruyter, 2008), 389–98.
20 T. G. Ashplant, G. Dawson and M. Roper, 'The Politics of War Memory and Commemoration: Contexts, Structures and Dynamic', in *The Politics of War Memory and Commemoration*, eds T. G. Ashplant, G. Dawson and M. Roper (London: Routledge, 2000), 3–85.
21 R. Eyerman, *Cultural Trauma: Slavery and the Formation of African American Identity* (Cambridge: Cambridge University Press, 2001); J. Alexander, 'Toward a Theory of Cultural Trauma', in *Cultural Trauma and Collective Memory*, eds J. C. Alexander, R. Eyerman, B. Giesen, N. Smelser and P. Sztompka (Berkeley: University of California Press, 2001), 1–59.
22 See Badsey (2001).
23 D. MacLeod, 'We should all wear our poppy with pride', *The* Sun, 7 November 2009. Available HTTP: <www.thesun.co.uk/sol/homepage/news/scottishnews/2718786/Donald-MacLeod-column.html> (accessed 22 May 2013).
24 M. Giannangeli, 'Helmet study "wastes cash"', *Daily Express*, 15 January 2012. Online. Available HTTP: <www.express.co.uk/news/uk/295713/Helmet-study-wastes-cash> (accessed 22 May 2013).
25 J. Rentoul, 'As ever, Tony Blair is David Cameron's Guide', *The Independent*, 3 March 2013. Online. Available HTTP: <www.independent.co.uk/voices/comment/as-ever-tony-blair-is-david-camerons-guide-8517959.html> (accessed 15 April 2013).
26 R. Behr, 'Cameron's cavalier style has the Tory infantry feeling like lions led by a donkey', *New Statesman*, 24 January 2013. Available HTTP: <www.newstatesman.com/politics/politics/2013/01/camerons-cavalier-style-has-tory-infantry-feeling-lions-led-donkey> (accessed 28 March 2013).
27 H. Hasan, 'David Aaronovitch's own "magical thinking" on Afghanistan', *New Statesman*, 24 July 2009. Online. Available HTTP: <www.newstatesman.com/blogs/dissident-voice/2009/07/afghanistan-aaronovitch-war> (accessed 28 May 2013).
28 Michael Jack (Conservative), *Hansard*, HC Deb vol. 373 col. 1039, 1 November 2001.
29 P. Thomson, 'It's your duty to wear it; No poppy? No excuse', *Sunday Sun* (Newcastle-Upon-Tyne), 7 November 2010, 22.

30 Anon., 'Even a cursory glance at the viewing figures for ITV's Sunday night bodice ripper Downton Abbey proves our fascination with the past', *Belfast Telegraph*, 18 November 2010, 22.
31 Baron Astor of Hever (Conservative), *Hansard*, HL Deb vol. 732 col. 415, 10 November 2010.
32 See S. Boyle, 'We are not very Abbey', *The Mirror*, 12 October 2011, 8; N. Murfitt, 'Downton's Somme – a field near Ipswich', *Mail on Sunday*, 7 August 2011, 8.
33 See S. Schama, 'No downers in Downton', *The Daily Beast*, 16 January 2012. Online. Available HTTP: <www.thedailybeast.com/newsweek/2012/01/15/why-americans-have-fallen-for-snobby-downton-abbey.html> (accessed 28 March 2012).
34 See Wilson, 115.
35 Anon., 'The war over pity', *The Economist*, 17 August 2006. Online. Available HTTP: <www.economist.com/node/7804031> (accessed 10 September 2006).
36 After P. Nora, 'Between Memory and History: Les Lieux de Mémoire', *Representations* 26 (1989): 7–10.
37 R. Hanks, 'All go on the Western Front', *The Independent*, 22 April 2002, 19.
38 E. Hanna, *The Great War on the Small Screen: Representing the First World War in Contemporary Britain* (Edinburgh: Edinburgh University Press, 2009).
39 J. Corrigall, 'Sermon for Remembrance. Ipswich Unitarian Meeting House', 11 November 2012. Online. Available HTTP: <www.unitarianipswich.org.uk/sermons/sermon_for_remembrance.pdf> (accessed 10 March 2013).
40 J. Rushton, 'Remembrance Sunday. The Parish Church of St John-at-Hampstead', 11 November 2012. Online. Available HTTP: <www.hampsteadparish church.org.uk/data/sermons_2012.php?id=457> (accessed 10 March 2013).
41 W. James, *Pragmatism and the Meaning of Truth* (Cambridge, MA: Harvard University Press, 1996), 43.
42 See Eyerman, 13.
43 T. Stoppard, *Parade's End: Adapted for Television* (London: Faber and Faber, 2012), 64.
44 Cited in L. Armstrong, 'Christopher is not just another toff in a period drama ... he's truly heroic', *The Sun*, 3 August 2012. Online. Available HTTP: <www.thesun.co.uk/sol/homepage/showbiz/tv/4469147/Benedict-Cumberbatch-says-his-TV-role-in-Parades-End-is-toughest-yet.html> (accessed 12 November 2012).
45 A. Hickling, 'Oh what a timely play', *The Guardian*, 26 February 2003. Online. Available HTTP: <www.guardian.co.uk/stage/2003/feb/26/theatre.artsfeatures> (accessed 13 August 2006).
46 R. Beste and J. Shallice, 'Oh what a lovely war in Afghanistan: we're staying till the job is done', *Stop the War Coalition*, 8 December 2011. Online. <www.stopwar.org.uk/index.php/afghanistan-and-pakistan/976-oh-what-a-lovely-war-in-afghanistan> (accessed 12 February 2013) [no longer available online].
47 K. Walker, 'Oh! What a lovely war: Liam Fox and his lucky aides direct the conflict in Libya from a Spanish hotel – at the taxpayer's expense'. *Daily Mail*, 9 August 2011. Online. Available HTTP: <www.dailymail.co.uk/news/article-2023900/Libya-Liam-Fox-directs-conflict-Spanish-hotel-taxpayers-expense.html> (accessed 12 February 2013).
48 K. Griffiths, 'Oh what a lovely war on terror it's been for Halliburton', *The Independent*, 27 March 2005, 15.
49 A. Stephens, 'Oh, what a lovely war for profits: Pharmaceutical firms, IBM, General Motors, even the cabbage growers – they've all benefited since 11 September', *New Statesman*, 19 November 2001, 15.
50 See Ferguson.
51 S. Žižek, *For They Know Not What They Do: Enjoyment As a Political Factor* (London: Verso, 2002).
52 Alexander, 1.

53 J. Breuer and S. Freud, *Studies on Hysteria, Standard Edition* (London: Hogarth Press, 1893–95); C. Caruth, *Unclaimed Experience: Trauma, Narrative, History* (Baltimore: Johns Hopkins University Press, 1996), 17.
54 P. Novick, *The Holocaust in American Life* (Boston: Houghton Mifflin, 2000), 214.
55 N. J. Smelser 'Psychological Trauma and Cultural Trauma', in *Cultural Trauma and Collective Memory*, eds J. C. Alexander, R. Eyerman, B. Giesen, N. Smelser and P. Sztompka (Berkeley: University of California Press, 2001), 31–2.
56 See Bond, 1.
57 See Corrigan, 5.
58 Todman, ix–x.
59 Wertsch, 15.

4 Teaching and remembrance in English secondary schools

Ann-Marie Einhaus and Catriona Pennell

Practices of remembering the First World War range from the informal to the ritualized, and are more often than not institutional. Some families in Britain still have a vivid culture of personal, familial remembrance of their own war story, recently evidenced in Jeremy Paxman's interviews with surviving eyewitnesses and relatives in *Britain's Great War* (BBC, January–February 2014), as well as the BBC's flagship 'World War One At Home' series featuring 1,400 case studies in a sequence of television and radio documentaries (BBC, February–November 2014). Many more, however, will not have such direct links to the war, either because no records were kept, no relative was traceably involved, their ancestors opposed the war, or they come from a migrant background with little involvement in the First World War. These Britons' ability to relate to and remember the First World War in meaningful ways is dependent on other forms of exposure and other ways of transmitting memories of the war. For many, the classroom is an important site of exposure, particularly at secondary level, where the First World War and its literature have remained central though not mandatory features since the introduction of the National Curriculum in 1988.[1] This chapter looks specifically at the relationship between teaching and memory formation in England as an example of other such forms of transmission and remembrance. We investigate the classroom and the secondary-school environment more generally as sites where collective memory of the war is shaped and transmitted, and where making the war matter to new generations of pupils is of particular importance. Our chapter provides some insights into front-line teaching practices on the eve of the centenary and enquires into how these are interlinked with the way the war continues to be remembered in the twenty-first century. During the series of war centenaries from 2014 to 2018, the conflict is likely to be of increased interest to teachers, particularly in the light of the UK government's plans to send a minimum of two pupils and one teacher from every state-funded secondary school in England to visit battlefields of the Western Front between 2014 and 2019.[2] However, challenges in teaching the First World War abound. Choices have to be made about which aspects of the topic to cover and the most appropriate teaching materials. A balance needs to be reached that enables students to relate to the subject of the war and its literature, while encouraging them to exercise their critical and analytical skills in a sufficiently objective manner.

There appears to be an implicit assumption in Britain – recently voiced by public figures such as then Secretary of State for Education, Michael Gove, and BBC veteran presenter Jeremy Paxman – that secondary school pupils studying the First World War in English literature and history lessons are taught a fixed canon of topics, mainly the war poets and the Western Front.[3] These tropes and clichés do not, however, reflect the advances made in academic research over the past thirty years, nor do they necessarily reflect the complex and diverse teaching practices one finds in many English secondary schools.[4] Academic researchers are rarely aware of what is actually going on in the secondary-school classroom and it is all too tempting to succumb to simplistic assumptions about what is being taught in schools and how this may affect the war's popular remembrance. Between February 2013 and December 2014, a new research project funded by the British Arts and Humanities Research Council (AHRC) explored how secondary-school and Further Education teachers of English and history teach the First World War. The scope of the project, which was exploratory in nature, was limited to England for practical reasons, and sought to establish a view of teaching practice relating to the First World War, via a workshop, online survey and regional focus groups. Through these forums it examined goals and motivations, challenges and opportunities faced by teachers who transmit knowledge (and thus 'memory') of the war to the next generation. The survey was publicized widely, through targeted e-mail newsletters, professional associations, adverts in professional magazines and national newspapers, social media and a range of other formal and informal networks, and recruited a total of 451 respondents across two separate, subject-specific sets of questions (pathways), one for English teachers and one for history teachers.[5]

The survey, which was created and publicized in tandem with the Institute of Education (University of London), represents views from at least 307 history departments and at least 60 English departments, approximating around 4.6 per cent of all history departments and 0.9 per cent of all English departments in secondary schools in England.[6] The sample of respondents, in which English teachers were noticeably less prominent, was otherwise roughly representative of the teacher population in England in terms of its distribution of gender, ethnicity, full-time versus part-time and trainee versus fully qualified status.[7] Given that the survey was detailed and relatively time-consuming, its results can be seen as a snapshot view of teaching practice among teachers with particular interest in the First World War.[8] However, respondents – and particularly the high percentage of heads of department who completed the survey – revealed insights into larger institutional practices, offering a representative idea of what was happening in English secondary-school classrooms leading up to the 2014 centenary.

What is being taught in classrooms in England?

The most striking characteristic of our results overall was the diversity of teaching practices even across our relatively small sample of respondents. Although expected topics and texts such as trench warfare and the war poets featured prominently in the results, they were by no means the only texts and topics taught. Nor were they taught, necessarily, in an uncritical manner. Qualitative responses and focus group interviews in particular showed that where such 'canonical' texts and topics are taught, they are often used to rouse interest and/or open up debates about established ideas about the war, rather than relied upon as the sole evidence in and for teaching. The top five topics for teaching stated by respondents in the History Pathway were (1) trench warfare at 96 per cent, (2) origins and causes of the war at 94 per cent, (3) the Western Front at 85 per cent, (4) propaganda at 84 per cent, and (5) new technology and its impact at 76 per cent. Arguably, these topics replicate the way the war is most commonly covered in popular media and literature. At the same time, they also represent the experience of war closest to home for England. Moreover, whereas teaching focused solely on these top five topics would be problematic in its narrow focus on only one theatre of war and potentially (though not necessarily) centred too exclusively on the English, or British, experience of war, there is evidence that most teachers cover these five main bases alongside a wide variety of other topics. Teachers who teach the Western Front, trench warfare and propaganda are likely to also cover all or any of the following options selected by survey respondents: how and why the war ended, social and political change connected with the war (such as women's changing position in society), and/or consequences of the war and links to other wars (specifically the Boer War and Second World War). Warfare at sea, at other fronts away from the Western Front and in Africa was referred to by 24 per cent, 21 per cent and 6 per cent of respondents, respectively, while war on the home front featured particularly prominently, with 69 per cent of respondents stating they were likely to teach it. A significant percentage of teachers also cover the First World War in relation to other events in the period, such as the Easter Rising of 1916 or the Russian Revolution at 21 per cent, and colonialism/decolonization at 17 per cent. Further free-text responses referenced a number of additional topics covered in relation to the First World War, from in-depth studies of the Battle of the Somme and individual decision-makers such as Haig, to an investigation of imperialism, 'the rise in national movements in the 20th century (Italy, Spain, Germany, Middle East, Africa etc.)', conscientious objectors, 'methods of recruitment', 'diverse experiences of WWI e.g. Empire troops, Walter Tull etc.', and the impact of the war on the school's local area. Other respondents stated that they incorporated explorations of changing interpretations of the war up to the present day, its impact on poetry and music and the topic of aerial warfare. Seen in conjunction, the picture painted by these responses is diverse and appears to represent genuine endeavours to combine canonical aspects with lesser known facets of the war's experience. At GCSE and A-Level (or equivalent qualifications), a number of exam boards appear to encourage the teaching of the First World War in tandem with other topics or issues by offering options ranging from general courses on twentieth-century British and world history to courses on conflict more generally, medical history (in which the First World War features as a catalyst for innovation), international relations, and Russian or German history.

Among English Pathway respondents, the top five authors likely to be taught were in fact a top eight, with several authors tied in fifth place. Perhaps unsurprisingly, the war poets and popular children's writer Michael Morpurgo top the list: (1) 97 per cent were likely to teach Wilfred Owen, followed by (2) 86 per cent for Siegfried Sassoon, (3) 60 per cent for Michael Morpurgo, (4) 55 per cent for Jessie Pope, and (5) a shared 36 per cent for Robert Graves, Pat Barker, Isaac Rosenberg and Edward Thomas. Jessie Pope, as the only contemporary woman in this list, is most often included in anthologies and textbooks either with recruitment poems such as 'The Call', which form a convenient patriotic counterpoint to Owen's 'Dulce Et Decorum Est', or with her poem 'War Girls', used to illustrate the diversity of women's involvement in the war effort.[9]

The dominance of these well-known writers is at least partly due to their long-standing inclusion in teaching anthologies, textbooks and exam board materials and presence in schools' stock cupboards: notoriously pressed for time, teachers will understandably turn to more easily accessible writers and texts.[10] In addition, the poetry of Owen, Rosenberg and Thomas in particular is nuanced, relatable and of high aesthetic appeal, rendering it easy for pupils to exercise their analytical skills. Survey responses show, however, that teachers by no means rely exclusively on such well-known writers. Not only are literary texts supplemented by historical material and audio-visual sources; additional texts by lesser-known war writers are also employed comparatively. Contemporary and retrospective writers such as Frederic Manning, Vera Brittain and Susan Hill feature further down on the lists of writers likely to be taught, and free-text responses also named nurse-poet Eva Dobell, socialist Margaret Cole and New Zealander James Keir Baxter next to more familiar names like Rupert Brooke, Rudyard Kipling and Thomas Hardy. Although our data does not specify particular formats in which such additional writers are taught, it is easy to imagine longer, more challenging texts about the First World War – such as Frederic Manning's *Her Privates We* (1930) – taught in extracts alongside more accessible material. In a move similar to the teaching of less-well-known topics alongside the staple diet of Western Front and trench warfare in history classrooms, such a complementary approach may ensure a much broader, less biased coverage of literary responses to the war, especially given restricted classroom time and practical limitations on the number of texts pupils can usefully read and process.

Teachers' goals and motivations for teaching the First World War

Across both the History and English Pathways, the top five motivations for teaching were the same: (1) 99 per cent of history respondents and 93 per cent of English respondents considered the First World War important to pupils' education overall, (2) 95/91 per cent respectively considered the war to be part of national collective memory, (3) 90/85 per cent identified personal interest as a key motivating factor, (4) 96/78 per cent saw the First World War as crucial to pupils' understanding of the twentieth century, and (5) 92/73 per cent taught the war because their department had made it part of their scheme of work.[11] In addition, 95 per cent of our English Pathway respondents considered First World War literature an important part of the literary canon.

The top ten goals (or desired outcomes) as opposed to motivations among History Pathway respondents were:

1 Development of contextual understanding (97 per cent)
2 Link First World War with subsequent events of the twentieth century (96 per cent)
3 Development of critical skills (95 per cent)
4 Provide pupils with key facts about the war (90 per cent)
5 Illustrate use/impact of propaganda (88 per cent)
6 Elicit a personal response from pupils (84 per cent)
7 Widen understanding of the war beyond what is usually covered in the media (83 per cent)
8 Educate pupils about the cost of war (82 per cent)
9 Demonstrate changes in attitude to war (80 per cent)
10 Illustrate the wide range of reactions to a major event (76 per cent).

This list indicates that teaching goals are a far cry from attempting a simple moral lesson and promoting a knee-jerk reaction to the First World War as futile slaughter. Rather, comments in the free-text sections of the survey and in focus groups showed that many teachers distinguish clearly between illustrating the cost of war and labelling it as groundless or futile, particularly in areas where pupils are likely to have relatives serving in the armed forces, or where teachers themselves have links to the military. In the general comments invited at the end of our survey, one respondent observed: 'Some very interesting questions. One point, horror and futility are quite clearly different things. Whilst the war may well have been horrifying, it was not necessarily futile.' This point was echoed by another teacher, who noted, 'I felt some of the questions were a bit "loaded" especially those dealing with "futility" of war', and a third teacher – notably in the English Pathway – stated that:

> I really didn't like this question's wording: Illustrating the horror/futility of war. It implies that these two things are synonymous and that the futility of war, all war, is a given. Whilst I appreciate that a sense of futility and disillusion pervades much scholarship and literature related to WWI, as the wife of a serving member of the armed forces, I do not like the implicit suggestion that the sacrifices my husband and those like him make on a daily basis are born of 'futility'.

Similarly, the desire to motivate students and elicit a personal response, although important, does not seem to outweigh more dispassionate and subject-specific aims, such as the transmission of key facts to help pupils understand the course of twentieth-century history and aid their development of critical and reflective skills.

Among English Pathway respondents, the top ten goals involved no fewer than four ties:

1 Elicit a personal response from pupils *and* Development of contextual understanding (98 per cent)
2 Demonstrate changes in attitude to war (96 per cent)
3 Development of critical skills (92 per cent)
4 Demonstrate changes in poetic language/technique *and* Widen understanding of the war beyond what is usually covered in the media (90 per cent)
5 Educate pupils about how texts form or reflect values such as duty and sacrifice (88 per cent)
6 Show how it changes the way we think and write about war *and* Demonstrate the futility of war (86 per cent)
7 Explore the effect of intense/common experience on literature (84 per cent)
8 Illustrate the wide range of reactions to a major event (80 per cent)
9 Illustrate use of literature for propaganda *and* Educate pupils about the cost of war (78 per cent)
10 Explore personal development in reaction to hardship (72 per cent).

In contrast to History Pathway respondents, a larger percentage of English Pathway respondents (86 per cent) appear to consider it important to portray the war as futile rather than educate their pupils about the costs of war (78 per cent) divorced from value judgment. Coupled with the two most commonly named aims – that is, eliciting a personal response from pupils and developing their contextual understanding of (war) literature – this greater stress on futility is potentially problematic, in that it may represent a widespread temptation to put students' emotional involvement with the text and an appreciation of a simplified version of the war's myth before a more nuanced understanding of the First World War. It could be argued, however, that an in-depth, nuanced understanding of the conflict cannot be a priority in the English literature classroom, where teachers' primary focus has to be on inspiring an interest in literature generally, and fostering a culture of engagement with literary material. The potential of war poetry in particular to shape the war's remembrance is somewhat unfortunate, as it is most likely to be encountered in a setting that necessarily emphasizes its literary and emotive nature over its complex place in the experience and memory of the First World War. While our survey findings show that many teachers do try to put the trench poets in perspective, it seems desirable to foster a stronger practice of cross-curricular work in secondary schools, to ensure that where First World War literature is taught, it is linked to history teaching, rather than leaving the task of establishing context to hard-pressed English teachers who may lack the time, knowledge and training to do justice to the subject of war.

The second and third goals in the list above – demonstrating changing attitudes to war and the development of critical skills – also tie in with two key handicaps in the way First World War writing is commonly taught in schools. On the one hand, poetry units are also the most obvious teaching context in which teachers can choose to cover literature of the First World War,[12] and the teaching of First World War poetry in particular continues to rely largely on the use of teaching anthologies, often compiled by or for specific exam boards. Such teaching anthologies tend to fall back on received wisdom about First World War writing, shaped by influential studies like Paul Fussell's *The Great War and Modern Memory* (1975), now frequently seen as contentious and limited among academic critics.[13] As a result, First World War poetry in many cases continues to be taught – and viewed – as a journey from naïve patriotic enthusiasm to the realization of futility and profound disillusionment, neglecting the vast range of other, far more nuanced positions expressed in literature of the time.[14]

On the other hand, the aim of using First World War literature to promote the development of critical skills reflects the status of war writing as a means rather than an end – if, as the list above suggests, eliciting personal responses from students is the most important goal in teaching literary texts even for teachers wishing to facilitate more generic learning processes, then war poetry like Owen's and Sassoon's offers an ideal combination of emotionally appealing material coupled with a rich array of stylistic, contextual and semantic features for analysis. The great popularity of Michael Morpurgo's novels, particularly *War Horse* (1982) and *Private Peaceful* (2003), serves to aggravate these problems. One teacher at our London focus group noted, and others agreed, that pupils were fairly likely to have read some Michael Morpurgo in their own time prior to being taught about the First World War in school, meaning that unguided reading may already have established a set view of the war's experience in pupils' minds, even before they are exposed to any sort of critical commentary by either English or history teachers. Even where Morpurgo's novels are read as part of a teaching unit, however, the combination of his targeted appeal to young readers, his exploitation of simple emotional responses to death and hardships, and his novelization of the kind of simplified version of the war that informs teaching anthologies and media representations of the First World War is likely to cement a narrow, entirely morally grounded view of the war in pupils' minds.[15] An English teacher participant in our focus groups stated that 'Morpurgo works with Key Stage 3 simply because the imagery is so vivid. … It's that hook to associate yourself with the situation – he's so good at allowing the students to relate to another youngster.'[16] The same teacher, however, showed keen awareness that despite the appeal of Morpurgo and other contemporary writers, their work helped to drown out original voices of the First World War by offering a new, easily accessible 'sanctioned view' of the war's experience.

The benefits and disadvantages of teaching Morpurgo's version of writing about the First World War to young adults perfectly encapsulate the central dilemma of teaching the war through literature. Any desire to do justice to the wide range and complexity of the war's experience – which is not adequately represented in any of the popular teaching texts – is in perpetual conflict with the need to engage and enthuse pupils increasingly unskilled in reading, and in need of emotional hooks to facilitate engagement with literature (and indeed history). The picture is further complicated where teachers feel a strong personal obligation to combine their teaching of the war's literature with a lasting moral lesson. A teacher's indignant letter to the *Observer* newspaper in the course of a January 2014 controversy surrounding the use of allegedly unpatriotic sources, sparked by then Secretary of State for Education, Michael Gove, illustrates this central dilemma. She stated:

> I have taught English in several state comprehensives, to students of many different abilities and nationalities, for more than 30 years. The most compelling texts were invariably those which emphasised the horror and futility of the first world war [sic]. The literature of endurance, heroism and despair has captured the imaginations of students from all cultures and ranges of ability. ... I taught Michael Morpurgo's *War Horse* to a group of year eight students who had hitherto shown no interest in reading. They were gripped by the intensity of the battle scenes, and the relationship between man and horse. A mixed-ability year seven class impressed Ofsted because all the students were able to reinterpret 'Dulce et Decorum Est' in their own words. The power of this literature is that it conveys so poignantly the horror, the shocking loss of life, and the anger and frustration of the poets, novelists and dramatists. These great writers have not 'belittled Britain', Mr Gove, they have immortalised the Great War, they have passed on their reflections to all our children. I, and all my colleagues, will continue to do the same.[17]

At the same time, it is important to bear in mind that not all teachers feel compelled to teach the literature of the First World War as a literature illustrating futility and disillusionment.[18] As Andrew Bradford, Chair of Examiners at OCR (Oxford, Cambridge and RSA Examinations, a UK-based exam board), pointed out in a BBC feature on war poetry, the job of English teachers and exam boards

> is to offer interesting poems, which use vivid language and show how poetry works. It's not the role of English to give a wider and balanced picture of the war, although OCR have set poems that offer different responses to the war.[19]

While many English teachers may agree with the letter-writer to *The Observer*, others are likely to hold with either Bradford's emphasis on aesthetics rather than history, or with those of our respondents who feel frustrated with the limits imposed upon their teaching of war literature in terms of nuance and breadth of coverage: as one comment pointed out, some teachers explicitly '[w]ould love to see a much wider range of texts available and move away from Owen and Sassoon and [towards a] greater inclusion of women's writing'.

Challenges and opportunities

Given that there does seem to be interest and motivation to move beyond the established canon and the limited 'popular' version of the First World War, and that this interest is voiced among both history and English teachers, the question arises how this interest can translate into broader changes to the way the war is taught and remembered. Individual examples of best practice in terms of teaching about the war are encouraging, but teaching can only contribute to significant changes in remembrance if such innovation is more widespread, and not limited to particularly motivated teachers.

Practical obstacles to wide-ranging and nuanced teaching of the First World War abound. In focus groups history teachers in particular complained about time constraints, though figures provided in response to the survey show that, due to the large number of topics and volume of material to be covered, even English teachers often do not have much time to develop their teaching of First World War writing beyond a few token texts. Although teaching hour data is hard to code due to its extreme diversity, it emerged that history teachers can, on average, devote between six and fifteen hours in total to the First World War between years 7 and 13 (not including pupils' homework and independent study time), with figures for years 9, 12 and 13 the highest.[20] In comparison, English teachers have between eleven and thirty-five hours at their disposal – with the caveat, however, that this only applies to schools where the First World War is taught as a distinct topic in English literature, and that the highest number of hours only occurs at Sixth Form level (years 12 and 13) if pupils pursue a First World War themed A-Level course. There are many more schools where First World War writing is covered as part of a differently themed unit, and where consequently little time can be devoted to contextualization.

This latter problem takes us to the second major practical obstacle, namely curriculum constraints. The English literature curriculum in England does not specify the study of First World War literature as mandatory, but if First World War writing is taught as part of an exam board course for school-leaving qualifications such as the British GCSE (General Certificate of Education), A-Level (General Certificate of Education Advanced Level), or equivalents, the course of teaching is circumscribed by the (often, though not always, problematic) choices and materials specified by the relevant exam board.[21] In the case of history, it is important to clarify that it is not a mandatory subject for any pupil in English secondary schools above fourteen years of age. The National Curriculum, which constitutes formal, government-approved specification of aims and contents for teaching, is in a period of major reform and subject to frequent reconfiguration; the latest version was due to go live in September 2014.[22] However, the National Curriculum guidance for history remains consistent in specifying the Holocaust as the only prescribed content at KS1–3;

in other words, the First World War is not a mandatory subject.[23] At KS4 and above, the content is set by the exam boards,[24] guided by government guidelines.[25] Taking the Edexcel GCSE specification as an example, the First World War appears as an optional part of 'History A' (Modern World History) and 'History B' (Schools History Project).[26] Sixth Form (or KS5) history is also made up of four units (the fourth being an independent study chosen by the pupil) and, overall, consists of many more options than at KS4. For example, the exam board AQA (Assessment and Qualifications Alliance) specification alone includes forty-four options within units 1–3. Taking the narrow view that the First World War is limited by the chronology of 1914–18, the topic could appear in nine of these forty-four options.[27]

In addition to external constraints, teachers of both subjects face the potential problem of a lack of expert knowledge about the First World War's history and/or literature. Although a number of our survey respondents cited their degree-level studies as a lasting influence on their teaching of the war, not every teacher will have studied the First World War in depth while at university, and the problem is potentially aggravated by the time that has passed since teachers took their degrees. While it can be seen as part of a teacher's job to acquire knowledge necessary to teach new texts and topics – and the vast majority of teachers are expert autodidacts – the staggering range of available resources on the First World War can make self-directed acquisition of subject expertise more difficult. The recurring issue of motivation is also applicable to this type of Continued Professional Development (CPD). The teachers who participated in our project were precisely those professionals who would voluntarily undertake additional study in their spare time. Those teachers who are less motivated generally or not interested in the First World War specifically are unlikely to keep up-to-date with the latest research on the topic. Even teachers who do wish to stay abreast of the subject face a number of obstacles. Academic resources can be costly to access where schools do not have a well-stocked library and/or subscriptions to scholarly journals and databases such as JSTOR, and free resources available online can be of highly variable quality. Time constraints mean it is sometimes difficult to attend conferences, exhibitions, public talks and other such events that may enrich an individual teacher's understanding of the conflict and its literature. At the same time, choice of resources, and choice of which aspects of the war and its literature to cover, are always necessarily guided by the 'tyranny' of league tables (and the need to attain good results in all subjects), as well as the need to motivate pupils whose lack of family links to the First World War means they approach the war as something to which they do not automatically attach any personal relevance.[28]

Despite these numerous challenges, the survey also highlighted a range of opportunities for teachers to contribute to memory building and remembrance by innovative teaching. One way of making a change in teaching without having to significantly change texts or topics is to approach canonical materials explicitly from the perspective of memory studies. Challenging pupils to reflect on *why* a Wilfred Owen poem, a Morpurgo novel or a television series like *Blackadder Goes*

Forth presents the war in a certain way can already effect a new level of reflection, and may contribute to changes in the way these sources are perceived.[29] The competition that teachers face with regard to media representations of the war – ranging from books to video games and television – can thus be utilized to encourage a critical interrogation of how the war is represented (and remembered) around them. This kind of approach is perhaps harder to implement, particularly where exam board specifications restrict history teachers in their freedom of movement around specific areas within First World War history. Even where such restrictions apply, however, there may be room to explore additional, more diverse or complex topics through extra-curricular activities or Gifted and Talented initiatives.[30] Teachers who completed the survey seemed to find many creative ways of exploring the war through extra-curricular activities such as school project weeks, trips or assemblies. These activities also seemed to offer the best opportunities for cross-curricular work, as a number of free-text answers and focus-group contributions specified that battlefield trips or project days are a time where all subjects come together and approach the war from their various disciplinary angles. While the cost of battlefield tours is prohibitive for many schools, field trips per se need not be expensive: survey results showed that while the greatest number of field trips went to the battlefields, 40 per cent of English Pathway respondents and 30 per cent of History Pathway respondents had also taken pupils to regional or national museums within the UK, to local cemeteries or memorials, theatre performances, talks or lectures. Such talks and lectures can, for instance, be arranged through local museums or universities, and it seems desirable to promote such links further, both in terms of offering talks for pupils and opportunities for high-quality CPD for teachers.[31] Pupils' individual research projects as part of coursework assessment also offer opportunities for branching out and diversifying teaching, particularly given the digitization and free availability of a wealth of primary resources.[32]

Conclusions

Looking at the data made available through our survey, what conclusions can we draw about the ways in which teaching the war influences how it is remembered in England? The First World War appears frequently in teaching, but it seems that it does so by volunteerism rather than conscription: the war as a topic is popular but not mandatory, and not every pupil in England will encounter the First World War during their time in secondary school. The response to our project, however, indicates that the war is a topic that many teachers of history and English literature in England are committed to teaching.[33]

Where pupils do encounter the First World War in the classroom, their exposure appears likely to be far more nuanced than commonly expected. In contrast to recent surveys on the war's remembrance carried out by the think tank British Future and the UK-based opinion-pollster, YouGov (on behalf of the British Council),[34] which suggest that Britons still understand the war more or less exclusively through ideas of 'mud, blood and poppycock', our survey results have shown a diversity of approaches to which pupils are exposed and that teachers are willing to take. The bottom line is that in teaching, more than any other field, the First World War has to be reinvented for each new generation – the further away we move from the original event, the more teachers have to work to make it matter. Like war memory itself, teaching of war changes constantly and never remains static for long.

The war's centenary in this light is a mixed blessing. It helps to ignite interest, but often this is an interest in state-led ceremonies, local projects, documentaries and coverage that frequently look conservative and traditional in their approach, reaffirming Anglo-centric views of the war that gravitate around the Western Front.[35] Furthermore, there is a real danger that pupils as well as the general public are going to become weary of the war in the course of more than four years' relentless exposure. This threat of over-exposure only highlights, however, the need for ongoing creativity in dealing with the war if we are to see its remembrance kept alive. Keeping the war's remembrance relevant for young people demands a constant re-invention of what is taught. The changing personal and professional backgrounds of teachers are equally bound to be in constant flux, changing the way different generations of teachers approach the First World War and their reasons for teaching – or indeed not teaching – the war.

Cross-curricular and extra-curricular teaching appears to offer creative solutions to successful teaching of the war in English schools.[36] We have seen that where nuanced, innovative teaching already happens successfully it often happens outside the classroom and its curriculum constraints, but nevertheless in a school environment, offering a potential solution to many of the challenges raised above. Opportunities to complicate and diversify teaching about the war exist even within the restrictions of curriculum, time, money and league-table pressures, but these are located primarily in extra-curricular settings, such as trips, attending public talks, independent projects and collaboration with local universities, amongst many other examples. One history participant at the Exeter focus group, who was already utilizing the expertise of a First World War academic at the local university to support extra-curricular activities, said:

> The history curriculum as dictated by exam boards is outdated. Examiners are more often ex-teachers than subject specialists. Up-to-date historical debate is nodded at in A-Level mark schemes but not rigorously enforced. Bringing third year undergraduates into my classes allowed me to expose my pupils to the web of experience, which was the First World War. The [undergraduate] students excelled at bringing to a classroom level the idea of a multi-faceted experience of the conflict.[37]

Paradoxically, our investigation of how the war is transmitted in the classroom has suggested that opportunities to broaden the war's remembrance at present often lie *outside* rather than *in* the classroom. Our research has revealed that teachers' manifold attempts to keep their students' remembrance of the war alive by maintaining interest in the subject frequently involve extra-curricular activities. Ultimately, the war's teaching, like its remembrance, will depend for its survival over the next hundred years on treading a fine line between emotional appeal and historical complexity.

Notes

1 The National Curriculum was introduced in England, Wales and Northern Ireland, as a nationwide curriculum for primary and secondary state schools following the Education Reform Act (1988). It does not apply to independent schools, which may set their own curricula, but ensures that state schools of all Local Education Authorities have a common curriculum. Academies, while publicly funded, have a significant degree of autonomy in deviating from the National Curriculum. The purpose of the National Curriculum was to standardize the content taught across schools to facilitate assessment, which in turn enabled the compilation of league tables detailing the assessment statistics for each school. While only certain subjects were included at first, in subsequent years the curriculum grew to fill the entire teaching time of most state schools.
2 See 'First World War Centenary Battlefield Tours Programme'. Online. Available HTTP: <www.ioe.ac.uk/study/87073.html> (accessed 21 February 2014).
3 See Tim Shipman, 'Michael Gove blasts "Blackadder myths" about the First World War spread by television sit-coms and left-wing academics', and Michael Gove, 'Why does the Left insist on belittling true British heroes?', *Daily Mail*, 2 January 2014. Online. Available HTTP: <www.dailymail.co.uk/news/article-2532923/Michael-Gove-blasts-Blackadder-myths-First-World-War-spread-television-sit-coms-left-wing-academics.html> (accessed 1 April 2014); and '"Poetry is no way to teach the Great War" Paxman says schools should address the important issues rather than fixating on horror, writes Nicola Woolcock', *The Times*, 14 March 2014, p. 3.
4 Scholars who have so far considered the influence of teaching on the memory of the First World War, such as Ian Beckett, Brian Bond and Gary Sheffield, have overwhelmingly relied on anecdotal evidence, which can only capture isolated views and dates quickly. See Ian F.W. Beckett, *The Great War: 1914–1918*, 2nd ed. (Harlow: Longman, 2007); Brian Bond, *The Unquiet Western Front: Britain's Role in Literature and History* (Cambridge: Cambridge University Press, 2001); Gary Sheffield, *Forgotten Victory: The First World War, Myths and Realities* (London: Headline, 2001).
5 The English Pathway had 45 complete plus 53 partial responses, the History Pathway 228 complete plus 125 partial responses.
6 There were 4,204 state-funded schools with secondary-age pupils in England as of December 2013, including academies and free schools (source: e-mail inquiry to the Department for Education, Curriculum Policy Division, 30 December 2013). In addition, 2,413 independent schools were recorded in the January 2013 school census. See Department for Education, National Statistics on schools, pupils and their characteristics: January 2013, last updated 12 July 2013, specifically 'National tables: SFR21/2013', table 2a. Online. Available HTTP: <www.gov.uk/government/publications/schools-pupils-and-their-characteristics-january-2013> (accessed 7 January 2014).
7 For a full description of the survey and its publicity, please refer to the project report for the AHRC-funded project 'The First World War in the Classroom: Teaching and the Construction of Cultural Memory'. Online. Available: <http://ww1intheclassroom.exeter.ac.uk> (accessed 30 May 2014).
8 The fundamental problem for any voluntary survey is that it captures data from a self-selecting audience. In our case, this audience consisted of teachers who not only teach the First World War or its literature, but have a particular interest in reflecting on their teaching of this topic. In our initial workshop and focus groups, the problem of reaching

a wider audience of 'disengaged' colleagues was raised repeatedly by teacher and academic participants. Possible solutions include shorter, more regionally concentrated surveys and higher incentives, but such measures cannot yield the same in-depth information as a detailed national survey.

9 For an example of such a limited inclusion of Pope's poetry, see David Roberts' anthology *Minds at War: The Poetry and Experience of the First World War* (Burgess Hill: Saxon, 2003), which first appeared in 1996 and explicitly targets an audience of teachers and pupils, as well as Christopher Martin's *War Poems* (London: Collins, 2004), which targets both GCSE and A-Level students.
10 Unsurprisingly, the writers listed above were also identified as the most likely to be found in stock cupboards, alongside R.C. Sherriff's play *Journey's End* (1928).
11 The lower percentage rating for English Pathway respondents on point 5 may be explained by the fact that while in England the First World War is part of the National Curriculum for History, this is not the case in English literature, where teachers usually have to make a conscious decision to teach war writing as part of units on other topics, unless their department adopts an exam board option with a First World War literature focus at either GCSE or A-Level.
12 The 2007 National Curriculum for English at Key Stage 4 featured the First World War only as a potential topic, naming authors such as Wilfred Owen, Siegfried Sassoon, Edward Thomas, R.C. Sherriff and Pat Barker as examples of writers suitable for study. Drafts of the new English curriculum for Key Stage 4, to be implemented in September 2014, initially explicitly included 'representative poetry of the First World War' under subject content (see Department of Education, 'English Programme of Study for Key Stage 4, February 2013', p. 4. Online. Available: <https://media.education.gov.uk/assets/files/pdf/e/english%20-%20key%20stage%204%2005-02-13.pdf> (accessed 7 January 2014)). This soon changed, however, to the generalized stipulation of 'a selection of poetry since 1850' and 'British fiction or drama since the First World War'. See Department of Education, 'English Literature GCSE subject content and assessment objectives', June 2013, p. 4. Online. Available HTTP: <www.gov.uk/government/uploads/system/uploads/attachment_data/file/206144/GCSE_English_Literature_final.pdf> (accessed 7 January 2014).
13 For example, see Robin Prior and Trevor Wilson, 'Paul Fussell at war', *War in History* 1 (1994), 63–80.
14 See also former English teacher Dr George Simmers, 'How the First World War is Taught', *Great War Fiction* blog, 21 January 2014. Online. Available: <http://greatwarfiction.wordpress.com/2014/01/21/how-the-first-world-war-is-taught/#more-3728> (accessed 12 February 2014). On the merits of First World War popular fiction, see Jane Potter, *Boys in Khaki, Girls in Print: Women's Literary Responses to the Great War 1914–1918* (Oxford: Oxford University Press, 2005), and her recent podcast, 'Popular Fiction in World War One'. Online. Available: <http://podcasts.ox.ac.uk/popular-fiction-world-war-one> (accessed 22 February 2014).
15 Michael Morpurgo's popularity as a First World War writer rocketed as a result of the 2011 film adaptation of his 1982 novel, *War Horse* (the novel sold 60,000 copies in the fortnight surrounding the film's release; total sales worldwide up to that point had been 50,000). He is now a regular feature of the UK's centenary commemorations, speaking at conferences aimed at teachers considering their practice during the centenary, as well as being able to access national platforms to voice his opinions, such as the *Guardian* newspaper. See Tim Masters, 'War Horse film boosts book sales', *BBC News*, 27 January 2012. Online. Available HTTP: <www.bbc.co.uk/news/entertainment-arts-16750325> (accessed 26 July 2013); 'First world war centenary is a year to honour the dead but not to glorify', *The Guardian*, 1 January 2014. Online. Available HTTP: <www.theguardian.com/world/2014/jan/01/first-world-war-centenary-michael-morpurgo> (accessed 22 February 2014).
16 Commonly abbreviated to KS3, Key Stage 3 is the legal term for the three years of schooling in state-funded schools in England and Wales, normally known as Year 7, Year 8 and Year 9, when pupils are aged between eleven and fourteen.

17 Letter to *The Observer*, Tilly Baker, Brighton, 12 January 2014. Online. Available HTTP: <www.theguardian.com/theobserver/2014/jan/12/the-big-issue-first-world-war-teaching> (accessed 18 January 2014).
18 See, for example, the free-text comment on the survey from the English Pathway quoted above.
19 See Ian McMillan's feature 'Has poetry distorted our view of World War One?' for *BBC iWonder* (© BBC 2014). Online. Available HTTP: <www.bbc.co.uk/guides/z38rq6f> (accessed 24 February 2014).
20 In England, Key Stage 4 comprises years 10 and 11, while years 12 and 13 constitute Sixth Form. Year 7 pupils will on average be eleven years of age, fifteen years in year 10, and eighteen in year 13.
21 The General Certificate of Secondary Education (GCSE) is an academic qualification awarded in a specified subject, generally taken in a number of subjects by students aged 14–16 in secondary education in England, Wales and Northern Ireland. It was introduced in 1986 replacing the former O-Level/CSE qualifications. On completion of secondary education, and pre-university education, the next stage of qualification is the General Certificate of Education Advanced Level or, more commonly, the A-Level. The qualification is generally studied for over two years and split into two parts, with one part studied in each year.
22 See 'Curriculum and Qualifications'. Online. Available HTTP: <www.gov.uk/government/publications/national-curriculum-in-england-history-programmes-of-study> (accessed 28 July 2014).
23 See 'National curriculum in England: history programmes of study'. Online. Available HTTP: <www.gov.uk/government/publications/national-curriculum-in-england-history-programmes-of-study> (accessed 21 February 2014).
24 For history (in England), these are Edexcel, OCR (Oxford, Cambridge and RSA Examinations) and AQA (Assessment and Qualifications Alliance).
25 Examination boards in the UK are private, profit-making organizations, responsible for the setting and awarding of secondary-education-level qualifications, such as GCSEs and A-Levels. Broadly speaking, the UK has always had two separate school systems: one for England, Wales and Northern Ireland; and one for Scotland. As a result, two separate sets of exam boards have been developed. Though the exam boards have regional roots, they are all – in theory – available nationally. Most offer a range of qualifications, though not all boards offer every qualification in every area. Schools and colleges have a completely free choice between the boards, depending on the qualification offered. Most schools use a mixture of boards for their GCSE qualifications, with a similar situation existing at A-Level.
26 Edexcel's Schools History Project is a GCSE qualification consisting of four equally weighted units (assessed through examination and controlled assessment) that encourages students to study history from four different angles: change and continuity over a long period of time; in-depth study of a short period; source analysis; and different views of history. For more information, see 'GCSE from 2009 – History B'. Online. Available HTTP: <www.edexcel.com/quals/gcse/gcse09/history/b/Pages/default.aspx> (accessed 21 February 2014).
27 See 'History (2040)'. Online. Available HTTP: <www.aqa.org.uk/subjects/history/a-level/history-2040> (accessed 21 February 2014).
28 See, for example, Graeme Paton, 'League tables are a tyranny, says head', *The Telegraph*, 29 April 2008. Online. Available HTTP: <www.telegraph.co.uk/news/1906395/League-tables-are-a-tyranny-says-head.html> (accessed 21 February 2014).
29 For vocal evidence of such practice, see Louise Birch, 'History in the classroom: a teacher speaks', *The History Vault*, 5 (February 2014). Online. Available HTTP: <www.thehistoryvault.co.uk/history-in-the-classroom-a-teacher-speaks> (accessed 24 February 2014).
30 'Gifted and talented' is a term used in UK schools to describe children who have the potential to develop significantly beyond what is expected for their age. 'Gifted' refers to a

child who has abilities in one or more academic subjects, such as English or mathematics. 'Talented' refers to a child who has skills in a practical area such as music, sport or art. By identifying these children, further support and opportunities can be offered to them.
31 Such CPD could potentially take the form of allowing teachers to audit individual MA-level courses, as well as dedicated study days on the First World War offered, for instance, by the University of Wolverhampton's First World War Research Group as part of a series of events to mark the centenary of the outbreak of the First World War. Following calls from survey and focus group participants for better access to expert speakers, the project website now incorporates a growing list of 'Willing Experts' happy to assist schools in their teaching of the war. See 'The First World War in the Classroom. Willing Experts'. Online. Available: <http://ww1intheclassroom.exeter.ac.uk/resources/willingexperts> (accessed 30 May 2014).
32 First and foremost among these is the new crowd-sourced, pan-European database *Europeana 1914–1918*. Online. Available: <http://europeana1914-18.eu/en> (accessed 30 May 2014). See also the digital archives at the University of Oxford which are already frequently utilized by English teachers, in particular 'The First World War Poetry Digital Archive'. Online. Available HTTP: <www.oucs.ox.ac.uk/ww1lit> (accessed 30 May 2014). Also the British Library portal, 'First World War'. Online. Available HTTP: <www.bl.uk/world-war-one> (accessed 30 May 2014). History teachers also cited as valued repositories for freely available primary sources the multi-media site 'firstworldwar.com'. Online. Available HTTP: <www.firstworldwar.com/index.htm> (accessed 30 May 2014). Also 'The World War I Document Archive'. Online. Available: <http://wwi.lib.byu.edu> (accessed 30 May 2014).
33 A number of focus group participants (mainly history teachers) talked about a sense of 'duty' and 'responsibility' in teaching the First World War and found it difficult to imagine the subject being taken off the curriculum entirely.
34 See Jo Tanner (ed.), 'Do mention the War: will 1914 matter in 2014?', British Future, August 2013. Online. Available HTTP: <www.britishfuture.org/articles/do-mention-the-war> (accessed 22 February 2014). Also Anne Bostanci and John Dubber, 'Remember the world as well as the war: why the global reach and enduring legacy of the First World War still matter today', British Council, January 2014. Online. Available HTTP: <www.britishcouncil.org/organisation/publications/remember-the-world> (accessed 22 February 2014).
35 In November 2011, Dr Andrew Murrison, MP for South West Wiltshire and Special Representative for Centenary Commemorations in the UK, described the types of centenary plans the British government would support as 'A tapestry of very local, very grassroots commemorations that will be drawn together in some sort of national framework'. Any sense of international collaboration was tacked on in a rather tokenistic manner. See 'Dr Andrew Murrison MP discusses the UK's centenary plans', *Centenary News*, 10 November 2011. Online. Available HTTP: <www.youtube.com/watch?v=VTOdYUTGnGA> (accessed 24 April 2012).
36 Examples of extra-curricular initiatives from our focus groups include field trips to the battlefields in which teachers from any subject can participate as long as they are prepared to offer an exploration of the war from the vantage point of their discipline; and war-themed project days or weeks in which all participants work together to explore the war from different angles.
37 The origins of this research project lie, in part, in Catriona Pennell's evolving relationship with local schools. Undergraduate students on her module 'The First World War: Interrogating the Myths' design and deliver (as part of their assessment) a 60-minute workshop to local Year 9 or 10 history pupils, with the support and guidance of both the schoolteacher and university lecturer. See 'First World War school workshops'. Online. Available: <http://humanities.exeter.ac.uk/history/undergraduate/cornwall degrees/schoolworkshops> (accessed 22 February 2014).

5 Museums, architects and artists on the Western Front
New commemoration for a new history?

Annette Becker[1]

Pour Ken Inglis, qui m'a appris à regarder la mémoire

> Museums, cemeteries! They are truly the same thing, in their sinister ranks of bodies ignorant of who or what lies next to them. ... In fact the habit of daily visits to museums, libraries and academies (those graveyards of vain efforts, those calvaries of crucified dreams, those registers of shattered spirits!) ... is for artists the equivalent of parents' extended guardianship of intelligent young people, drunk with their talent and ambitious determination ... And then come the righteous incendiaries with scorched hands! ... and you can start off with burning the library shelves! Turn the canals round to drown the museum vaults!
>
> Marinetti, *Manifesto initial du futurisme*, 1909[2]

This statement by the Italian futurist followed closely on another: 'We want to glorify war – the only hygiene in the world – militarism, patriotism, the destructive action of anarchists'.

Artists must always be taken seriously: Marinetti's non-future indeed became the future of the war. Beginning in 1914, and far more intensively after 1918, the cemeteries and all reminders of the war on the Western Front became memorials and museums; Marinetti had won the argument – but it related to a tragedy with ten million dead. His fellow-countrymen of today's Italy have developed the concept of the *Museo al aperto*, or 'open museum', to describe these areas where the residue of wars and of mass death forms sites of commemoration, mourning and the unwavering focus of despair. Perhaps the impossibility of projecting the self into a too-painful past underlies this intensive process of heritage-making which has grown in importance since the 1990s, in the adaptation of sites which have become cemeteries, either original or replacement, and hence memorials and museums. Does the use of the present as a museum represent an attempt to rediscover the past? Or is this anyhow impossible?

This is how architects and artists occupy these old sites of war that are now 'sites of memory'. Here they can present their messages on site, direct to the casual visitor who encounters and rediscovers the war that is past, together with the art of today. In France and Belgium, the nations of the Western Front, public commissions from local communities – in France the departments and regions, in Belgium the two regions of Flanders and Wallonia – have taken on this double market, memory and art. The Franco-Belgian organization 'Interreg 14–18 Mémoire', under the slogan of 'Une ligne de front, un passé, un avenir' (A single front line, a past, a future), brought together twenty-one partners, large museums or smaller interpretation centres from the North Sea to the Chemin des Dames.[3] In the name of the 'duty to remember' and in the frequent but not universal forgetting of the duty of history – the wandering and wayward memory is so much easier to manipulate than the rigid critique of historicity – the Great War has re-emerged spectacularly in the collective conscience along the old Western Front since the end of the 1980s and in many of the formerly active belligerent nations.

The uniqueness of France – followed by Belgium – is that the greater part of the main front line of the Great War lay on its soil, on which the world's armies contended. In this sense, it is not the nation which is at war in the world, but the soil of France that became the world territory of the world war. A UNESCO committee is now classifying the traces of battlefields, under the heading of 'Landscapes and Sites of Memory of the Great War'. This classification through the cultural organ of the United Nations is designed to express awareness that men came from the entire world to fight and to die on the Western Front: the physical reminders are, above all, graves, the reason for the particular strength of historical, memorial, political, editorial and media aspects.[4] There may be consensus on the suffering and the mourning, visible in the very numerous war memorials erected in communes and the battlefields in the 1920s, but many other aspects of the understanding of the war have long remained controversial: in this chapter we will cover the length of the Western Front to show the assaults of memory reconstructed and deconstructed, from national controversy to the internationalization of memory, as embodied and represented in works of art and museums.[5] Suffering has been rendered universal, facilitating narratives of European unity and internationalization of the war story in public, while marginalizing to the point of denial the hatreds that had so animated the belligerents. Alternative narratives are thus rendered anti-victim in complexion. Nevertheless, more recent examples of commemorative art have not only continued to struggle with representations of destruction, but have acknowledged the war's totality, and the breadth and endurance of its impacts.

Between sacrifice and pacifism, from controversy to appeasement

We are still haunted by the long-term memory of the First World War, with its periods of suppression or oblivion, our thinking confused by the later horrors and large-scale massacres of the Second World War, followed in turn by the wars of decolonization – not to mention current warfare.[6] In France, to celebrate the anniversaries of the war, in the years ending in 4 (1914), in 8 (1918) and in 6 (Verdun in 1916), the Presidents of the Republic – François Mitterrand in 1984, Jacques Chirac in 1996 and 2006,[7] Nicolas Sarkozy in 2008, François Hollande for the centenary of 1914 – or, in one case, a prime minister

(Lionel Jospin at Craonne in 1998) – have taken direct control over memorial projects, whether they are short-term or intended to be permanent features of the landscape.

Without any doubt the most important example of recent memorial art on the Western Front is the Chemin des Dames, which in France has risen from a secondary site of memory (after Verdun or even the Somme) to become the leading location for a France united over the sufferings of the war and of those men/soldiers who realized very early that rejection of the war was the only way to comprehend their experience. This *aggiornamento* of memory has taken not quite twenty years, from 1998, when Prime Minister Lionel Jospin initiated his own distinctive way to commemorate the eightieth anniversary of the armistice, to the centenary commemorations of 2014.

Jospin's originality in 1998 was to seek out contemporary artists who had responded particularly strongly to the site of Craonne village on the Chemin des Dames. The woodland here has grown up again over the lost village, which has been reconstructed elsewhere because all that remained of it was a vast cemetery; they spoke of the contrast between the beauty of flourishing nature and the horror of the suffering. In his 'Ils n'ont pas choisi leur sépulture' (They did not choose their tomb) Haïm Kern created an imaginative work designed not to remain as a permanent foreign element in the woodland – now a magnificent arboretum – but to be an enduring link between the living and the dead. It was the sufferings and conditions surrounding the death of soldiers in the First World War which moved the artist and, particularly, the proliferation of unknown soldiers, pulverized beneath the unimaginable power of the artillery. 'I want this sculpture to be physically close to these men so that they return to us, from the earth to the light, standing out in the mesh of history.'[8] 'The mesh of history': heads are caught in the mesh of a bronze net, always the same, always different: set at different heights and angles, they never catch the light, or the shadows, in the same way (Figures 5.1 and 5.2). Farmers along the 'red scar' of the old front line still continue to plough up bits of metal, barbed wire, pieces of bone. But they never recover faces. Haïm Kern restores a face, a life, to those who were lost in their hundreds of thousands, swallowed up in earth and fire. The net of the sculpture becomes a metaphor for mourning, grieving without end, mesh by mesh, inextinguishable. In choosing to show no uniform or mark of affiliation, but only faces, the artist humanizes the sufferings of the Great War – this time of mass death, all the more unbearable in its reversal of the natural order of the generations, with sons dying before their parents.

From the very moment the work was commissioned, before the artist himself knew what he would express, the Prime Minister was determined to make a significant speech at its inauguration. The sculpture was to have a political purpose: it would become the 'monument of monuments' designed for the whole nation. *Le Monde* obliged, declaring that the time had come to 'restore the mutineers' of 1917 to national memory.[9] Lionel Jospin spoke of a 'sacred site'. Defining the site at such a symbolic level seemingly left little space for critique or challenge. And yet the 'sacred' has been interpreted differently at

Figure 5.1 Haïm Kern, 'Ils n'ont pas choisi leur sépulture' (They did not choose their tomb), Chemin des Dames, 1998. © Annette Becker

both ends of the political spectrum. Haïm Kern's sculpture has been vandalized several times by partisans of military order and/or from the extreme right, who see the sculpture – which shows only the suffering of the war – as a three-dimensional rejection of heroism and patriotism. Such violence against a work of art in the public space, an extremely rare event, reflects the magnitude of the issue at stake, even though the artist's sculpture was merely the pretext for this French-on-French attack. In addition, the facts that the artist's first name, Haïm, happens to echo the Hebrew word for 'Life', and that his place of birth was Leipzig, from where he fled with his parents in 1933, were undoubtedly not without significance in some of the attacks.

More significantly, however, the sculpture has acquired a nickname – 'The Mutineers' monument'. This characterization has been adopted by peace-minded observers and pacifists, who have created a model and a hope for those who were capable of rejecting the war while it was in progress.[10]

94 *Annette Becker*

Figure 5.2 Detail, Haïm Kern, 'Ils n'ont pas choisi leur sépulture' (They did not choose their tomb), Chemin des Dames, 1998. © Annette Becker

Between 1914 and 1918 all combatants wondered how it was possible to undergo so much and still continue to fight and suffer while, increasingly, they were convinced of the absurdity of their sacrifice. Still bewildered by their own violence, for the most part it was only after the war that they became aware of another possible form of messianism, that of the total rejection of all war. In this conception, everyone killed between 1914 and 1918 is indiscriminately described as a 'victim' – as confirmed by the inscriptions on so many war memorials. Victimhood was also applied to the civilians behind the front line area, or in the occupied regions which had suffered great material damage. In today's commemorative awareness, this status is more acceptable than being an agent of suffering and death. Death is always suffered, always anonymous, never inflicted: the individual is, always, the victim. Unless of course we are concerned with the leaders, shown as commanders of the massacre, or executioners; the dialectic of generals either as mutineers or butchers is thus imposed.

Contrary to belief in the 1990s, the Great War became a past which was unacceptable, at least in France. Under the circumstances, the past then became deeply contested. This controversy evolved from the fact that some wished only to see heroes and disregard the suffering while others had compassion only for the exemplary victims – men killed in great numbers in the chaos of the opening stages of the war, and the mutineers of 1917 – and ignored the consent and sufferings of the greatest number, whose commitment to the war was difficult to assimilate. Each individual is so afraid of not having suffered enough in this century of total war that the 'complicity of victims' acquires a scale that is sometimes excessive.[11] For pacifist activists, surely the 'mutineers' – relating more to ideological ritual than to the historical reality of the refusals to obey orders in the French army of 1917 – were, in their very revolt, the precursors of European unity?[12] And surely the Nivelle offensive had been the 'first crime against humanity', as described by the Mayor of Craonne himself?[13]

The imperatives of promoting a united Europe were well served by the common narrative, even before the events of 1998. At Verdun in 1984, François Mitterrand and Helmut Kohl took each other by the hand in Douaumont military cemetery, giving some slight impression that the depth of past conflict, which could no longer be expressed in Europe, was being channelled into domestic, French-on-French, controversies. And yet a new consensus has emerged as the centenary approaches. This was visible in 2008 in the two speeches by Nicolas Sarkozy – one of the fiercest opponents of Jospin's remarks in 1998 on the 'reinstatement of everyone in the national memory'. In March that year, at Les Invalides, at the national funeral of the last surviving French soldier Lazare Ponticelli (with a predestined first name, 'he who would rise again'), a volunteer soldier of Italian origin, the President emphasized the values of heroism and sacrifice; in November, at Douaumont, he spoke of the suffering of the combatants – French, European, from the entire world. 'Underlying each loss, in the heart and in the soul of every widow and every orphan, there was a suffering which has never died away. These wounds, these sufferings, we must never forget a single one of them.'[14] He clothed his remarks in the language of universal victimhood. The time for argument was over, everything had been recovered and used by the politicians, sometimes causing great harm to pacifist militants who would have chosen to contest the point. The two narratives – of heroism and of suffering – now coexisted in a shared victimhood, and made impossible a pacifist critique that recognized the agency of all soldiers in killing, as much as suffering.

In the work of artists and architects, however, such readings are still possible. The Caverne du Dragon on the Chemin des Dames, a quarry turned into wartime barracks and later transformed into a museum, 'bears witness movingly' to the soldier's life on this section of the front.[15] The route of the visit is mainly underground, and there is much emphasis on the mutinies of 1917. The architect, Nasrine Seraji-Bozorgzada, has set her elegant and very modern building in today's peaceful landscape. It is also one of the few places on the old front line which mentions African soldiers: a work by Christian Lapie was installed here in 2007, 'the constellation of grief'. Nine trunks of calcified timber, the faces of men without features, universal faces, stand out very tall and very black, in the horizontality of the white chalk landscape, as if risen from the poem by Senghor, 'Hosties noires' in 1938:

> Hear me, Tirailleurs from Senegal, in the solitude of the black land and of death
> In your solitude without eyes, without ears, more than in my dark skin in the depths of the Province
> Without even the warmth of your comrades lying close against you, as once they were close in the trench, or in the village councils
> Hear me, black-skinned infantrymen, even though you have no ears and no eyes in your three-fold enclosure of night.

As well as recalling the specificity of the African troops, the work renews the pacifist memorial struggle on this section of the front: General Mangin's 'Black Force' took a large part in the Chemin des Dames and on 16 and 17 April 1917 the losses among the ill-prepared African soldiers, who suffered greatly from the cold, were crushing: of the 15,000 dead of the offensive, 6,000 were African. Pacifist and anti-racist struggles come together in this part of the front, the 'butchers' of the whites are also described as the 'grinders of the blacks'.

While the controversies over the 1998 memorial had subsided, the issue itself remained. In November 2013 the socialist president François Hollande demanded that 'a place be accorded to the history of the men shot for mutiny, in the Army Museum at Les Invalides which tells the story of the war'.[16] The narrative of terrible injustices – the men shot (or not), for example – was shifted from its original setting, the Western Front, to Paris, at the centre of power, but in a museum.

France and the Chemin des Dames have no monopoly on this view, both compassionate towards the combatants and, in the near absence of perpetrators, 'politically correct'. Everywhere, more has been seen of the Christmas Truce of 1914 and episodes of fraternization than of hatred of the enemy;[17] for however painful it may be, it is easier to accept that one's grandfather or father was killed in the anonymity of battle, under artillery and gas attack, than to admit that he himself could have killed, even that he could have seen this as part of his normal and ordinary patriotic duty.

The political efficacy of this approach is easily apparent. For 2014 the region of the Nord-Pas-de-Calais has decided to commemorate all the dead among all the fighting men in the battles of Artois and the north of France, without distinction of nationality, in 'homage to the lasting peace established on the continent of Europe'. Alongside a vast French military cemetery and the group of Catholic commemorative buildings at Notre Dame de Lorette – the church, the lantern tower of the dead and the ossuary, dating from the 1920s – the modern memorial with its own interpretation centre will present a very up-to-date view of the war to mark the centenary of its outbreak. No distinction of nationality or religious affiliation will appear; the carved names will record simply those who died there. François Hollande has given this central vision of the centenary his official approval, with the announcement that he will inaugurate this new memorial on 11 November 2014. 'It is true that it was one side against the other, for their own nation, that these young men died. It is in the name of shared humanity that they will henceforward be brought together.'[18] As this shows, the intention is not to offer further explanation for the terrible struggle of the early years of the century, but to exonerate it: commemoration has become a sort of reparation, offered by the living to the dead, in a desire to bring all the sacrifices together. The emphasis lies on the feelings and perceptions of today, as stated in the very new interpretation centre of the Great War at Ploegsteert, near Comines in Belgium: 'An approach that is humane, interactive and moving showing a world in change'. The cover photograph on the brochure is entirely typical of this new tourism of remembrance which wishes to participate directly in the historical experience: seen from behind, in jeans and colourful clothes, the visitors seem to be going back into history – a trench photograph in black and white where the combatants are drawn up opposite each other. Everywhere, experience – as in *Plugstreet 14–18 Experience* or *The Passchendaele Experience* – and feeling are designed to dominate. *Plugstreet 14–18* opens with a phrase by Peter Englund – as definitive as it is questionable: 'When an event or an epoch has moved beyond living history it becomes ineluctably and irretrievably history and nothing but history', but the selected commentaries are typical of the approach through generalization: 'The Great War turned 60 million men into cannon fodder.'[19]

What dominates the efforts of museums and politicians on the brink of the centenary is that all the combatants were the same men, dead together, for a cause that no one now wants to identify historically. They have in common their death at that time, here on this terrain, where they are now the watchmen of peace and strong emotion, examples of universal reconciliation in the rediscovered peace. The architects invited to compete for the new memorial at Lorette have been forced into marvels of invention to find enough space for the 600,000 carved names: an immense circular structure won the day, with its inner and outer walls entirely covered with names – the circle standing as a symbol of the globe, of the world war. For the second characteristic of these new sites of memory is their internationalization.

How to represent the internationalization of suffering

The memory of the Western Front has clearly not waited for the centenary to become internationalized. During the post-war years graves were identified by nation, with steles, memorials and individual carved names marking a sacrifice for nation or empire. And the Unknown Soldier – British, Italian, Belgian – became the symbol for all the dead: he alone had no name, for he had all names. Since the end of the 1980s museums have appeared along the line of military cemeteries and memorials, established in the 1920s and 1930s, defining the old Western Front as it was remembered by its former combatants. Since the late 1980s, three great buildings have engaged in the presentation of 'historical' 'war narratives' – as in the Historial de la Grande Guerre in Péronne and In Flanders Fields museum in Ypres, both set up in the 1990s and then re-imagined for the centenary, and the more recent Musée de la Grande Guerre du Pays de Meaux. The three have experienced varying degrees of success in presenting the war in international context.

The Historial is entirely tri-national: French, British and German. It shows the societies at war, with their soldiers and their civilians, through interaction: as the visitors move through the museum they follow the course of the war, from the pits set in the floor at the centre of the halls – symbolizing the trenches – to the showcases displaying objects from the fully mobilized civilian societies. The museum was conceived as a setting for encounter and dialogue between objects of daily life and works of art. The collections have been used imaginatively so that each object retains its own individuality while the totality illuminates the story of those who lived through the tragedy of 1914–18, from the military, domestic and occupation fronts to the prison camps for captured soldiers. The scale ranges from the very near – Péronne and the Somme – to the most distant, the remainder of France, and still further: the European war, the world war. There is the range of ages and types: from Australians to Senegalese infantrymen, or from the German mother in Hamburg to the Russian child. The aim of the museum is to immerse the visitor in a 'total' experience of total warfare.[20]

The central hall makes use of the contrast between the verticality of photographs and postcards showing the contemporaries of the pre-war world, not knowing what awaits them, looking directly at the visitors with great innocent eyes, and the horizontality of the engravings by the German artist Otto Dix who went through the whole war. Dix was not ready to create his fifty engraved moments of horror and suffering until 1923–24, after careful reflection. He knew too much. The whole museum, the whole war, can be seen from this central hall. This dark and sombre space is the heart of the cyclone, like Otto Dix's representation of the war.

At the In Flanders Field museum the interaction is more military, with the museum located in Belgian territory but designed above all – hence its name – for the British visitors who come in search of understanding of the battles of Flanders. On leaving the museum, they are invited to tour the battlefields of the Salient, and their visit to the museum includes the Menin Gate, a few hundred metres away, where the Last Post is sounded in a dramatic ceremony every night. The museum operates through complete interactivity for the visitors-turned-participants: as they enter the In Flanders Fields display they receive an electronic bracelet in the shape of a poppy (the symbol of this museum, as it is of the Historial de la Grande Guerre – the Somme and Flanders under British patronage). This is their *open sesame* to pass through the gateway of the history of the war. Everything is dark and the main 'attractions' consist of models – such as the presentation of the Battle of the Yser and the deliberate protective flooding of the land – and the films which narrate tales of life at war. The magnificent collections of soldiers' notebooks, weapons and other objects are integrated into this audio-visual presentation and the commentaries, given in four languages (Dutch, French, English and German), stress the sufferings of the combatants and civilians caught up in the war. Undoubtedly this death-focused atmosphere transmits something of the war and its human cost, but at the same time the persistent electronic presentations and the continuous soundtrack turn the exhibition into a vast television or computer screen, so familiar to modern visitors that the 'disturbing strangeness' of history risks being completely lost. Visitors might feel something of the empathetic experience of war, but critical understanding remains more remote and difficult.

The museum at Meaux opened in 2008 with great ambitions, based on its setting at the site of the battles of the Marne, and close to Paris. Unfortunately, despite or because of its magnificent collection, it is not easy to grasp the intellectual message of the museum which begins with a lengthy re-run of Franco-German hatreds which were somewhat out of date by the time of the world war. The visitor is faced with a pile of objects which are intended to speak for themselves, with a leaning towards uniforms and weapons – it could be a museum of battles. But there is no interpretation of these particular battles, of tactics or strategy, still less the ebb and flow of war or relationships between the rear areas and the front, the European centre and the rest of the world. Between the piles of objects and the trenches reconstructed in the old style, the very modern technology, the fascination with weapons and the very prominent anti-militarism of the designer Tardi, the impression is one of a museum full of internal oppositions. Who used these weapons? Why? What are we to make of these people – our ancestors – today? One gets the impression that historians have not been consulted, as they were at Péronne and Ypres, and an overriding urge to mark the centenary with a commercial angle informs the nature of this museum experience.

Other and more local interpretation centres have appeared, responding to the ever-growing number of visitors from all over the world who are deeply interested in their own national origins and their grandparents' and great-grandparents' participation in the war, seeking some kind of intelligibility from the ground itself. Here we have a paradox of commemoration: just as all the soldiers gradually came to see each other as brothers, today's visitor is more inclined to seek a sense of sharing in the soldiers' suffering. Each of the national elements is determined to find self-identification ever more clearly in commemoration as it is inscribed on the battlefields. The fiction of the Unknown Soldier in Westminster representing all the soldiers of the British Empire could no longer be accepted by the Commonwealth nations which have each buried their own Unknown Soldier at Canberra, Wellington or Ottawa; similarly, we are witnessing a re-nationalization of sections of the Western Front in the interpretation centres located near the old memorials of the 1920s to explain each individual nation's part in the war.

The Canadians were the first to create their own national commemoration at their two heroic locations, Beaumont-Hamel in the Somme (for Newfoundland) and Vimy in the Pas de Calais. South Africa has had to transform its approach to the war which recognized only whites until Nelson Mandela came to power, with a new museum centre at Longueval in the Somme. Under the flag of the new nation it states that 'this museum commemorates the 25,000 South African volunteers, men and women of all races and all regions, who fell in the course of the two world wars and the war in Korea'. Elsewhere, the Indians serving with the British Expeditionary Force were a visible reminder of colonial history; the British Empire had a certain advantage over the French, who have always encountered greater difficulty in revisiting their colonial past. The greatest novelty on the Western Front was undoubtedly the Chinese presence: men who brought a reminder from twentieth-century China of the former 'coolies', employed in service corps by the British and French armies. Deaths among these men were mainly caused by the Spanish flu epidemic in 1918–19. The modern authorities of the second greatest world power have rediscovered this Chinese presence on French soil – for example in the cemetery at Noyelles-sur-Mer in the Somme – and, having ignored the graves for ninety years, adorn them with vast wreaths, tracing a shared origin with the proletariat so often swept up in China and used in war, and with the traders of the new all-conquering China.

The rediscovery and re-appropriation of one of the most complete sections of the Western Front belongs to the Australians, in two forms: the celebration of Anzac Day at Villers-Bretonneux has become a very substantial affair, attracting thousands of pilgrims on 25 April every year for ceremonies at 5.00 am; while excavations at the rediscovered burial site near Fromelles, DNA research into descendants and the creation of a new cemetery have galvanized Australian memory of the Western Front. The opening of a new museum in April 2014 promises to complete the Australian itinerary, 'from shadow to the light'.[21] Its logo references Peter Corlett's sculpture, 'Cobbers' (Figures 5.3 and 5.4) – of which a cast stands next to the Shrine of Remembrance in Melbourne. It recalls the founding myths of Australian war memory: the dreadful day of the Australian troops' first battle on the Western Front, and the humanity and brotherhood among the rescuers summoned by the cry 'Don't forget me, Cobber.'

After the Treaty of Versailles, each of the former adversaries maintained its own cemeteries and set up memorials in its own style along the old line of the Western Front, on sites donated by France and Belgium. The British chose a large number of small cemeteries strung out like links in a chain across the landscape, creating British terrain 'For King and Country'. The Americans, late arrivals in the war and who suffered fewer casualties, established the very large cemeteries and memorials which still occupy stretches of land on the former front lines in the Aisne and Argonne. They seem to proclaim that 'we are still here', a diplomatic expression of ambitions displayed in the graves, despite repatriation of thousands of bodies.

Figure 5.3 Peter Corlett, 'Cobbers', Fromelles Memorial Park, 1998. © Annette Becker

For the Germans, once the principle of military cemeteries was accepted, it was understood that they should occupy the smallest area possible, hence the cemeteries with very few individual graves – black in colour, the condemnation of defeat – and vast mass graves. This pattern then encouraged them to a degree of competition, to establish memorial forms less imperial and imposing than the British, French or Americans, and set out in the cemeteries. The most extraordinary work of art of the era is Käthe Kollwitz's creation at Vladslo in Flanders: parents – herself and her husband – kneel weeping beside their son's grave, now photographed and displayed life-size in the In Flanders Fields museum. Up to the present day, however, despite the great care and continuing maintenance evident in these cemeteries in the form of 'groves for heroes', Germans visitors are still rarely seen. The Western Front continues overwhelmingly to belong to the victors. Even if the great museum and interpretation centres give them their space – German historians worked on the design of the Historial de la Grande Guerre alongside their international

Figure 5.4 Detail, Peter Corlett, 'Cobbers', Fromelles Memorial Park, 1998. © Annette Becker

colleagues – no modern structure has been designed by the Germans of today for the Western Front. For the vast majority of Germans the Second World War undoubtedly continues to occlude the memory of the preceding global conflict – but they also do not necessarily feel welcome on the Western Front, where, a century later, they are still 'the enemy'. A recent controversy over German remains in the ossuary at Douaumont is a good example: the director of the ossuary found himself severely criticized for his decision to add the carved names of German soldiers who were killed on the battlefields of Verdun. One correspondent to the director wrote that everyone is in favour of 'reconciliation over the graves' – but:

> reconciliation does not mean forgetting. For me this gesture is a betrayal of the memory of all the *poilus* who fought, who were killed or who were wounded on the battlefields.
> We cannot forget the destruction, nor the sufferings of the population living in the occupied zones.[22]

This correspondent's letter has the merit of setting out clearly the contradictions of commemoration: reconciliation, he says, should not be dependent on the forgetting of specific sufferings. To accuse the Germans rather than 'the war' is an outdated nationalist anachronism in 2014, but entirely in the spirit of the hatreds of 1914–18, themselves in danger of being not simply overcome, but denied. And it also raises the question of civilians who were caught up in the war and the occupation – equally terrible but often forgotten on the Western Front – where it is the combatant memory which takes centre stage.

'Nothing is more powerful than the surviving traces'[23] – what contemporary artists show us

In late 1916, Guillaume Apollinaire published a book on which he had been working since before the war, *Le poète assassiné*. Wounded in the war, trepanned and suffering the trauma of being buried in the trenches, Apollinaire – an ordinary combatant and avant-garde poet – now became one of the inventors of modern commemoration. The semi-urban-myth literature of 1913 was overtaken by the seriousness of the war as the poet's premonition of 'the great killing' turned to full-scale reality. Chapter XVIII, 'Apothéose', describes the construction of the commemorative monument to the hero, 'Croniamental/Apollinaire'; in the dialogue between Tristouse and the Bird of Benin – representing Picasso, all women and anyone commissioning works – it also gives advance warning of proposals for memorials to commemorate all the combatants of the war:

> 'I must create a statue for him' said the Bird of Benin, 'for I am not only a painter but also a sculptor ... '
> 'Where? ... the government won't give us a site. Times are bad for poets.'
> 'So they say ... But perhaps it's not true. ...'
> 'What sort of statue? ... Marble? Bronze?'
> 'No, that's too old-fashioned ... I must create a profound statue out of nothing, like poetry and like the war.'
> 'Bravo! Bravo! ... A statue made of nothing, a void, it's magnificent, and when are you going to sculpt this?'
> 'Tomorrow, if you wish; ... I will carve this profound figure. ... '
> Next day the sculptor returned with workmen who clad the well with a wall of reinforced cement, eight centimetres thick, except for the base which was 38 centimetres thick, so effectively that the void took the form of Croniamental, the hole was full of his ghost.[24]

From Apollinaire to the works of contemporaries that were equally conceptual, everyone understood that the combatants of the First World War would be no more than phantoms. For a century now, artists have sought to master the war-catastrophe which dislocated the world and its beings, between sufferings, cruelty, violence and negligence. Now we see the generation – born during or after the Second World War, born of the war, or another war, or sometimes without war – which devotes its labours to the relationships between art, memory and oblivion. Each confronts the difficulty of representing acts of violence: the very claim that forms of war violence can be shown asserts the possibility of seeing what, paradoxically, represents the absence of direct vision, the destruction of individuals as well as objects.[25] This explains why many have expressed a sort of rage at seeing objects, museums and memorials apparently claiming to take the place of memory and to be capable of acting as substitutes for men and their absence. Against this, art prefers 'deep holes' and 'ghosts', between rehabilitation and disappearance. None the less, as the Great War returns to general awareness a new wave of contemporary creations has burgeoned on the Western Front. A generation of French and foreign artists remembers that the war was global, and in many respects total. All stumble over the difficulty of representing bodies that have suffered violence, and their forms of art therefore often prefer to show the traces of death, entering a debate which is both political – in the urban setting – and aesthetic.

Above all they have shown the totalization of the war, demonstrating their recognition that women, children and landscapes were transformed or destroyed, as well as men. All have shown in one way or another, whatever the chosen medium, that the First World War was a tragedy and that the working of mourning and of memory should never be kept apart from reflection on their counterparts: oblivion and suppression. In 1998, for example, Bosnia was in everyone's mind – and equally Sarajevo in 1914. Reflecting on her commission from Lionel Jospin in 1998, the artist Christine Canetti wrote:

> I have stolen this profoundly hateful subject, evocative of loss, solitude, abandonment, death. This commission has enabled me to refocus on 14–18 and to see in these violent stakes the same atrocities and wrongs as in the modern wars, a mere two hours away from us ... Working on the themes of memory, the passage from life to death, I like to delve into history ... the artist sometimes feels useless. And it is this 'work of transcription' which relocates him in his role of intercessor with its social mission.[26]

In giving voice to the women of the occupied territories in a work made of glass, symbol of fragility and tenacity, Christine Canetti has successfully restored the balance between front and rear, speaking of the 'domestic front' and the specificity of the dramas of the occupied peoples, of women in these occupied populations.[27]

Alain Fleischer has felt that he was 'under the gaze of the dead' while exploring the battlefields, hence the title of his work.[28] He has photographed the gaze of the soldiers hundreds of times as he reproduces snapshots of the time. At the moment of exposing the work – in both senses of the word, but alas only once in Arras in 1998 – hundreds of racks of developed images awaited the viewers: and in the red light of a photographic laboratory large enough for a battlefield, the eyes emerge bit by bit, the eyes of men whose gaze seems never to have existed except for this death. The ever-open eyes of Alain Fleischer's soldiers are, as he says, 'practically immaterial ... the opposite of a memorial to the dead. They did not know that this would be the last photograph taken of them.'[29]

Figure 5.5 Ernest Pignon-Ernest, Bois de Soyécourt, Somme. © C.A. Becker

The artists reveal the blindness of war, in one way or another: Ernest Pignon-Ernest's trees of bronze, permanently broken and incapable of growth (Figure 5.5), are a metaphor of the conflict – the artist who has always drawn human bodies, tortured, violated, excluded, decided that he could not show soldiers' bodies. He therefore chose to cast the stumps of twenty-year-old trees in bronze: 'Nature has won all this, life wins the day. The trees are growing on the bodies of those who died there. Bodies, flesh, blood, soil'.[30] He may be likened to Paul Nash, whose tree stumps were metaphors for mutilated men. The English language, which refers to *stomp* and *stump*, is particularly striking with this alliteration. The novelist Edith Wharton was very successful in demonstrating this incredible transformation by war of men and nature in 1915:

> Our road ran through a bit of woodland exposed to constant shelling. Half the poor spindling trees were down, and patches of blackened undergrowth and ragged hollows marked the paths of the shell. ... there was

something humanly pitiful in the frail trunks of the *Bois Triangulaire*, lying there like slaughtered rows of immature troops.[31]

Contemporary artists confirm the mourning and the loss in their work: they come the nearest to modern preoccupations with the fate of bodies and souls in the First World War. The Forester's House at Ors, in the Department of the Nord, where the poet Wilfred Owen was killed in the final days of the war, has been transformed by the British artist Simon Patterson, who reflected at great length on the place of art in the public sphere. The roof has been reconstructed in the form of an open book, Owen's poetry is projected onto the walls and read by Kenneth Branagh; the cellar where Owen is said to have written his final letter home is preserved as it was. The memory of the war should be as close as possible to reality – memory bearing witness – and sublimate the horror in emotion. Here the work, in this squared-off sculpture-house of dazzling white, Patterson's 'bleached bone', offers with remarkable soberness the impossible acceptance of the life cut short, through sounds, silences and words: the light appears to come from the poetry itself:

My friend, you would not tell with such high zest
To children ardent for some desperate glory,
The old Lie: Dulce et decorum est
Pro patria mori.

Like the combatants of the time, artists come from the whole world: the internationalization of contemporary art, visible in the Biennales of the great cities of the world, expresses the globalization of the conflict that is now one hundred years old. Some sample works shown on the Western Front, and also in Wellington, Cape Town or in New York, seem to signify these commemorative routes through and for the eye, recalling the eyes of the combatants and of those whom they have loved, lost or rediscovered, transformed by the war, between wounding and trauma.

The New Zealander Kingsley Baird, with his work 'Tomb' (2013) – exhibited in France at the Historial de la Grande Guerre de Péronne, in Germany and in Wellington – presents the dead of the war to the living (Figure 5.6). In choosing a material from an intimate setting, the kitchen, the little 'Anzac' biscuits, he blends the military front with the domestic front, men and women – the women who traditionally remain in the kitchen and the men who travel far away to defend (or believe they are defending) their shared values. Baird knows that in reality these Anzac biscuits did not exist during the war, that they are a typical 'invented tradition', an act of memory from the 1920s. Each biscuit represents the uniform, represents a man, one, plus one, plus one … . Each of these men was 'eaten' by the war. In modern warfare, the enemy is no longer consumed – except where the extreme situations of famine and/or hatred have led there: it is the whole of warfare in itself that has turned cannibal.

Figure 5.6 Kingsley Baird, 'Tomb', 2013. © Yazid Medmoun, Historial de la Grande Guerre

Baird brings together layers of memory, history and anthropology to represent the complexity of the war. Were not the fighting men of the Australian and New Zealand Army Corps – of European origin but also Maori or Aboriginals – like all the other British and Allies with whom they fought side by side – convinced that they were representing Civilization in the face of barbarians, those whom they called the Huns, their German enemies? 'Tomb', in its sophisticated composition, its 18,000 biscuits – in the mutability of chance and necessity, the number of New Zealanders who died in the Great War – shifts from the singular which represents the multiple, the unknown soldiers, to the multiple which represents the singular, a single soldier in a single grave. 'Tomb' is also full of voids, the 18,000 biscuits that can never fill this hole, it is there, infinite, like the void of the *Poète assassiné*.

Kader Attia brings the facially wounded soldier brutally into the Great War in most contemporary art, like the Documenta XIII in Kassel with the 'Reparation', at MOMA in New York with 'Open Your Eyes' (2010); on

108 *Annette Becker*

several screens, he brings photographs of 'mended' soldiers, with scars and striking deformities, face to face with African objects with obvious repairs: men and objects are stitched together, hybridized, between traditional cultures and colonial borrowings, between war and peace. In the photographs picked out from the archives of military hospitals, the broken faces are like objects in every way, broken and patched up in the reserves of colonial museums, far from the 'aesthetics of purity'[32] preached at the time. The form of surgery known as 'restorative' is often compared to more craftsman-style repairs and the synthesis is achieved through photographs of colonial soldiers wounded in the face during the war. The work obliges the spectator, horribly ill at ease in front of the photographs, to reflect on medical and military ethics, on trauma and impossible healing: for neither the repair of bodies nor that of souls is still imaginable after the war, in the whole world.

The emphasis of so much contemporary memorial art on damaged bodies, and the effort to represent destruction, reflects that growing recognition of the war's totality, and its expanding affective circles. The South African artist Paul Emmanuel reflects on the bodies of the combatants, on wounding, on physical and mental fragility faced with the technology of industrial death. His installation 'Lost Men' presents a trail of banners on which photographs of parts of his body are reproduced after the names of dead soldiers have been recorded on them. Matrices of lead print are sunk, like temporary sculptures, into the artist's shoulders, thighs, thorax, face and shaven skull. The naked body represented by enlarged fragments where the bruise-inscriptions are clearly visible, the delicate fabric selected for the reproduction and to quiver in the wind, all proclaim human fragility and vulnerability. Paul Emmanuel wishes to reflect on age, the youth of the soldiers, their masculinity, their virility, and on race: this white body, his own, also bears the name of dead soldiers from South Africa, and by analogy the process recalls the branding of slaves. In 2014, the installation was at Thiepval, close to the grand architecture of the triumphal/mourning arch bearing the carved names of thousands of British soldiers, the missing of the Battle of the Somme. Paul Emmanuel recalls this in his own way with some of the bodies in his work marked 'unknown soldier'. Lutyens, the architect, designed the monument in such a way that the summit of the arch can never be completely resolved: it will always be possible to add another stone; the mourning of the stones is infinite. And for all those who explore the Western Front, however they do it, the traces of the Great War are always infinite.

Notes

1 Translated from French by Helen McPhail, with many thanks from Annette Becker.
2 *Le Figaro*, 20 February 1909.
3 Several very well documented maps have been published recently, including one from the Institut national de l'information géographique et forestière (France), *Grande Guerre 1914–1918, 'Evénement, tourisme, mémoire'*, 2014.
4 See the French publication of a vast album of 335 pages, *2014, Centenaire de la Première Guerre mondiale* (Paris: 14–18 Mission Centenaire, 2014), which refers to an

'unprecedented cultural dynamic of combatant memory', 14. Many internet sites are worth studying independently.
5 The case of Belgium, and the controversies around Wallonia/Flanders, deserve an article to themselves. See Karen Shelby's chapter (Chapter 10) in this book.
6 It is not only the memory of the First World War but of the entire twentieth century that is now examined in this light. See Paul Ricoeur, *La mémoire, l'histoire, l'oubli* (Paris: Seuil, 2000), published in English as *Memory, History, Forgetting*, translated by Kathleen Blamey and David Pellauer (Chicago: University of Chicago Press, 2004).
7 See Annette Becker, 'Verdun, les religions, l'Europe, 1916–2006' in *Actes du Colloque 'les religions de l'Europe'*, dir. Jean Dominique Durand, 2007.
8 Haïm Kern in 1998, cited in *La Lettre du Chemin des Dames, Bulletin d'information édité par le Conseil Général de l'Aisne*, special issue no. 3 (November 2006), 2.
9 Wrapper on the newspaper *Le Monde*, 6 November 1998: 'La République honore les mutins de 1917'.
10 Nicolas Offenstadt, *Les Fusillés de la Grande Guerre et la mémoire collective (1914–1999)* (Paris: Odile Jacob, 1999).
11 Jean-Michel Chaumont, *La concurrence des victimes: génocide, identité et reconnaissance* (Paris: La Découverte, 1997).
12 Leonard V. Smith, *Between Mutiny and Obedience. The Case of the French Fifth Division during World War I* (Princeton: Princeton University Press, 1994); and Leonard V. Smith, *The Embattled Self. French Soldiers' Testimony of the Great War* (Ithaca: Cornell University Press, 2007).
13 Noël Genteur, mayor of Craonne, replied to Lionel Jospin: 'The dignity that you bestow, today, on the *poilus* is the measure of your humanity' [at these sites] 'the first crime against humanity remains unpunished.'
14 Nicolas Sarkozy, 11 November 2008, Douaumont.
15 Brochure of the Caverne du Dragon, the museum of the Chemin des Dames.
16 François Hollande, 7 November 2013.
17 See for example Christian Caron's film *Joyeux Noël*, 2005.
18 François Hollande.
19 *Plugstreet 14–18 Experience*, opened in November 2013.
20 Jay Winter, 'Designing a War Museum: Some Reflections on Representations of War and Combat' in *Memory, Mourning, Landscape*, eds Elizabeth Anderson, Avril Maddrell, Kate McLoughlin and Alana Vincent (Amsterdam: Rodopi, 2010), 1–19.
21 Museum brochure. See Annette Becker, Lucy Noakes, Bruce Scates, *Fromelles 1916–2016*, in preparation.
22 Letter to the Director, Verdun ossuary, protesting the inscription of German names in the ossuary. Personal communication with the Director.
23 Alain Fleischer interviewed in Michel Quinejure's film *Quatre artistes sur les traces de la Grande Guerre*, DAP, 1998.
24 Guillaume Apollinaire, *Le poète assassiné*, Oeuvres en prose, vol. 2 (Paris: Gallimard, La Pléiade, 1991), 300–1.
25 Octave Debary and Annette Becker (eds), *Montrer les violences extrêmes: Théoriser, créer, muséographier* (Paris: Editions Creaphis, 2012).
26 Christine Canetti, 'Cinq artistes pour la commémoration de la Grande Guerre' *14–18 Aujourd'hui, Today, Heute* 3 (2000), 230–5.
27 Work set in Armentières, 'Parlez-vous?'.
28 Alain Fleischer, interview.
29 Ibid.
30 Ernest Pignon-Ernest interviewed in Michel Quinejure's film *Quatre artistes*.
31 Edith Wharton, *Fighting France, from Dunquerque to Belfort* (New York: Charles Scribner's Sons, 1915), 165–6 (22 June 1915, in the north of France).
32 The expression comes from Kader Attia commenting on his work at a conference in Beaubourg Metz in September 2012.

6 Music and remembrance
Britain and the First World War

Peter Grant and Emma Hanna

In his research using a Mass Observation study, John Sloboda found that the most valued outcome people place on listening to music is the remembrance of past events.[1] While music has been a relatively neglected area in our understanding of the cultural history and legacy of 1914–18, a number of historians are now examining the significance of the music produced both during and after the war.[2] This chapter analyses the scope and variety of musical responses to the war, from the time of the war itself to the present, with reference to both 'high' and 'popular' music in Britain's remembrance of the Great War. We argue that music has not been incidental but central to remembrance and the contestation of war memory, sometimes assuming a critical role in the debate over remembrance practices. The tensions and developments in ways of remembering the war have been consistently reflected in the musical responses both of participants themselves, and subsequent generations. Since the 1960s, changes in popular music have seen the war reinterpreted through a variety of genres, often very much within the dominant cultural representation of the war, emphasizing loss and futility. In this sense the majority of modern popular music follows precisely the pattern noted by Dan Todman in *The Great War: Myth and Memory* (2005) in relation to literature and film. Yet important dissident voices continue, even today, to question the accepted meanings of the war, and the sources of that wisdom, and to suggest that debate is hardly over.

It is important for historians to recognize the power of music. The emotional potency of music surpasses the capabilities of visual images or written texts; it is an intrapersonal process, a social phenomenon, and a product of cultural influences and traditions.[3] In order to fully appreciate the power and impact of music in the remembering of 1914–18 it can be helpful to use existing models of understanding memory and remembrance. Maurice Halbwachs expounded his thoughts on memory practices in the 1920s, published posthumously as *On Collective Memory* (1950), and was followed by studies into historical narratives, myths, traditions, rituals and ceremonies, by theorists such as Barthes, Foucault, Lacan and Nora. Following Nora we can understand musical pieces as modes of remembrance, as *Lieux de Mémoire* (sites of memory).[4] An interdisciplinary study of this nature may also refer to Clifford Geertz in order to understand the historical context of human behaviour by underlining that music and poetry are part of the 'thick description' of Britain's modern memory of the First World War.[5] The music inspired by the conflagration of 1914–18 reminds us of music's capacity to 'incite and to calm, to preach and to moralize, to jeer and to cheer, and finally to lament and to memorialize. Collectively, it offered a heady mixture that traversed the entire landscape between heaven and hell.'[6]

In this more longitudinal study, we can see that music has also been a powerful tool in setting the parameters of popular remembrance. Britain's modern memory of the First World War has been dominated by a handful of 'war poets' who fought in the trenches.[7] A relationship between music and poetry began during the early stages of the fighting, and persisted through the following decades. Thus the changing nature of the war poets' relationship to remembrance is also reflected in the changing interaction between music and the remembrance of the war. We discern three main phases of 'musical memory' which are broadly chronological:

1. Music from the war itself, a potent way for participants to recall their experiences.
2. Music written specifically to inform the practices of remembering.
3. Music as a commentary on/response to the war.

These three categories allow us to render the contest between different forms of music for public dominance in remembering the war. They also provide a foundation for tracing developments over time, showing that music has provided a forum in which the remembrance of war has been shaped, debated, consolidated and challenged for a century.

Music during the war

Music produced in Britain during the war is differentiated on the one hand by 'soldier songs', produced both in the trenches and at home, and on the other by efforts to memorialize experiences of loss and grief. Soldier-composed songs were often based on existing popular songs or hymns and were collectively or anonymously composed usually with many variants. The gap between soldier-composed and professionally composed songs is far narrower, and the two are less distinct, than many often think. Several songs often understood as composed in the trenches are nothing of the sort.

> The coming and going between the two genres was continual. Soldiers sang the latest music-hall or variety songs at concert parties ... music-hall or variety artists adapted soldiers' songs for commercial production; record companies rushed to record soldiers singing 'trench songs'.[8]

The most common themes found in the songs of the war are morale-boosting, looking forward to better times ahead and the dream of home. Songs also mocked the Germans and took a sardonic view of authority, and at least 20 per cent of soldiers' songs were humorous in content.[9] Remembrance as a theme is virtually absent from both soldier- and professionally composed songs: as Mullen observes, 'the classic tone of a First World War song is jaunty, the romantic tone is rare, and the tragic is absent'.[10]

Yet soldiers' experiences – and indeed civilian experiences – could also give way to much more open expressions of war's pain in music. It is a common misconception that until Britten's *War Requiem* 'virtually all Anglophone composers shunned settings of the raw-edged anger expressed by Owen and Sassoon'.[11] Contrary to Glenn Watkins's assertion, the first settings of Sassoon's poems, 'Butterflies', 'Idyll', 'Everyone Sang' and 'A Child's Prayer' were by Cyril Rootham in 1920–21. Rootham's 'For the Fallen' (1915) is the earliest example of the relationship between music and wartime verse. Composed just months after the poem's publication in September 1914, his setting of Laurence Binyon's verses was one of the first pieces of 'formal' or 'classical' music to be written on the war. Rootham was followed closely by Edward Elgar's choral setting of the same poem in *The Spirit of England* (1915–17). Elgar's setting ultimately overshadowed Rootham's work, though many critics thought Rootham's 'shows the greater respect for Binyon's poem'.[12] Elgar also produced *Fringes of the Fleet*, featuring Kipling's verses. And these were not simply academic pieces: Elgar's settings were widely performed and popularly acclaimed. For his part, Rootham's approach to 'For the Fallen' is far from celebratory or morbid but deeply contemplative and captures some of the ambiguities of the poem – death *and* glory – which were reprised by Rootham's pupil Arthur Bliss in *Morning Heroes* (1930).

Beyond responding to the war's poetry, the idea of composing a requiem had occurred to composers of many nationalities throughout the war, all of whom sought to shape the rites of commemoration. Most wanted to create musical memorials whose tone would be appropriate to the scale of sacrifice. In France, Maurice Ravel, who served as a truck driver near Verdun, composed *Le Tombeau de Couperin*, a suite for piano, between 1914 and 1917. *Tombeau* is a musical term, popular in the seventeenth century, meaning a piece written as a memorial, and Ravel dedicated each movement to a friend who had been killed in the fighting. Frederick Delius, who was too old to fight and at the outbreak of war had moved to southern England, dedicated a requiem (1914–16) to 'the memory of all young artists who have fallen in the war'. A confirmed atheist, Delius completed the half-hour long piece before his nephew was killed fighting for France in 1918. The text was written by his German-Jewish friend, Heinrich Simon, who was inspired by the writings of Friedrich Nietzsche and Arthur Schopenhauer. The Russian composer Alexander Kastalsky's *Requiem for the Fallen Heroes of the Allied Armies* (1916) was performed in Birmingham in November 1917 under the direction of Henry Wood.[13] Charles Villiers Stanford's organ sonata *Eroica* (1917) was followed by *At the Abbey Gate* (1918), the latter performed at the Albert Hall as the opening piece of the annual performance of Elgar's *Dream of Gerontius*. Both these and many inter-war works varied between the personal and intimate and monumental works of collective mourning which attempted to depict the scale of the war.

Music in the inter-war years

Composers' efforts to grapple with the scale of sacrifice, and to engage with the intimacy of loss, continued after November 1918. Gustav Holst dedicated his *Ode to Death* (1920) to the memory of his friends, particularly the composers George Butterworth, killed on the Somme in August 1916, and Cecil Coles, killed in April 1918. While British music lost several young composers, many survived the war and resumed their work. Ralph Vaughan Williams, who had served on the Western Front in the Royal Army Medical Corps, and as an Artillery officer, was deeply affected by the events he witnessed, in addition to the loss of his close friend Butterworth. As a result Vaughan Williams's musical language changed to reflect his experiences and emotions in a rapidly changing world.[14] The 'Pastoral' symphony was inspired by his service in France, and was first performed in London in 1923. The use of a natural trumpet in the second movement playing out-of-tune partials provides echoes of some of Vaughan Williams's wartime memories; the trumpet motif is also a mediated version of the traditional Last Post sounded every night in the trenches, and in remembrance of the fallen since 1914, played every Armistice Day and at the Menin Gate in Ypres every evening. The symphony was received with some puzzlement by both public and critics alike for its apparent one-paced approach: 'it's in four movements and they are all slow. I don't think anybody will like it much', the composer remarked.[15] Fellow composer Constant Lambert, however, called it 'one of the landmarks of modern English music' and it led to Vaughan Williams's first invitation to the USA where he conducted a performance with the New York Symphony Orchestra.[16]

Besides the persistence of personal tributes to the dead, we also see much more ambitious efforts to shape public remembrance of the war through music. The composer John Foulds's war service involved dedicating a large part of his time to the musical activities of the Young Men's Christian Association (YMCA). The charity had been quick to recognize the power of music for Britain's war effort, and their Music Department's motto – 'Whatever cheers the warrior helps to win the war' – underpinned their wartime mission.[17] It was during his time with the YMCA that Foulds composed his *World Requiem*. This was to be the largest composition he would write both in terms of length and the unprecedented number of performers required. It would be the centrepiece of the first commemorative musical event staged at the Royal Albert Hall on Armistice Night 1923. It was organized by Foulds and his partner, the musician Maud MacCarthy. MacCarthy was an Irish-born professional violinist with links to prominent socialists and members of the suffragette movement.[18] This led them to compile a text that attempted a universal, non-denominational pacifism which, in turn, later caused problems for the reception of the work. The phrase 'Festival of Commemoration' was first used by MacCarthy, who appears to have been the driving force behind the Albert Hall Armistice Night concerts in the mid-1920s. Foulds and MacCarthy remain relatively neglected figures despite their key roles in establishing the ways in which the war was remembered in the early 1920s.[19]

The *World Requiem* was a monument in musical form, and ambitious both in its production and its seeking of a wide audience. The dedication in the score reads 'A tribute to the memory of the Dead – a message of consolation to the bereaved of all countries.' A presentation copy of the programme is entitled 'A Cenotaph in Sound. In Memory 1914–18.'[20] With a running length of approximately two hours, it was written for 1,200 singers and instrumentalists. The piece used texts from multiple literary sources, including the Bible, *Pilgrim's Progress*, Hindu poetry and some contemporary free verse; it made use of both Foulds's pioneering of the quarter-tone, and a Middle Eastern instrument called the Sistrum.

Foulds had some success in his aims. In the spring of 1921 he submitted his *World Requiem* to the British Music Society, an organization of prominent English musicians including Adrian Boult, Arnold Bax and Arthur Bliss. After some consideration they informed Foulds that their committee would allow *World Requiem* to be given under the auspices of the British Music Society. The committee secretary reported that they

> lay great stress on the advisability of giving the work in a Cathedral, in preference to a performance in a concert room. Should it be possible to arrange such a performance in St. Paul's Cathedral or Westminster Abbey they will do all they can to make the event a national one ... we were very much impressed with the work and feel sure that it will not be unworthy of the great occasion.[21]

Indeed, it was suggested that the *World Requiem* should be performed in Westminster Abbey in November 1921.[22] Such a debut did not occur but the Society supported the first performance, along with the British Legion who adopted the composition for the Armistice Night performance at the Royal Albert Hall in 1923. It was agreed that royalties from the annual Armistice Night performances would be donated to the Legion for an initial term of five years.[23] In 1924 there were discussions about performances of the *World Requiem* taking place in Seattle, Vancouver, Sydney and Bombay. BBC radio broadcasts were also mooted.

The piece was not only heard but performed at much more local levels. Ahead of the second performance of the *World Requiem* at the Royal Albert Hall on Armistice Night 1924, Douglas Haig requested that it should be performed by regional choirs throughout the United Kingdom every Armistice Day to bring the nation together in a communal act of remembrance, and to raise money for the welfare of ex-servicemen and their dependants. Haig asked local choirs

> to establish and maintain in your district annual Festival Commemoration Performances of all or portions of this work, in aid of my appeal for

ex-servicemen of all ranks, their dependents [sic] and the widows and orphans of the fallen. Such performances ... would at the same time constitute social musical events in honour of those who fell in the Great War.[24]

Haig's encouragement spoke to the power of music in British popular culture and, more specifically, in remembrance of the war itself. The work received a positive public reception in more traditional ways, too, as the *Times* reviewer commented favourably: 'in the opinion of many musical connoisseurs the "World Requiem" has met the need of a national memorial in poetry and music, and has truly been called "a Cenotaph in sound"'.[25] In this sense, such memorials in music should not be considered incidental accompaniments to other forms of remembering, but a form with the potential for a genuine mass audience, especially via broadcast radio. By 1925 the *British Legion* magazine asserted that 'Never before has the whole Nation – nay the whole Empire – shown itself so completely in unison in its desire to do homage to the dead whilst assisting the living.'[26]

Yet Foulds's and MacCarthy's efforts did not proceed without controversy, especially over what was appropriate to remembrance, and whose memories the music of remembrance would privilege. At first the *World Requiem* was enthusiastically received as a key element in the Festival of Remembrance itself; however, as the 1920s progressed it fell out of favour, its sombre tone not entirely in keeping with what was thought appropriate, notably by the British Legion who had agreed to sponsor the performance. By 1927, the ways in which Britain publicly commemorated the war were a matter of considerable contention between those who wanted to mourn, and a large number of veterans who wished to celebrate their survival. The first Armistice Nights had often been 'celebrated' with 'Armistice Jazz' concerts and balls. Author and former officer Charles Carrington recalled that

> the Feast-Day became a Fast-Day and one could hardly go brawling on the Sabbath. The do-gooders captured the Armistice, and the British Legion seemed to make its principal outing a day of mourning ... many soldiers found it increasingly discomforting, year by year.[27]

The role of music in remembrance was at the heart of this debate. Throughout the 1920s the national newspapers, notably the *Daily Mail* and *Daily Express*, disputed the appropriate tone of Armistice Day, set against a backdrop of class antagonism, unemployment, strikes and economic instability. Previous celebrations had been deemed too elitist and favouring of those who could afford travel to London.[28] By 1927 the Home Office, War Office and Admiralty agreed that the ex-service community should be more fully represented at the Cenotaph, and British Legion Headquarters were asked to organize an ex-servicemen's parade past the monument.[29] Leading figures of Britain's musical establishment no longer deemed Foulds's piece appropriate as the nation's musical memorial. Foulds's work was deemed too middle brow for the establishment and too 'high' for many of the veterans and the general public. While MacCarthy was convinced there had been 'back door business' to discredit Foulds, the accounts of the British Legion also suggest that the piece was too expensive to produce and was running at a considerable financial loss.[30]

In 1927 the *Daily Express* secured the Royal Albert Hall for its own Armistice Night concert. The paper's two-year sponsorship of the event marks a clear, but temporary, change in tone of the character of British national remembrance and was described as a 'rally' which featured 'community singing' of old wartime songs. Huge demand for tickets indicated not only the strength of nostalgia for wartime bonds, but the importance of music in facilitating it. Places were limited to those who had served in war areas and British Legion Headquarters allotted seats for the event by Divisions, 'a system which provided many instances of men meeting again, wartime pals whose very existence had in some cases been forgotten since a "blighty" had parted them "somewhere on the Western" or other "Front"'.[31] The centrality of music to remembering becomes clear in writer and veteran H.V. Morton's response. His review of the event bubbled over with nostalgia as he described 10,000 people, the majority men, in the Albert Hall under flags which had been used in the war. The pageantry was only part of the equation, though. Once the music started – with 'Pack Up Your Troubles' – Morton and his fellow ex-servicemen

> found ourselves back in 1914 ... We did not realise until last night that the songs we sang in the Army are bits of history. In them is embalmed that comic fatalism which carried us through four years of hell. ... above all, the memory of the men we knew so well, men better than we were, nobler, finer, more worthy of life, who slipped into the silence of death.[32]

Morton concluded with the plea that the event

> must not die. It must become part of Armistice Day. Every year we must sing these songs again. In singing them we draw nearer to the men who died; in singing them we show to the world a thing that is visible only once a year – the splendid heart of England.[33]

The contest over the appropriate music of public remembrance was hardly decided by the ascendancy of soldiers' nostalgia in the Legion's Armistice Night singing. The BBC continued to broadcast the Armistice Night singing every year from 1927, but by 1936 the Corporation's officials referred to the annual event as a 'British Legion sing-song'. An internal memo in the BBC archives suggested that more sombre music should be played along with readings from the Bible to 'wash out the taste of the super-sentimental orgy from the Albert Hall and reset the frame for these readings'.[34]

More in line with this sentiment was Arthur Bliss's *Morning Heroes*, first performed in 1930. In a similar vein to Foulds's *World Requiem* it contains a mixture of textual sources, including the first musical setting of a Wilfred

Owen poem, ('Spring Offensive'), as well as extracts from fellow war poet Robert Nichols, the *Iliad* and poems by Walt Whitman and Li-tai-Po.[35] Bliss was himself a veteran of the trenches and his diaries are no less candid than many more well-known memoirs. Bliss's wartime service had already found its way into his incidental music composed for a 1921 production of Shakespeare's *The Tempest*. After the loss of his brother on the Somme, Bliss suffered from survivor's guilt coupled with frequent nightmares in which he was back in the trenches even though 'we knew the armistice had been signed'. Composing *Morning Heroes* was thus a cathartic experience that proved effective in ridding him of the flashbacks.

Morning Heroes is thoroughly immersed in allusions and emotions which writers, following Fussell, have claimed had fallen out of common currency by the time of the work's composition. Despite referencing Owen, Bliss's music was more equivocal on how the war ought to be remembered than later and more culturally dominant texts would suggest. The juxtaposition of the *Iliad* extracts with the more nuanced poems of Walt Whitman, together with those of Owen and Nichols, provides contrasting views of war, even though Bliss's choice of poem is one of Owen's more reflective. Representing these 'two sides' of the war was very common in the immediate post-war period, and we also encounter it with regard to wartime cinema.[36] Contemporary reviewers regarded this as a strength, and praised the mixture of texts as 'natural and right'. They found 'shifting emphasis from the personal to the collective experience of war, and their reflection of Bliss the man' appropriate in the musical structure.[37] Bliss was himself very well aware of the possible controversy the use of Homeric texts might cause:

> A few may even call it a glorification of war ... I make no defence of my choice of this subject, as I have no political views to put forward, no moral prejudices to air, no theories indeed of any kind to expound. I have been guided entirely by my aims as an artist, for whom other considerations than the aesthetic do not exist ... War begins with glamour as surely as it ends with the reckoning; and perhaps the end of war will not come till by some miracle we can reverse the order, and see the bill first.[38]

In the early twenty-first century Bliss's romanticism and ideas of beauty can sound inappropriate and outdated. Yet the persistence of more traditional forms is understandable in the sense that it offered comfort. It is telling that, for example, both Arthur Bliss in *Morning Heroes* and Ralph Vaughan Williams in *A Pastoral Symphony*, both of them war veterans, utilized a pastoral mode in their work rather than turning to more modernist forms.[39] Bliss was seeking for that comfort in his work, and to express the inverse of so much suffering at the front:

> I found in France, as so many others did, that the appreciation of a moment's beauty had been greatly intensified by the sordid contrast

around ... the sheer joy of being alive was the more relished for there being the continual possibility of sudden death.[40]

Post-1945

The public dimensions of the struggle over war memory through interwar music were assured by the centrality of music to public services and festivals. Yet remembering the war had little or no resonance in the popular music of the period. The most popular music genres of the day – ragtime, jazz and, later, swing and 'crooner' ballads – did not lend themselves to contemplation of historical themes. This was the province of the folk or protest song, or occasionally the comic song, which in the 1920s and 1930s were more concerned with political issues such as unemployment. The advent of a second world war saw the resurrection of some tunes and scatological soldier songs of 1914–18, amid the new conflict's more sadly sentimental strains of 'We'll Meet Again'. Besides that brief resumption, the music of the Great War would not be revisited on any scale until the 1960s and the fiftieth anniversary of the conflict. The popular music hall ditties and soldiers' songs returned to ironic effect in Theatre Workshop's *Oh, What a Lovely War!*, developed into a film of the same name in 1969 by Richard Attenborough, to the extent that we might struggle to appreciate their once genuine popularity.

The fate of Foulds's and Bliss's efforts was sealed earlier, first by their inability to meet the mood of commemoration after 1945, and then more emphatically by Benjamin Britten's *War Requiem* (1962). *War Requiem* has become Britain's accepted 'cenotaph of sound', due in great part to Britten's setting of Wilfred Owen's poetry, which, since the 1960s, has been privileged as the British voice of 1914–18, though it was written to mark the experience of 1939–45. Britten had been a self-exiled conscientious objector during the war, and his career by the late 1950s was only then recovering. It may well have been Britten's pacifism, perfectly suited to the anti-war mood of the post-1945 world, that led the Arts Committee at Coventry Cathedral to invite him in 1958 to write something for the consecration of the new cathedral.[41] Destroyed by Luftwaffe bombs in November 1940, Coventry's modern cathedral would open in May 1962 with the first performance of the *War Requiem*. Britten's piece juxtaposed popular war songs and religious texts with the addition of poetry by Wilfred Owen as tropes to the Latin Requiem Mass. His choice of the poetry of the Great War helped the piece to transcend its immediate origins: not only were further performances in Dresden contemplated, but also at that iconic site of Britain's Great War, Ypres.[42]

The *War Requiem* came before the majority of the 1960s cultural works that cemented the popular view of the war as 'useless slaughter' and its 'message' is clearly one of universal abhorrence of war rather than being a specific critique of 1914–18. The power of Britten's work in setting the parameters of 'serious' music that has followed, in multiple genres, cannot be underestimated, though we should note that it was only one of many factors in the transformation of war memory occurring in the 1960s. These included not only the fiftieth anniversary of the war and a spate of publications, but the war generation themselves entering retirement, and their children becoming more interested in elements of parents' lives which had often been hidden.[43]

Following the fiftieth anniversary of the war, the late 1960s witnessed a significant flowering of musical endeavours contemplating 1914–18, and a definite shift to a conception of the war which left little room for levity in its remembrance. That transition becomes clearer when we observe that the first notable post-1945 newly composed popular song in Britain about the First World War is Flanders and Swann's 'The War of 14–18' (1964), which combines elements of music hall (though filtered through a middle class lens) and is a loose translation of a French *chanson* by Georges Brassens. Also one of the first anti-Vietnam War songs, it was released as a single with 'Twenty Tons of TNT', another humorous anti-war song, on the reverse. Flanders and Swann were hardly obscure artists, but the tenor of the record was out of kilter with what became the dominant voice of the 1960s. *Oh, What a Lovely War!* infused the music of the war itself with deep and angry irony, and the folk genre reflected the shift clearly, as it turned to the war as a tragedy, in which the world before 1914 was lost. Ralph McTell's 'England 1914' (1969) takes up Edward Grey's supposed comment on the 'lamps going out all over Europe'. Set on the eve of war, 'the gas-lamps stand like soldiers; His warnings to the wind', but McTell goes on to suggest that with virtually continuous conflict somewhere since 1914 the lamps have never been re-lit. In the same year Sussex folk singer Shirley Collins's highly innovative *Anthems in Eden* took up the concept of a 'lost' England. Stringing together a number of well-known English folk songs, including 'The Blacksmith', 'Lowlands Away' and 'Staines Morris', the climax of the work is 'Dancing at Whitsun': a song of remembrance and loss where 'The fields they are empty' with 'No young men to tend them' as they have been 'wasted in battle'.

Rock musicians were also in contemplative mood regarding the Great War. In the late 1960s, developments in popular music, under the influence of pioneers such as Bob Dylan and the Beatles, saw the lyrical content of songs become more diverse, and this has meant a much more willing engagement with war in popular music. Treatment of the Great War in song could invoke further shifts: very frequently bands and singers take on a different persona when it comes to their songs about the war, often reverting to a more folk-based approach considered suitable for the subject. The Zombies' 'Butcher's Tale (Western Front 1914)' – actually set in 1916 during the Battle of the Somme and attacking pro-war Anglican clergymen familiar from the poems of Sassoon and the Attenborough film – is significantly different to the soft, psychedelic rock of the rest of the album on which it features. Some were thinking on grander scales than individual songs. The Pretty Things' seminal 1968 album *S.F. Sorrow*, often described as the first 'rock opera' or even the first concept album, tells the story of a twentieth century 'everyman' including his participation in a war that, chronologically, has to be the First World War.

the following year the Kinks released their concept album *Arthur (or the Decline and Fall of the British Empire)* which, as the title suggests, attempted to chart the story of Britain from 1914 to the present. The songs describe the England Arthur once knew, and in dealing with the war 'Yes Sir, No Sir' tells of the individuality that is left behind when the soldier volunteers, or is called up. With a reference to another famous war song Ray Davies skilfully sums up the plight of the recruit: 'Pack up your ambition in your old kit bag'. 'Some Mother's Son' refers to the death of Arthur's brother in the war, a sign again of rock's maturing, and of the terms in which the war could be addressed.

Since these pioneering contributions there have been a steady stream of songs that make reference to the war. Significant artists, whose styles range from punk to progressive rock to death metal, include Billy Childish, whose songs often have both musical and lyrical references to wartime satire and music hall, and Gary Miller, formerly of the Whisky Priests.[44] Since the mid-2000s there has been a very significant increase in output: the average number of songs released annually worldwide about the war prior to 2003 was under twenty. Since then it has often been above one hundred a year. This has largely been due to the development of new musical genres that are easy to self-produce (often by a single person with just a keyboard and a computer), are possible to make widely available (via the internet) and accept the war as potential source material. Commercially, the trend is similar: a search of iTunes or the Amazon music store reveals well over a hundred songs related to Remembrance Day alone and an equal number of albums. They contain selections that have been anthologized as appropriate for remembrance in general or Remembrance Day itself, from readings of the war poets, through 'great classics' (such as Holst's *Planet Suite* or Fauré's *Requiem*) to 'Flowers of the Forest', 'Amazing Grace' and Ennio Morricone's 'Cavatina'. Often they are explicitly released for incorporation within group or personal acts of remembrance around 11 November or as fund raisers for military charities (*Music for Heroes* or *The Poppy Girls*, both 2013, for example). Of the ten best-selling recordings of Britten's *War Requiem* on Amazon, no fewer than six were recorded in 2012 and 2013.

While one might easily point out that the musical approach to the Great War is almost universally serious, this does not necessarily mean uncritical, nor that there is no differentiation in attitudes towards war and its remembrance in contemporary music. One trend is easy enough to trace, echoing as it does the popular sentiments surrounding remembrance as it has developed over the past several decades. Among those to take a reverential tone in remembering the war are former Dire Straits frontman Mark Knopfler's 'Remembrance Day' (2009) which features his distinctive guitar style in a slow, pastoral elegy about those servicemen who lost their lives from a single English village. In a similar vein Radiohead's 'Harry Patch (In Memory of)', recorded shortly before Patch's death in 2009, adapts Patch's words, and features Thom Yorke's vocals against a relatively simple string arrangement by Jonny Greenwood. All proceeds were donated to the Royal British Legion, and its critical reception was often laudatory. Marc Richardson compared it musically to Samuel Barber's

'Adagio for Strings' whose melancholy strains have accompanied many solemn cultural events from Oliver Stone's film *Platoon* to commemorations of 9/11.[45] Luke Lewis in *New Musical Express* and Simon Vozick-Levinson in *Entertainment Weekly* both saw resemblances to Wilfred Owen's 'Dulce et Decorum Est'.[46]

Others continue to mine the rich vein of myth of the 1914 Christmas truce. The Buff Medways' – one of Billy Childish's bands – 'Merry Christmas Fritz' (2003) is only one in a long line that includes Jona Lewie's anti-war novelty hit 'Stop the Cavalry' (1980), Paul McCartney's 'Pipes of Peace' (1983) and The Farm's 'All Together Now' (1990). In more 'serious' music the theme persists too: Kenneth Puts's Pulitzer-Prize-winning opera *Silent Night* was based on the 1914 Christmas truce, and inspired by Christian Carion's 2005 film *Joyeux Noël*. So embedded has the literary conception of the war become that the Pulitzer officials described *Silent Night* as 'a stirring opera that recounts the *true* story of a spontaneous cease-fire among Scottish, French and Germans during World War I, displaying versatility of style and cutting straight to the heart' (our emphasis).[47] Puts has been creative in having the truce initiated by a pair of opera singers, one a Swedish soprano, though what survives is the dominant tale of an unsympathetic higher command, and the futility of the struggle.

Whilst these examples remain firmly within the dominant discourse of remembrance there are also a number of songs that take Remembrance Day as a starting point for a sharp critique of remembering the war, though they too tend to remain within the idiom of the war poets. These stretch back to the late 1970s when punk rock emerged. Among several punk bands to cover the topic are Bristol-based Disorder in their 1983 EP *Perdition*. They sandwich a trip to the trenches in all its blood and gore between a cynical pair of verses 'on Poppy Day' with 'polished medals on display' in a raw and bitter snarl of rage against the waste of human life and its sanitization in the modern ceremony. Veteran folk/protest singer Leon Rosselson takes the same material but approaches it from an ironic, blackly humorous standpoint. His 'Remembrance Day' (2009) is set at the annual Cenotaph ceremony attended by the Queen and dignitaries. As the two minutes' silence begins the narrator hears a voice rising up that represents 'the voice of the fallen'. In many hands this 'ghost' would deliver portentous words of warning or tendentious political slogans. In Rosselson's the voice of the dead soldier rejects the ceremony and exclaims 'stuff it up your arse'. This song is one of few popular songs to capture the black humour of soldiers' songs of the trenches. Even as it suggests the hypocrisy of the occasion as 'a strange aroma of corpses hung round the Cenotaph' Rosselson's characteristically good-natured delivery and rather jaunty tune retain the ironic humour.

Though several of the above songs begin to question received views of the war and its modern remembrance, there are two British artists in particular whose work stands out as going a step further to re-configure the myths into a new artistic statement. In the mid-1980s together with bands such as Napalm Death and Carcass, Bolt Thrower (Figures 6.1 and 6.2) 'combined punk and early death metal to develop an extreme sound that has been widely

Figure 6.1 Bolt Thrower in performance. Courtesy of Bolt Thrower

Figure 6.2 Bolt Thrower, publicity shot for *Those Once Loyal*. Taken at the Royal Artillery Monument, London. Courtesy of Bolt Thrower

influential'.[48] They have built their career around songs relating to war in its varying forms, both in fantasy and reality.[49] Two albums in particular, *For Victory* (1994) and *Those Once Loyal* (2005) focus on the Great War.

Music and remembrance 123

The artwork of the latter features Gilbert Ledward's highly realistic frieze of an 18-pounder gun in action from the Guards Memorial in St James Park, London. Bolt Thrower's contemplation of war in general, and the Great War in particular, is both complex and distinctive. They avoid simple stereotypes and instead express the ambiguities of warfare, as horrifying and exhilarating, insane and necessary. Similar ambiguities occur in the works of Siegfried Sassoon and Wilfred Owen who both wrote of their utter contempt for the mindlessness of war, but both remained with (or returned to) their regiments and fought with distinction. In this sense Bolt Thrower are probably more representative of the totality of Owen's and Sassoon's work than virtually any other artists and they go beyond simply raging against war and its destructiveness. They are hinting at constructive, cooperative alternatives, returning to representations of the war more akin to those of Foulds or Bliss.

There are signs too that popular music can move beyond the parameters of remembering set by the war poets, and interrogate modern Britain's relationship with the Great War. Award-winning singer/songwriter P J Harvey wrote her 2011 album *Let England Shake* after spending a considerable time researching the history of war, most notably the Gallipoli campaign, as well as more recent first-hand accounts from Iraq and Afghanistan.[50] The album received critical acclaim as a serious commentary on both war and England's military past.[51] Critic Dorian Lynskey called it 'an eloquent and multivalent song suite about war and national identity, drawing inspiration from poems, paintings, diaries and news reports'.[52] Perhaps more pleasing for Harvey was the story of 'an old soldier ... who served as an officer in Northern Ireland, [who] was deeply struck by how vividly the album conveyed military experience, describing Harvey ... as "the first rock-and-roll war artist"'.[53]

Let England Shake is one of the very few examples of rock music that is able to approach the complexity of Foulds and Britten, and by extension the war itself. A lingering pride in the country's military achievements is accompanied by Harvey's questioning of the role of memory and remembrance. 'The Glorious Land' states 'our land is ploughed by tanks and feet, feet marching', and while 'Hanging in the Wire' references typical Great War imagery, Harvey still escapes the 'straight jacket' of cultural myth that has ensnared so many performers. Part of the reason is that her sources are not the obvious ones. Among her influences were the work of Harold Pinter, the poetry of T.S. Eliot, the paintings of Salvador Dali and Goya, and music by the Doors, the Velvet Underground and the Pogues.[54] Notable by their absence are the war poets. Indeed, Harvey's interrogation of remembrance becomes much more direct: 'On Battleship Hill' examines the emotions of 'battlefield tourists' today. In a Proustian image the song links the scent of wild thyme with the recognition that over the years even the destruction wrought by the First World War is being eradicated by nature. Its pastoral imagery links time and remembrance in a complex relationship: should we remember or make a conscious decision to forget? Because the song directly reflects the experience of today's tourists it has powerful resonance as it challenges the motives for such 'pilgrimages'. Do we visit the sites of former conflicts for positive or negative reasons? Are we 'bearers of the flame' or mere ghouls? What exactly should we remember?

Conclusion

Since the early 1960s Britten's *War Requiem* has become the paradigm for musicians in both classical and popular genres of music. It has also contributed its part to the popular myth of the war as a futile slaughter, helping to further sanctify a small number of selected poems by Owen, Sassoon and others as key reference points. As recent performances show, the work is still emotionally potent for audiences: 'tears threatened to become sobs, and self-restraint made just listening hard work'.[55] Nevertheless, *War Requiem* and so much of the continuing musical response to the Great War operates within the constraints of a popular memory defined by the war poets. Only occasionally have musicians broken free from 'the weight of silent dead', as P J Harvey puts it, to produce works that challenge or question the cultural norm. They remind us that music too is a powerful medium through which the remembrance of the Great War has been shaped and challenged for a century, and that the nature of war memory has never been so solid as the canon of remembrance music might suggest. During the years of the war's centenary, BBC Radio 2 has commissioned 'The Ballads of the Great War' which will showcase fifty specially commissioned new songs by the cream of British folk songwriters. This is a continuation of the trend which sees popular rather than classical artists leading the way; and, in their very different styles, contemporary musicians may be in the vanguard of a group of revisionist artists who are working in parallel with the scholarship of the revisionist historians of the last twenty years.

Notes

1 John Sloboda, 'Everyday Uses of Music Listening: A Preliminary Survey', in *Music, Mind and Science*, ed. Suk Won Yi (Seoul: Seoul National University Press, 1999), 354–5.
2 Kate Kennedy and Trudi Tate, 'Literature and Music of the First World War', *First World War Studies* 2:1 (2011), 1–6. Exceptions include Jeffrey Richards, *Imperialism and Music: Britain 1876–1953* (Manchester: MUP, 2002); J.F.G. Fuller, *Troop Morale and Popular Culture* (Oxford: Clarendon, 1990); Glenn Watkins, *Proof Through the Night: Music and the Great War* (California: University of California Press, 2003).
3 Nico Frijda's Foreword in *Handbooks of Music and Emotion: Theory, Research, Applications*, eds Patrick N. Juslin and John A. Sloboda (Oxford: OUP, 2010). Also see Tia DeNora, 'Emotion as Social Emergence: Perspectives from Music Sociology' in Patrick N. Juslin and John A. Sloboda (eds), *Handbooks of Music and Emotion: Theory, Research, Applications* (Oxford: Oxford University Press, 2010), 159–60.
4 Michel Foucault, *The Archaeology of Knowledge* (Paris: Editions Gallimard, 1969) and the multi-volume work by Pierre Nora (ed.) *Lieux de Mémoire* (Paris: Editions Gallimard, 1984–92).
5 Clifford Geertz, *The Interpretation of Cultures* (New York: Basic Books, 1973).
6 Watkins, 7.
7 Paul Fussell, *The Great War and Modern Memory* (Oxford: OUP, 1975); Martin Stephen, *The Price of Pity* (London: Leo Cooper, 1996); Stephen Badsey, '*Blackadder Goes Forth*

and the Two Western Fronts Debate', in *The Historian, Television and Television History*, eds Graham Roberts and Philip M. Taylor (Luton: Luton University Press, 2001); Dan Todman, *The Great War, Myth and Memory* (London: Hambledon, 2005).
8 John Mullen, 'Propaganda and Dissent in British Popular Song during the Great War', *Revue Interdisciplinaire 'Textes & contextes'* 6 (2011): 'Discours autoritaires et résistances aux XXe et XXIe siècles', 6 décembre 2011. Online. Available: <http://revueshs.u-bourgogne.fr/textes&contextes/document.php?id=1478 ISSN 1961-991X> (accessed 28 July 2014).
9 Ibid.; John Nott, *Music for the People: Popular Music and Dance in Interwar Britain* (Oxford: Oxford University Press, 2002), 209.
10 Mullen, 26.
11 Watkins, 49.
12 Daniel M. Grimley, 'Music in the midst of desolation: structures of mourning in Elgar's The Spirit of England', in *Elgar Studies*, eds J.P.E. Harper-Scott and Julian Rushton (Cambridge: Cambridge University Press, 2007), 225; A.J.B. Hutchings, 'The Music of Cyril Bradley Rootham', *The Musical Times*, 79:1139 (January 1938), 20; Diana McVeagh, 'Edward Elgar', in *The New Grove: Twentieth Century English Masters* (London and Basingstoke, Papermac, 1986), 19.
13 Watkins, 422.
14 Wilfrid Mellers, *Vaughan Williams and the Vision of Albion* (London: Barrie & Jenkins, 1989), 260–1.
15 James Day, *The Master Musicians: Vaughan Williams*, rev. ed. (London: J.M. Dent, 1975), 38, 44; Simon Heffer, *Vaughan Williams* (London: Phoenix, 2000), 56.
16 Hubert Foss, *Ralph Vaughan Williams* (London: George G. Harrap, 1950), 51.
17 Cadbury Research Library, YMCA/K/6/1; Motto of the YMCA Music Department as quoted by Percy A. Scholes, 'Music and the Fighting Man', *The Red Triangle* 2 (September 1917–August 1918), 191–3.
18 Malcolm MacDonald, *John Foulds: His Life in Music* (Rickmansworth: Triad Press, 1975).
19 The *World Requiem* is given a cursory mention in Samuel Hynes' *A War Imagined: The First World War in English Culture* (London: Bodley Head, 1990), 275–6, and also a brief mention in Watkins, 422 and Richards, 159–60. Also see James G. Mansell, 'Musical Modernity and Contested Commemoration at the Festival of Remembrance, 1923–27', *The Historical Journal* 52:2 (2009), 433–54.
20 BBC Written Archives Centre: Composer John Foulds, 1924–38, File I.
21 British Library Manuscripts 56482: Letter from A. Eaglefield Hull, Hon. Director, British Music Society, 29 April 1921.
22 British Library Manuscripts 56482: Letter from Arthur Snow to John Foulds, 15 March 1921.
23 MacDonald, 26.
24 British Library Manuscripts 56482: Letter from Douglas Haig (Appeal Department, British Legion) to Secretary of a Musical Competition Festival.
25 MacCarthy-Foulds Papers – Borthwick Archive: *The Times*, 10 November 1924, 19.
26 *British Legion* 5:6 (1925), 1.
27 Charles Carrington, *Soldier from the Wars Returning* (London: Hutchinson, 1965), 258.
28 Adrian Gregory, *The Silence of Memory: Armistice Day 1919–1946* (Oxford: Berg, 1994).
29 Royal British Legion: General Secretary's Monthly Circular for November 1927 and *British Legion* 7:5 (November 1927), 1.
30 BBC Written Archives Centre: Composer John Foulds 1924–38, File I, Letter from Maud Foulds to Mr Boult, 9 December 1931.
31 *British Legion* 7:6 (December 1927), 1.
32 Ibid., 149.
33 Ibid., 149.
34 BBC Written Archives Centre: internal memo, A.D.M. to Herbage and Reybould, 21 August 1936, R 34/227/2.

35 Owen's poetry (as well as that of Sassoon, Brooke, Binyon, Graves and others) was also included in BBC Remembrance Day broadcasts from 1930; Gregory, 139.
36 See several of the contributions to Michael Hammond and Michael Williams (eds), *British Silent Cinema and the Great War* (Basingstoke: Palgrave Macmillan, 2011).
37 'H.G.', '"Morning Heroes": A new symphony by Arthur Bliss', *The Musical Times* 71:1052 (1 October 1930); extracts from Arthur Bliss's war diary of 1915 quoted in Andrew Burn, '"Now, Trumpeter for thy Close" The Symphony "Morning Heroes": Bliss's requiem for his brother', *The Musical Times* 126:1713 (November 1938), 666.
38 'H.G.'
39 Eric Saylor "It's Not Lambkins Frisking At All": English Pastoral Music and the Great War', *Musical Quarterly* 91:1/2 (Spring/Summer 2008), 40–1.
40 Cited in Saylor, 43.
41 Britten–Pears Foundation: Correspondence – Benjamin Britten to Coventry Cathedral Provost, R.11: Letter from BB to John Lowe (BBC, Birmingham) 8 October 1958.
42 Britten–Pears Foundation: Correspondence – Folder 2 – Coventry Cathedral correspondence, R.11: Letter from BB to Provost of Coventry Cathedral 13 October 1965 and Letter from BB to Hans Keller 14 December 1965.
43 Todman, 29.
44 Gary Miller, 'Reflections on War'. Online. Available HTTP: <www.garymillersongs.com/reflections-war.php> (accessed 16 November 2012).
45 Wikipedia entry, 'Harry Patch (In Memory Of)'. Online. Available: <http://en.wikipedia.org/wiki/Harry_Patch_(In_Memory_Of)> (accessed 16 November 2012).
46 Ibid.
47 Tom Huizenga, 'Kevin Puts Wins Music Pulitzer for World War I Opera "Silent Night"'. Online. Available HTTP: <www.npr.org/blogs/deceptivecadence/2012/04/16/150764941/kevin-puts-wins-music-pulitzer-for-world-war-i-opera-silent-night> (accessed 7 January 2014).
48 Keith Kahn-Harris, *Extreme Metal: Music and Culture on the Edge* (Oxford: Berg, 2007), 109.
49 Ibid., 36–7.
50 'Local Rock Star P.J. Harvey Talks to *The News*', *Bridport and Lyme Regis News*, 26 January 2011.
51 It was named 'album of the year' by sixteen publications and won the prestigious Mercury Prize for 2011. Jason Dietz, '2011 Music Critic Top Ten Lists', 7 January 2012. Online. Available HTTP: <www.metacritic.com/feature/music-critic-top-ten-lists-best-albums-of-2011?tag=supplementary-nav;article;2> (accessed 11 November 2012). It was not quite so successful commercially, peaking at no. 8 in the UK and 32 in the US album charts.
52 Dorian Lynskey, *33 Revolutions Per Minute: A History of Protest Songs* (London: Faber and Faber, 2012), 684.
53 Neil McCormick, 'P J Harvey: Masterpiece of the first rock-and-roll war artist', *Daily Telegraph*, 20 July 2011. Online. Available HTTP: <www.telegraph.co.uk/culture/music/rockandpopfeatures/8650329/P.J-Harvey-Masterpiece-of-the-first-rock-and-roll-war-artist.html> (accessed 15 March 2013).
54 *Bridport and Lyme Regis News*.
55 David Nice, 'War Requiem, BBCSO, Bychkov, Royal Albert Hall', theartsdesk.com, 11 November, 2013, Online. Available HTTP: <www.theartsdesk.com/classical-music/war-requiem-bbcso-bychkov-royal-albert-hall> (accessed 7 January 2014).

Part 3
The return of the war

7 'Now Russia returns its history to itself'

Russia celebrates the centenary of the First World War

Karen Petrone

In the past twenty-eight years, rulers in Moscow have undergone a cycle of revolutionary transformation and upheaval, followed by an era of retrenchment and stabilization. In order to understand the preparations for the centenary of the First World War in Russia, it is essential to understand the place of the centenary in this cycle of social, political and cultural change.[1] When Mikhail Gorbachev lifted censorship restrictions, ushering in an era of 'glasnost' or 'openness', shortly after coming to power in 1985, he unleashed a torrent of repressed historical memory that questioned Soviet interpretations of all events in Russian and Soviet history and ultimately undermined the legitimacy of the Soviet state. During this revolutionary period and in the first decade or so of the new Russian state under Boris Yeltsin, historical narratives were in flux, and the range of what could be said about historical events was greatly enlarged as new standard narratives had not yet emerged to replace the old.

In the past decade or so (corresponding with the Putin era), Russian state officials and the leaders of the most popular political party, United Russia, have worked very hard to promote their particular version of Russian national identity. Narratives about and interpretations of twentieth century Russian history are absolutely central to this nationalist identity project, and so there is an increasing tendency toward 'official' historical narratives that discredit and replace other possible narratives. Unlike in the Stalinist 1930s, when tight censorship removed undesirable narratives from public discourse altogether, the current moment is one in which official narratives are gaining more prominence and media exposure, but the alternative narratives have not entirely disappeared. In this environment, state authorities are using the official celebration of the centenary of the First World War as an opportunity to bring interpretations of the war into alignment with nationalist Russian narratives that seek to build a positive national identity, reassert Russian national pride, and affirm Russia's status as a European power.

In addition to understanding the immediate Russian context for the centenary, it is also important to understand that the historical meanings ascribed to the First World War have always been profoundly different in the countries that emerged from the Austro-Hungarian, Ottoman and Russian Empires from those in western Europe, the United States and the countries of the British Commonwealth.

In the countries that were created as a result of the First World War, the narratives about the relationship of the war to the new national identities have always been extremely complex. For example, the new interwar Polish state had to contend with the fact that the First World War was a fratricidal war in which Poles in the Russian Empire and Poles in the Austro-Hungarian Empire killed one another. The legacy of this war did not easily fit into new national narratives and so the Polish state emphasized other events such as the Soviet–Polish War to celebrate national valour instead.[2]

This was most certainly the case in the Soviet Union as well. Lenin and the Bolsheviks had opposed the First World War from the beginning as an 'imperialist' war and had advocated 'turning the imperialist war into a Civil War'. The Russian Revolutions of 1917 and the Russian Civil War became central to official Soviet historical narratives, while the First World War was de-emphasized, though not entirely forgotten.[3] Like the years from 1985 to the present, the first two Soviet decades saw an era of transformation and turmoil in historical narratives, followed by an era of retrenchment. The variegated and complex Soviet memory of the First World War in the 1920s and early 1930s that contained both patriotic and pacifistic elements was suppressed by Soviet censors in the second half of the 1930s, and reduced to a narrow swath of official (and tendentious) patriotic discourse in the years leading up to the outbreak of the Second World War.[4] In the post-war period, the overwhelming destruction of the Second World War eclipsed the First World War nearly completely, to the point where, when historian Catherine Merridale in 1997 and 1998 asked Russian adults to recall the three most deadly wars in Russia's twentieth century, 'almost no one even mentioned the war of 1914. To some, indeed, my [Merridale's] mentioning it came as a surprise. "Oh, that!"'[5] Thus, another crucial aspect of the centenary is that the organizers and participants consciously understand it to be the recuperation of a national past that has been lost.

But, as historians well know, recapturing a lost past is never just a matter of simple recovery. This chapter proceeds from the premises that all memory is contested memory, and that within Russia, different constituencies of varying influence are building multiple versions of the memory of the First World War with variable levels of success.[6] It examines several of the paradoxes and complexities of recuperating the First World War as a defining event in the current historical moment. There are two historical layers of complexity here; the first is that the Soviet state found the legacy of the First World War complex and difficult to incorporate into its narratives. The second is that the Russian state, in turn, finds the legacy of the Soviet state complex and difficult to incorporate into *its* narratives, so Russian officials are reaching back to the First World War as a heroic moment that helps them to neutralize and displace the history of the Russian Revolution and Soviet rule from their current national narratives.

This chapter focuses on state-sponsored attempts to construct an 'official' history of the First World War. Because there is an extensive public sphere in Russia today in which myriad interpretations of the First World War can be found, it is important to acknowledge that this chapter concentrates on the most 'official' of the new narratives, influenced by Russian state cultural institutions. There are many other types of alternative narratives that could be found in the Russian public sphere. If one were to study academic discourse about the First World War in scholarly literature and as presented at scholarly conferences, for example, one would find a much more nuanced and complex treatment of the war than that which appears in this chapter.[7] Likewise, private Russian citizens, like people all over the developed world, have an unprecedented ability to pursue a wide variety of aspects of First World War history and share their findings (whether historically sound or controversial and conspiracy driven) via the internet. What I am trying to investigate here, however, are the ways in which Russian political and cultural elites seek to shape the public view of the First World War through the centenary, and (as much as I am able) the extent to which this version of the war is gaining public purchase.

In the course of this examination, I will explore the early stages of a number of memorial projects to begin analyzing who the possible winners and losers might be in these contests for meaning. Until the centenary actually takes place in the years 2014–18, one cannot know which constituencies will have been most successful in promoting their visions or the extent to which the Russian population will have embraced one vision of the First World War over another. Still, by investigating and documenting the plans for the centenary, I can identify different interested constituencies, assess their relative strengths, and begin to show their successes and failures in shaping plans for the centenary events. Eventually, it will also be possible to compare these plans with the actual events, to see the extent to which the projects were successfully carried out.

Because the history of the First World War was long obscured and ignored in the Soviet Union, this war has emerged as a very significant historical event in post-Soviet Russian memory, second only in importance to the two 'Patriotic' or 'Otechestvennye' victories against Napoleon in 1812 and against Hitler in 1941–45.[8] New history standards link the promotion of students' patriotism to 'pride in the military victories of their ancestors' and historians are exploring the possibilities for placing the First World War into this category of 'victory'.[9] Yet, the new historical approach to the era of the First World War, the Russian Revolutions of 1917, and the Russian Civil War remains somewhat ambivalent. The plans for new educational materials describe 1914–21 as the 'Years of Great Shocks'. On the one hand, the new standards recognized that the revolutions of 1917, because of their 'influence on the processes of world history' were among the most important events of the twentieth century. Yet the standards also describe the Russian Civil War as tragic and catastrophic for the Russian population, and argue that the First World War led to militarization of the economy, a strengthening of state regulation, and the rise of dictatorial regimes, not just in the Soviet Union but all over Europe. While plans for the centenary of the First World War are now underway, there do not yet seem to be any analogous plans for formal commemoration of the centenary of the Russian Revolutions of 1917.

The preparation for the centenary of the outbreak of war in August 1914 has accelerated the process of official Russian historical remembrance of the First World War. Some key events include the designation of 1 August, the anniversary of Germany's declaration of war on Russia, as the Day of Remembrance of Russian (Russkikh) Soldiers Who Fell in the First World War;[10] the building of a monument to the heroes of the First World War in Moscow's Victory Park on Poklonnaia Gora (Homage Hill) due to open on 1 August 2014; and the opening of a Museum of the First World War in the Martial Chamber at Tsarskoe Selo, the former summer residence of the Romanovs. Harkening back to Tsarist usage, the permanent exhibit of the museum is tentatively called 'Russia in the Great War'.[11] There will be numerous other events between 2014 and 2018 including the production of a feature film on the Women's Battalion of Death, an all-female volunteer unit formed in 1917, numerous museum exhibitions including international ones as well as exhibitions at the national and local levels, a wide range of scholarly conferences, the creation of a large 'new contemporary audio-visual resource' that 'will unite historical information not only from Russia, but also from many European countries',[12] and the development of a variety of informational websites such as '1914.histrf.ru', sponsored by the Russian Military History Society.

The speaker of the State Duma, Sergei Naryshkin, who is also the chairman of the newly recreated Russian Historical Society, is leading efforts to restore the First World War's place in Russian history. He is now a member of the Organizing Committee of the Celebration of the Centenary of the First World War, charged by Dmitrii Medvedev to plan the commemorations of the anniversary of the First World War. It was also Naryshkin who, on 1 August 2013, for the first time in the history of post-revolutionary Russia, laid a wreath on behalf of the Russian government at the obelisk in Moscow's Memorial Park Complex of the Heroes of the First World War dedicated to 'those who fell in the World War 1914–18'. Naryshkin aims to bring 'the memory of that war to every person, to our youth' so that 'the First World War will no longer be a forgotten war among our people'.[13] Academic Aleksandr Chubar'ian of the Russian Academy of Sciences explained that the laying of the wreath on the Day of Remembrance of Russian Soldiers Who Fell in the First World War was a 'symbol of restoring historical justice in relation to our heroes and victims of that great war'.[14]

Naryshkin's dual role as Speaker of the Russian Parliament and Chairman of the new Russian Historical Society is also worth considering. Although he is not trained as an historian, Naryshkin led the Presidential Commission to Counter Attempts to Falsify History between 2009 and 2012, when it was disbanded. In 2012, The Russian Historical Society was recreated as a successor to the Russian Imperial Historical Society (1866–1917). According to its website, the goal of the society is to

> unite the forces of society, the government, scholars, artists and lovers of history for the formation of an all-Russian historical culture on the basis of

objective study, the illumination and popularization of Russian and World History, and the conservation of national memory.[15]

This organization is instrumental in the writing of new school textbooks and the creation of new national history standards. According to *Moscow Times* journalist Natalya Krainova, the new history curriculum endeavours to 'reinforce Russians' patriotism, as well as ... overcome ethnic tensions and raise the country's profile worldwide and with its former Soviet allies'.[16] The Historical Society is also the successor to the President's Commission in that it seeks to police the boundaries of history to 'counteract dilettantism and attempts to falsify historical facts'.[17]

Another organization active in the centenary is the newly resurrected Russian Military History Society (originally in operation from 1907 to 1917), whose members were decorated by Vladimir Putin in March 2013 for their research, their 'active work in patriotic education of the young people ... and perpetuating the memory of the fallen defenders of the Fatherland'.[18] The chairman of this organization is the Minister of Culture, Vladimir Medinskii (who has recently made international headlines by insisting that the famous Russian composer Petr Chaikovskii (Tchaikovsky) was not gay).[19] Thus it is clear that the efforts to commemorate the First World War are being organized by key state officials as part of a larger national project to create a usable past to further the national goals of the contemporary Russian state.

In an interview about the First World War, presumably for foreign consumption on Radio 'Voice of Russia' in March 2013, Viacheslav Nikonov, a Doctor of History and the head of the Russian World Foundation (Russkii mir), an organization dedicated to the promotion of Russian culture around the world, declared:

> It was a glorious war in which the heroism of our ancestors revealed itself. They demonstrated strength of spirit, defending Russian (Rossiiskie) national interests from the obviously aggressive German and Austro-Hungarian sides. A large number of our fellow countrymen perished. And, at the same time, the Russian Federation is one of the few countries on the planet where the war left its traces, but there is not one monument to the heroes of the First World War; there is not one properly organized military cemetery. And, as is well-known, the war isn't over until the last soldier is buried. If things had gone differently in February 1917, then the war might have ended quite differently. And, without a doubt, Russia would have been in the camp of the victors.[20]

Nikonov's statement captures several aspects of the paradoxical nature of the First World War that will likely shape the coming commemoration of its centenary: Russia's international status as simultaneously victor and vanquished; the difficulties of depicting the First World War as a glorious war; the relationship between the First World War and the Revolutions of 1917; the inevitable connection of the memory of the First World War to the memory of the Second World War.

Although I would argue that the national component is the most critical aspect of the centenary, there is a compelling international component as well, as Russia claims the right to be an honoured partner in the international commemoration of the First World War. Materials about the centenary emphasize that without Russian participation in the war, the Triple Entente could not have gained victory over the Triple Alliance, just as the Allies could not have defeated Nazi Germany in the Second World War without the Soviet Union. While Nikonov revealed a xenophobic undertone by pointing to German and Austro-Hungarian aggression, a speech by Medinskii at an international meeting with French delegates emphasized cooperation. The French indicated that the Russians would be invited to participate in the centenary celebration of the Battle of the Marne 'at the highest possible level', and in return, the Russians would invite the French Minister of Culture to the dedication of the national First World War memorial in Moscow in August 2014. The remembrance of the First World War not only affirms Russian martial valour for a domestic audience, but also emphasizes to an international audience that Russia is an indispensable player in twentieth century Europe.

Medinskii bemoaned the fact that Russia had never before taken part in the international commemoration of the war even though, 'Our country endured the greatest losses; it took part in the coalition of victors, but ended up declaring itself defeated by the force of internal cataclysms. Now Russia returns its history to itself.'[21] This remarkable statement illustrates the Russian Minister of Culture's desire for Russia to be seen as a victor and to celebrate victory with its allies on the winning side of the war, as well as his recognition that Russia's internal conflicts caused defeat. Whereas in 1917, Medinskii saw Russia as robbing itself of the victory it deserved, first through revolution and then when the Soviets suppressed discussion of Russia's wartime heroism, now the Russian state was reclaiming that victory for the Russian people, declaring themselves victors both abroad and at home.

This notion of victory is tied very closely to an emerging view of the war as a heroic one in which Russian soldiers fought valiantly and demonstrated 'mass heroism'.[22] This stands in contrast both to long-standing Western notions that the Russian soldier fought poorly in the First World War and Soviet claims that after a very brief period of chauvinistic fervour, the Russian soldier refused to fight. Medinskii underlined the fact that 'the current generations should not forget the heroism of our soldiers, the self-sacrifice of thousands and tens of thousands of Russian heroes'.[23] Nikonov began his remarks on Radio 'Voice of Russia' with this striking pronouncement: 'It was a glorious war in which the heroism of our ancestors revealed itself.' For almost one hundred years, all of the combatants of the First World War have been debating the extent to which the First World War could be called a 'glorious' war. Certainly, the dominant interpretation in the Soviet Union was that the First World War was not a glorious war but rather illegitimate imperialist bloodshed that employed the workers of the world as 'cannon meat'. Furthermore it is universally recognized that after a few early victories, the Russian Empire endured a disastrous and humiliating year of defeats. Many historians agree that the economic and political mobilization in 1915–16 significantly improved the Russian war effort, but also argue that this mobilization put into play the societal forces that ultimately destroyed the Tsarist government in February 1917.[24] While there is no doubt that many Russians fought effectively and heroically in the First World War, and the Russians won some substantial victories, it is, nonetheless, not particularly easy to construe the Russian war effort in general as a glorious success. This tension between 'heroic war' and the war as an empire-destroying national failure is a central problem in contemporary remembrance of the war. It is hard to imagine an effective commemoration that does not in some way acknowledge the costs as well as the glories of the Russian First World War.

In the post-Soviet era, nationalism has become an incredibly important element in constructing new post-Soviet identities, and there is no doubt that a renewed Russian nationalism is a central mobilizing component of contemporary Russian state power. Nationalism in Russia is all the more effective because it is embraced by both the state and many of its citizens. To reinscribe the First World War into a narrative of Russian honour and national pride, centenary events will have to emphasize the positive efforts of the Tsarist state and military. This will require a good deal of effort and constant reinforcement on the part of those constructing memory, as the events of the war do not always easily lend themselves to this interpretation. Nikonov's remarks clearly express this version of the war, stating that the Revolution of February 1917 robbed Russia of the opportunity to join the camp of the victors. The piece that aired in March 2013 on Radio 'Voice of Russia' further explained that, 'The facts show, that up until the moment of the February Revolution, Russia was ready for the successful continuation of military action.' Thus, the liberal and democratic Provisional Government shares blame with the Bolsheviks for Russia's loss. The reporter Mikhail Aristov then went on to quote Winston Churchill who said that Russia suffered an unjust fate because she suddenly fell to the ground when she was already holding victory in her hands.[25]

The First World War website of the Russian Military History Society has one webpage entitled 'forgotten victories'. The very existence of this page demonstrates that one of the goals of the site is to reclaim the First World War as a site of military glory for Imperial Russia. This page describes a number of battles in which the Russian Imperial Army fought bravely. While some of these events may have been tactical victories, they were strategically insignificant. Since the webpage also acknowledges these larger strategic failures, its prose is somewhat ambivalent in staking a claim for Russian success. For example, a narrative of the Defence of Osovets Fortress (September 1914–August 1915), describes the heroic conduct of the Russian troops during a 190-day siege, asserting that the soldiers in the fortress 'fulfilled their duty to the end'. After a German gas attack killed many soldiers, the gravely wounded survivors of the 13th company repelled the enemy during the so-called 'attack of the corpses'. The soldiers advanced 'with the traces of chemical burns on their faces, wrapped in rags. They spit blood, literally spitting out pieces of lung onto their bloody shirts.' The account then explains that the fortress 'was abandoned only on the 23 (10) of August in light of the general retreat of the troops of the North-western front'.[26] Thus the narrative reveals that despite the suffering of the Russian troops and their successful defence of the fortress, the fortress did not ultimately remain in Russian hands.

One of the other battles commemorated on this same webpage was the famous Brusilov Offensive in the summer of 1916, though it is a stretch to call this victory 'forgotten' as it was one of the few episodes in the war that Soviet propagandists later claimed in their attempts to prove that they could beat Germans. This battle is the only First World War battle mentioned by name in the new Russian history standards.[27] Because of General Aleksei Brusilov's success in breaking through the Austrian lines, the Germans had to transfer a considerable number of troops away from the Verdun Campaign in order to save the Austro-Hungarians from defeat. The webpage quotes a German scholar's assessment of the situation:

> If, in this critical moment at the beginning of June, the Anglo-French troops had begun a decisive offensive, then, even if they had not achieved a breakthrough immediately, they would have tied up the Germans on the Western Front, so that the German High Command would not have been able to satisfy Austria-Hungary's persistent demand for help.[28]

In this formulation, it is the failure of the British and the French to take advantage of Brusilov's success that ultimately caused the failure to eliminate Austria-Hungary from the war and the prolongation of the fighting for two more years. As in Soviet Cold War interpretations of the delay in opening a second front in the Second World War, it was the Entente's (Allies') failure to act that forced Russia (the Soviet Union) to bear the brunt of the war. In this particular case, it also meant that Brusilov's brilliant success, which had been achieved at a high human cost, could not be sustained. These examples demonstrate that this representation of Russia's First World War as a glorious war has to be carefully parsed and qualified, as the realities of the war were complex, and do not lend themselves easily to a straightforward narrative. The current complexities of the relationships between Russia and its European allies lead to further complications in the narration of their collective endeavours in the First World War. Yet, one has to recognize that the anti-British and anti-French tone is sometimes counterbalanced and contradicted by Russia's satisfaction at being included in the international community of the victors of the First World War.

All the heroes identified on the 'forgotten victories' webpage are generals except for Koz'ma Kriuchkov, a much-celebrated Tsarist hero from the first weeks of the war who appeared frequently in Tsarist-era pulp literature, broadsheets, movies, and even circuses and variety shows.[29] Kriuchkov was a Don Cossack who became the first St George Cavalier of the war by ostensibly killing eleven Germans in one battle. The short biography on the website next to Kriuchkov's picture casts some doubt on this version of events by saying that he 'in one battle, according to the disseminated version, killed eleven Germans with his own hands'. The inclusion of the words 'according to the disseminated version' is an acknowledgment that the 1914 description of these deeds was most likely exaggerated. Yet the rest of Kriuchkov's biography describes the battle in detail and the warrior's modesty thereafter. The decision to include Kriuchkov valorizes the brave Cossack warrior, skilled in battle and afraid of nothing. All of these 'victories' demonstrate the ability of Russians to fight well, even under incredibly difficult circumstances. With the exception of casting blame on the other members of the Entente, none of these biographies delve very deeply into the circumstances within the Tsarist Army that prevented it from taking full advantage of the brave fighting of its soldiers or the conditions on the home front that led to the breakdown of the war effort. A popular nostalgia for the pre-Soviet era (not necessarily shared by professional historians and educators) sometimes prevents analysis of the very complex problems that Tsarist Russia faced on the eve of and during the First World War.

Another problem area for the centenary is the relationship between the war and the revolution, and by extension the relationship between the Russian Revolution and the contemporary Russian state. Twenty-two years after the fall of the Soviet Union, Russia and its citizens hold very complex attitudes towards the Soviet past. Some Western commentators have even argued that the failure to come to terms with the mass crimes of communism 'has contributed to a situation in which the average Russian is as powerless before the apparatus of the state as was a citizen of the Soviet Union'.[30] The centenary of the First World War will necessarily shed light on the Russian Revolution and its effects, because, in the contemporary moment, it is very difficult to explain the First World War in positive terms without referencing the revolutionary transformations it put into motion.

Contemporary Russian analysts (justifiably) blame Soviet policies for erasure of the First World War from Russian consciousness. They see Soviet interpretations of the war, including that it was 'imperialist' and 'mistaken', as a 'distortion of the true historical picture', and they seek to debunk and revise Soviet views of the war.[31] Echoing Weimar-era discourse in Germany, the new revisionist narratives see the revolution as a kind of 'stab in the back' that snatched victory away from a glorious and heroic Russian national army. While some analysts pointed, like Nikonov, to February 1917 as the key turning point in the war, Vladimir Putin himself focused on the Bolshevik signing of the Treaty of Brest-Litovsk in March 1918 as the moment of ignominy. He stated in June 2012 that 'the Bolsheviks committed an act of national betrayal' in signing the Treaty. According to Putin, the First World War was unique in that the Bolsheviks capitulated to the losing side, 'and shortly thereafter it [Germany] capitulated to the Entente'.[32] The contemporary narrative squarely blames the Revolutions of February and October 1917 for turning

Russia's potential victory into military defeat, even though the Putin government certainly does not repudiate everything Soviet.

Recent remembrance of the First World War thus echoes some of the themes of the Russian émigré literature of the 1920s and 1930s. Historian Aaron Cohen has argued persuasively that 'the public language of the military emigration was suffused with traditional images of military virtue and patriotism, a strong religious sensibility, and, less often, a nostalgic reverence for the monarchy'.[33] These elements have also surfaced in recent commemorations as part of contemporary Russian military-patriotic discourse. In the middle of the 1990s, White Russian émigrés took part in planning the First World War memorial chapel in Moscow's Memorial Park Complex of the Heroes of the First World War.[34] On the Russian Military History Society's webpage featuring 'Heroes of the First World War', out of the six men whose biographies I could find (out of seven men featured), one died during the First World War, one emigrated before the Civil War, and four fought with the Whites.[35] Thus the recuperation of the history of 'heroes' of the First World War like M. V. Alekseev, N. N. Iudenich and Koz'ma Kriuchkov means embracing the leaders of the anti-Bolshevik movement as central figures to be honoured in the new Russian history. Because the new definition of a hero is one who fights valiantly for his country, it can encompass both Whites and Reds, and create a new patriotic narrative without necessarily disavowing the Soviet legacy. This rehabilitation of the Whites has been underway for some time and is also evident in popular films like the 2008 *Admiral*, about the naval commander Aleksandr Kolchak.

The current recuperation of the war as a heroic event embraces a certain nostalgia for the Romanov monarchy. One of the main foci of the centenary, thus far, seems to be the creation of a First World War Museum in Tsarskoe Selo, the Russian 'Versailles' – a state museum-preserve outside of St Petersburg. This aspect of the centenary affirms that the grandeur of the Imperial Russian monarchy is the legacy of contemporary Russians in spite of the Soviet interlude. The new museum will be housed in the Martial Chamber, a complex that was built in 1913–17 to house a collection of military documents, trophies and art given to Tsar Nicholas II by Elena Tretiakova (the sister-in-law of the founder of the Tretiakov gallery). Architect Semen Sidorchuk designed the museum complex in the Russian Revival style and, in 1915, Nicholas II began collecting First World War military trophies there. The museum remained open only until sometime in 1919, when it was closed and its collections were dispersed.[36]

The museum, whose goal is to educate future generations by transmitting 'the feeling of the World War I era graphically and emotionally', opened again in August 2014. Vladimir Putin publicly announced that he would be attending the opening of this museum 'without fail', making it the highest-profile centenary event of 2014. There are indications, however, that the process of creating a museum may not be going smoothly. Prominent on the museum's web page is a call for the donation of artefacts: 'any objects from the WWI period, including documents, photographs, matchboxes, bandage packs, badges and tags, field radios, telephones, kitchens, etc.'. The web page promises that 'if donators (sic) wish, their names will be mentioned in the related sections of the exhibit'. The massive dislocations in twentieth century Russia and the lack of attention to the First World War have led to a scarcity of such artefacts. In an article on the RiaNovosti website on 14 March 2013, an employee of the museum admitted that the renovation of the building and exhibit space had been underway for many years, but 'we are having difficulty finding artefacts, and for that reason, the interactive exhibits will be the most important'.[37] Here, technology (while no doubt much more expensive) has to be deployed to take the place of authentic objects from the First World War era. That there are insufficient physical exhibits available for even the most high-profile First World War museum in the Russian Federation indicates the long-term absence of the First World War from Russian consciousness and the difficulty of returning the First World War to a prominent place in Russian memory. Scholars and curators will have to turn to synthetic recreations and digital media, which may, ultimately, be more effective in attracting Russian youth than traditional exhibits. Despite difficulties in obtaining authentic artefacts, the centenary offers an opportunity for the contemporary Russian state and its people to connect back to the glories of the Imperial period and to heroize the loyal servitors of the Tsar who fought against the Reds.

A fourth area of complexity in celebrating the First World War centenary is the relationship of the First World War to the Second World War. In the contemporary Russian moment, the one Soviet-era narrative that has remained central to Russian state and national identity is the narrative of the 'Great Patriotic War of the Fatherland'. After 1945, but especially in the Brezhnev era, both the Soviet state and then eventually the Russian state embraced the Second World War as a legitimating and heroic war. The massive devastation that the Second World War wrought on the Soviet population and the enormous sacrifices they made to defeat Nazi Germany led to a melding of popular and official commemorations of that war that to this day remain particularly powerful.[38] Furthermore, the common experience of fighting in (and winning) the Second World War has been used by the post-Soviet Russian state to make overtures of friendship to Ukraine and Belarus, for example. Accusations of collaboration with the Nazis, on the other hand, are often used to tar the political enemies of Russia in the Baltic states and elsewhere. The Second World War remains a central element of Russian identity and a touchstone for defining 'us' versus 'them'.

The tremendous power of the Second World War as a mobilizing force casts a long shadow over attempts to commemorate the First World War. It is likely to be difficult for organizers to keep their focus exclusively on the First World War. One recent example of this combining of commemorations for the First World War and the Second World War is Moscow's Memorial Park Complex of the Heroes of the First World War, completed in 2004. Despite the fact that the complex was built to honour the First World War dead, there is nonetheless also one small stele dedicated to 'the eternal memory of the heroes who fell in the Great Patriotic War, 1941–45'. Not only will contemporary First World War memory overlap in complex ways with memory of the Russian Revolution, it will also have to navigate through the powerful currents of the memory of the Second World War.

In Europe and the United States, when cities and towns commemorated the dead of the Second World War, very often they just added the names of the fallen to their already existing First World War monuments. In contemporary Russia, this process is running in reverse, with a monument to the First World War being added to the Second World War Memorial Complex in the Victory Park at Poklonnaia Gora. Currently, Victory Park is a combination of memorial park and fairgrounds in which a variety of holiday events, concerts and mass festivals take place. It is also the site of a Second World War memorial obelisk, the Central Museum of the Great Patriotic War, and an Orthodox church, mosque and synagogue dedicated to the fallen of the Second World War. There are also a variety of other monuments including ones dedicated to the victims of Nazism, the missing in action, and to the fallen 'internationalist' soldiers who fought in Afghanistan.[39] The proposed First World War monument will therefore be one of just a few monuments in the park not dedicated to the Second World War.

Building a monument 'To the soldiers who fell in the years of the First World War' was first proposed by members of the Russian Military History Society whose family members had died in the war. Artists submitted contest entries, and in April 2013, the public were invited to vote for their favourite submissions on the Russian Military History Society website. There were thirty-two projects in the first round of voting, and fifteen in the second round. The voting for finalists ended on 16 September 2013, at which point the final decision was made by a jury that took into account the views of the Moscow City Government and the results of the internet voting. The names of the artists were kept secret so that the members of the jury could 'impartially and objectively' make their choice.[40] In the end, the jury chose a very prominent Russian artist, People's Artist of the Russian Federation, Andrei Koval'chuk. Koval'chuk has been the chairman of the Union of Russian Artists since 2009 and, in 2007, he was awarded the Governmental Prize of the Russian Federation. Koval'chuk is the creator of many well-known monuments and his sculpture 'In the Battle against Fascism We Were Together' already stands on Poklonnaia Gora.[41]

A news release from 18 September 2013 described the bronze and granite monument: 'In the centre of the sculptural composition ... is a soldier in a field uniform with a St George Cross on his chest. Behind the main sculpture, against the backdrop of a Russian flag, soldiers armed with bayonets are depicted.' The soldier will stand between four and five metres high and the flag composition up to twelve metres high. According to the Russian Minister of Culture, the monument will be built exclusively with contributions from the public 'on principle', while the city will provide money for upkeep of the site.

This idea of public financial sacrifice is an important aspect of the Russian leadership's endeavours to engage Russian citizens in the national cause. As of 1 June 2014, more than fifty-six million rubles or more than $1,600,000 dollars had already been collected from private individuals, businesses and institutions. Medinskii expressed confidence that 'the needed sum would be collected'.[42] The news release emphasized the public's participation both in choosing the monument and in spontaneously supporting it through financial contributions. The webpage has a prominent invitation 'to take part' in building the monument and the most recent contributors are thanked by name on the webpage. The webpage invites contributors to explain why they contributed, and several of them have posted pictures of family members who fought or died in the war. Thus the monument reflects individual, personal and family memory as well as the official memory of the Russian nation.

The white, blue and red flag with the Imperial Double-Headed Eagle dominates the composition of the winning monument and in the original project, this flag dwarfed the individual soldier who was supposed to be 'in the centre of the sculptural composition'. Perhaps to address this problem, later renditions of the project, as of June 2014, place the soldier on a pedestal (approximately 6–7 metres high) adorned with a St George Cross (Figure 7.1). Another new addition to the composition is a wall (approximately a metre high) in front of the tricolour flags inscribed with the words 'To the Heroes of the First World War'. The rear side of the flag shows a cavalry charge of soldiers on horseback with lances and swords drawn. The front side shows foot soldiers advancing with bayonets, followed by an image of civilian suffering during the war. A pieta-like mother mourning her son forms the bridge between the battlefield and the home front, which is represented by an

Figure 7.1 Winning design in the First World War monument contest held by the Russian Military History Society. Courtesy of the Russian Military History Society Monument Contest Archive

Orthodox Church, clergy, women and children. The winners of the second and third prizes employed classical themes. The central figure in the second-place submission was a Winged Victory with her flag at her feet. The third-place submission contained classical columns and a statue of soldiers.[43] The base of the statue was decorated with a pieta-like image of a mother mourning a dead soldier.

Although the news reports and the website emphasized popular participation in choosing the monument, Koval'chuk's composition was only the fifth most popular with 13,071 votes. The expert jury and the Moscow city officials thus elevated Koval'chuk's project over four other proposals with many more votes. Neither of the two top vote getters in the second round (with 48,439 and 48,029 votes, respectively) was included in the final three. The most popular design encased the soldier within a globe, depicting him underground. A variant of this monument placed a pieta-like mourning mother and dying son inside the globe. The winning monument also had fewer votes in the second round than either the eventual second-place winner (42,782) or third-place winner (34,355). Without access to the jury deliberations, I cannot do more than speculate about why Koval'chuk's project was successful. All of the designs reveal the tensions between images of heroic soldiers and sombre depictions of mourning, reflecting the complicated nature of the First World War. The winning design embraced multiple aspects of the war, introducing the traditional element of holy war, emphasizing the heroic nature of the soldiers and their national identification through the inclusion of the tricolour flag and the St George Cross, and also recognizing the sorrow and sacrifice of war through the image of the mourning mother. It is the most dynamic of the most popular compositions, with soldiers, cavalrymen and the flag all in motion.

I have spent the last decade researching how the Soviet state repressed the memory of the First World War starting in the late 1920s, and how the Soviet state was particularly vigilant in eliminating any interpretation of the war that espoused pacifism or acknowledged the horrors of war. I find several aspects of the upcoming centenary notable. The first is the extent to which institutions directly tied to the Russian state are controlling the major activities of the centenary and how these institutions openly acknowledge their intentions to serve as gatekeepers against the 'falsification' of history. The organizers of the upcoming centenary, while claiming to restore the memory of the war to the Russian public, are constructing a version of history that nevertheless omits many significant aspects of the First World War experience. The depiction of the war as a heroic, glorious and patriotic event overlooks many of the complexities of 1914–18. The voting for the monument, for example, shows that the public is divided between seeing the war as heroic or as a tragic loss of life. While discrediting the Soviet version of the war (as a senseless bloodbath), Russian leaders have themselves created a version of the war that highlights the valour and prowess of heroic Russian sons. This version construes every soldier as a willing and patriotic participant in the war.

This view of the war privileges the heroic male soldier. It places primacy on the field of battle and on patriotic heroism without examining the day-to-day experiences of soldiers or the circumstances that prevented them from achieving victory. This new version of the war at times has xenophobic overtones. The vision of the war promulgated by the centenary could turn out to be every bit as one-sided as the Soviet version. It remains to be seen, however, whether the public, seemingly more attuned to the tragic elements of the conflict, will embrace this version of the war.

Notes

1 I am grateful to the participants in the September 2013 Midwest Russian History Workshop at Indiana University for their comments and suggestions, many of which have been incorporated here. I am also grateful to Ryan Voogt for his assistance with the research presented here. Many thanks also to Bart Ziino for his helpful comments. I am using 'First World War' throughout this chapter as a direct translation of the Russian 'Pervaia Mirovaia Voina' in use today. In 1914, the Russians called the war 'Velikaia Voina' or 'Otechestvennaia Voina', the 'Great War' or the 'Patriotic War'. In the Soviet period, the war was often known as the 'World Imperialist War'. Both the heroic and the negative connotations in these appellations have generally been jettisoned in current use in favour of the neutral 'First World War'.
2 See for example Melissa Bokovoy, 'Commemorating Serbia's Wars of National Liberation 1912–18', and Maria Bucur, 'Commemorations of December 1, 1918 and National Identity in Twentieth Century Romania', in Maria Bucur and Nancy Meriwether Wingfield eds, *Staging the Past: The Politics of Commemoration in Habsburg Central Europe, 1848 to the Present* (West Lafayette, IN: Purdue University Press, 2001), 236–54; 286–326.
3 See Frederick C. Corney, *Telling October: Memory and the Making of the Bolshevik Revolution* (Ithaca, NY: Cornell University Press, 2004).
4 See Karen Petrone, *The Great War in Russian Memory* (Bloomington, IN: Indiana University Press, 2011).
5 Catherine Merridale, *Night of Stone: Death and Memory in Twentieth-Century Russia* (New York: Viking, 2000), 100.
6 Here I am drawing on Alon Confino's useful definition of memory. See Alon Confino, 'Collective Memory and Cultural History: Problems of Method', *American Historical Review* 102:5 (December 1997), 1391. For a helpful discussion of the process of Soviet memory construction see Lisa A. Kirschenbaum, *The Legacy of the Siege of Leningrad, 1941–1945: Myth, Memories, and Monuments* (New York: Cambridge University Press, 2006), 5–6.
7 For a sampling of the most recent Russian scholarly work on the First World War translated into English, see *Russian Studies in History* 51:4 (Spring 2013), with an introduction by guest-editor Joshua Sanborn, 'Twenty-First-Century Views of Russia's Great War Effort', *Russian Studies in History* 51:4 (Spring 2013), 3–6.
8 The Russian word 'Otechesvennyi' is connected to the idea of 'Otechestvo' or Fatherland. Soviet discourse referred to the country both as the 'Rodina' or Motherland and 'Otechestvo' or Fatherland.
9 Russian Historical Society, 'Istoriko-kul'turnyi standart'. Online. Available: <http://histrf.ru/ru/biblioteka/book/istoriko-kul-turnyi-standart> (accessed 3 March 2014).
10 There are two adjectives to denote Russian. The one used here, 'Russkii', indicates Russian ethnicity; the other adjective, 'Rossiiskii', denotes all citizens of the Russian Empire whatever their ethnicity. Note that here the former version of the adjective is used.

11 *Vesti*, 'V Rossii otmechaiut Den' pamyati voinov, pavshikh v Pervoi mirovoi voine', 1 August 2013. Online. Available HTTP: <www.vesti.ru/doc.html?id=1112563&cid=7> (accessed 30 October 2013); Russkiy Mir Foundation, 'K stoletiiu Pervoi mirovoi voiny rossiya snimet fil'm o 'Batal'onakh smerti', 20 May 2013. Online. Available HTTP: <www.russkiymir.ru/russkiymir/ru/news/common/news40218.html> (accessed 24 July 2013); *Rosbalt*, 'Na Poklonnoi gore poyavitsya pamyatnik geroyam Pervoi mirovoi voiny', 24 July 2013. Online. Available HTTP: <www.rosbalt.ru/moscow/2013/07/24/1155943.html> (accessed 30 October 2013); Russkiy Mir Foundation, 'Museum Dedicated to World War One to Open at Tsarskoye Selo', 4 June 2013. Online. Available HTTP: <www.russkiymir.ru/russkiymir/en/news/common/news10423.html> (accessed 24 July 2013).
12 *Ria Novosti*, 'K 100-letiiu s nachala i mirovoi voiny sozdadut audiovizual'nyi resurs', 1 August 2013. Online. Available: <http://ria.ru/society/20130801/953515282.html> (accessed 30 October 2013).
13 *Novosti@mail.ru*, 'K 100-letiiu s nachala i mirovoi voiny sozdadut audiovizual'nyi resurs', 1 August 2013. Online. Available: <http://news.mail.ru/society/14150233> (accessed 30 October 2013).
14 *Novosti@mail.ru*, 'Naryshkin vozlozhil venok k obelisku pogibshim v Pervoi mirovoi voiny', 1 August 2013. Online. Available HTTP: <news.mail.ru/inregions/moscow/90/society/14147359> (accessed 30 October 2013).
15 Russian Historical Society (Rossiiskoe istoricheskoe obshchestvo). Online. Available: <http://rushistory.org> (accessed 30 October 2013).
16 Natalya Krainova, 'New Way of Teaching History to be Finalized by Next Month', *themoscowtimes.com*, 23 October 2013, Issue 5241. Online. Available HTTP: <www.themoscowtimes.com/news/article/new-way-of-teaching-history-to-be-finalized-by-next-month/488397.html> (accessed 29 October 2013).
17 Russian Historical Society, 'Tseli i zadachi RIO'. Online. Available: <http://rushistory.org/?page_id=23> (accessed 30 October 2013).
18 'Meeting with Founding Congress of the Russian Military Historical Society participants', 15 March 2013, The Embassy of the Russian Federation to the United Kingdom of Great Britain and Northern Ireland: Diplomacy Online. Online. Available HTTP: <www.rusemb.org.uk/press/1128> (accessed 30 October 2013).
19 Sara C. Nelson, '"Tchaikovsky Was Not Gay", Insists Russian Culture Minister Vladimir Medinsky (But Putin Says He Was)', *Huffington Post UK*, 19 September 2013. Online. Available HTTP: <www.huffingtonpost.co.uk/2013/09/19/tchaikovsky-not-gay-russian-culture-minister-vladimir-medinsky-n_3953476.html?utm_hp_ref=uk> (accessed 30 October 2013).
20 Mikhail Aristov, 'Podgotovka k stoletiiu Pervoi mirovoi voiny', *Radio Golos Rossii*, 4 March 2013. <http://rus.ruvr.ru/2013_03_04/Podgotovka-k-stoletiju-Pervoj-mirovoj-vojni> (accessed 29 October 2013). While the statement that there is 'not one monument to the heroes of the First World War' is hyperbolic, as in fact there are several monuments in Moscow's Memorial Park Complex of the Heroes of the First World War, for example, Nikonov is certainly correct that traces of the First World War have largely been erased from the Russian landscape. On the Memorial Park Complex, see Petrone, 292–300.
21 Website of the Institute of Social-Economic and Political Research, 'Memorial'naia programma k stoletiiu Pervoi mirovoi voiny: pervaia v Rossii za sto let', 21 October 2013. Online. Available HTTP: <www.odnako.org/blogs/show_30568> (accessed 29 October 2013).
22 *Russian Historical Society*, 'Kontseptsiia novogo uchebno-metodicheskogo kompleksa po otechestvennoi istorii'. Online. Available HTTP: <http://histrf.ru/ru/biblioteka/book/kontsieptsiia-novogho-uchiebno-mietodichieskogho-kompliksa-po-otiechiestviennoi-istorii> (accessed 29 October 2013).
23 'Memorial'naia programma k stoletiiu Pervoi mirovoi voiny'.

24 Peter Gatrell, *Russia's First World War: A Social and Economic History* (Harlow, UK: Pearson, 2005), 264–75.
25 Aristov, 'Podgotovka'.
26 Russian Military History Society, 'Zabytye pobedy'. Online. Available: <http://1914.histrf.ru/war/chronicle> (accessed 30 October 2013).
27 Russian Historical Society, 'Kontseptsiia novogo uchebno-metodicheskogo kompleksa po otechestvennoi istorii'.
28 Russian Military History Society, 'Zabytye pobedy'.
29 Hubertus Jahn, *Patriotic Culture in Russia during World War I* (Ithaca, NY: Cornell University Press, 1995), 24.
30 David Satter, *It Was a Long Time Ago, and It Never Happened Anyway: Russia and the Communist Past* (New Haven, CT: Yale University Press, 2012), 300.
31 Aristov, 'Podgotovka'.
32 Maria Antonova, 'A Century Late', *Russian Life* (September–October 2013), 15.
33 Aaron J. Cohen, 'Oh That!: Myth, Memory, and the First World War in the Russian Emigration and the Soviet Union', *Slavic Review* 62 (Spring 2003), 75.
34 Petrone, 298–300.
35 Russian Military History Society, 'Geroi Pervoi mirovoi voiny', Online. Available: <http://1914.histrf.ru/heroes> (accessed 30 October 2013).
36 Tsarskoe Selo State Museum-Preserve. Online. Available: <http://eng.tzar.ru/museums/palaces/alexander_park/landscape_park/martial> (accessed 30 October 2013).
37 *Ria Novosti*, 'Putin priedet na otkrytie muzeya geroyam i Pervoi mirovoi voiny d Tsarskom sele', 14 March 2013. Online. Available: <http://ria.ru/society/20130314/927341900.html> (accessed 24 July 2013).
38 See Kirschenbaum for a discussion of this process. See also Nina Tumarkin, *The Living and the Dead: The Rise and Fall of the Cult of World War II in Russia* (New York, NY: Basic Books, 1994).
39 GBU Poklonnaia Gora. Online. Available HTTP: <www.poklonnaya-gora.ru> (accessed 30 October 2013).
40 ITAR/TASS, 'Rossiiskim geroiam i voinam, pavshim v gody Pervoi mirovoi voiny'. Online. Available: <http://tvkultura.ru/article/show/article_id/96147> (accessed 29 October 2013).
41 Russian Military History Society, 'Na Poklonnoi gore vybrali luchshii pamyatnik geroyam Pervoi Mirovoi', 18 September 2013. Online. Available: <http://histrf.ru/ru/rvio/activities/news/item-140> (accessed 30 October 2013).
42 ITAR/TASS.
43 Russian Military History Society, 'Pobediteli Konkursa'. Online. Available: <http://1914.histrf.ru/monument/voting> (accessed 3 June 2014).

8 Çanakkale's children
The politics of remembering the Gallipoli campaign in contemporary Turkey[1]

Vedica Kant

Carved into the hillside on the Asian side of the Çanakkale Straits, visible to every visitor who crosses the famed Hellespont, is a verse by the Turkish poet Necmettin Halil Onan that underscores the importance of this geographical landmark in the Turkish republic's imagination (Figure 8.1). The inscribed lines read:

> Dur yolcu! Bilmeden gelip bastığın
> Bu toprak, bir devrin battığı yerdir.

Roughly translated they say, 'Stop traveller! This land which you unknowingly tread on is where an epoch lies.' The subsequent lines of the poem, which are not engraved into the hillside, perhaps even more aptly capture the place the Çanakkale campaign has acquired in Turkish history. 'Bend down and lend your ear', the poem continues, 'for this silent mound is the place where the

Figure 8.1 'Dur Yolcu!' Verse carved into the landscape visible to every visitor crossing the Dardanelles. © Vedica Kant

heart of a nation sighs.' Çanakkale resonates in this way not just because of its intrinsic importance, but because it is linked to a powerful narrative of the origins of the Turkish republic and its key figure, Mustafa Kemal (later Atatürk). In this narrative, the defence of Çanakkale stands as the first instance of the nationalist awakenings of the Turkish people, followed by the War of Independence and the creation of the republic in 1923. This potent story of historical origins has endured, though not without subtle change, to the present. This chapter is concerned with the creation of the Çanakkale myth in the early years of the republic, and with how the narrative around Çanakkale has changed and shifted over almost a century. It argues that despite greater acknowledgement of ordinary soldiers, and a more substantive challenge to the Kemalist narrative by the Islamist Justice and Development Party (AKP), that myth has proved deeply resilient, limiting the terms in which the significance of Çanakkale can be contested and reoriented in Turkey.

The Çanakkale narrative has three main phases in its shaping and perpetuation. Until 1950 Turkey was a single-party state in which Atatürk and his Republican People's Party (CHP), played a critical role in moulding the nation according to their vision, and crafting a national historiography that supported their aims. At the centre of that power was the personality cult of Atatürkism, which had at its disposal the institutional powers of the state and its military to insist that the formation of the republic established a complete break with the past and a rejection of the decadent and untenable Ottoman way of life. While state activism around Çanakkale diminished after the advent of multi-party politics in 1950, the period from the late 1980s onwards saw a revitalization of public interest in Çanakkale and increasing memorial activities through private agencies and individuals. This process occurred in tandem with the increasing influence of neoliberalism, the opening up of the Turkish economy and consequently greater civil society activism. Though this period was marked by a wider veneration of the ordinary Turkish soldier, the broader contours of the Kemalist Çanakkale story remained largely intact.

In recent years, however, the ascendancy of the AKP, in power since 2002, has precipitated a resurgence of government interest in how Çanakkale should be memorialized. With its mixture of neoliberalism and soft Islamism, the AKP has reduced the stranglehold of the military over politics and begun to challenge more strongly than ever before the ideals of Kemalism and the Atatürk personality cult. Since coming to power the AKP has championed a more inclusive Ottoman identity: for the AKP it is not the six centuries of Ottoman rule that were an anomaly but rather the first eighty years of the Turkish republic. Çanakkale remains important in this vision because it is seen as the last site of Ottoman glory in all its multi-ethnic, multi-national and religious connotations. In the official literature announcing the development of a new exhibition centre at Çanakkale the Prime Minister Recep Tayyip Erdoğan stated, 'The victory at Çanakkale has an extremely important place in the soul of our nation, not just as a glorious memory of our past, but also as one of the strongest sources of inspiration in our march towards the future.'[2]

Yet despite the resources at its disposal and its increasing authoritarianism, the AKP's rhetoric on Çanakkale has not gone unchallenged. This is in large part due to the resilience of the Kemalist narrative and the way Atatürk's role in the war is remembered. But it is also because of the multitude of non-state voices and alternate perspectives that have also entered the debate over how Çanakkale should be remembered since the liberalization of the economy. The AKP has accessed the public space available to project its own narrative of Çanakkale, but it remains constrained by the power of the Kemalist framing of Turkish history.[3] The contest over Çanakkale is, then, hardly settled.

Establishing the Çanakkale myth: the historiography of the Kemalist state

Mustafa Kemal's centrality to the Çanakkale story was never simply assured by his exploits in 1915, but required cultivation over time. Indeed Kemal initially received little public recognition. At a ceremony in Istanbul in 1916 to celebrate the Çanakkale victory, Kemal's name was not even mentioned, while in the *Harp Mecmuası* (*War Magazine*) published by the war ministry, his name was mentioned only once with respect to Çanakkale.[4] This owed something to his difficult relationship with War Minister Enver Paşa, and Kemal was only able to really bring attention to his exploits first in the March 1918 issue of the Turkish nationalist magazine *Yeni Mecmua* (*The New Review*), which commemorated the third anniversary of the naval battle in the Dardanelles. The issue ran an interview with Kemal, which had been secured through the work of a number of publicists who had been employed to get his name out. This interview was the first articulation of the popular perception of Kemal as the victor of Çanakkale and the saviour of Istanbul. As such it was an important moment in building Kemal's public reputation as a great commander and in giving him the legitimacy that he would need to steer the War of Independence. It was in this interview that Kemal could begin to articulate his own version of Çanakkale, including the now legendary, though misquoted, order to his men in the face of the Allied landing: 'I do not order you to attack, I order you to die. In the time it takes us to die, other troops and commanders can come and take our places.'[5] Now, Kemal could insist that: 'At that moment, we won.'[6]

'Nationalism is not the awakening of nations to self-consciousness; it invents nations where they do not exist', noted Gellner.[7] In his seminal work Anderson puts the emphasis on imagination and creativity in constructing the nation, rather than thinking of the nation as a false construct.[8] In the Turkish case, such imagination was harnessed soon after the consolidation and creation of the new republic in 1923. As the only war front in which Ottoman soldiers saw success during the First World War, Çanakkale became an important symbol of courage and self-sacrifice and provided inspiration and a source of possibility during the years of the Turkish national movement. Parmaksız notes that the victory became the basis of a new national myth for the Kemalist state in which

Çanakkale was a symbolic historic breakpoint with the Ottoman Empire. Accordingly it was at Çanakkale that the Ottoman Empire made way for the Turkish republic, which committed itself to a modernist future and stressed the importance of breaking links with the past.[9] Yet such a break with the past was more difficult to achieve in practice, especially when a large number of the republican elite, Kemal included, had been so deeply entrenched in the Ottoman system from which they had built their authority. This was specifically true of Mustafa Kemal's achievements at Çanakkale and goes some way in explaining the war's co-option in the narrative of the new republic.

If this view of events could be hammered home with such force it was because, as Zürcher notes, Turkey by 1925 was not just a one-party state but also effectively a dictatorship.[10] By 1926 statues of Kemal were already being erected in the major towns and he was presented as the father of the nation, its saviour and its teacher. In 1934 parliament bestowed on him the surname 'Atatürk', literally the 'Father of the Turks'. By the 1930s a set of ideas that together formed *Kemalizm* (Kemalism) or *Atatürkçülük* (Atatürkism) slowly evolved. These ideas formed the basis for indoctrination in schools, the media and the army and were also accompanied by the personality cult that grew up around Mustafa Kemal during and even more so after his lifetime.

In addition to Atatürk's role in the campaign another factor that aided the co-option of the Çanakkale myth was the fact that the groundwork for the choice of Çanakkale as such an important national myth had already been laid during the war years themselves. Hanioğlu notes a common saying in the aftermath of the victory that the Ottoman army had fought 'seven nations' and emerged victorious.[11] The fact that the Allied forces comprised English, Australians, New Zealanders, Irish, Scots, Indians, Gurkhas, Egyptians, French and Senegalese helped Ottoman propaganda present the victory as one of Turkism: 'the miracle of the Turk against all odds'.[12] This undoubtedly made it easier for the new Turkish state to co-opt Çanakkale into its own narrative given that it was already seen as a spectacular success and especially as it was setting out to build a specifically Turkish nation on the ruins of the multicultural Ottoman Empire.

Jay Winter has argued that remembrance consists of negotiations between a multiplicity of groups, including the state, though obviously all the partners are not equal.[13] In early republican Turkey the state had the authority and resources to push forward its imperatives on its own, including its version of the past. The importance of Çanakkale in the new republic's imagination of itself can be gleaned from the fact that the topic was introduced in the school-level history syllabus as early as 1927. This is perhaps unsurprising if one takes into account the importance attached to Çanakkale by the Kemalists as a break with the Ottoman Empire and as the site where Turkish nationalism had its first stirrings. The topic was introduced in the university history syllabi in 1934 as part of the compulsory subject 'The History of the Turkish Revolution' which sought to teach how the new state was established.[14] Unsurprisingly, in the official history the topic is covered with a particular focus on Mustafa

Kemal and with stress on the campaign as a pivotal point for Turkey. Some of the figures used by the textbooks in discussions of the topic highlight these points.[15] Of particular interest is one claim that more than 100,000 teachers and graduates of the civil service died in the campaign when in actual fact only 7.5 per cent of the entire population of Turkey was literate at the time. The figures bear highlighting because they are an example of ways in which the state stressed not just the losses suffered in the campaign, but also how much work the new republican regime had to put in to rebuild the country, thus making both the victory and the foundation of republican Turkey a truly remarkable achievement.

In addition to its use of the educational system the new republic also had at its disposal the media to propagate its vision of the Çanakkale campaign. The anniversaries of important battles in the campaign – especially 18 March (the day of the naval victory), 25 April (the day Atatürk repelled the invading Anzacs), and 9 and 10 of August (the anniversary of the Anafarta victory, the Turkish reference to the victory at Suvla Bay) – became opportunities to recount the Çanakkale victory as Atatürk's deliverance of Istanbul and Turkey. Such articles were de rigueur on important anniversary days for most of the period of high Kemalism in the 1930s. A front-page article in the state organ *Cumhuriyet* on 25 April 1936, for example, was simply titled, 'The anniversary of a great day' with a subheading 'Atatürk saved Istanbul on 25 April 1915.' The article continued:

> There are days in the lives of countries that must never come to be forgotten. That day, when Atatürk was still a young general, he saved Çanakkale and Istanbul. This was not the fortune of a first rescue but the auspicious beginning of a series of rescues.[16]

Another front page article published on the twentieth anniversary of the Anafarta victory stressed '20 years ago today Atatürk saved Çanakkale, Istanbul and Turkey.' The article continued in a similar vein to most commemorative writings on Çanakkale:

> 20 years ago today Monday the 9th of August and again 20 years ago tomorrow Tuesday the 10th of August 1915 the man God created to save Turkey saved Çanakkale and Turkey for the second time. He wrote the Anafarta victory with a golden pen, no, not a golden pen but with the clean blood of the Turks.[17]

Undoubtedly, this kind of heavy rhetoric helped in making Çanakkale an emotional cornerstone of the story of the republic. At this time *Cumhuriyet* also emphasized the Western Allies' underestimation of the Turkish army, on account of its poor performance in the Balkan Wars, thus identifying those losses with the Ottoman Empire while claiming the victory at Çanakkale for the new state.

In addition to intertwining the legends of Atatürk and Çanakkale tightly together, the late 1930s onwards also saw what one could term the 'Atatürkization' of the battlefields of Çanakkale itself. Atatürk himself set a conciliatory note for the Turkish commemorative presence on the peninsula in the 1930s, which was almost certainly a function of his reorientation of Turkish society towards the secular West.[18] A narrative of forgiveness and friendship worked well to support those aims and in a sense fit with the Kemalist tenet – 'Western in spite of the West'. Whereas for someone like nationalist poet Mehmet Akif Western civilization was a 'single-toothed monster' representing the Christian aggressor on the battlefields of Çanakkale, Atatürk embraced all the dead of the campaign in a speech delivered on his behalf for the visit of a British delegation in 1934. In it, he famously declared:

> Those heroes that shed their blood and lost their lives are now lying in the soil of a friendly country. Therefore rest in peace. There is no difference between the Johnnies and the Mehmets to us where they lie side by side here in this country of ours. You, the mothers, who sent their sons from far away countries, wipe away your tears. Your sons are now lying in our bosom and are in peace. After having lost their lives on this land, they have become our sons as well.

Adrian Jones argues that one reason Atatürk went out of his way to honour the invaders was because he had come to realize that they had unknowingly prompted the Turks to shape a new kind of nation.[19] Further, the Australians and British may have been Turkey's adversaries in war, but they were members of the larger 'civilization to which the new Turks aspired to belong'.[20]

Atatürk had set the tone for the atmosphere of commemoration at the battlefields, but he also soon became a very visible presence on site. In 1939 the Turkish government sponsored a monument overlooking the southern part of the peninsula, inscribed with a quote from Atatürk; today a number of monuments with quotes from Atatürk and Atatürk statues dot the battlefields (Figure 8.2). These monuments serve as a lingering reminder of just how intertwined Çanakkale's history is with the story of Atatürk himself and hint at the difficulties that might be involved in challenging the very entrenched narrative surrounding his deeds in Çanakkale.

In 1944 an architectural competition opened to determine a design for a major martyrs' memorial on the southernmost tip of the peninsula. Bozdoğan notes that the competition was part of a process (that included the earlier competition for the design of Atatürk's mausoleum, the Anitkabir) very much in the nationalist mode wherein monumentality, national symbolism and power constituted the primary architectural preoccupations.[21] By the mid-to-late 1940s, however, the enthusiasm for this kind of modernist architecture, and indeed the modernist legacy, had been lost. Atatürk had died in 1938 and there was popular frustration and anger against the CHP. In 1950 Turkey held free and fair elections and for the first time the CHP was ousted from

152 *Vedica Kant*

Figure 8.2 Atatürk memorial on Çanakkale battlefields. Atatürk quotes and statues dot the peninsula and serve as a reminder of how his personality is intertwined with Çanakkale's history. © Vedica Kant

power. Perhaps unsurprisingly, around the same time funds for the memorial dried up and the project eventually had to be funded through a popular fundraising campaign spearheaded by the daily *Milliyet*.

It says a lot for the strength of the Çanakkale narrative that it motivated people to donate towards the building of the monument, but one can view the martyrs' memorial as a last flourish of Kemalist modernism and its undiluted version of Çanakkale's history. The Çanakkale martyrs' memorial reflects Turkish pride in their humanitarian behaviour, but also asserts their pride in the victory. The monument, which is more than 40 metres in height, comprises four large columns capped by a 25-metre square concrete slab. Reliefs on the base depict scenes of the Turkish victory but also showcase meetings between erstwhile enemies. The memorial dominates the entrance to the Straits and is still the largest and most striking visual monument on the peninsula. It is, in a sense, a startling symbol of the hold of the Kemalist ideology over Çanakkale.

Remembering history: public re-engagement with Çanakkale

After the 1960s memorial activity regarding Çanakkale, even on the peninsula itself, continued largely through private agencies such as the 'Society to Assist the Memorials of the Çanakkale Martyrs' which erected monuments to mark the significant sites of resistance to the Allied naval attack in March 1915 and the landings of 25 April.[22] This process continued intermittently until the 1990s, which marked a period of increasing public interest in Çanakkale. One factor was the increasing profile of Anzac commemorations on the peninsula and the very large-scale activities that marked the seventy-fifth anniversary commemorations in 1990.[23] This increased public interest was also in keeping with broader changes in Turkish society where the ideology of neoliberalism that had been pursued since the mid-1980s not only opened up the economy, but also brought with it a greater focus on individual agency by introducing new boundaries and concepts such as voluntarism, choice and privacy which in turn led to a privatization of state ideology.[24]

Anzac commemorations have been held at dawn on 25 April each year since 1934, but the ceremony has not always drawn as many tourists as it does today. In 1957 for example, only fourteen people took part in the official dawn ceremony. The 1990 commemorations drew in 1,000 attendees;[25] in 2015 this number will have increased to 10,500, limited by ballot. This increasing interest of Australians and New Zealanders has had a two-fold impact. One is directly on the peninsula's local economy, making it more reliant on tourism revenues and tying it in more closely to the memorialization of Çanakkale.[26] The second has been to create a greater interest among the Turkish public at large about the campaign. Writing in *Hurriyet* in 2001, the journalist Emin Çölaşan noted:

> We have reached a state where we have broken away from our history. Even recent history does not interest our society at all. But, [on the other hand] every year the sons of strangers along with groups of thousands of people are coming to Çanakkale from the other end of the world in the month of April and organizing commemoration ceremonies for their fathers who fought and died there.[27]

This renewal of interest in Çanakkale led to initiatives by both the state and non-state actors that broadened the way in which Çanakkale was memorialized. As domestic tourism to the battlefields increased, both the land and sea battles associated with the campaign began to be celebrated with grand ceremonies. The newspaper *Hürriyet* and the Association of Turkish Travel Agencies (TÜRSAB) came together to spearhead a campaign for an official commemoration of 18 March as Çanakkale Martyrs' Day under the slogan 'The ANZACs commemorate, why shouldn't we?' In June 2002 the Turkish parliament established 18 March as Martyrs' Day. In passing the legal amendment, parliament noted that commemorative activities had been diffuse in nature, contained to the security forces, and had failed to create a large enough public impact. Now, commemorative activities were to be concentrated on a single day with the participation of the public, civil society organizations and the state itself.[28] *Hürriyet* and TÜRSAB played an important role along with state authorities in organizing the first Martyrs' Day ceremony in 2003, in which 3,500 students from the 81 provinces of the country participated, along with a number of state officials.[29]

In addition to the recognition of a single Martyrs' Day commemoration, this period also saw a broader, more democratic veneration of the sacrifices of the ordinary soldier or '*Mehmetçik*'. In 1992 a cemetery commemorating 600 Turkish soldiers was established at the Çanakkale Martyrs' Memorial and in the same year a series of statues of Turkish soldiers appeared in the landscape, bringing to life the ordinary *Mehmetçik* and aspects of the Çanakkale mythology. For example, it was around this time that the statues of Seyit Ali Çabuk (an artilleryman whose superhuman efforts to lift shells to feed guns helped repel the Allies) and Hüseyin Kaçmaz (the last Turkish veteran of the campaign, who also fought in the Turkish War of Independence, Figure 8.3) were erected on the peninsula.

Figure 8.3 Statue of Hüseyin Kaçmaz, the last Turkish veteran of the campaign, who also fought in the Turkish War of Independence. © Vedica Kant

This humanization of the campaign can also be seen in the large number of films, documentaries and television shows that have been made about Çanakkale since the 2000s. Tolga Örnek's 2005 documentary *Gelibolu* made use of extensive archival material to bring to life the experience of the campaign, and quickly became the most watched documentary in Turkish history, recording 555,149 viewers in a span of five weeks.[30] A spate of movies about Çanakkale are also due for release in the run-up to the centenary of the war, with three released already in 2012–13. Though none of these films have been blockbuster successes, in aiming to showcase the lives of ordinary soldiers and humanize the war they operate at a slight remove from the Kemalist narrative that has been pre-eminently concerned with the story of Atatürk's success in the campaign.

State vs government: The AKP's challenge to Kemalist historiography

Despite increasing public interest and the opening up, indeed the privatization, of the narrative associated with Çanakkale since the 1990s, the official contours of Turkish historiography around Çanakkale remained broadly unchanged. This can be explained by the fact that despite the advent of democracy and multi-party politics since the 1950s, the hold of the Kemalist narrative was maintained by the regular intervention of the army. Turkey has witnessed military coups in 1960, 1971 and 1980, and several other military interventions in parliamentary rule. During this period the Constitutional Court has also shut down twenty-four political parties, despite their electoral victories, largely because they were perceived to be too Islamic. Jenny White notes that since the 1960 coup there has been a long-standing split between the state and popularly elected governments. While the state (and its institutions such as the military, judiciary and education administration) sees itself as the protector of the secular national identity and cultural and territorial integrity of the nation-state as established by Kemalism, governments represent the interests of their electorate, a large majority of which is devout and conservative.[31]

It has only been under the rule of the current incumbent, the Justice and Development Party (AKP), that Kemalism has come to be challenged more vigorously than ever before. The AKP was one of the more moderate offspring of the Islamist parties of the 1990s, blending neoliberal economic policies with soft Islamism. The party won the November 2002 elections and has remained in power through three election cycles, increasing its share of the vote to 49.9 per cent in 2011. This success in electoral politics and indeed in eroding the power of the military – on which front the AKP has been more successful than any other political party or organization in Turkey – has only added to a confrontation between the AKP's politics and ideology and the initial conception of the Turkish republic.

What the AKP has managed to do is to challenge the notion of the emblematic secular Turk and to develop an alternative definition of Turkishness and the nation that is not encumbered by the Kemalist vision of an embattled nation but rather 'as a self-confident successor to the Ottomans in a rediscovered (and reinvented) past'.[32] White terms the AKP's ideology a sort of 'Muslim nationalism', whose vision for the future is shaped by an imperial Ottoman past overlaid onto the republican state framework but divorced from the Kemalist state project. A result of this overt ideology has been the fact that the very basic tenets of the state as established by Kemalism – from state ideology and foreign policy to everyday lifestyle – are being contested.

Most importantly, this 'neo-Ottomanism' brings Islamic faith and identity back into the public sphere, and insists that the Kemalist era marked a period of detachment, in which the nation lost its links with its glorious past.[33] Ahmet Davutoğlu, the AKP Foreign Minister, has called on Turks to rediscover their ancient values while calling the twentieth century 'only a parenthesis'.[34] Neo-Ottomanism has also encouraged Turks to rediscover their imperial legacy. While such an approach is not one that aims to replace ties with the West with ties with the East, it is strongly rooted in pride over the imperial and multinational Ottoman legacy and stresses a common Muslim identity that binds Turkey with the larger Middle East and North Africa. Such an agenda also has ramifications closer to home. Because neo-Ottomanism rejects the assimilative nationalism of Kemalism it is more at peace with the imperial and multinational legacy of Turkey, and therefore it opens the door for a less 'ethnic' and more multi-cultural conceptualization of 'citizenship'. This is particularly important in defining relations with Turkey's Kurdish minority, and the AKP has made significant strides on this front because it sees no major threat behind Kurdish cultural rights and the expression of Kurdish national identity, as long as Kurds maintain a sense of loyalty to the Republic of Turkey.[35]

Because the AKP is expansive in its attempts to fashion the republic according to its ideology, these shifts in state ideology and agenda during the party's time in power have also had a visible effect on the events the state celebrates as central to Turkish identity and the ways in which these are celebrated. Instead of focussing on commemorating the 1923 foundation of the nation, for instance, the new Turks pay more public tribute to events like the 1453 conquest of Istanbul and the birthdate of the Prophet Muhammed.[36] They cannot ignore, however, the myth of Çanakkale, so squarely associated with Atatürk and the founding of the Turkish republic. This is not simply because Çanakkale represents a powerful and entrenched foundation story. It is also because the number of visitors – domestic and international – that the site attracts has grown with public interest in the campaign, thus presenting the AKP with an important audience for its ideology.

As already noted, the heavy-handed Kemalist narrative surrounding Çanakkale had already softened due to a weakening of the Kemalist hold over Turkish politics from the 1950s onwards. While the individuals who fought the campaign have received more attention, the central tenets of the story, however, remained largely unchanged, and it has only been under the AKP regime that there has been a renewed flurry of government-led activity on the peninsula and in terms of referencing the story. On the one hand this is because of the approaching centenary of the campaign. On the other it is clear that there is a renewed emphasis on the Ottoman nature of the campaign (both by stressing the Islamic character of the Turkish campaign and the presence of many post-imperial nationalities who fought there) that is very much in tune with the AKP's rhetoric and agenda. Speaking at the March anniversary celebrations in Çanakkale in 2013, for example, Prime Minister Erdoğan said:

> The martyrs here are not the members of a single race. They are the architects of a great nation. The martyrs are the heroes that shaped our understanding of a nation. They are the children of people from all over Turkey, the Balkans, the Middle East and Africa. There are Turks here at this cemetery, and Bosniacs, and Kurds. There are people who believed in the same values. Çanakkale is a victorious page in our history, but it is also a light for us today.[37]

Such an emphasis on celebrating the non-Turkish Ottoman troops who fought in Çanakkale is markedly different both from the perception of these troops during the war itself and of the Kemalist regime, which generally propagated the view that the Arabs had betrayed the Turks in the war.[38] This shift could also be seen during the ninety-eighth anniversary celebrations of the naval victory at Çanakkale. As part of the celebrations a number of events were organized across the country and the Çanakkale Governor's Office specifically printed banners in Kurdish and Arabic to invite the residents of Turkey's south-east to join the celebrations, with the Governor highlighting that it was symbolically important to address everybody in their mother tongue.[39] Further, and significantly, a number of representatives of countries from the former Ottoman Empire took part in the 2013 Anzac day commemorations, including several from the Balkans, North Africa and the Middle East.

The example of the symbolic cemetery that was opened in a space bordering the area of the Çanakkale Martyrs' Memorial in 2007 further elucidates the above points.[40] The cemetery is characterized by row upon row of glass tombstones with the names of the fallen etched on both sides of the glass (Figure 8.4). The abundance of names re-emphasizes the thousands of soldiers who gave their life for the victory. Though statues of Atatürk are present at the memorial, these rows of tombstones emphasize the loss of life and visually and spatially compete with the idea that Çanakkale was a victory won by one man alone. It is also divided into province-specific plots, and in addition to the many parts of modern-day Turkey, an entire area of the cemetery is reserved for soldiers from countries formerly part of the empire. This stress on the multi-ethnic (and multi-national) character of the campaign allows for Çanakkale to be reimagined not just as a war that was important for the Turks but also for other Muslims. To emphasize the point, the Prime Minister recently invoked Çanakkale to justify Turkey's involvement in the current conflict in Syria. He argued that a number of nationalities, including Syrians, fought beside the

Figure 8.4 Glass tombstones at the symbolic cemetery, opened in 2007. The tombstones create a strong sense of loss and challenge the notion that the victory was Atatürk's single-handed accomplishment. © Vedica Kant

Turks in Çanakkale and that it was Turkey's duty now to fight on their side. At the 2013 commemoration ceremonies at Çanakkale there were also two flags to recognize the Syrian dead, the official one and the flag of the armed Free Syrian Army rebels fighting against the Bashar al-Assad regime.

Perhaps the most cogent encapsulation of this new narrative around Çanakkale is the Çanakkale Epic Promotion Centre. The centre, which was first envisaged by Prime Minister Erdoğan during a visit to Çanakkale in 2003, cost approximately US$50 million dollars to build and was inaugurated in June 2012. Spread over four floors it recreates the story of the campaign through a series of eleven thematic 3-D montages. The narrative of the war proffered here also stresses the multi-national character of the campaign. While Atatürk is hardly ignored, the narrative never focusses solely on his part in the course of events. A section focussing on the memories of the war quotes a number of letters written by family members to soldiers who were fighting on the front. The letters quoted are heavy in religious imagery and terminology. The war, for example, is being fought for 'the protection of religion and the nation'; the terms '*jihad*', '*gazi*' and '*şehit*' (martyr) come up frequently. The final section of the concluding montage, termed 'Turkey from 1915 to today', explicitly states that the sacrifices of those who fought at Çanakkale have helped forge modern Turkey, and links Çanakkale to the economic, social, military and diplomatic successes of the AKP. *Gazi* Mustafa Kemal is given thanks but the visual images are of Prime Minister Erdoğan and President Abdullah Gül leading Turkey to higher levels of success.

On exiting the theatre after the final montage the visitor is greeted by a mural that takes up an entire wall, showing a whole regiment of Turkish soldiers on the battlefield deep in prayer. This stress on the religious nature of the campaign has been quite marked during the AKP rule. Prime Minister Erdoğan is on record terming the campaign in Çanakkale 'a crusade'. Yet while the emphasis on the religious aspect of the campaign is a definite departure from the Kemalist narrative of Çanakkale, in fact the politics of the Young Turk period and the hazy early years of the republic make such appropriation particularly easy. This Ottoman Muslim nationalism continued to hold sway throughout the war, which was officially declared a *jihad* and partly fought out as a brutal ethnic/religious conflict in Anatolia and beyond. The appeal of such an ideology is easy to understand given that the empire had lost most of its European provinces and needed to mobilize the population. The national resistance movement that Atatürk led in Anatolia after 1918 very much carried on in this vein, at least initially.[41] Mustafa Kemal's adoption of the religiously tinged title of *gazi*, for example, aimed to give him and his movement greater legitimacy. Bozdoğan also notes that nationalist poems of Mehmet Akif Ersoy (who also wrote the Turkish national anthem before his falling out with Atatürk over the secular reforms) are full of religious codes adapted to the new nationalist consciousness.[42] For example, Ersoy terms the soldiers who fought in Gallipoli (and the War of Independence) 'as glorious as the lions of Bedr', a reference to the holy wars of the Prophet, and the Kaaba in Mecca as their gravestone. This vocabulary can still be seen on the battlefields, and it is this vocabulary that is referenced by the AKP.

By invoking this religious tenor of the early republic, the AKP is following in the footsteps of its predecessor Islamist parties, which found legitimate political space – especially after the military intervention of 1997 – by highlighting the Islamic aspects of the foundational moment, rather than simply idealizing the Ottoman period when Islam was the official religion of the state.[43] In a similar way, the AKP has begun to challenge the secularist monopoly over Çanakkale, by engaging with the broader context of the original Kemalist narrative, in which Çanakkale is a foundational episode in the creation of the nation. In this the AKP example adheres closely to Smith's argument that, while on the one hand creating nations is a recurrent process that has to be renewed periodically, such nation-building activities also operate within a definite tradition. The nation is not built anew by each new generation.[44] Atatürk's role in the victory at Çanakkale has been so successfully established as a foundational cornerstone of the republic that it simply cannot be removed from the historical narrative. Instead the narrative has been appropriated to comply with the ideological criteria of the current government. In 2012 the AKP started organizing an annual 'Breaking the fast with the menu of martyr's programme' in the month of Ramadan, where thousands of attendees break their daytime fast with rye bread, cracked wheat soup and water, the supposed menu of Ottoman soldiers on the battlefield.[45] Further, Parmaksız argues that though the AKP was not in power when Martyrs' Day was instituted in 2002, the ceremony has become an important part of the way in which it commemorates Çanakkale. For the AKP, 18 March is not a day to celebrate a victory but rather a day of pain, to mourn and commemorate the loss of empire, and a day that symbolizes modern Turkey's break with the past.[46] This begins to explain the importance of Çanakkale – despite its associations with Atatürk and the founding of the republic – as an important opportunity for the AKP to advance its own rendering of the wartime past.

It is important to note, however, that by the time the AKP came to power in late 2002, there was already a great deal of public interest and activity with regard to Çanakkale. As such, a space had already been created for memorial activity that was not directly controlled by the state even though such activities largely occurred within the broader Kemalist narrative. The AKP has had significant success in imaginatively challenging the Kemalist hegemony in remembering Çanakkale. Despite its own tendency towards greater authoritarianism, however, the AKP cannot simply control commemorative practice and thought. The AKP continues to face challenges to its rendering of the story of the campaign and its remembrance not just by Kemalists, but also other groups and parties who represent alternate viewpoints that don't fit neatly into the secular vs Islamic narrative. Most significant here are the experiences of Armenians. In the first instance, the presence of Armenians in the Ottoman army at Çanakkale challenges the conception of the war as a *jihad*. For example, on 18 March 2013, the anniversary of the Turkish naval victory, the Armenian Turkish newspaper *Agos* ran a story with the headline 'Çanakkale's non-Muslim martyrs who have been forgotten.'[47] The article noted that,

> the [story of] the non-Muslim soldiers of the Çanakkale campaign is a topic that is passed over every year on 18 March without any mention. The story of these non-Muslims who went to Çanakkale to 'defend the nation' throws light on an aspect of history that has been concealed carefully. The fact that 82 out of the 215 doctors who died up to 1918 were Armenians is enough to explain some things.

More difficult still are the persistent reminders that 2015 also marks the centenary of the Armenian genocide.[48] Recently, Prime Minister Erdoğan issued a statement that urged people to talk about and remember their losses 'with maturity'. While a major departure for the way in which Turkey has so far dealt with this chapter of its history, it still stopped short of terming the events of 1915 a genocide.[49] The statement and the focus on Çanakkale as a symbol of Turkish loss and mourning as part of the planned 2015 commemorations in front of a very international audience can be seen as a way to counter the commemorations of the Armenian genocide that will also be generating a lot of international attention.[50] Parmaksız has noted that even though for the AKP the republic is a direct continuation of the Ottoman Empire, it still distances itself from the issues of the Armenian genocide.[51] The official position was encapsulated by the Foreign Minister Ahmet Davutoğlu: '1915 represents the deportation for the Armenians but at the same time it represents Çanakkale for us.'[52] He has further noted, 'We will make the whole world recognize (the importance of) the year 2015. Not as the anniversary of a genocide as claimed and slandered by some, but as a nation's great resistance, as the anniversary of the Çanakkale resistance'.[53]

According to Jay Winter it is not the injury of war but rather its dramatic nature and earthquake-like quality that fuels a continued fascination with the topic.[54] In recent years, especially with the upcoming centenary, the First World War in particular has been the subject of such a memory boom. Turkey is no different, especially because the war had such momentous outcomes. In the case of Çanakkale, in particular, the drama is intense, the victory was won against all odds, and the war had an unimaginable impact in bringing to an end the Ottoman Empire and bringing to life the new Turkish state. It is therefore natural that the Kemalist state focussed on the story of the campaign to lend a particular emotional weight to the story of the birth of Turkish nationalism by linking that birth with the trenches of Çanakkale. It is also just as natural that the AKP has sought to leave its stamp on the narrative of the campaign so that the story reflects its agenda of a more inclusive Turkey domestically, and a Turkey that invokes brotherly feelings amongst its immediate neighbours. Yet there are clear challenges to just how successful the AKP will be in stamping its mark on the way Çanakkale is remembered.

In the summer of 2013 the AKP faced its most serious challenge of its time in power when protests broke out over the government's decision to destroy a park to reconstruct an Ottoman barracks and build a new mosque in the heart of Istanbul's Taksim Square. The protests were linked to issues of authoritarianism, corruption, commercialization of public space and lack of transparency in decision-making. But another important fact was the concern amongst a large number of protesters that the plan to reconstruct an Ottoman-era building that had been pulled down by the Kemalist regime to refashion Taksim as a modern space was a symbolic, if not so subtle way, for the AKP to refashion the square in line with its own ideology. The protests spread to cities and towns across the country; five people were killed during the protests and around 5,000 detained, many for extended periods.[55] The reformulation of how Çanakkale is remembered is not as contentious an issue as those that caused the Gezi Park protests. The protests are a reminder, however, that the AKP's attempts to push forward its own ideologies will be neither easy nor without challenge. There remains considerable space for the contestation of Çanakkale, and the stakes are high. Even though the Çanakkale campaign took place a century ago, the debate over the meaning of the war and its appropriate memorialization has never been more insistent.

Notes

1 In Turkish, the Gallipoli campaign is referred to as the *Çanakkale Savaşı*, the Çanakkale War.
2 Türkiye Cumhuriyeti, Orman ve Su İsleri Bakanığı Doğa Koruma ve Milli Parklar Genel Mudurlügü, 3. Online. Available: <http://canakkaledestani.milliparklar.gov.tr/dosya/GELIBOLU.pdf> (accessed 10 October 2013).
3 See N. Ökten, 'An endless death and an eternal mourning: November 10 in Turkey', in *The Politics of Public Memory in Turkey*, ed. E. Özyürek (Syracuse: Syracuse University Press), 96.
4 Andrew Mango, *Atatürk* (London: John Murray, 2004), 158–9.
5 Mango (147) argues that Atatürk's memory was probably influenced by the fact that almost the entire 57th regiment was wiped out in the fighting. He notes that Atatürk's real order as found on the body of a dead Turkish soldier was as follows, 'I do not expect that any of us would not rather die than repeat that shameful story of the Balkan war. But if there are such men among us, we should at once lay hands upon them and set them up in line to be shot!'
6 S.M. Hanioğlu, *Atatürk: An Intellectual Biography* (Princeton: Princeton University Press, 2011), 84.
7 E. Gellner, *Thoughts and Change* (Chicago: University of Chicago Press, 1964), 169.
8 B. Anderson, *Imagined Communities: Reflections on the Origins and Spread of Nationalism* (London: Verso, 2013).
9 P.M.Y. Parmaksız, 'Çanakkale Bellek Savaşı', in *Neye Yarar Hatıralar? Bellek ve Siyaset Çalışmaları*, ed. P.M.Y. Parmaksız (Ankara: Phoenix Yayýnevi, 2012), 288–9.
10 E.J. Zürcher, Turkey: A Modern History (New York: I.B. Taurus, 2004), 187–91.
11 Hanioğlu, 77.
12 Ibid., 78.
13 J. Winter and E. Sivan (eds), *War and Remembrance in the Twentieth Century* (Cambridge: Cambridge University Press, 1999), 30.
14 S. Zeyrek, 'Liselerde Okutulan Türkiye Cumhuriyeti ve Atatürkçülük Adlı Ders Kitaplarında Çanakkale Savaşları', *Ankara Üniversitesi Türk Ýnkýlâp Tarihi Enstitüsü Atatürk Yolu*, 10:40 (2007), 708–9. Online. Available: <http://dergiler.ankara.edu.tr/dergiler/45/790/10140.pdf> (accessed 15 October 2013). In 1981 when the course was made independent of the history syllabus and renamed 'The History of the Turkish Revolution and Atatürkism', the topic of Çanakkale was included in the introductory chapter on the disintegration of the Ottoman Empire, but with a note specifying, 'Special attention should be paid to the Çanakkale battle.'
15 Ibid., 715.
16 A. Daver, 'Şanlı bir günün yıldönümü: Atatürk 25 Nisan 1915 te Istanbulu kurtarmıştı', *Cumhurriyet*, 25 April 1936, 1.
17 A. Daver, 'Anafataların yıldönümü', *Cumhurriyet*, 9 August 1935, 1.
18 B. Ziino, '"We are talking about Gallipoli after all": contested narratives, contested ownership and the Gallipoli Peninsula', in The Heritage of War, eds M. Gegner and B. Ziino (London: Routledge, 2011), 146.
19 A. Jones, 'A note on Atatürk's words about Gallipoli', *History Australia*, 2:1 (2004), 104.
20 S. Bozdoğan, *Modernism and Nation Building: Turkish Architectural Culture in the Early Republic* (Seattle: University of Washington Press, 2001), 108.
21 Ibid., 290.
22 Ziino, 147.
23 Ibid., 148; N. Yazıcı, 'A critical approach to the instruction of the Dardanelles campaign in secondary education curricula and text books' (in Turkish), *Hacettepe Üniversitesi Eğitim Fakültesi Dergisi*, 28:2 (2013), 537. Online. Available HTTP: <www.efdergi.hacettepe.edu.tr/201328-2NEVİN%20YAZICI.pdf> (accessed 15 December 2013).
24 E. Özyürek, 'Public memory as political battleground: Islamist subversions of republican nostalgia', in *The Politics of Public Memory in Turkey*, ed. E. Özyürek (Syracuse: Syracuse University Press, 2007), 4.

25 Yazıcı, 537.
26 Ibid., 537.
27 Quoted in ibid., 538.
28 Parmaksız, 290–1.
29 Ş. Ordu, '18 Mart'ta şehitler herkesi Çanakkale'ye çağrıyor', *Hürriyet*, 4 February 2003.
30 Yazıcı, 539.
31 J. White, *Muslim Nationalism and the New Turks* (Princeton: Princeton University Press, 2013), 33. Zürcher (182) notes the fact that Kemal was not associated with a very definite ideology that could be discredited (unlike Fascism, National Socialism and Marxism–Leninism) has meant that his personality cult could survive changes in the political climate. It has also ensured that Kemalist ideology has not yet become a dead letter and that the Kemalist narrative of Turkish history is still surprisingly entrenched.
32 White, 9.
33 S. Çağaptay, *Islam, Secularism and Nationalism in Modern Turkey: Who Is a Turk?* (London: Routledge, 2009), 162; Parmaksız, 295–6.
34 Quoted in E. Batuman, 'Ottomania: A hit TV show reimagines Turkey's imperial past', *New Yorker* 90:1 (17 February 2014), 57.
35 Ö. Taspinar, 'Turkey's Middle-East policies: Between Neo-Ottomanism and Kemalism', *Carnegie Papers* 10 (2008), 15. Online. Available: <http://carnegieendowment.org/files/cmec10_taspinar_final.pdf> (accessed 15 October 2013).
36 White, 9.
37 *Today's Zaman*, 'Turkey commemorates martyrs slain at Çanakkale battle', 18 March 2013. Online. Available HTTP: <www.todayszaman.com/news-310110-.html> (accessed 15 October 2013).
38 Jones, 105; Zürcher, 176–7.
39 M. Güler, 'Banners to be printed in Kurdish, Arabic for Çanakkale celebrations', *Today's Zaman*, 6 March 2013. Online. Available HTTP: <www.todayszaman.com/newsDetail.action;jsessionid=A+yYz1hytk16NGrAdi8JnPLG?newsId=308973&columnistId=0> (accessed 15 October 2013).
40 This cemetery replaced an existing cemetery that was laid out in the shape of a crescent moon. The individual tombstones simply had the name 'Mehmet' and the name of the soldier's province of origin on it. 'Mehmet'in adı var!', *Radikal*, 15 March 2004. Online. Available HTTP: <www.radikal.com.tr/haber.php?haberno=109667> (accessed 15 October 2013).
41 H. Kayali, *Arabs and Young Turks: Ottomanism, Arabism and Islamism in the Ottoman Empire, 1908–1918* (Berkeley: University of California Press, 1997), 148; Zürcher, 277.
42 Bozdoğan, 44–5.
43 E. Özyürek, *Nostalgia for the Modern: State Secularism and Everyday Politics in Turkey* (Durham: Duke University Press, 2006), 136.
44 A. Smith, *The Ethnic Origin of Nations* (Oxford: Blackwell, 1988), 206.
45 A. Aktar, '18 Mart Zaferi'nin unutulan kahramanları yahut, Çanakkale bir 'Haçlı Seferi'midir', *Taraf*, 18 March 2014, 13.
46 Parmaksız, 294–6.
47 E. Ertanı, 'Çanakkale'nin unutturulan gayrimüslim şehitleri', *Agos*, 18 March 2013. Online. Available HTTP: <www.agos.com.tr/haber.php?seo=canakkalenin-unutturulan-gayrimuslim-sehitleri&haberid=4692> (accessed 15 October 2013).
48 'Çanakkale 2015'e hazırlanıyor', *Agos*, 24 July 2012. Online. Available HTTP: <www.agos.com.tr/haber.php?seo=canakkale-2015e-hazirlaniyor&haberid=2127> (accessed 15 October 2013).
49 S. Arsu. 'Turkey offers condolences to Armenians over killings', *New York Times*, 23 April 2014. Online. Available HTTP: <www.nytimes.com/2014/04/24/world/europe/turkey-offers-condolences-to-armenians-over-killings.html?emc=eta1&_r=1> (accessed 25 May 2014).

50 T. Akçam, 'Where do I stand in the Torosyan debates?' Online. Available HTTP: <www.tanerakcam.com/debates/where-do-i-stand-in-the-torosyan-debates> (accessed 15 March 2014).
51 Parmaksız, 296. Since the Kemalist view is that the republic was not an inheritor of the Ottoman legacy, the claim that Turkey had no responsibility for the genocide in 1915 is at least intellectually coherent.
52 'Davutoğlu: 1915 bizim için Çanakkale'dir', *Sol Portal*, 5 March 2010. Online. Available: <http://haber.sol.org.tr/devlet-ve-siyaset/davutoglu-1915-bizim-icin-canakkale-dir-haberi-24901> (accessed 15 March 2014).
53 Aktar, 13.
54 Winter, J. (2006) *Remembering War: The Great War between Memory and History in the Twentieth Century* (New Haven: Yale University Press, 2006), 6.
55 Batuman, 51.

9 Commemoration and the hazards of Irish politics

Keith Jeffery

It has been asserted that the First World War was the single most significant all-Ireland experience of the twentieth century,[1] and that the impact of the war and its legacy affected Ireland politically more than any other single event or series of events. But even to make an assertion of this sort can raise the hackles of some nationalists for whom events within Ireland will always take priority over any wider experience. The proclamation of 'the Irish republic as a Sovereign Independent State' in Dublin on Easter Monday, 24 April, 1916, at the beginning of a week-long uprising against British rule over Ireland, is taken to be the foundation-point of the independent Irish state.[2] Although the 'Easter Rising' was a failure at the time, it provided an exemplary model for the 'Irish War of Independence' of 1919–21 which secured a substantial measure of autonomy for around three-quarters of the island, first as the 'Irish Free State', with the status of a dominion of the British empire (analogous to Canada or Australia), and subsequently (from 1948) as a fully independent republic. It is an article of republican faith that the inspiration and legitimation of the republic is essentially and uniquely the product of Irish circumstances and Irish history. The preamble to the 1916 proclamation makes this perfectly clear. 'Irishmen and Irishwomen', it begins, 'in the name of God and of the dead generations from which she receives her old tradition of nationhood, Ireland, through us [the rebels], summons her children to her flag and strikes for her freedom.'[3]

Clearly the 1916 Rising was primarily an Irish affair, but it would not have occurred without the circumstances of the First World War. Rather than seeing the Rising as an exclusively Irish event, and only peripherally (if at all) as part of the wider conflagration, it can only be properly understood in the context of the war, which provided both the moment and the mode for its planning and execution.[4] It had long been a staple of Irish nationalist strategy that 'England's extremity was Ireland's opportunity', and the titanic global struggle in which 'England' (actually the United Kingdom, which, of course, at the time included all of Ireland) was engaged provided a marvellously tempting moment for Irish separatists to strike. And there was at least some help to be had from Germany. In the 1916 proclamation the leaders of the Rising mentioned that they were supported by 'gallant allies in Europe'. While the leading Irish republican, Roger Casement, had tried (with very little success) to recruit

Irish-born British soldiers in German prisoner-of-war camps to join an 'Irish Brigade' to fight against the British, a boat-load of arms was sent from Germany but intercepted before the munitions could be landed. The war itself, embodying the use of lethal violence for political ends, also provided a pattern of action for Irish republicans. The notion of Dublin 1916 as a Great War battle was sustained at the time by comparisons with the Western Front. After the Rising had been suppressed and parts of central Dublin destroyed in the fighting, the city was likened to towns in the Western Front battle-zone, as, for example, 'Ypres on the [river] Liffey'.

The wartime circumstances of the Rising had an important effect on how it was suppressed by the British authorities, who certainly believed it to have had German backing. Engaged in an existential struggle on the Continent, the British government was hardly going to treat the Dublin Rising either as some routine matter of Irish political excitement, or, indeed, with any political sophistication. The primary requirement was to suppress the outbreak as quickly and effectively as possible. In the short-term this was certainly achieved. Military rule was established, the rebels crushed and exemplary punishment by military courts-martial meted out. Of the 187 people tried after the Rising, 88 were sentenced to death. But justice was tempered with mercy, and of these only 15 were executed (all by firing-squad). Casement, tried for treason in London, was hanged a few months later. But the executions in Dublin, especially, turned the rebel leaders into martyrs in the cause of an independent Irish republic and contributed to the sea-change in nationalist public opinion which helped the Sinn Féin party to win an overwhelming majority of the Irish nationalist seats in the 1918 United Kingdom general election.

For Ulster unionists, who wanted at least their part of north-east Ireland to remain within the United Kingdom (and certainly not languish, as they thought would be the case, under a Dublin 'Home Rule' parliament), there was also a moment in 1916 which was to become stitched into their own communal political identity and tradition. On the opening day of the great Battle of the Somme, 1 July 1916, units of the 36th (Ulster) Division suffered extremely heavy casualties. If, as some nationalists argued, there was a 'blood sacrifice' for the Irish republic at Easter 1916, then on 1 July there was a similar sacrifice by unionists for their own political aspirations. During and especially after the war, unionists also asserted that Britain owed a debt to Ulster for coming to its aid at its time of need. In the planning and erection of the 'Ulster Tower', at Thiepval on the Somme, a memorial to the Ulster Division, the Belfast press characterised the division's men as 'sons of the Imperial province' – Ulster – 'laying down their lives gladly in defence of the Empire'. 'To break pledged faith with the living is dishonourable' declared the *Belfast Telegraph* in November 1921, 'to break it with the dead is atrocious ... Ulster men died in the belief that, as they had given their all, the country for which they had died would not forget that their shed blood was given for a United Kingdom.' Affirming the unionists' own desire for autonomy the *Telegraph* solemnly declared that 'under no circumstances will we submit to a [Dublin] Parliament in which rebels would be the masters, and where neither our lives nor our liberties would be safe'.[5]

The unionists got their way with the emergence in 1921 of a six-county 'Northern Ireland', a region with devolved local power within the United Kingdom, though this was at the cost (or at least the limitation) of the liberties of the Catholic, predominantly nationalist, community who comprised a third of the population. Socially and politically unsustainable, the unrealised national aspirations of the minority contributed powerfully to the social and political violence with which Northern Ireland was periodically afflicted, especially in the thirty years of the 'Troubles' from 1969.

The years 1914–18 showed Ireland both at its most united – at the start – and at its most divided – at the end. The commemoration of the events of those years, the war as a whole, its battles (especially the Somme) and the 1916 Rising, has been intensely politicised ever since in a variety of different ways. In the aftermath of the Great War and for much of the twentieth century, war commemoration (and the lack of it) was subsumed within the dominant competition between nationalism and unionism in Northern Ireland, and in the construction of a secure autonomous identity in independent Ireland. More recently, aspects of the commemoration itself have been enlisted into a reconciling political agenda, which, however praiseworthy, has not been completely unproblematic. This contemporary narrative of healing, moreover, serves to highlight a continuing struggle with the past in Ireland. 'Healing' is hardly complete or without continuing dissent, and the coming series of centenaries (including both the war and the Rising, inseparable as they are, along with those of the Irish War of Independence and civil war which followed) will test the durability and acceptance of that narrative.

There has been a widely held assumption that a 'national amnesia' about the First World War obtained in at least nationalist Ireland until perhaps the 1980s. In a famous, posthumously published essay, '1916 – myth, fact and mystery', F. X. Martin described the attitude of Ireland's governments to the constitutional nationalist Irish Parliamentary Party as the 'Great Oblivion'. Contrasting the support for constitutional nationalism with that for separatist republicanism, Martin observed that 'how little hold the Irish separatists had on the people can be clearly shown by cold statistics – in mid-April 1916 there were 265,600 Irishmen serving, or in alliance, with the British forces'. At the same time there were an estimated 16,000 Irish Volunteers in the separatist paramilitary organisation. Thus, for every Irishman with the separatists, 'there were sixteen with the British; over eighty per cent of the people', he continued, 'were in sympathy with England's war effort'. Martin observed that currently (he was writing in the mid-1960s), in independent Ireland it was 'difficult to find men and women who will acknowledge that they are children of the men who were serving during 1916 in the British Army'. This, he wrote, 'is the "Great Oblivion", an example of national amnesia'.[6] Reflecting on these matters in 2014, the celebrity Irish broadcaster, Gay Byrne, whose father (and seven uncles) served in the First World War, said he remained 'angry that his father's experience' and that of other Irishmen was 'written out of Irish history' after the war had ended. At a school run by the Christian Brothers in the 1940s, Byrne recalled that 'we heard all about 1916 and everybody ... but not one single mention ever was there of the Great War. It was as if it never happened.'[7]

The idea of 'national amnesia' has had considerable currency, especially among cultural commentators,[8] but it does not quite match the historical reality. From the early 1920s to the late 1930s the Great War was widely commemorated across Ireland. There were large public demonstrations on Armistice Day (tens of thousands paraded in Dublin in the 1920s), official Irish government representatives laid wreaths at the London cenotaph, the Fianna Fáil government after 1932 provided a publicly acknowledged state subsidy for the completion of the Edwin-Lutyens-designed Irish National War Memorial at Islandbridge in Dublin, and Eamon De Valera himself – one of the leaders of the 1916 Rising but by now prime minister of the Irish Free State – agreed in principle to attend the opening of the memorial (though the onset of the Second World War prevented this).[9] This is not to say that Ireland's engagement with the First World War was enthusiastically and openly commemorated and celebrated in the ways which have more recently become commonplace. The real watershed in the public acknowledgement of nationalist Ireland's engagement with the Great War took place during the Second World War,[10] when independent Ireland declared its neutrality. Suddenly, from the autumn of 1939, gathering at a war memorial to remember individuals who had served in the British armed forces became politicised in a way it had not been hitherto and, worrying that these rituals might challenge the state's neutrality, the government prohibited Remembrance Day parades in Dublin during the war years. From the 1940s to the 1960s (when Martin wrote his essay) – and beyond – there was indeed a greater degree of disengagement, even 'forgetting', about the issue. This phenomenon was powerfully reinforced during the Northern Ireland 'Troubles' for thirty years from 1969, when the commemoration of Irishmen fighting in British uniforms (in any war), which was often accompanied by British military rituals and iconography in the wearing of uniforms and medals, and the use of military flags and banners, was politically and socially problematic during a period when violent conflict existed between some Irish people and 'Crown forces' (primarily the British army and the Royal Ulster Constabulary).

The effective withdrawal of nationalist Ireland (at least as formally represented by political leaders north and south of the border) from the commemoration of either world war after 1945 had the effect of reinforcing the perception in unionist Northern Ireland that war service had essentially been a unionist affair. This was despite the fact that British army infantry regiments with an Irish designation – the Irish Guards, Royal Irish Fusiliers and Royal Inniskilling Fusiliers especially – continued to draw many recruits from the Republic of Ireland. In the late 1950s, for example, the Royal Irish Fusiliers found that a quarter of their officers and over forty per cent of the men were from the Republic.[11]

The focus of commemoration on war memorials had some negative results in Ireland, where the associated rituals – especially their military dimension – could for some identify the events less with remembrance of some past conflict and its human costs than with current, violently disputed political issues and identities. War memorials, especially in independent Ireland, were neglected, vandalised and sometimes attacked. The Limerick war memorial was blown up by republicans in August 1957. The South African War memorial in Connaught Avenue, Cork, and the First World War memorial in Drogheda were vandalised on a number of occasions. The head of the statue of the military trumpeter at the memorial in The Moy, County Tyrone, was knocked off in the early 1990s (and since replaced). The most shocking and costly attack was the bombing by the Provisional IRA on 8 November 1987 of the Remembrance Sunday ceremony at the war memorial in Enniskillen, County Fermanagh, when eleven people were killed and sixty-three wounded. On the same day, eighteen miles from Enniskillen at the village of Tullyhommon, a second and much larger IRA bomb, also targeting a Remembrance Day ceremony, failed to detonate.[12]

The 'Poppy Day bombing' in Enniskillen, widely regarded as one of the very worst atrocities of the Troubles, had a devastating effect on attitudes towards the IRA, especially in the Republic, where widespread revulsion and condemnation undermined any residual mainstream support for militant republican violence and fed into efforts to find a peaceful solution to the conflict. Reactions to the event went far beyond mere political circles. One of the most poignant stories to come out of the Enniskillen bombing was that of Gordon Wilson, a local shopkeeper, who was attending the service with his daughter Marie, a nurse. Both were caught in the blast and Marie was fatally injured. Trapped under the rubble, father and daughter held hands as she died. Wilson's astonishing response to the tragedy – he said 'I bear no ill will. I bear no grudge' – carried a powerful, Christian message of forbearance and forgiveness. The internationally famous Irish singer Chris de Burgh wrote a song, 'At the War Memorial', which referred to Marie's last words, as reported by her father: 'Daddy, I love you very much':

> And her words did more to make us one,
> Than a hundred years of a bomb and gun,
> Let the so-called patriots
> See what they have done![13]

Following Enniskillen, indeed, there was increased participation across Ireland in Remembrance Day ceremonies. One remarkable public effect of the event was a sharp rise in the number of poppies sold and worn in the South. Before street sales in the Republic of poppies were given up in 1971, approximately 25,000 had been sold annually. When they were resumed in 1988, some 45,000 poppies were sold.[14]

There was a marked revival of interest in Ireland's involvement with the First World War from the late 1980s onwards. In part this reflected wider trends in

Britain and elsewhere. It was also a manifestation of a growing popular interest in genealogy and family history, which, combined with the facts that the Great War was the first mass national war, and that participation was very well recorded, made it irresistibly fascinating. Some public commentators, too, notably the journalist Kevin Myers in Dublin, had begun to raise the subject of Ireland's role in the First World War, and its widespread neglect in popular memory. In 1998 Myers recalled that in the late 1970s, when he had first raised the issue, there had been what appeared to be 'an informal community of silence' concerning Ireland's engagement with the Great War, primarily stemming from a narrow sense of 'Irishness' which itself largely depended on 'anti-Britishness'. But over the years since, he asserted that 'a broader sense of Irish identity, freed by the European dimensions of Irish life and separated in time from the obligatory obeisances of post-colonial political culture' had enabled a broader, more tolerant and accepting attitude to emerge.[15]

In 1990 the 'Somme Association' was formed in Northern Ireland 'to ensure that the efforts of Irishmen to preserve world peace between 1914 and 1919 are remembered and understood'. From the start there was a praiseworthy, though clearly political, cross-community agenda: 'to co-ordinate research into Ireland's part in the First World War and to provide a basis for the two communities in Northern Ireland to come together to learn of their common heritage'. The significant aspect of the Somme Association was not the interest in the Somme, which for decades had been the central focus of Ulster unionist war commemoration, but the widening of its scope beyond the Protestant and unionist community, a trend which began to surface in the South, too, where military history enthusiasts, many of whose forebears had served in British army regiments, began to form groups devoted to the history of Irish infantry regiments which had been disbanded in 1922, in the wake of Irish independence.

In 1992 a Royal Munster Fusiliers Association was founded with the aim of perpetuating 'the memory and traditions of the regiment', a British army formation disbanded in 1922. Such a development could not have happened in times when the British army was seen as an enemy of 'the Irish people', and it reflected a progressive normalisation of relations between Ireland and Britain. The notion that a common heritage for Irish people from differing political standpoints might be found in British army service suggested that the recovery of this particular slice of Irish history might contribute towards the improvement of relations between nationalists and unionists. In January 1997 a Royal Dublin Fusiliers Association was established to remember 'those who have been forgotten for a long time, particularly the tens of thousands of Irishmen and indeed many women, who fell in the First World War'.[16]

As people in the Irish Republic began to rediscover the involvement of forebears in the First World War, the commemoration of that war started to be integrated into public life much more fully than hitherto, or at least ever since the late 1930s. In 1993, for the first time, the head of state, President Mary Robinson, attended a Remembrance Day service in St Patrick's (Protestant)

Cathedral in Dublin. First World War memorials in the Republic began to be refurbished, starting with the Irish National War Memorial, which had fallen into some disrepair. Under a Fianna Fáil government it was restored in the 1980s and part of Edwin Lutyens' original scheme not built in the 1930s, an ornamental circular shelter or 'temple', was completed and declared open in June 1994 by the then Minister of Finance, Bertie Ahern. It was, wrote Kevin Myers, an event which would have been 'inconceivable' only six years before (when the restored memorial park had been opened).[17] Ahern took a personal interest in the First World War. In November 2000, by which time he was Taoiseach, he agreed to launch this author's book on *Ireland and the Great War* at the National Museum of Ireland's new military history gallery, and he later named the volume as his 'Book of the Year', generously describing it as 'a must-read for lovers of Irish history'.[18]

Commemoration of the First World War began to be drawn into a wider, more general commemoration of all Irish people who had died in war. The Great War memorial in Cahir, County Tipperary, was rededicated in 1996 'to commemorate the men and women of this district who fought and died in all military conflicts worldwide'. Demonstrating the hybrid ways in which these monuments can be used, when visited in June 1999 someone had laid a wreath of red poppies at the memorial with a card on which was written: 'To the Memory of All Freedom Fighters'. In 1996, too, marking the eightieth anniversary of the Battle of the Somme, as well as the traditional 1 July events in Northern Ireland which commemorated the involvement of the Ulster Division, a service was held at the Irish National War Memorial on 8 September to remember the largely nationalist 16th (Irish) Division's part in the battle.

The most outstanding manifestation of this new engagement with Irish Great War commemoration has been the Island of Ireland Peace Tower, erected at Mesen in Belgium close to the site of the Battle of Messines in 1917, where the 36th (Ulster) and the 16th (Irish) Divisions had fought alongside each other (Figure 9.1). Inspired by a cross-community reconciliation project based in Derry and led by Paddy Harte, a Fine Gael TD (member of the Dáil), and Glenn Barr, a former paramilitary and loyalist politician, the tower was dedicated on the eightieth anniversary of the Armistice, 11 November 1998, by President Mary McAleese, Queen Elizabeth II and Albert II, King of the Belgians. It was the first time the heads of the Irish state and the United Kingdom had joined in any sort of war commemoration, reflecting the way in which the First World War could be used for purposes of national, as well as local, reconciliation. But it also illustrates how, at that time, such joint national activity could only really take place on politically neutral territory. There was (as yet) no combined Irish and British war commemoration, at least at the highest political level, in Ireland or Britain. Currently the Peace Tower sits at the centre of a 'Peace Park', which contains a very ambitious 128-bed 'Peace Village' and International School for Peace Studies which opened in June 2006. It comprises part of the 'Messines Vision', and is substantially funded by the European Union Programme for Peace and Reconciliation. The aim is to

Figure 9.1 Island of Ireland Peace Tower at Mesen/Messines, dedicated 11 November 1998. © Keith Jeffery

host courses for groups from divided communities from Europe and beyond with 'a unique and completely experiential learning programme' which 'uses the events of the Great War (1914–18) to engage participants in learning about their shared history, cultural heritage, peace and reconciliation, and the futility of war'.[19]

The reconciling potential of war commemoration has been manifest in community initiatives in various parts of Northern Ireland. A proposal was made in Newry, County Down, in the late 1990s to add names to the town's war memorial, a scaled-down replica of Edwin Lutyens' Cenotaph in London, which had originally been erected in 1938. This could have been a divisive exercise, potentially enabling unionists to celebrate service in the British armed forces of people from a region close by the internal Irish frontier with some deep nationalist–unionist antagonisms. The nationalist-run local council decided to commission research to establish how many casualties from both world wars had come from the district. This project was undertaken by the (then) assistant Community Relations Officer, Colin Moffett, who imaginatively cast the definition of 'war casualty' as widely as possible. There was a wonderful response to advertisements placed in the local press seeking names and personal stories, with individuals bringing in not just family narratives but historical artefacts of many sorts. Moffett eventually came up with 373 names of men and women, too many to be inscribed on the war memorial, but whose names and stories were included in a well-illustrated publication containing the names of casualties, not just those killed on active military service, but also, for example, Newry-born victims of the Second World War London Blitz and (Newry being a seaport) a significant number of merchant mariners, including five Newry sailors among the crew of the Cunard liner *Lusitania*, sunk by a German U-Boat in May 1915.[20] This Newry initiative is an admirable model for a democratic and inclusive local study, which, far from being a divisive exercise, proved to be quite the opposite. At the book's launch in November 2002 representatives attended from across the political spectrum, including the local Sinn Féin MP, Conor Murphy.

The progressive engagement of Irish republican politicians with Great War commemoration is one of the more remarkable features of recent years. During the late 1990s there was movement on the part of some Sinn Féin politicians to engage with war commemoration. In 1995 Tom Hartley, a Sinn Féin councillor in Belfast and an active local historian, attended a Second World War commemoration (including veterans and Holocaust survivors) at the Irish National War Memorial at Islandbridge in Dublin. It was an important departure in Sinn Féin practice and the first involvement at a location widely regarded in republican circles as 'British'. The first Sinn Féin lord mayor of Belfast, Alex Maskey, took office in 2002 just a month before the annual 1 July Somme commemoration ceremony held at the Belfast Cenotaph and traditionally attended by the 'first citizen'. Maskey (whose maternal grandfather had served in the British army during the First World War) did not participate in the main ceremony (where if he had done so a counter-demonstration was threatened) but, with some republican colleagues, laid a wreath at the cenotaph at nine o'clock in the morning of 1 July, two hours before the main event. Even this was extremely controversial, but it was justified by Maskey as commemorating 'the common humanity at the centre of all this'.[21]

Since then republicans have become more closely involved in war commemoration throughout Ireland, though stopping short of any full participation in 'British military commemorations'. Richard Grayson has identified four clear themes of this participation. First, the Great War has to be seen as 'part of a multi-layered narrative of Irish history'. Second, is respecting individual soldiers 'on their own terms'. Third (and Grayson was writing in 2010), 'the existing public commemorations cannot be inclusive if they remain in their current form'. Fourth, he identified a less explicit 'need to understand the political pressures which resulted in nationalists enlisting, for example, to fight for the "freedom of small nations"'.[22] This last consideration is, of course, one where historians of Ireland and the First World War have an important role to play in recovering and explaining the motivations behind enlistment during the war.[23] On being elected lord mayor of Belfast in July 2013, the Sinn Féin politician Mairtin O Muilleoir declared that he would review the policy whereby Sinn Féin representatives did not attend Remembrance Day events. He said he was 'already in discussion with the Royal British Legion to create a Remembrance Day event he could attend' and he travelled 'in hope believing politics is the art of the possible'.[24] O Muilleoir was as good as his word and on 11 November 2013 he became the first Sinn Féin lord mayor to attend the ceremony. He did it, he said, as representative of all the citizens of Belfast and 'to show respect to the unionist tradition'.[25]

In the twenty-first century fresh initiatives have continued in the matter of Irish Great War commemoration. Astonishingly, new memorials to the First World War are still being erected. In Killarney, County Kerry, on 24 September 2009, a wholly new memorial was 'erected in memory of those from Killarney and surrounding areas who served and died in the 1914–18 war' (Figure 9.2). This memorial complements an adjacent memorial erected in 1902 to soldiers of the Royal Munster Fusiliers (the local regiment) who had died in British imperial conflicts in Burma, West Africa and South Africa. The Great War memorial was unveiled by President McAleese who congratulated the war memorial committee for 'healing' the memory of Killarney's Great

Figure 9.2 Killarney First World War memorial (dedicated 2009). The Irish inscription reads 'Light them to eternal paradise'. © Keith Jeffery

War dead 'and drawing them back into memory and drawing them back into the community'. Illustrating the increased Irish interest in the conflict, the event was attended by members of the Irish Great War Society, a re-enactment group dressed in replica First World War uniforms, 'representing Irish First World War heroes'.[26] Representing (though not perhaps very deliberately) a rather different strand of Irish political life, there was also a local band named after the Kerry-born Thomas Ashe, an Irish republican who died in Mountjoy Gaol, Dublin, on 25 September 1917. Ashe had been a participant in the 1916 Rising whose death sentence had been commuted to penal servitude for life. He was released in June 1917, but after making a seditious speech, was re-arrested, convicted and sentenced to a further period in gaol. Demanding 'prisoner-of-war' status, he began a hunger strike on 20 September and died five days later after having been force-fed.[27] Ashe, therefore, could be regarded as a war casualty of sorts, but undeniably one who had died in the Irish struggle for freedom from British rule. To find him, therefore, associated (however vestigially) with a First World War memorial is an indication of the extraordinary distance Irish public political life has travelled since the revolutionary years and the Irish War of Independence.

These memorials have not been confined to Ireland. On 24 March 2010 President McAleese unveiled another brand-new monument, at Green Hill cemetery by Suvla Bay in Gallipoli, dedicated to soldiers of the 10th (Irish) Division. President McAleese referred to a 'deficit of remembrance' which had afflicted Irishmen who had fought 'for the British Empire', but who had returned to Ireland to 'considerable ambivalence and even hostility about their role and their sacrifice'. Now, however, 'distance of time and changing historical context' allowed a contribution to be made 'to the much needed healing of memory on our own divided island'. This dedication took place during a two-day pilgrimage to the Dardanelles to commemorate the ninety-fifth anniversary of the Gallipoli campaign in which the President of the Somme Association, the Duke of Gloucester, planted four myrtle trees – one for each of the ancient provinces of Ireland – also at the Green Hill cemetery. At the ceremony, Dr Ian Adamson, Chairman of the Association, remarked on President McAleese's role 'in bringing the two communities in Northern Ireland closer together, particularly through the establishment of the Irish Tower at Messines in Belgium'. He also explicitly linked the event at Green Hill with the Northern Ireland peace process:

> Sons of Ulster, soldiers of Ireland. Do not be anxious. The War is over – both here and in your beloved Ireland. The Western Front is no more and Ireland, at last, is at peace with herself and with her people.[28]

The battlefields of the Great War still provide convenient 'neutral territory' for joint Irish–British and nationalist–unionist commemorations of Ireland's engagement with the Great War, as demonstrated by President McAleese at Mesen/Messines in November 1998 and at Gallipoli in March 2010, and more recently by the Irish Taoiseach, Enda Kenny, and the British Prime Minister, David Cameron, in Flanders in December 2013. Together they visited the Irish Peace Tower; the grave of the nationalist leader John Redmond's brother, Willie Redmond; the Menin Gate at Ypres; and Tyne Cot Commonwealth War Cemetery. The rhetoric was one of common Irish and British experience, its reconciling potential and the aspiration that the now peaceful relations between the two countries and peoples could act as an exemplar for wider European and world peace. Kenny, reported the Irish national broadcaster Radió Telefis Éireann, was 'the first ever Taoiseach to lay a wreath at a British and Commonwealth cemetery'. Arriving at a European Union summit in Brussels after his visit to Flanders, Kenny reflected: 'The thought crossed my mind standing at the grave of Willie Redmond that that was why we have a European Union and why I'm attending a European Council.'[29]

Not all of the renewed memorial building passes without criticism. In September 2009 Republican Sinn Féin (a splinter group opposed to the Northern Ireland 'peace process') described the unveiling of the new Killarney memorial 'to Irish men who fought and died in the British Army ... as an insult to the many Irish men who were executed by the same British Army'. The local Republican Sinn Féin chairman, John Sheehy from Listowel, said 'It would be a far more meaningful gesture for those behind this project to consider a memorial to the Irish men who ignited the flame of liberty for Ireland during those years. This event', he added, 'smacks of historical revisionism or else it is another stunt devised to lure tourists to the Killarney area. Either way this ceremony should be boycotted by all nationally minded people.'[30]

The most powerfully symbolic manifestation of the normalisation of relations between independent Ireland and the United Kingdom, in which commemoration of the First World War and the Irish revolutionary years played a central part, occurred in May 2011 when Queen Elizabeth II made the first-ever state visit of a British monarch to the Republic of Ireland. As with all such occasions, the formal events were extremely carefully choreographed. On the first day the Queen laid a wreath at the Irish National Garden of Remembrance in Parnell Square, Dublin, which is dedicated 'to the memory of all those who gave their lives in the cause of Irish Freedom'.[31] This was hailed as an extraordinary moment in the Dublin press. 'Moment of Healing' read the front-page headline in the best-selling Irish newspaper, the *Irish Independent*. 'Queen bows her head to fallen heroes in symbolic act of reconciliation', it continued.[32] The next day, again accompanied by President McAleese, she went to the Irish National War Memorial Gardens at Islandbridge, where both heads of state laid wreaths to other dead Irish soldiers. Again, the Dublin press welcomed the events as having a transcendentally healing quality. 'Sombre remembrance of the war dead in the hush of Islandbridge', reported the *Irish Times*.[33] Yet, among the widespread assumptions that, in this dual commemoration, the war dead of Ireland could be combined in an inclusive historic community reflecting the aspired-for mutual tolerance and inclusivity of twenty-first-century Ireland, North and South, some indications remained that (in Northern Ireland at least) the divisions of the war and revolutionary years had not quite entirely been swept away. The main nationalist newspaper in Belfast, the *Irish News*, significantly reported the Islandbridge event as: 'Queen lays wreath to honour Irish killed fighting for *Britain*',[34] which was not, for example, how the nationalist leader John Redmond had seen it at the start of the war, or, indeed, the Cork Independent Ex-Servicemen's Association in the 1920s. Redmond's opinion, powerfully expressed in a famous speech at Woodenbridge, County Wicklow, on 20 September 1914, was that it was as much an 'Irish war' as a British, and that 'the interests of Ireland – of the whole of Ireland – are at stake in this war'. Asserting an *Irish* moral imperative to have participated in the war, nationalist ex-servicemen in Cork in 1925 chose a dedication for their war memorial 'in memory of their comrades who fell in the Great War fighting for the Freedom of Small Nations' (Figure 9.3).[35]

The commissioning and dedication in June 2013 of a new war memorial for Wexford men who died in the First World War provides a further instructive

Figure 9.3 Cork City war memorial as restored in 2008, reproducing the original 1925 inscription, and subsequent addition of 1939–1945. © Keith Jeffery

example of how far commemoration in the Republic of Ireland has come in recent years. It had been calculated that over 800 men from Wexford town and county in south-east Ireland had died in the war. But no memorial had been erected. One of the most famous Wexford casualties was William Redmond, Member of Parliament (in the United Kingdom House of Commons) for the borough and younger brother of John Redmond.[36]

Announcing the war memorial project, the Mayor of Wexford, Councillor Jim Allen, noted that his own great grandfather, Michael Golden, had died in the war 'when his ship was sunk by a submarine as it returned from Gallipoli',[37] and 'like many in Wexford we have nowhere to pay our respects to those who died. This [memorial] will fulfil that need.' Allen added that 'while the plans might stir some controversy, it was time to move on'.[38] In fact, and unlike the Killarney memorial in 2009, there appears to have been no opposition whatsoever. This might reflect a more relaxed attitude among republicans generally to Great War commemoration and analogous events, as illustrated during Queen Elizabeth's state visit to Ireland in May 2011 and her visit a year later to Northern Ireland when she and the Sinn Féin leader Martin McGuinness publicly shook hands. There may well be, too, a more accommodating attitude in Wexford than in Kerry to the political and commemorative use of public space. Three days after it was announced that the war memorial would be sited in Redmond Square in the centre of Wexford, on 11 May 2013 the local Sinn Féin organisation used the square for a 'black flag remembrance event ... to mark the 32nd anniversary of the death of Bobby Sands', a celebrated IRA volunteer who died on hunger strike in prison in Northern Ireland. At the protest, local Sinn Féin Councillor Anthony Kelly said that it was 'encouraging to see the interest that people have in the iconic figure of Bobby Sands ... [and] in the history of the 1981 hunger strike and the ultimate fate of the ten men who lost their lives in that terrible prison protest. Thirty two years after his death Bobby Sands is as relevant as ever.'[39]

In a ceremony jointly sponsored by Wexford Borough Council and the Royal British Legion of Wexford, the Great War memorial was dedicated on 23 June 2013.[40] It consisted of a stone panel set into the pavement with the inscription: 'Wexford Remembrance. In memory of all from the Town and County of Wexford who fought and died during the Great War 1914–18.' The wording of the memorial, which was decided in consultation with the British Legion, might be considered sufficiently ambiguous – 'who fought and died during the Great War 1914–18' – as to include the combatants on *both* sides in the Easter Rising of 1916. Potentially even more inclusive was the phrasing used on the cover of the dedication ceremony brochure: 'To the sacred memory of all Wexfordmen who sacrificed their lives in defence of freedom 1914–18'. This was reinforced by elements of the dedication service itself. The bidding prayer urged those present to 'remember with thanksgiving and sorrow those whose lives, in world wars and conflicts past and present, have been given and taken away in the cause of justice and freedom'. The lesson, from St John's Gospel, chapter 15, verses 12 to 17, embodied the sacrificial understanding so long associated, not just with Great War dead, but also with the Easter Rising 'martyrs': 'There is no greater love than this; that a man should lay down his life for his friends.' The predominant message in the prayers was one of peace, embedded in the service with a repeated collective response of 'God give peace'. The petitions in turn bade the participants to pray for 'men and women' who had 'died in the violence of war'; for the bereaved; for 'all members of Armed Forces, whether peace-keeping or peace-making who are in danger this day'; for 'civilians whose lives are disfigured by war or terror'; for 'peace-makers and peace-keepers'; and, finally, for 'all who bear the burden and privilege of leadership'.

The British Legion was represented by its president in the Republic of Ireland, Major General The O'Morchoe, a retired British army officer and the holder of an ancient Irish clan title. The colour parties who paraded to the memorial site carried Irish national and service-association flags, as well as a British Legion flag with the Union Jack in the upper left corner. That the event had official sanction was confirmed by the presence of uniformed Irish army personnel (including musicians), the mayor of Wexford (with other local representatives) and an Irish government minister, Brendan Howlin (Minister for Public Expenditure and Reform), who read the scripture lesson. The playing of the 'Last Post' and 'Reveille' confirmed the military dimension of the programme, as did the inclusion of the Irish national anthem, which itself explicitly celebrates martial service ('Soldiers are we, whose lives are pledged to Ireland'). The dedication comprised a Christian religious service and was explicitly ecumenical, with Roman Catholic and Protestant (Church of Ireland) clergy officiating. In sum, the day's event was as traditional as war memorial services ever are, and, in the spirit which now almost invariably characterises such events in Ireland, it sought to be as inclusive as possible: Catholic and Protestant; matching military display with high hopes for peace; 'Irish' and 'British', though, in the end, and perhaps inevitably, more of the former than the latter. While the chief intention was to commemorate (and, indeed, celebrate) the Wexford men who had served in British uniform in the 1914–18 conflict, in participation and ceremonial, the affair was predominantly, if not essentially, Irish. We may, therefore, see here the incorporation at last of Irish First World War service into the communal civic culture of the modern independent Irish state, in a way which the Cork Independent Ex-Servicemen's Association had asserted in 1925, but which could not actually be possible until the entrenched political positions and passions of the revolutionary years had passed away.

Sinn Féin's apparent silence in Wexford about the matter of Great War commemoration does not at all indicate any lack of interest in Ireland's history. Planned commemorations of the other 1981 Hunger Strikers who followed Bobby Sands demonstrate the party's very active engagement with history for political purposes. In March 2014, moreover, Councillor Kelly proposed a motion in the Borough Council to convert the town's historic old gaol into a museum. 'As we approach the decade long period of commemoration which will no doubt be associated with the centenary of our rising, war of independence and civil war', he said, 'it would be fitting for Wexford to have a museum which could educate people in a mature and non biased fashion about what really happened during this troubled period.'[41]

While the phrase 'what really happened' has for historians a Rankean resonance, implying an obligation to establish the 'historical facts' of the past ('wie es eigentlich gewesen'), in this specific Irish context it embodies a clear political agenda and transmits an instructive imperative that any such museum should inculcate the 'true' (and necessarily uplifting) narrative of the heroic assertion and achievement (if only partial and, perhaps, interim) of national independence. Nevertheless, the aspiration towards objective history is not lightly to be dismissed, and it is echoed in the commendable injunction – 'Start from the historical facts' – in the guidance for the 'Decade of Centenaries' developed by the Northern Ireland Community Relations Council in conjunction with the grant-giving Heritage Lottery Fund. Anticipating that community groups would wish to mark the centenaries of some very contentious events in Irish history, as well as that of the First World War (and might seek public funding to support this), from late 2010 the two organisations 'began working together in order to stimulate a conversation about "Remembering in Public Space"'. They did 'not seek to stop groups and communities remembering in their own way', but argued 'that there needs to be a contextualisation and discussion about how we remember periods and events and what the historic record tells us'. Out of this process, they developed four principles: '(1) Start from the historical *facts*; (2) Recognise the *implications* and *consequences* of what happened; (3) Understand that different *perceptions* and *interpretations* exist; and (4) Show how events and activities can deepen *understanding* of the period'. All of this has to be 'seen in the context of an "*inclusive and accepting society*"'.[42]

In keeping with their first principle, during 2013 the Community Relations Council sponsored a 'Marking Anniversaries Lecture Series', distributing videos, podcasts and DVDs of the events, and in February 2014 the Heritage Lottery Fund announced the first grants to local groups specifically working on the First World War. The funding was to be used 'to explore a range of themes including the role of Nationalists in the First World War, the forgotten histories of locally buried war dead and the impact of the war on soldiers, their families and home communities'. The titles of two projects indicate activity across the Northern Ireland political spectrum. One is 'The forgotten men of Dundonald cemetery', by the 'Lagan Village Somme Society', clearly biased (though not necessarily exclusively) towards the history of the 36th (Ulster) Division (Figure 9.4). Another is 'Belfast Nationalists and WW1', which speaks for itself politically, and the findings of which would be 'used to create exhibitions and slideshows to raise awareness of this shared heritage and stimulate fact-based public debate'.[43]

These initiatives in Northern Ireland are matched by similar efforts in the Republic. In 2012 an official 'Decade of Centenaries' programme was established by the Irish Department of Arts, Heritage and the Gaeltacht, directed by

Figure 9.4 Orange banner commemorating the 36th (Ulster Division) on the first day of the Battle of the Somme, 12 July 2012. © Keith Jeffery

an all-party group of politicians, advised by an 'Expert Group', comprising eleven academics. In classic government corporate-speak this body was set up to 'work with stakeholders from representative bodies and the community and voluntary sector to facilitate commemorative initiatives'. Among the activities proposed was the 'development of access to historical records and primary sources from the time period' and to 'bring forward a series of public exhibitions and public discussions'. As in Northern Ireland, the programme would 'encompass the different traditions on the island of Ireland and aims to enhance understanding of and respect for events of importance among the population as a whole'.[44] 'Universities Ireland', the network of university leaders across the island of Ireland, has also set up a 'Historians Group' to co-ordinate 'a multi-annual programme of activities … to reflect on the 1912–23 period in Irish history'. The aim 'is that this will be a high-level, scholarly and sustained initiative, and thus a unique contribution to reflection on a decade of history-changing events by the island's intellectual leaders'. As well as conferences and seminars, among the activities sponsored are 'research scholarships for young historians' and lobbying archives 'to enhance access to key historical materials from the period'.[45]

All this embodies an undoubted public good, but, as with the Northern Ireland activity, there is also an implicit political agenda and a clear anxiety to pre-empt any overly (party) political commemoration and, in effect, fill the Irish 'commemorative space' with officially approved activities lest something more unsuitable might occur. While this all provides work for professional historians, there is a danger that, despite the explicit obeisance to 'the historical facts' and 'high-level' scholarship, they may be drawn into officially sanctioned activities with an officially sanctioned agenda which prioritises a separate and distinct public good of inclusivity, understanding and mutual respect.

Greatly critical of the role some historians took in the official programme of commemoration for the bicentenary of the 1798 Rising, the Cork historian Tom Dunne, wisely quoting John A. Murphy (another Cork historian) that the historian's first duty 'is to historical research not historical healing', has warned about the potential dangers of subordinating historical scholarship to any official line.[46] Equally concerned about the mutually corrupting potential of history and commemoration, David Fitzpatrick, a historian with an extremely distinguished record studying the Irish revolutionary period, has observed the dangers for historians of engaging with official commemorative programmes. 'Whereas good historians try to establish what happened, how and why (no matter how painful and depressing their findings may be),' he writes, 'good commemorators use "history" to pursue meritorious political, social or therapeutic objectives. Though often morally desirable, the use of history to promote intercommunal or international reconciliation may involve the suppression of ugly or inconvenient facts.'[47] Another commentator, David Rieff, in reflections specifically aimed to contribute to the Irish discussion and drawing on experience in the Balkans, has cast doubt on the utility of commemoration at all, however carefully modulated it might be. 'The problem with historical memory, as exercised by groups anyway,' he writes, 'is that it tends to be high on grievance but low on forgiveness.'[48]

As we well know, the Irish revolutionary period, and the Great War, have enough ugly and inconvenient facts, lethal violence, atavistic hatreds, sectarian and ethic animosities, and so on, to fill libraries of academic historical works. So, too, are there plentiful reservoirs of Irish grievances to be remembered and perhaps reanimated in the commemorative process. The 'Decade of Centenaries' and the commemoration of contentious events in Ireland's past, thus, provides for Ireland's professional historians serious challenges, pitting their academic duty of scholarship against the political objectives (however desirable or therapeutic) of their political masters (and perhaps those of their institutional managers too). It remains to be seen how well they rise to their own 'decade of challenges'.

Notes

1. This is the underlying contention of my book: Keith Jeffery, *Ireland and the Great War* (Cambridge: Cambridge University Press, 2000).
2. See Fearghal McGarry, *The Rising* (Oxford: Oxford University Press, 2010), for a first-class account.
3. An image of the original proclamation may be found at <www.nli.ie/1916/pdf/1.intro.pdf> (accessed 23 March 2014).
4. I argue this point in my essay 'The First World War and the Rising: mode, moment and memory', in *1916: The Long Revolution*, eds Gabriel Doherty and Dermot Keogh (Cork: Mercier Press, 2007), 86–101.
5. Quoted in Catherine Switzer and Brian Graham, '"Ulster's love in letter'd gold": the Battle of the Somme and the Ulster Memorial Tower, 1918–35', *Journal of Historical Geography* 36 (2010), 189.
6. F. X. Martin, '1916 – myth, fact and mystery', *Studia Hibernica* 7 (1967), 7–124.
7. 'Gay Byrne reveals his father's trauma from experiences in First World War', *Irish Times*, 5 April 2014.
8. See, for example, Declan Kiberd, *Inventing Ireland* (London: Jonathan Cape, 1995), 239.
9. Jeffery, *Ireland and the Great War*, 109–23; Jane Leonard, 'The twinge of memory: Armistice Day and Remembrance Sunday in Dublin since 1919', in *Unionism in Modern Ireland*, eds Richard English and Graham Walker (London: Palgrave, 1996), 99–114.
10. A point I make in Jeffery, *Ireland and the Great War*, 134–5.
11. Keith Jeffery, 'The British army and Ireland since 1922', in *A Military History of Ireland*, eds Thomas Bartlett and Keith Jeffery (Cambridge: Cambridge University Press, 1996), 447.
12. AP news archive, 'Police: IRA planted bomb in town near Enniskillen that didn't explode', 11 November 1987. Online. Available HTTP: <www.apnewsarchive.com/1987/Police-IRA-Planted-Bomb-in-Town-Near-Enniskillen-That-Didn-t-Explode/id-61973ff2d09ef7925a981f7ee2ea991f> (accessed 1 April 2014).
13. Paul Clark, 'Two traditions and the places between', in *Towards Commemoration: Ireland in War and Revolution, 1912–1923*, eds John Horne and Edward Madigan (Dublin: Royal Irish Academy, 2013), 69.
14. Leonard, 110.
15. Kevin Myers, 'The Irish and the Great War: a case of amnesia', in *Ideas Matter: Essays in Honour of Conor Cruise O'Brien*, eds Richard English and Joseph Morrison Skelly (Dublin: Poolbeg Press, 1998), 103–8.
16. Jeffery, *Ireland and the Great War*, 137. Other Irish regimental associations have subsequently been formed. See 'Regimental Associations, Museums and Websites'. Online. Available HTTP: <www.irelandww1.org//?s=regimental+associations> (accessed 30 April 2014).
17. *Irish Times*, 2 July 1994.
18. *Irish Times*, 9 December 2000.
19. Quotes from International School for Peace Studies, 'The Messines Experience'. Online. Available HTTP: <www.schoolforpeace.com/content/project-summary/33> (accessed 5 April 2014).
20. Colin Moffett (ed.), *Newry's War Dead*, Newry: Newry and Mourne District Council, 2002.
21. Richard Grayson, 'The place of the First World War in contemporary Irish republicanism in Northern Ireland', *Irish Political Studies* 25:3 (2010), 334–5.
22. Ibid., 335.
23. Catriona Pennell, *A Kingdom United: Popular Responses to the Outbreak of the First World War in Britain and Ireland* (Oxford: Oxford University Press, 2012), provides an excellent recent analysis.
24. *Belfast Telegraph*, 19 July 2013.
25. BBC News Northern Ireland, 'Sinn Fein lord mayor at Belfast Armistice Day ceremony', 11 November 2013. Online. Available HTTP: <www.bbc.co.uk/news/uk-northern-ireland-24898648> (accessed 6 April 2014).

26 *Irish Times*, 25 September 2009.
27 'Thomas Ashe', in *Dictionary of Irish Biography: From the Earliest Times to the Year 2002*, eds James McGuire and James Quinn (Cambridge: Cambridge University Press/Royal Irish Academy, 2009), vol. 1.
28 For a report on President McAleese's speech, see 'McAleese tribute to Gallipoli victims', *Irish Examiner*, 25 March 2010. Online. Available: HTTP: <www.irishexaminer.com/ireland/mcaleese-tribute-to-gallipoli-victims-115437.html> (accessed 30 May 2014). For Dr Adamson's remarks, see 'Gallipoli', 30 March 2010. Online. Available HTTP: <www.ianadamson.net/myblog/2010/03/30/gallipoli> (accessed 5 April 2014).
29 'Kenny and Cameron make "poignant" joint visit to WW1 sites', RTÉ News, 19 December 2013. Online. Available HTTP: <www.rte.ie/news/2013/1219/493745-enda-kenny-david-cameron> (accessed 6 April 2014).
30 'RSF object to Killarney war memorial', *Irish Republican Bulletin Board*, 10 September 2009. Online. Available: <http://admin2.fr.yuku.com/reply/61531#.U2D-oY9OXIU> (accessed 30 April 2014).
31 Office of Public Works 'Heritage Ireland' website. Online. Available HTTP: <www.heritageireland.ie/en/Dublin/GardenofRemembrance> (accessed 7 April 2014).
32 *Irish Independent*, 18 May 2011.
33 *Irish Times*, 19 May 2011.
34 Emphasis added; *Irish News*, 19 May 2011.
35 Jeffery, *Ireland and the Great War*, 13, 129–31.
36 For Redmond, see Terence Denman, *A Lonely Grave: The Life and Death of William Redmond* (Dublin: Irish Academic Press, 1995), 85, 130.
37 This is not quite as Mr Allen described it. Leading Seaman Michael Golden (husband of Mary Golden of Wygram Place, Wexford) went down with the troopship HMS *Louvain*, torpedoed in the Aegean Sea on 20 January 1918. See Commonwealth War Graves Commission casualty details. Online. Available HTTP: <www.cwgc.org/find-war-dead/casualty/3046141/GOLDEN,%20MICHAEL> (accessed 24 March 2014).
38 *Gorey Guardian*, 8 May 2013. Online. Available HTTP: <www.independent.ie/regionals/goreyguardian/news/memorial-to-honour-the-wexford-800-29230950.html> (accessed 24 March 2014).
39 'Bank holiday traffic met by black flag protest', 11 May 2013. Online. Available: <http://wexfordsinnfeinnews.blogspot.co.uk/2013/05/bank-holiday-traffic-met-by-black-flag.html> (accessed 24 March 2014).
40 Details taken from the brochure for the 'Ecumenical Dedication Ceremony of Remembrance and Wreathlaying', 23 June 2013.
41 'Council agree to feasibility report on Wexford Gaol Museum', 11 March 2014. Online. Available: <http://wexfordsinnfeinnews.blogspot.co.uk/2014/03/council-agree-to-feasibility-report-on.html> (accessed 24 March 2014).
42 Community Relations Council, 'Marking anniversaries' (emphasis in original). Online. Available HTTP: <www.community-relations.org.uk/programmes/marking-anniversaries> (accessed 6 April 2014).
43 Heritage Lottery Fund, 'Five projects to explore First World War heritage', 21 February 2014. Online. Available HTTP: <www.hlf.org.uk/news/Pages/FWWHeritageNI.aspx#.U2ERfl9OXIU> (accessed 6 April 2014).
44 Decade of Centenaries programme. Online. Available HTTP: <www.decadeofcentenaries.com/about> (accessed 6 April 2014).
45 'Background note' on 'Reflecting on a decade of war and revolution in Ireland 1912–23' conference programme, Dublin, 23 June 2012. See also <www.universitiesireland.ie/2014/05/conference-reflecting-on-a-decade-of-war-and-revolution-in-ireland-1912-1923-the-road-to-war> (accessed 6 April 2014).

46 Tom Dunne, 'Commemorations and "shared history": a different role for historians?', *History Ireland* 21:1 (January/February 2013), 10–13. For his critique of the 1798 commemoration, see Tom Dunne, *Rebellions: Memoir, Memory and 1798* (Dublin: Lilliput Press, 2004).
47 David Fitzpatrick, 'Historians and the commemoration of Irish conflicts, 1912–23', in *Towards Commemoration*, 132.
48 David Rieff, *Against Remembrance* (Dublin: The Liffey Press, 2011), 121.

10 Little Flemish Heroes' Tombstones
The Great War and twenty-first century Belgian politics

Karen Shelby

The Great War affected the Kingdom of Belgium in ways not experienced by other belligerents. Entirely occupied but for a small corner in the northwest region, the great material devastation induced poverty, starvation and exile. Over 35,000 soldiers and 20,000 civilians died. Belgium's cultural and geographical character also produced a unique experience both during the war, and in commemorative practices after the armistice. In 1914, Belgium was a country divided. It was home to three cultural and language groups: the Dutch-speaking Flemish in the north, the French-speaking Walloons in the south and a smaller group of German-speakers in the east. French was the de facto language of administrative and public affairs. The Great War served to exacerbate the tensions for members of the Flemish community against French-language hegemony. In the trenches, Flemish cultural organizations emerged, publishing trench journals that spoke to a specific *flamingant* (Flemish-minded) perspective, while a visual culture with overt Flemish propaganda addressed perceived Flemish disenfranchisement in the Belgian army. This also served the development of a Flemish memory and history of this war, separate from any Belgian national memory of the war. This chapter examines the expression of that memory of war through the history of a tombstone – the most prominent object of a plastic commemorative practice. This was the *heldenhuldezerk* (hero's tombstone) (Figure 10.1), created as a sentimental gesture that marked the Flemish soldier with his language and culture – a Flemish language and culture distinct from that of French-dominated Belgium. The *heldenhuldezerken* have been utilized in the past nearly 100 years in order to facilitate a specific Flemish-minded ideology, against a largely fragmented national commemoration of the war in Belgium.

Initially a mark of cultural allegiance, and surprisingly tolerated by the Belgian army, the *heldenhuldezerken* evolved to serve as a covert, and then, at the end of the war, overt political symbol. While the Belgian state itself struggled to formulate and commemorate a *Belgian* experience in the war, a small, but vocal, group of Flemish veterans insisted on the need to physically manifest a distinctive Flemish experience of the war. The memorials created and the rituals enacted, especially in western Flanders during and after the war, produced signs and symbols that continue to resonate in contemporary Flemish

Figure 10.1 Heldenhuldezerken possibly in Oeren. Courtesy of the ADVN (Archive and Documentation Centre for Flemish Nationalism), VFFY 20/02.

and Belgian political discourse. Against the backdrop of an attempt at an official Belgian commemorative practice, this chapter examines why the Flemish felt compelled to create parallel remembrance monuments and rituals. Flemish nationalist commemorative practices, while visually and compellingly different, were not necessarily at odds with the overall sentiment expressed by Belgian officialdom, which, like its counterparts in Great Britain and France, sought to celebrate the end of the war while underscoring the sorrow and losses experienced by the Belgian people.

German invasion forced Belgium's entry into the war, and by October 1914, German forces occupied the majority of the country. This reality meant that a high proportion of Flemish volunteers from the unoccupied northwest populated the Belgian army after October 1914, though they remained commanded by French-speaking officers. In his appeals for volunteers, King Albert alluded to more rights for Flanders and the Flemish after the war and, thus, some

Flemish men responded to this specific aspect of his plea. The Belgian defenders were separated from the Germans by the flooding of the IJzer Plain during the Battle of the IJzer (October 1914). As a result, the zone was far less active than the infamous Ieper (Ypres) Salient to the south. The men had more time on their hands, which was filled, for the Flemish soldiers, by educational meetings organized by Flemish priests and former university students. A mid-nineteenth-century Flemish Movement had lobbied for language rights, among other issues, during these years and these concerns were carried into the Belgian trenches. Many of the meetings served to educate the men in Flemish literature and history, framed within a pious Catholic rhetoric. As the war progressed Flemish grievances against the Belgian army grew: letters to the King underscored Flemish soldiers' discontent at their perceived status as second-class citizens in the Belgian army and within Belgium as a whole. Soldiers' gatherings became political in nature and many of the Flemish soldiers who had enlisted without a particular Flemish-minded conscience became *flamingant*, narrowing their allegiances to their own language and cultural community. In 1915, these smaller groups fused in a new organization: the Front Movement (*Frontbeweging*). The King acknowledged some of the complaints received, but overall, his attitude was punitive and he placed much of the blame on the Flemish priests: 'The clergy has been most imprudent in releasing, or at the very least exploiting, a current, the effects of which it no longer has the power to control.'[1]

The Belgian army regarded *flamingant* activities, however minimal their impact in the larger military sphere, as undermining a unitary Belgian identity forged against German occupation. King Albert and his commanders took action to quash any voice of protest and curtail the insubordination in the ranks.[2] Nevertheless, political essays continued to appear in the Flemish-minded trench journals and *flamingant* graffiti served to engage the cause in a public discourse. The Flemish soldiers who ignored a cease and desist directive from their commanding officers and persisted in their activism were disciplined and some were incarcerated in work camps in northern France. For their part, the Front Movement categorized the Flemish soldiers who died in the war, and in particular a select group of ten, as martyrs to a cause – a Flemish cause – with little regard to the overall consequences of the war effort. During the Great War, much of the Flemish nationalist spirit went hand in hand with a fervent Catholicism – a relationship that has roots in the nineteenth-century Flemish Movement.[3] As a result, priests, such as Cyriel Verschaeve, were instrumental in leading the soldiers toward the Flemish cause and underscoring the sacrifice inherent within *flamingant* activities. The Flemish-minded soldiers, turning a blind eye to the military implications of their insubordination, saw this disciplinary action as a suppression of their Flemish voice and those who died were co-opted as martyrs for a righteous cause. The activities of the Front Movement were curtailed by the crackdown, but the *flamingant* cause had spread to occupied Belgium, where the even more vigorous Flemish 'Activists' collaborated with the Germans to form the *Raad van Vlaanderen* (Council of Flanders), and declare an independent Flanders in December 1917.[4] This contrasted with the more moderate demands of members of the Front Movement, the majority of whom sought Flemish autonomy within the Kingdom of Belgium. The two groups manipulated the *heldenhuldezerken*, and other *flamingant* symbols, as ends to different means after the war – a difference that continues to reflect their disparate ideologies into the present day.

Belgian or Flemish: burial during the war

Because almost the entirety of Belgium was under occupation during the war, by necessity large orderly burial plots were created along the Belgian Front. The graves in these cemeteries were marked by black wooden crosses inscribed in French: *Mort pour la Patrie*. Members of the Front Movement, however, objected to being interred beneath an inscription in a language neither they nor the majority of their mourners spoke and undertook to bury *flamingant* soldiers under a grave marker dedicated in Flemish. They founded the *Comite voor Heldenhuldezerkjes* (Committee for the little Flemish Heroes' Tombstones) on 15 August 1916 specifically to secure an appropriate symbol for the Flemish war dead. They chose a design by volunteer Flemish soldier Joe English, who served as a war artist for various Flemish-minded groups, including the Front Movement. His drawings articulated the goals of the Flemish soldiers in *flamingant* trench journals published along the Belgian Front. The son of an Irishman and a Flemish mother, English travelled to Ireland on several occasions to stay with his father's family. During these visits he may have noted how the Irish High Cross, the foundation of the *heldenhuldezerken*, figured in Irish Catholic commemorative practice. In the late nineteenth century, the High Cross, along with the shamrock and the harp, was adopted by the Irish as a cultural symbol in order to distance themselves from British influence. English looked to the Irish High Cross as one of the inspirations for the Flemish dead, but incorporated two signs of the nineteenth-century movement into the *heldenhuldezerken* design. The first is the *blauwvoet*, a sea bird. This was the emblem of the *Blauwvoeteri* (1875), a student group led by Albert Rodenbach, a leader in the revival of Flemish literature. The *blauwvoet* announces the coming of a storm, an apt reference to the energy the student movements generated for the Flemish Movement as it gained momentum in the late nineteenth century.[5] The second symbol is the AVV–VVK (*Alles voor Vlaanderen – Vlaanderen voor Kristus*/All for Flanders – Flanders for Christ). The priest Frans Drijvers coined the slogan for the pro-Catholic Flemish journal *De Student* in 1881. In the repurposing of these two symbols, the *Comite voor Heldenhuldezerkjes* forged a deliberate continuity with the past in the interest of creating nationalist loyalties in the present. The slogan also identified the Flemish as, first and foremost, Catholics, dying for a cause they believed to be rooted in their God-given rights as articulated by the priests in the nineteenth-century Flemish Movement.

As a grave marker, this modified High Cross combined with the AVV–VVK and the *blauwvoet* bird immortalized the Flemish dead as martyrs and they were referred to as the IJzer symbols in the subsequent literature. One of the dead, Renaat De Rudder, is even referred to as the Saint of the IJzer. The Flemish martyrs became the platform upon which the Flemish nationalist movement, largely suppressed under Belgian military rule during the war, would flourish in visibility and influence in the postwar years. In support of this ideology, a line from a poem by the poet-priest Cyriel Verschaeve – highly involved in the Front Movement – was added to the print images of the *heldenhuldezerken*.

> Here lay their bodies as seeds in the sand
> Hope for harvest, O Flanders-land.[6]
> [*Hier liggen hun lijken als zaden in 'tzand.*
> *Hoop op den oogst, O Vlaanderland.*]

An article in *Belgische Standaard* in April 1917 suggests that at first Cyriel Verschaeve and the *Comite voor Heldenhuldezerkjes* did not necessarily consider the new tombstone an exclusively Flemish matter.[7] Indeed, some Walloon soldiers purchased *heldenhuldezerken* for their Flemish mates and some Walloons were even buried beneath *heldenhuldezerken*. In an article in *Ons Vaderland* only two months later, however, on the National Day of Flanders, Verschaeve framed the symbolism of the new tombstones differently: 'it is a cross. On the graves of heroes nothing else can be placed.'[8] Such statements stressed that these Flemish tombstones were for Flemish soldiers, sponsored by their Flemish comrades or their kin – a necessary gesture challenging the Belgian army that had systematically and deliberately stymied the Front Movement's efforts at a discourse with King Albert, ignored the demands in the *flamingant* journals, and eventually incarcerated some of their Activists. It was in the *heldenhuldezerken* that the Front Movement thought their presence would be permanently and visibly acknowledged.

But on the nights of 8 and 9 February 1918, thirty-six *heldenhuldezerken* were defaced in the Oeren–Alveringem cemetery. The AVV–VVK inscription was filled in with concrete. It was never clear who the perpetrators were and the Belgian army refused to open an investigation.[9] Members of the Front Movement widely held the Belgian army responsible. Two days later the AVV–VVK was assertively re-written twice as big with black paint. Photographs of the damaged headstones that appeared in the newspapers *Ons Vaderland* and *De Belgische Standaard* incited a nationalist response, and the images continued to be reproduced in pro-Flemish propaganda long after the war (Figure 10.2). *Ons Volk* recalled in August 1935, 'how their graves were violated'.[10] The images of these tombstones continued to circulate in the promotions for an annual IJzer Pilgrimage (the *IJzerbedevaart*), which was established in 1919, and throughout the twentieth century underscored the perceived victimization in the ongoing struggle for either Flemish autonomy within Belgium, or indeed a complete separate Flemish state. In twenty-first-century Flanders, it is predominantly the Flemish separatists that persist in using these images in *flamingant* propaganda. This visual culture has not been adopted by the official Flemish political parties,

Figure 10.2 A damaged *heldenhuldezerk* in the Oeren–Alveringem cemetery, 1918. Courtesy of the ADVN (Archive and Documentation Centre for Flemish Nationalism), VFA 228.

such as the Nieuw-Vlaamse Alliantie (New Flemish Alliance) and the Vlaams Belang (Flemish Interest). But the politicians from these parties do participate as members of the Flemish community at a second annual pilgrimage that began in 2003, called the IJzerwake (Vigil on the IJzer [River]), where the images of the *heldenhuldezerken* and other symbols from the Great War feature prominently in the ritual programme.

A Belgian-centred postwar commemorative practice

At the close of the war in 1918, Belgians commenced a commemorative process that remained uncertain about how to marry the two groups that made up its mourning rituals – the civilians and the soldiers. In the West, only in France were Belgium's 23,700 civilian deaths surpassed.[11] King Albert returned to

Brussels on 22 November 1918, where in his famous 'Discours du Trône' he paid tribute to the sacrifices of the soldiers, but followed with homage to the civilians who had been deported or killed during the massacres of August 1914. In 1919 national funerals were held, well-attended by the public, local and national authorities and high-ranking church officials, for civilians who had been executed by the Germans.[12] It was not until 1922, responding to veteran pressure and public opinion, that the country conducted a funerary procession for the Unknown Soldier in Brussels.[13] At the same time, veneration of soldiers was complicated by acknowledging that so much of the fighting in Belgium had been conducted by its allies. Still today, memorial services are held nightly at the Menen (Menin) Gate, the memorial in the Flemish city of Ieper (Ypres) raised to remember the British and Commonwealth soldiers who were killed in combat in the area. Even choosing which date to officially remember the war indicated an inability to come to a national consensus on what aspect of the war to officially and publicly privilege. The majority of belligerents chose the end of the war: 11 November. Belgium chose 4 August – the beginning of the war – in order to emphasize the patriotism Belgians demonstrated in joining up to serve their country. But as noted by Rosoux and Van Ypersele, five years later this day had become synonymous with the suffering imposed on the country during those long years of 1914–18.[14] The date was switched to 11 November and Parliament declared the day a public holiday.

This same ambivalence is reflected in the failure to raise a traditional war memorial in the form of a stone monument. While memorials tend to commemorate the dead, monuments tend to serve the nation in commemorating itself. How exactly was Belgium to commemorate itself in a permanent statement in monumental form? A stalwart nation that endured German occupation? A nation bolstered by the sacrifice of its citizens and soldiers? Belgium's strategies after the war focused on the immateriality of memorials: King Albert's 'Discours de Trône'; parades including the funerary procession for the Unknown Soldier; or specific calendar days chosen to observe anniversary dates such as the observance of the Armistice. In addition, the government discouraged the construction of war memorials to commemorate local individuals, including non-soldiers, in the villages across Belgium.[15] But there is evidence that this dictum was ignored in those small communities, especially Flemish communities, with the resulting statues tolerated by Belgian officials. For example, in the town of Alveringem the Statue to the Military Victims of Alveringem was dedicated in 1923. In addition, smaller monuments, such as the Memorial Grave in Remembrance of the Military Victims of Zillebeke (dedicated in 1926 in the parish cemetery), dot the Belgian landscape. But it is in the IJzertoren (Tower along the IJzer, Figure 10.3), that instructions from Brussels were ignored in a very public and political manner. Over 100,000 people attended the inauguration of this monument in 1930, suggesting that in Flanders, at least, there was no ambiguity in the need for a physical memorial to serve both as a space for provincial grief and as a focal point for a national spirit.

Figure 10.3 The IJzertoren, 23 August 1936. Courtesy of the ADVN (Archive and Documentation Centre for Flemish Nationalism), VFFY 37/119

The IJzertoren stands in contrast to Belgium's broader inability to arrive at a consensus as to how to honour the war. This seven-storey monument was conceptualized in 1925 and raised in Diksmuide, a central site on the Belgian Front, in memory of the Flemish men who died in the war and who, posthumously, were enrolled in the nationalist *flamingant* cause. Thus the IJzertoren quickly evolved, becoming a symbol for Flemish emancipation enfolded within the political and cultural position of Flanders within the Kingdom of Belgium. In contrast, it was not until 1935 that the Infantry Memorial of Brussels, designed by Edouard Vereycken, was dedicated in front of the Palais de Justice de Bruxelles, in memory of the Belgian foot soldiers who fought in the First World War and later the Second World War.

No distinction is made here between Flemish and Walloon, or Dutch and French. So what do the Flemish memorials, the *heldenhuldezerken* and the IJzertoren, accomplish in Flanders and in Belgium as a whole? Do they provide a parallel memory or a counter-memory?[16] Or did they begin as the first and evolve into the second?

The sentiment behind the creation of memorials ranges from personal expression to institutional proclamations. Because of the number of civilian deaths, postwar national identity became fixed in the personal local or provincial identities across Belgium.[17] Due to the rise in a Flemish consciousness during the war years, however, the memorials in Flanders were, in particular, rooted in that regional context. These local acts of commemoration in Flanders also served to underscore the sacrifice of Flanders and the Flemish for a Flemish nation and not the Belgian state. The IJzertoren, indeed, highlighted specific individuals whose *flamingant* exploits only resonated with a select group in the Flemish community. These Flemish 'heroes' were, for the most part, unknown to those in the Belgian Parliament (both the Flemish and the Walloon representatives), although, through the activities of the Front Movement and Activists, the dogma behind the nationalist rhetoric of these individuals was familiar. Their *flamingant* associations and sacrifice were later recalled in the late 1920s as leading to the Dutchification of Flanders. In light of the attempts to suppress the Flemish voices in the Belgian trenches and the postwar repercussions faced by the collaborationist Activists, it is curious that the *heldenhuldezerken* and the IJzertoren were tolerated. Nevertheless, the King himself gave no sign of acknowledging a particular Flemish memory and commemorative practice.

In the 1920s the belligerent countries undertook the formidable task of exhuming their dead buried along the Western Front and re-interring them in state-sponsored military cemeteries. By the mid-1920s the gravestones in the British and French burial grounds all demonstrated a homogenous gravestone design.[18] But in most of the Belgian military cemeteries two different grave markers provided a visible indication of difference in national allegiance. During the early months of 1923, rumours again prompted a panic among the Flemish veterans that the Belgian government was going to impose a uniform design for all soldiers who fought in the war and that the *heldenhuldezerken* were ultimately to be removed. The Minister of Defence, Pierre Forthomme, was indeed concerned to incorporate all sacrifice within a single symbol. Standardized headstones would help to produce 'a uniform appearance of our military cemeteries, of the cemetery of the brave, who all perished for the same task'.[19] But Forthomme also noted that each of the new stones would contain a small, hollow space into which family members could choose to place either a cross (Walloon) or a lion (Flemish) indicating cultural affiliations. This concession to Flemish concerns demonstrated a consciousness in the Belgian Parliament of a parallel memorial programme and the willingness to at least give a measure of acknowledgment to the differences in the two language and cultural communities.

Many, if not the majority, of the Flemish families were not politically driven by the separatist politics to which their sons were exposed at the front, and were unaware of the goals of the Front Movement. This affected the reburial of those under *heldenhuldezerken* at the close of the war, with the creation of the nine military cemeteries to contain the bodies of all Belgian soldiers, both Flemish and French-speaking. Most of the fallen Flemish men were not buried beneath a Flemish cross. Since soldiers' comrades had largely sponsored the *heldenhuldezerken* during the war, many families were not inclined to insist upon one during the relocation process. Others, through language and literacy barriers, lost the opportunity to preserve the *heldenhuldezerken* under which the soldier was buried. In addition, on 27 May 1925, Minister of Defence Albert Hellebaut, a war veteran, ordered that *heldenhuldezerken* not claimed by families be crushed and utilized in the construction of a road in Adinkerke. Outraged Flemish veterans perceived this as a new attack on the *heldenhuldezerken*, and an overt effort at suppression by the Belgian government. Accounts of the exact numbers of the destroyed tombstones vary. According to the IJzer Pilgrimage Committee over 600 of 800 stones were destroyed. The Belgian army placed the number at 140 stones out of a total of 400.[20] Whether the *heldenhuldezerken* were destroyed deliberately as a hostile act or not, indignation spread among the Flemish-minded population at the perceived 'desecration'. Thus the story of the Belgian attempts to symbolically, and literally, crush Flemish-minded ideologies and activities was later incorporated into the narrative of the IJzertoren, adding to the mythology of the deaths of the Flemish men.

Outrage was sufficiently strong to ensure that on 10 July, under the direction of a new Minister of Defence, the destruction of the *heldenhuldezerken* ceased. In 1927 the IJzer Pilgrimage Committee decided to extend the *heldenhuldezerken* to all Flemish veterans. This decision emphasized the postwar efforts of the veterans in the *flamingant* cause, including the preservation of the *heldenhuldezerken*, the organization of the IJzer Pilgrimage and the creation of the IJzertoren. Several veterans served in the postwar political parties demanding more autonomy (some also served in the right-wing separatist parties during the 1940s that collaborated with the Nazis). The *heldenhuldezerken* were placed on graves in the parish cemeteries since the military cemeteries were reserved for those who died during the war. Cyriel Verschaeve, for instance, received a *heldenhuldezerk* in 1973.[21] Over the next ten years new commemorative *heldenhuldezerken* were placed on the graves of soldiers who died during the war who did not initially receive such acknowledgment. But the fears regarding any possible changes implemented by the Belgian military, and not discounting the possibility of further defacement of the tombstones, gave rise to a new initiative in Flemish commemoration – the creation of a permanent memorial marker for all of the Flemish dead.

A seven-storey *heldenhuldezerk*

The members of the Front Movement were dismayed by the damage to the *heldenhuldezerken* in Oeren–Alveringem in 1918. But the systematic destruction of the *heldenhuldezerken* at the hands of the Belgian government was alarming. On 31 August 1924, the IJzer Pilgrimage Committee proclaimed a permanent pilgrimage site and memorial in their decision to 'bring together the threatened gravestones of the *heldenhuldezerken* under the mantle of a gigantic cross'.[22] The proposed site, near the destroyed town of Diksmuide, was a strategic choice; it would remain under provincial Flemish jurisdiction, and not subject to any oversight by the Belgian military. Pilgrimages to the site were not held on 11 November, but in August, and occasionally on or near 11 July, to coincide with the National Day of the Flemish Community.

The design competition stipulated that the memorial incorporate English's *heldenhuldezerk*.[23] When the chosen design – essentially a seven-storey *heldenhuldezerk* – was presented to the public during the pilgrimage of 1925, the tower was described within the framework of the myths of the martyred IJzer symbols:

> Already five times the pilgrims from Flanders come to the Fields of the IJzer dead, where our best men bled out in days of youthful dedication and selflessness; they knelt on the many grave hills, more numerous each time, solemnly thinking about the idea these simple heroes had embodied until the end and that was imprinted in the crowns of the countless *heldenhuldezerkjes,* erected with piety by the comrades of the fallen for one last celebration and lasting testimonial: AVV–VVK.[24]

By the end of 1927, 120 of the smashed *heldenhuldezerken* had been incorporated into the walls of the inner rooms of the crypt.

The IJzertoren's commemorative politics were naturally grounded in the ideologies of the Front Movement. The IJzer Pilgrimage Committee dedicated the pilgrimage of 1923 to what was labelled a 'restitution of honour' for the so-called violated gravestones near the towns of Oeren and Alveringem.[25] On this occasion, veteran Hendrik Demoen accused the army of attempting to silence the Flemish ideologies and erase the members of the Front Movement even in death. He declared that 'Belgium did this … the oppressive and criminal Belgium, the Belgium of Cezembre, and of Orne, and of Fresne and Auvours [the internment camps in which some members of the Front Movement were incarcerated]; … the Belgium against Flanders and Christ.'[26] During the tenth IJzer Pilgrimage, on 18 August 1929, Filip De Pillecyn, a war veteran and one of the founders of the pilgrimage, speaking on behalf of VOS (*Verbond Der Vlaamsche Oud-Strijders* – The Union of Flemish Old Combatants), justified the cross shape of the memorial:

> The Flemish Cross of Diksmuide is … a summary of all the crosses that the Flemish people have had to bear. The cross of contempt by brothers from the same house; the cross of workers who were reined in as working cattle and drilled by foreign rulers; the cross of spiritual injustice and lastly the heavy cross of thousands of dead, young men.[27]

The Great War and Belgian politics   197

The martyrdom of the men and the subsequent martyrdom of the *heldenhuldezerken* damaged in 1918 and 1925 were aligned in the crypt, where ten *flamingant* soldiers (including Joe English) were buried, with the remnants of the broken *heldenhuldezerken*. In the 1930 pilgrimage poster a small black cross, topped with a soldier's helmet as one would find after a recent burial at the Front, is enclosed within a grey *heldenhuldezerk*, the tombstone that replaced the generality of the war dead with a definitive symbol of national allegiance (Figure 10.4). The IJzertoren rises, filling the visual field, from these two foundations. This symbolism is repeated on several other occasions reminding the pilgrims of the foundations of the object of their veneration. For example, in the 1936 poster, the base of the IJzertoren is filled with numerous *heldenhuldezerken* – for individuals honoured alongside Frans Kusters, one of the ten IJzer martyrs, whose portrait hangs above.

Figure 10.4 The 1930 poster for the IJzer Pilgrimage. Courtesy of the ADVN (Archive and Documentation Centre for Flemish Nationalism), VAFC 84.

The tower largely functioned, then, as a signifier of the struggle for Flemish autonomy and the efforts to sustain the memory of the injustices against the Flemish soldiers at the front. At the 1930 inauguration of the tower, Frans Daels, a veteran of the war and the first president of the IJzer Pilgrimage Committee, spoke of the tower as a 'monument of accusation' as it, along with the dead soldiers, accused those in power of having a lack of faith and honour.[28] The tales of the heroic deaths of the *flamingant* soldiers on the battlefields of the Belgian Front, the suppression of their native tongue, the humiliation of being buried under a French-language tombstone, and the indignity of having their tombstones defaced and destroyed, fuelled the separatist politics and underscored the feelings of a martyred people. The IJzertoren was raised as an enduring reflection of the sacrifice of the Flemish soldiers, both in the war and for Flemish autonomy within Belgium. Towering over the IJzer Plain, its verticality implied strength and permanence.

Another martyr to the cause

By the 1930s, the activities of the Flemish Movement, supported by the legacies of the nineteenth century and the Front Movement, had achieved recognition of the Flemish language in both legal and academic institutions. But for some members of the Flemish Movement this important transformation in Belgium was not enough. Since the nineteenth century two *flamingant* groups had co-existed: those who wanted more autonomy for Flanders within the framework of the already established Kingdom of Belgium and those who lobbied for a separate Flemish state. Under Nazi occupation from 1940, many Flemish nationalists again embraced collaboration with the Germans as a step toward Flemish autonomy. Thus, in the years of the Second World War, the IJzertoren came to represent the collaboration of a few Flemish nationalists with the German occupiers. Pilgrimage programmes changed to reflect Nazi pageantry, causing tension with the more moderately political Flemish. On 15 March 1946 the memorial was destroyed, by 'persons unknown', in a move calculated to disrupt the right-wing symbolism it had acquired during the war.[29] Popular belief again held the Belgian army responsible, though a hamstrung judicial inquiry turned up few legitimate suspects.

Flemings from all spectrums of the Flemish Movement publicly protested the destruction of the tower. The board of the *Het Vlaamse Kruis* (Flemish Cross) expressed its anger by insisting the tower was a sacred object and labelling the destruction as a blasphemous act of desecration, which violated the graves of the heroes who rested there as a symbol of Flemish greatness.[30] The choice of the word 'desecration' clearly placed the tower within the Christian context of its inception linked with the martyrdom of the Flemish soldiers. The stories of the defaced *heldenhuldezerken* in 1918 and the crushed *heldenhuldezerken* of 1925 surfaced in abundance in newspapers throughout the region. Many writers asserted that since the pieces of the crushed *heldenhuldezerken* from Adinkerke had been incorporated into the tower itself, these grave markers had been violated for a second time.

The IJzer Pilgrimage Committee immediately expressed its determination to rebuild. The reconstructed IJzertoren rose from the original fifty metres to eighty-five, some twenty-four storeys above the IJzer Plain. The original footprint of the tower remained, as a ruin (Figure 10.5). In the summer of 1948 a simple white cross with the AVV–VVK inscription was erected on top of the pile of rubble crowning the crypt. Inscribed on the cross was the verse that Cyriel Verschaeve – by then an infamous collaborator – had penned for the *heldenhuldezerken* during the First World War:

> Here lay their corpses as seeds in the sand
> Hope for harvest, O Flanders-land.

Figure 10.5 The *heldenhuldezerk* erected behind the ruins of the first IJzertoren. Courtesy of the ADVN (Archive and Documentation Centre for Flemish Nationalism), VFFY 62/09.

Circling this ensemble were the graves of the IJzer martyrs including Joe English and student soldier Firmin Deprez. Prone *heldenhuldezerken* marked the graves, while the walls of the reconstructed crypt were lined with more of the same. Above each grave an open shaft allowed direct light to fall on the graves of the martyred men of Flanders following the precepts of the martyrariums of the Middle Ages. The IJzer Pilgrimage Committee noted its pleasure with the results, noting 'above it all, between the stumps of the IJzer Tower, the delightful white cross of "*Heldenhulde*"'.[31]

The ruins of the IJzertoren and the *heldenhuldezerken* were utilized to the fullest extent in the pilgrimage propaganda during the next ten years. 'Resurrection!' ('*de Verrijzenis!*') was the theme of the first postwar pilgrimage in 1946; in 1952 organizers declared '*een Volk zal Nooit Vergaan*' ('A People Never Perish'). The pilgrimage poster featured a silhouette of the new tower rising from the rubble. The new monument was erected roughly 150 metres behind the site of the old tower. An allée of sorts led pilgrims through the crypt of the first IJzertoren to the entrance door of the second. Prone *heldenhuldezerken* lined this processional path. Symbolically, the remains from the first IJzertoren were carried to the new tower on funeral biers during subsequent pilgrimages filling the *heldenhuldezerken* that framed the sacred path. This act effectively collapsed into one sign the destruction of the *heldenhuldezerken* in Adinkerke and the destruction of the tower – a tower that was ostensibly created to protest further destruction of these memorial crosses. In 1965, the year the second IJzertoren was inaugurated, the poster featured a tower that dominates the visual field. A halo surrounds the *heldenhuldezerk* in a blaze of light – the resurrection was complete.

A new pilgrimage: the vigil to the IJzer

After the Second World War, the IJzer Pilgrimage struggled to shed the conflation of Flemish remembrance and nationalism with the appropriation of the IJzertoren and the *heldenhuldezerk* by the collaborators. In the late 1940s, the Pilgrimage Committee was purged of its right-wing members and the pilgrimage programme shifted to highlight the advances made by Flanders in achieving more autonomy within Belgium through a series of reforms in 1970, 1980, 1988 and 1993. The memorial aspect was not forgotten, but the victimhood framework that had guided many of the pilgrimages in the previous years was de-emphasized. Nevertheless, many still desired a separate Flemish state; opinion pieces condemned the decision and protesters disrupted the pilgrimage ritual on several occasions. In 1995, criticizing the recent changes made to the IJzer Pilgrimage programme, the *Vlaams Nationaal Jeugdverbond* (The Flemish National Youth Group – VNJ), under the slogan 'Truth to the IJzer Legacy', organized a pilgrimage of sorts in Steenstrate – an active battlefield during the war and the death site of two more of the IJzer martyrs, Edward and Frans Van Raemdonck. In August 2003, a new pilgrimage, the IJzerwake (IJzer Vigil), and site were officially established by Flemish separatists in order to commemorate Flemish nationalists of *both* world wars. In 2004,

IJzerwake President Johan Vanslambrouck[32] recalled as victims those who had worked with the National Socialists to forge a separate Flemish state and who were subsequently prosecuted as traitors:

> The repression from sixty years ago is not a footnote in our history. It was a deliberate and calculated attempt to negate all of the progress of the Flemish Movement. Numerous Flemings were forced from their country and many of them have since died far from Flanders ... Belgium is the only country in the world where the legal consequences of the postwar repression continue today. This shame must be erased by the only measure that so many years after the date could bring relief: total and unconditional amnesty.[33]

Vanslambrouck frames these individuals as more martyrs to the *flamingant* cause and thus their names become, in the twenty-first century, entangled with the IJzer martyrs of 1914–18. He reiterated, as truth, the great myths of the war: 'at the Front the [Flemish] soldiers were ignored, despised and humiliated' and 'even for the dead, Belgium could not pay its respect', reminding the pilgrims of the *'heldenhuldezerkjes* [that] were smeared or served as pavement'. In the early 2000s, in addition to the IJzer martyrs such as the Van Raemdonck brothers and Firmin Deprez, the IJzerwake consciously commemorated Staf De Clercq and Cyriel Verschaeve (the poet-priest from the Great War), two of the more infamous Second World War collaborators.

The political emphasis that formerly guided the IJzer Pilgrimage is now a prominent part of the IJzerwake, and it reminds us that some Flemings continue to perceive themselves as a persecuted minority. The IJzerwake originally drew its pilgrim base from the former members of the Vlaams Blok (Flemish Block), a xenophobic right-wing nationalist separatist movement, which was forced to disband in 2003. Re-organized as Vlaams Belang (Flemish Interest), these political groups initially funded the IJzerwake. But as the influence of the Vlaams Belang has waned in recent years, politicians from a variety of Flemish political parties have attended the IJzerwake. Politicians who have attended include several from the New Flemish Alliance (N-VA), currently the largest Flemish political party in Belgium: Jan Van Esbroeck; Karim Van Overmeire, formerly of Vlaams Belang; and Bart Denyn who, on his website, describes himself as a committed *flamingant*. According to the satirical journal *'t Pallieterke*, in 2013 more people from the N-VA, which advocates a gradual secession of Flanders from Belgium, attended than in years past. The call for Belgium's demise has been an integral part of the IJzerwake programme since its inception. The common plea in almost every presidential speech is for Flemish independence. In 2003, at the conclusion of his speech, Johan Vanslambrouck declared, 'Belgium must crack!' (*'België barst!'*), and again in 2005: 'An independent Flemish state is the only good solution. So that Flanders can live: Belgium must crack!' In 2007, Vanslambrouck underscored his plea for a separate Flanders by invoking the Great War and the primary role the actions of their separatist precursors played in the initial realization of this goal: 'Almost ninety years ago [those lobbying for a separate Flanders] … began the drive for Flemish independence … if Belgium keeps standing in the way of the development of Flanders, then Belgium has to disappear.' In 2009, IJzerwake President Wim de Wit did not couch this desire in any nostalgic rhetoric: 'Against Belgium, is as it should be! That is our ultimate mission; that is our duty! [It is] our duty and my duty, to destroy this Belgian State.' In 2013 Wim de Wit emphasized in his speech: 'We are going for an independent Flemish Republic. That is our future!'[34]

Since its inception the IJzerwake has utilized the symbols of the First World War in order to ground the pilgrims in what the organizers of the IJzerwake believe to be the goals of the Front soldiers – separatism and not autonomy, as interpreted by those in the IJzer Pilgrimage Committee. The *heldenhuldezerk* image has all but disappeared from the IJzer Pilgrimage publicity literature while the IJzerwake has embraced it as a central symbol. The podium at the IJzerwake generally features a *heldenhuldezerk* against a background of Flemish yellow. The pilgrimage posters and entrance tags recirculate the same images: a hand raised in the oath to Flanders, a *heldenhuldezerk*, and a rallying cry from the war, '*Hier ons bloed – wanneer ons recht?*' ('Here is our blood – when is our right?'). In 2003 a ghostly image of a defaced *heldenhuldezerk* was used for the annual poster (Figure 10.6). A large facsimile of a *heldenhuldezerk* is present at nearly all of the IJzerwake pilgrimages perhaps as a substitute for the real object of veneration – the IJzertoren. At the 2013 pilgrimage a large *heldenhuldezerk* was placed on the stage. But instead of the name of an individual soldier carved on the surface, '*Hier ons bloed – wanneer ons recht*' was substituted as a stand-in for all those who had died. What the IJzerwake Committee highlights as the inflammatory symbols of the Front Movement, the IJzer Pilgrimage Committee attempts to contextualize within the larger framework of the past 100 years of an evolving and complex Flemish nationalism. The goal is not to empty them of meaning, but to recognize and direct their power within the twentieth and twenty-first century Flemish Movement.

In 2010 the IJzer Pilgrimage Committee, under the direction of president Paul De Belder, secretary Dirk Demurie, curator Peter Verplancke and education director Steven Maes, instituted a new programme, which represented a deliberate re-evaluation of the symbolism of the IJzertoren and the IJzer Pilgrimage. A distinction was made between the IJzertoren as a memorial to the Flemish dead and the political rhetoric associated with the monument in various periods from the 1930s to its troubled relationship with a right-wing contingent during the Second World War and through the 1990s. Less emphasis was placed on the *heldenhuldezerk* as a symbol of Flemish oppression. The president's speeches focused on peace and the end of war and did not re-visit the histories of the martyred men that lay in the crypt. As of 2013 the IJzer Pilgrimage is no longer held in August, but on 11 November, Armistice Day. For the IJzer Pilgrimage Committee, the need for an annual pilgrimage, framed in a Flemish political message, is over. Federalism (autonomy) has been

The Great War and Belgian politics 203

Figure 10.6 The 2003 poster for the IJzerwake. Courtesy of the ADVN (Archive and Documentation Centre for Flemish Nationalism), VAFB 459.

established in Belgium and the IJzertoren can now be understood as simply a memorial to the Flemish men, honoured on Armistice Day, who died at the Belgian front supporting a platform of peace and the slogan 'No More War'.

To reinforce that perspective, in 2013, the IJzertoren was no longer visible during the ceremony. The symbol of the cult of the IJzer martyrs, the twenty-four-storey *heldenhuldezerk*, was obscured from view. The speeches took place in a tent. The prone *heldenhuldezerken* filled with the rubble from the martyred first IJzertoren were removed. The walkway that links the IJzer crypt with the IJzertoren was renamed the Via Dolorosa (road of sorrows). The names of eighty villages that suffered considerable civilian losses during the war were posted along the path, both Flemish and Walloon. The phrase used was 'the moving war' in reference to the war as it moved through Belgium, from August to October 1914, and ending with the armies entrenched on either side of the flooded IJzer Plain. The road of sorrows was to honour all those lost in the war, not just the Flemish. Perhaps in 2013, for the first time, there were as many French as Flemish speakers on the IJzer. Essentially the pilgrimage stayed Flemish, but with open hands toward Wallonia – sharing living quarters instead of existing almost as hostile neighbours.

It is unlikely that this will set the precedent for a resolution of differences within Flemish commemoration of the Great War. Certainly these gestures will continue to be absent from the IJzerwake programme: members of the *Vlaams Belang* and other right-wing groups spoke of treason when referring to the shift of the IJzer Pilgrimage from August to November, calling the change to 11 November 'a Belgian repossession' of the Flemish dead. On 11 November, they note, there are also 'Belgian commemorations'; they assert that the uniqueness of a Flemish day of commemoration will be subsumed in Belgian Armistice Day.[35] The difficulties the Museum aan de IJzer (housed in the IJzertoren) encountered in 2014 when developing a new exhibition, and indeed new narrative of the war, also exposed those continuing fault lines. Perhaps even more important is the continuing ambiguity over how to facilitate new traditions and a monument programme nationally. As we have seen, a standard, top-down, patriarchal and military-focused official memory struggled to emerge after the war in Belgium. Because the state did not *officially* suppress the municipal memories of the war, including the looming IJzertoren, it did not invalidate what Kirk Savage calls the 'inner' or vernacular memories of the war at the expense of the 'outer' memory.[36] Perhaps then, the 'counter-memory' of a Flemish memorial practice suggested by Marnix Beyen is not so much against Belgian memory and commemoration of the war, but a parallel memory – one that runs alongside official memory and speaks, in a specific, vernacular language to a specialized community as they continue to lobby, through a bloodless revolution, for more Flemish autonomy. This is not to argue that some of the tactics used, for example the actions of the Activists and collaborators in the two wars, were just – and it is clear that at several different points in the last 100 years the tone of the IJzertoren and the IJzerwake was anti-Belgian – but to emphasize that the lack of Belgian engagement with these municipal memories failed to challenge that message. Nevertheless, from the awkward memories of the Second World War, political parties emerged that led to the foundation of a federal Belgian state.

That process remains in tension. There has never been a hegemonic national memory in Belgium. Regional memories flourished in its place, and indeed produced stronger narrative structures and commemorative institutions. In Flanders, there are two groups that posit themselves as custodians of the memory of the Great War. The IJzer Pilgrimage Committee, organized specifically to care for the *heldenhuldezerken* after 1919 and subsequently the IJzertoren, seeks to depoliticize, or neutralize, the imagery of these two symbols in the interests of autonomy within federal Belgium. The other group asserts these memorials as a nationalist Flemish heritage. As the numbers of pilgrims to the IJzertoren diminish, attendance at the IJzerwake might increase (roughly 4,500 attended in 2013).[37] At the IJzerwake, more Flemish will be exposed to the *heldenhuldezerk* as a symbol of Flemish pride framed within a nationalist ideology. Perhaps these attendees do not embrace the separatist agenda espoused during the IJzerwake programme, but the subtle influence and strength of the visual culture at the Steenstrate meadow could serve to unduly influence the right-wing arm of the Flemish Movement. The politics of regional commemorative activity have gained importance due to, even driven by, the fragmented nature of Belgian remembrance nationally. Contesting national histories and the placement of politically charged landmarks implies far more than just, to paraphrase the anthropologist Katherine Verdery, restoring a truth, because it challenges the entire national lineage.[38] While there might be greater accommodation and complementarity in federal Belgium, the long histories of dissent that underpinned demands for both autonomy and independence remain strong.

Notes

1 Cited in Herman Van Goethem, *Belgium and the Monarchy: From National Independence to National Disintegration* (Antwerp: University Press Antwerp, 2011), 115.
2 For more information on the production of visual culture through the *flamingant* activities and the resulting repercussions imposed by the Belgian army see K. Shelby, *Flemish Nationalism and the Great War: The Politics of Memory, Visual Culture and Commemoration* (Basingstoke: Palgrave, 2014). On the Front Movement see D. Vanacker, *De Frontbeweging: De Vlaamse strijd aan de IJzer* (Koksijde: De Klaproos, 2000).
3 See Piet Couttenier, 'National Imagery in 19th Century Flemish Literature', in *Nationalism in Belgium: Shifting Identities, 1780–1995*, eds Kas Deprez and Louis Vos (Hampshire: MacMillan, 1998), specifically for information on Guido Gezelle, also a priest and a poet, who was instrumental in drawing attention to the issue of the rights of the Flemish to speak their vernacular language.
4 Shepard Clough, *A History of the Flemish Movement in Belgium: A Study in Nationalism* (New York: Octagon Books, 1968), 204.
5 The symbol comes from a poem penned by Rodenbach containing a line he borrowed from the novelist Hendrik Conscience: When the *blauwvoet* flies, there is a storm at sea! (*Vliegt de blauwvoet, storm op zee!*).
6 Vanacker, 30.
7 Thank you to Peter Verplancke, curator at the Museum aan de IJzer, for sharing his research with me.
8 'Het is een kruis. Op een heldengraf kan niets anders staan', Cyriel Verschaeve, 'Over Heldenhulde. Wat het gedenkteken is, dat geplaatst wordt', *Ons Vaderland*, Year 3, No. 784 (11 July 1917), 2.
9 *Bedevaart naar Vlaanderens Dodenveld* (Temsche, 1924), 174.
10 ' … en hoe hun graven zijn geschonden', *Ons Volk*, 11 August 1935, 507.
11 Statistics are compiled from *Belgique l'Annuaire statistique de la Belgique et du Congo Belge 1915–1919* (Brussels, 1922); The War Office, *Statistics of the Military Effort of the British Empire during the Great War 1914–1920* (1922), 237; Leo Grebler, *The Cost of the World War to Germany and Austria-Hungary* (New Haven: Yale University Press, 1940); and Michel Huber, *La Population de la France pendant la guerre* (Paris: Carnegie Endowment for International Peace, 1931).
12 See L. Van Ypersele and E. Debruyne, *De la Guerre de l'ombre aux ombres de la Guerre: l'espionage en Belgique durant la Guerre 1914–1918. Histoire et mémoire* (Brussels: Labor, 2004), 120–34.
13 Ibid. Quoted from S. Claisse, 'Ils sont bien merité de la Patrie! Monuments aux Soldats et aux Civils Belge de la Grand Guerre'. Unpublished doctoral thesis, Université Catholique de Louvain, Louvain-la-Nieve, 2006.

14 Rosoux and Van Ypersele, 'The Belgian National Past: Between Commemoration and Silence', *Memory Studies* 5:1 (2012), 47.
15 Ibid.
16 For an argument on the Flemish memorials as a counter-memory see M. Beyen, 'A Parricidal Memory: Flanders' Memorial Universe as Product and Producer of Belgian History', *Memory Studies* 5:1 (2012), 32–44.
17 V. Rosoux and L. Van Ypersele provide numerous examples of the localization of memory after the war, noting the emphasis on schoolbooks published in the different provinces that highlighted the 'heroes' of the region. See Rosoux and Van Ypersele, 48.
18 The history of the formation of the German cemeteries is more complicated and was not completed until mid-century.
19 'Om in onze militaire kerkhoven den gelijken aanblik te bekomen dien het wenschelijk is te geven ... ', in *Bedevaart naar Vlaanderens Dodenveld*, 181–3.
20 Vanacker, 438.
21 Because of his collaboration Versachaeve was forced to flee to Austria after the Second World War where he died in exile in 1949. His body was exhumed by the Vlaams Militanten Orde (VMO), a Flemish far-right-wing nationalist political group, and reburied in his home town of Alveringem.
22 ' ... onder de hoede van een reusachtig kruis, de bedreigde zerkjes van Heldenhulde bijeen te brengen', *De woeste aanslag op de Heldenhulde tombstoneszerkjes* (Temse, 1925), 11.
23 Robert and Frans van Averbeke of the van Averbeke Brothers Architectural firm from Antwerp were selected.
24 *Bedevaart naar Vlaanderens Doodenveld (1ste vervolg)* (Uitgave van het Komiteit der Jaarlijkesche IJzer-Bedevaart: Temse, 1925), 7.
25 *Bedevaart naar Vlaanderens Doodenveld (1ste vervolg: 1924–25)*, 146–80.
26 *Bedevaart naar Vlaanderens Doodenveld*, 175.
27 *Doodenveld* (6 de Verlog), 19 and 23.
28 *Zo leefde, zo sprak Profesor Frans Daels* (Diksmuide: s.d.).
29 Frank Becuwe and L. De Lentdecker, *Van IJzerfront tot zelfbestuur* (Veurne: Veurne Publishing, 1993), 31.
30 'De Verwoesting van de IJzertoren' and 'Motie aan het Vlaamsche Kruis', *Het Volk*, 29 March 1946. Translation by Bregtje Hartendorf.
31 *XXIe IJzerbedevaart naar Vlaanderens Doodenveld* (Diksmuide, 1930), 143.
32 Johan Vanslambrouck was the leader of *Voor Post* (For Post), a nationalist group founded in 1976 as a splinter from the *Volksunie* political party (People's Union). *Voor Post* follows in the tradition of *Verdinaso* (the VNV – Verbond van Dietsche Nationaal-Solidaristen), a Flemish nationalist movement with a fascist-inspired platform founded in the 1930s. The group proposed a Greater Netherlands, a nation state that would unite all Dutch-speaking countries in Europe.
33 All quotes are from the transcripts of the presidential speeches available online at 'IJzerwake'. Online. Available HTTP: <IJzerwake.org> (accessed 9 April 2014).
34 Correspondence between the author and Wim de Wit, September 2013.
35 Guy Tegenbo, '*Zomer eindigt laatste keer met IJzerbedevaar*', *De Standaard*, 23 August 2012.
36 Kirk Savage, 'History, Memory and Monuments: An Overview of the Scholarly Literature on Commemoration', online essay commissioned by the Organization of American Historians and the National Park Service (2006). Online. Available HTTP: <www.nps.gov/history/history/resedu/savage.htm> (accessed 9 April 2014).
37 www.ijzerwake.org.
38 Katherine Verdery, *The Political Lives of Dead Bodies* (New York: Columbia University Press, 1999), 41.

11 Between the topos of a 'forgotten war' and the current memory boom

Remembering the First World War in Austria

Sabine A. Haring[1]

In the centenary year of 2014 contributions to the history of the origins as well as of the causes and effects of the First World War can hardly be ignored.[2] Numerous new academic as well as popular publications and new editions of existing works are broadening our knowledge of the war. All the main daily newspapers in Austria are now reporting on the fronts and the hinterland between 1914 and 1918.[3] Different television channels are broadcasting numerous documentaries and films about the First World War.[4] Meanwhile, more than ninety-five years have passed since the end of the First World War, which is about four or five generations. Each generation – against the background of their different constraints and opportunities – knew and knows its own reconstruction of the war of soldiers, officers and civilians. The complete process can only be grasped as a social, inter-generational process of recording and passing on.[5] If one tries to understand the significance of the war from what exists as collective memory today, one may err massively: in Austria this war has long been subjugated to, and eclipsed by, efforts to reconstruct Austrian identity, especially since 1945. This does not however mean that it has actually become insignificant. Reconstructing memory of the First World War in Austria, as a process spanning generations, reveals significant contestation over its class bases, giving way to a safer Habsburg nostalgia after 1945, and the war's re-imagining as a much more Europe-oriented story today.

Context, time and memory

It is hardly controversial to observe that our relationship to the past – as individuals and societies – changes over time. This indeed is what we see over several generations in Austria since 1918. In the conceptual sense, memory is intimately connected to time. 'Time and identity', Aleida Assmann says, 'interfere actively with the remembrance process, which inevitably involves a shift between storing and recollecting'.[6] Furthermore, the individual memory process is influenced both by communicative and cultural memory. The former includes everyday communication, where communication functions by social interaction – among families, at the pub, in the village community – in ways that are 'arbitrary' and 'unorganized', not necessarily fixed in time.[7] In this context we might think of communication processes between parents and children or between grandparents and grandchildren. The war children of the First World War were the parents of those of the Second World War – examined in particular by the w2k (weltkrieg2Kindheiten – world war2childhoods) research group – who consciously and unconsciously passed their war memories on to their children.[8] To underline the interdependent nature of this exchange, Völter suggested speaking of a 'mutual establishing of generational experiences by running interaction' instead of a more formal and direct process of 'passing on'.[9] As shown, among others, by the study *Opa war kein Nazi* (Grandfather wasn't Nazi), at the level of everyday memory the image of National Socialist Germany is different from that of the current cultural memory.[10]

In Jan Assmann's influential framework, cultural memory is characterized by its distance from everyday communication. Cultural memory refers to events fixed in time, the meanings of which are constantly reconstructed to serve group identities in the present.[11] Memory is shaped by personal experience and reconstructed over time, and emotions 'contribute essentially' to 'mobilizing memories from the memory stores' or not mobilizing them.[12] 'Sometimes in the process of reconstructing', Jay Winter emphasizes, 'we add feeling, beliefs, or even knowledge we obtained after the experience. In other words, we bias our memories of the past by attributing to them emotions or knowledge we acquired after the event.'[13] Cultural memory draws on a range of media to transmit these reformulated understandings of the past in stable and accessible ways. These 'sites of memory' play a significant role in the 'construction' of individual and collective identities. Ritualized remembering in the form of celebrations of certain historical events or in the transmission of collective experiences at school, works as a society's 'site of memory': a place that functions to foster identification and provide orientation.[14] Archives, libraries and museums and also, in a 'metaphorical sense', diaries or 'new media' function in this way too.

Still the essential media of cultural memory are the 'canon of the classics', the 'museum' and the 'memorial'.[15] Canonized texts and authors are elevated from the normal variety of published texts and identified as being 'classical'; their 'value' is considered given, and their 'eternalness' praised. Canonized texts are passed on from generation to generation, while being discussed and reflected on again and again. At the museum, 'memories' of various kinds are collected and presented to the audience in a well-ordered, systematized way. Through memorials and ceremonies, again, certain events are made present: individuals, deeds or ideas are supposed to be 'heroically' eternalized or, alternatively, the wounds of the past are kept open in a 'traumatizing way'.[16] 'By its collective tradition, a society becomes visible: for itself and for others', Jan Assmann says, 'which past becomes visible there and which values emerge in its identifactory appropriation tells us something about that society and what it wants to be.'[17] This does not mean arbitrariness: cultural memory is fixed to historical events and reservoirs of knowledge.[18] Rather does it mean selection, context and suppression in the production of those memories and their fixtures. In all successor and former enemy states of the Habsburg Monarchy, the collective memory of the war was similarly complex and contested.

The first two decades after 1918

What then was the meaning of the collective memory of the war for German-speaking Austrians? Without claiming any classificatory completeness, the following examples represent some kinds of 'narrations' which Helmut Kuzmics and I believe to be important, as they reflect their respective position within the international and national network of relationships of nations and classes.[19] Austria within its current borders can actually be considered an indirect 'result' of the First World War. The combined experience of the lost war and the lost Monarchy (meaning a concurrent sense of a superior cultural heritage which had become idealized with time) has provided strong roots for Austrian cultural identity in contrast to Germany. This Austrian self-image is partly still in effect today. Significant for the study of the collective memory of all wars, but particularly of the First and Second World Wars, is the difference between victory and defeat.[20] There is the methodological question of how far we should extend the limits of war events. If we orient ourselves towards the original or the resulting conflict, it may be that the actual armed struggles constitute only a small part in the development of those identities, and the world-political effects of a devastating peace have bigger consequences. Hungary's fragmentation after the Trianon Peace Treaty is an impressive example. In this context, the famous question of war responsibility also plays an important role.[21] Whereas Austria's emaciated and ragged soldiers – many of them having spent time as prisoners of war – crept home with a feeling of shame, Italy's 'victory' at Vittorio Veneto allowed proud heroes to come home triumphantly; Mussolini's gigantic ossuaries speak a completely different emotional language to Austrian war memorials. The narrative of the First World War in school books, as well as in popular and academic historical research, was extensively shaped by the combination of the First World War and the end of the Habsburg Monarchy and, more generally, the fall of empires in central and eastern Europe. According to Werner Suppanz, this state cesura was an overwhelming experience which shaped the categories, constructions and interpretations of the common awareness as well as of historians.[22]

The manner of the war's conclusion made possible a series of narratives of the war in Austria. We need to think here not just of defeat on the battlefield, but of the destruction of monarchical power, and the strengthening of left-wing politics. This is critical to understanding the politics of memory in defeated states more generally. In literary terms, the sociologist Norbert Elias in his *Studies on the Germans* analysed two ways of German dealing with the war experience: literature in support of the war and literature dissenting from the war. The best-known work of the former is Ernst Jünger's *Storm of Steel*, and of the latter is Erich Maria Remarque's *All Quiet on the Western Front*.[23] Remarque discusses the nature of this war precisely by contrasting the celebration of courage and strength with identification with the wounded and dying enemy, thus not idealizing the suffering of the war by attributing an ultimate meaning to it (death for the fatherland). Accordingly, this book – like its British (Graves, Sassoon) or French (Barbusse, Chevallier) equivalents – could be employed to support pacifist propaganda and those groups spreading it, which again was regarded as 'treason' by their opponents. According to Elias, both reactions to the war are dependent on the different ways in which members of the Wilhelmine establishment and those belonging to weak groups of outsiders (such as workers or Jews), experienced the total defeat. Whereas the former, including court, nobility and bourgeois reserve officers, suffered from a 'traumatic shock' when they had to cope with this grave, unexpected defeat – 'like a runner crashing into a wall' – after the fall of the old regime, the latter were considerably stronger than before, at least in their own minds.[24] In Austria the day of the armistice could not lastingly develop into a national holiday, not only because it represented military defeat, but because both the bourgeois upper and middle classes and the members of the old elites perceived it as a defeat by the despised lower classes of their own society. In most successor states to the Monarchy the inner distribution of power among the classes was massively shifted by the war. Thus, apart from the level of tensions between nation-states, a sociological analysis of collective war memory must also consider class-based tensions within those states. From this alone the very different and often contradicting narrations of collective memory result.[25]

With regard to the Habsburg heritage and mythos between 1918 and 1945, Laurence Cole distinguishes three phases in its development and use. The first extended from 1918 to 1927, the second from 1927 to 1938, and the third from the Anschluss of 1938 to the end of the war in 1945.[26] During the first period the Habsburg mythos was radically disenchanted: large sections of the Austrian population and the Austrian government emphasized the break with the old regime and desired a closer connection with Germany. Only a small political movement – a heterogeneous group of monarchists – invoked the Habsburg heritage. After the fragile consolidation of the Austrian state the official memory culture began to change, and the second phase began. This period can be described as a span of nostalgia and rehabilitation first within society and later on in governmental politics. The government wanted to legitimize the 'Ständestaat' and simultaneously to distance itself from National Socialist Germany. In contrast to the population's polarization into different political camps, the Habsburg mythos symbolized an idyll without social and political conflicts. Thus, re-invoking the Habsburg heritage suited the authoritarian government. Emphasizing Austria's Habsburg history served to give the state a stronger 'Austrian profile', which in turn would give the regime historical legitimacy and a point of continued distinction from Germany. After the 'Anschluss' the memory of the Habsburg Monarchy was repressed. In 1945 the dynasty of the Habsburgs stood on the brink of oblivion.

The development of war memory after the First World War was fostered in Austria – as elsewhere – not only through war memorials, but through literature, including regimental histories and autobiographies of Imperial and Royal Army (*kaiserlich und königliche Armee* – k.u.k.) soldiers.[27] The latter especially was a form in which to contest the meaning of the war and its aftermath in public, though one might also acknowledge concerted efforts among dissenters to ignore the war altogether. Nevertheless, from the early 1920s, as Verena Moritz observes, a 'conservative turn' took place, which was advanced by, amongst others, numerous Habsburg officers.[28] In this context, regimental histories became an important memory source. From the early 1920s a significant number of regimental histories were published: for example the 1926 *Ehrenbuch der Heßer: Geschichte des altösterreichischen Infanterie-Regimentes Freiherr von Heß Br. 49*, or the 1928 *Die Deutschmeister. Taten und Schicksale der Infanterieregiments Hoch-und Deutschmeister Nr. 4 insbesondere im Weltkriege*.[29] The 'regimental history boom' increased during the 1930s, in which even more regimental histories were written, most of them by k.u.k. officers.[30]

This conservative rendering of the war had its uses in all the belligerents' societies, during and after the war, either for the purpose of raising their men's fighting-morale, or for selling the war to the general public or to a forgetful world continuing to live after the terrible events. In this context, one of the regimental histories written in 1931, the regimental history of the Styrian 3rd Riflemen (3er-Schützen), relates their changeful and cruel fate, in great detail and definitely not always in a palliating way. Austrian regimental histories were partly a form of rehabilitation after defeat, not shying away from the pain of the war, but insisting on the spirit and dedication of the Austrian soldier. Like the texts on so many war memorials, this remains a story of heroes:

> Just forward, to get out of hell into the open. – At last we reach the edge of town, the city is ours, but the comp. [company] consists of only a few now, however their spirit is unbroken. On the railway embankment there sit the Russians. One more 'hurrah' by the few voices left. The Russians, being ten to one, are running, seeking cover in potato and turnip fields, where they completely vanish from the eye, due to their earth-coloured uniforms. But still, the Styrians' hawk-eyes discover them. Calm as if being on the firing range, as if just being on a walk, we aim – and hit. Disturbed, the Russians run farther backwards.[31]

This book, largely addressed to veterans (whose patronage made its publication possible) and probably also their families, attempts a picture of classless cohesion within the unit. In this sense it offers an example to contemporary society, and is sympathetic to the memory of the Monarchy. Indeed, a Habsburg Archduke (Joseph) wrote a preface. The entire text does not show any German-national bias and is also not meant exclusively for officers. Officers and rank-and-file are presented as acting in concert; the former are not decried as failures, or for being stupid or failing their men. Sorrow and pain have their place in the narration; fear and 'cowardice' do not.[32] Regimental histories predominantly sketch an image of a homogeneous group kept together by a relationship of trust, reaching from the regiment's commander down to the common soldier. Even if sometimes a few feel insecure (mostly, however, this happens with other regiments), this we-community includes all front-line officers and common soldiers of a regiment, all of whom are frequently depicted as 'bold', 'daring' and 'tough'. Again and again mutual trust and a feeling of security are made topics of discussion – most of all in Regimental Adjutant Hermann Fröhlich's 1937 history of the 27th Regiment. Even if the numerous fluctuations resulting from losses and replacements lead to obvious changes of the group structure, it seems as if – if we follow the interpretation by Fröhlich, for example – the cohesion among the group was re-established within a very short time. Accordingly, Fröhlich's conclusion regarding the first period of fighting in 1914, until 3 September, reads as follows:

> It [the Regiment] had gone through these fateful days boldly, toughly, performing its duty, it had tested its willpower, its steadfastness, its readiness to sacrifice, it had gone through all hardships and tribulations, through all traumata like men and hardened by the suffering, and it had paid a considerable toll in blood. Haunted by disappointments, but with unbroken courage, trusting their power, their iron will, they were waiting for the renewed call – the Regiment.[33]

This intermingling of heroic epic with a tale of nameless, unspeakable suffering had its political expressions in the interwar period, as it informed right-wing politics, and indeed underpinned the ideals of a number of private armies. The existence of the *Heimwehr* (Homeguard), *Schutzbund* (Protective Federation) and the *Österreichische Legion* (Austrian Legion) who had their base in Germany, could hardly be explained without previous mass mobilization and war, and the idealization of that experience. This is not necessarily to say that these private armies were exclusively recruited from former front-line fighters and officers. But the need to give meaning to the terrible sacrifice, the cry for a restitution of honour and the example of the virtue of heroism are emotional realities which were passed on over the generations and became essential for right-wing political orientation in the inter-war period.

Apart from the regimental histories, a number of war memoirs were also published in the inter-war period, though a synthesis of Austrian war prose is still lacking.[34] Among the best-known authors in this context are Fritz Weber,[35] who was also re-edited after the Second World War, and the famous mountaineer and movie actor Luis Trenker.[36] These memoirs could serve that same rehabilitative agenda for a masculinity challenged by defeat and the traumatizing effects of war. As Christa Hämmerle emphasizes, these retrospective war memoirs had, among other roles, the function of

> re-establishing, re-erecting an idealized male image which had been destroyed by the actual war experiences or were at least suffering from a

crisis and to open up again new possibilities of identification, which seemed to be particularly urgent in the loser states.[37]

Their fighting and their suffering were not supposed to stay senseless and were supposed instead to point towards an open, once again heroic future.[38]

This format was also much more open to use in dissenting politics, as a sometimes more differentiated image of the war is sketched by diaries and autobiographies, which helps to expose the class basis of remembering the war, and denies the myth of homogeneity and classlessness in the war experience propounded by the regimental histories. Whereas in official and semi-official depictions comradeship is demanded, conjured and sometimes celebrated, in diaries and autobiographies we find different narratives concerning 'vertical loyalty'. For example Franz Matthias Hartinger, an 'Offiziersstellvertreter' (temporary gentleman) with the k. k. Landsturm-Infanterieregiment Laibach, in his diary speaks again and again of flogging and of soldiers having been tied to the post:

> The brutality exercised by this gentleman deserves to be nailed. There are no excuses for it, neither nervousness nor any other kind of suffering. Sergeants are being beaten until their blood runs down, the most evil bad names keep just flying like bullets on Podgora.[39]

Those who would be obliged to intervene in these brutalities are looking away: 'Everybody is keen on being awarded, but you won't see anybody taking care about the rank and file. I am lying on a meadow and I'm angry like a frog.'[40] A homogeneity of officers and rank-and-file which might indicate comradeship or exclusively 'good' superiors is not to be found in Hartinger's diary. The community of sacrifice, so central to that narrative and its interwar political expressions, is bluntly denied.

Of course Hartinger was not expressing something unique to Austrian experience: all armies of the era were class-structured, and as the war proceeded, inexperienced or brutal leaders provoked growing resentment. This attitude is connected with a humanist protest against the sacrifice and suffering of the war, which were perceived as senseless, and this sentiment had its expression both in the working class and elements of bourgeois society. Independent of working-class soldiers' correspondence, we can also detect a bourgeois–antifeudal–antiwar protest of an elaborated kind of pacifism in Austria, which had been in conflict with the army's post-feudal warrior code. One of its leading figures was the Jewish publicist and author Karl Kraus. His indictment of the war in the monumental drama *The Last Days of Mankind* (1918) spoke passionately to the inhumanity of what was happening in the war. Further, this strand of collective memory was significant for the development of an Austrian collective memory of the world war. Working-class hostility towards the Habsburgs and the bourgeois class, together with the pacifist and rebellious canon, and other texts oriented towards the humanist middle-class norms on which Kraus's work is based, were very important in producing a rejection of what George Mosse called 'the myth of the war experience' – the belief that the lost war had been meaningful and ennobling.[41]

If we compare the constellation in Austria to that in Germany, there is, however, a crucial difference. As Elias explains, the German elites in their effort to catch up and achieve predominance over Europe were stopped; thus they suffered a 'traumatic shock' with their defeat. Probably in dismembered Austria this shock was even greater, for the Empire had fallen apart; the nobility was homeless, and the bourgeois elites had been deprived of their ability to exercise power both externally and domestically.[42] Different from Germany, however, for the small new Austria 'revenge' was practically unimaginable – except by way of German-national revolution; thus the inter-war period also became a 'fight for Austrian identity' as it was described by Friedrich Heer, who depicted impressively the confusion surrounding Austrians' national identity after 1918 as an age-long conflict between a German and an Austrian orientation.[43] Thus we arrive at another type of narration of Austria's collective memory: sadness about the fall of the Monarchy. The paradigmatic text for this perspective is Alexander Lernet-Holenia's novel *Die Standarte* (*The Standard*). Its basic motif is sadness – not only about the dead but about the whole fallen Empire.

The 'forgotten war'

As Helmut Kuzmics and I emphasize in our book *Emotion, Habitus und Erster Weltkrieg*, in many respects the First World War in this part of Europe has been a 'forgotten war' for a long time; the battlefields in Poland, Ukraine, the Balkans, on the Isonzo or in the Alps are far less frequently visited than those on the former Western Front in France and Flanders. It is least forgotten at the Isonzo Front, that battlefield whose horror can be compared to Verdun, from where we know the movements and fates of individual regiments in as much detail as those that fought on the Somme. It is only there where cemeteries have been preserved similar to the notorious, endless rows of graves of British, French and German soldiers in the west.[44] However, the collective memory of the 'Great War' in central Europe is not dead. Since the end of the duopolies of the superpowers following the collapse of the Soviet Union and the regions it dominated, we have experienced a revival of 'forgotten' events, actions and emotions, which has opened the way for new perspectives on the First World War.

In most of the countries in central and eastern Europe, the traumas of the First World War were overshadowed by National Socialism and the Second World War. Compared with the academic efforts of other countries, research on the First World War in Austria has been relatively limited. Even official editions of files were published rather late and their size and range cannot be compared to those of Germany, Britain, or France. As Werner Suppanz observes, no academic historical publications about themes relating to the First

World War were printed in Austria between 1945 and 1958. During the 1960s only a few academic publications about the 'great catastrophe of the twentieth century' were published, whereas in the 1970s and 1980s a quantitative increase can be noted.[45] But there is a difference between academic historical research and memory and commemoration. In an ideal-typical way, Jost Düffler insists, the latter should be based on the former.[46] The reality, of course, is that the relationship is hardly so co-operative, and in Austria the reconstruction of memory over several generations has been marked by that process of diminishing recognition of the First World War and its meanings.

Nevertheless, while the First World War itself was largely neglected in cultural memory after 1945, the Habsburg myth played an important role in the process of identity formation in the Second Republic. It was no longer important in immediate political–ideological terms, but emerged more powerfully in the commercial entertainment sector, where it could exercise a degree of cultural power.[47] The absence of debate on the most recent past – that is on Austro-Fascism and National Socialism – was accompanied by a revival of older fields of reference. This nostalgia becomes particularly obvious in the numerous films of the 1950s, telling stories from the days of the Empire, in particular of their rulers, officers and bourgeois girls.[48] Between 1950 and 1959, without taking the genre of 'Heimatfilme' (films idealizing the rural regions of the home country) into consideration, Wendelin Schmidt-Dengler counts twenty-five films employing the 'ancient Austrian frame tale'.[49] These films, however, did not only influence contemporaries from Habsburg rule, but also those who were born later. Repeatedly shown on Austrian television, mostly on Saturday afternoons, for the generation born around 1970 these films were an integral part of their weekends. Connecting three generations – parents, children and grandparents – they helped produce a collective memory of a safer, idealized and very much Austrian past. The greatest commercial success of Austrian cinematography in the post-war period was the Sissi trilogy, directed by Ernst Marischka and with a young Romy Schneider in the role of Empress Elisabeth.[50] The image of Austria and Sissi presented therein was exported all across the world and became an important element of tourist marketing.[51] Internally these positive, completely uncritical, depictions of the Habsburg past helped in creating an emotional and symbolic bond to the Austrian state and with finally separating from Germany, both politically and also at the emotional level.

Despite this kind of inoculation against the recent past – and its avoidance of the war that ended the Monarchy, there were still those determined to remember the war of 1914–18. On the occasion of the 1965 television version of Josef Roth's *Radetzkymarsch*, today a nostalgic icon of Austrianism, the generation of First World War front-line fighters raised angry protests against what they – incomprehensibly these days – perceived as a disparagement of the 'Old Army'. This film version of Roth's novel, which is itself an expression of a deep longing for the Empire and of feelings of loyalty to the Habsburgs, was accompanied by fierce protest, showing that erasure of the First World War was hardly uncontested. For example, a former colonel wrote to the editors of the *Kronen-Zeitung*:

> Being a former professional officer of the Austro-Hungarian Army, I would like to comment on the TV broadcast 'Radetzkymarsch'. Among many people watching TV there had to be the impression that the officers of 1914 went to war full of pessimism, being aware that the fall of the Monarchy was certain. Actually, however, just the opposite was true! The morale of the officer corps and the rank and file was outstanding, and this was not changed by the defeats on the Eastern Front. After all, for four years this army, which is now so much abused and besmeared, fought against a superior enemy. ... Whoever constantly besmears the past, may not be surprised when in the present he will not get anything better.[52]

Along with such a defence of the spirit of the soldiers of 1914–18, reactions against 'defamation of the Emperor' were also a feature of letters to the editors, which indicates how much loyalty to the Monarchy still existed among the older generation. The former colonel went on:

> Further, how is it possible that ... old Emperor Franz Joseph was presented as a senile-naïve idiot, [and] the Austro-Hungarian officers however, with one purposeful exception, as drunken prowlers. The majority of the soldiers of World War I have fallen or have since died. However, those few who are still alive will remember who received them at the train stations when they were returning from the lost war. They will also remember who tore down their stars and badges.[53]

These reactions show the great significance honour had for the former officers of the Austro-Hungarian army; the reserve officers' corps of the Austrian Federal Army also expressed sharp protest against 'the defamation of the comrades from the "Old Army"'. A number of people even identified this film with 'class hatred'; they called it an attack on officers, nobility and Emperor. This was the last flickering of collective memory of the First World War and the old army; despite its vehement defence, in the following years it disappeared, as did the nostalgically glorified operetta army of the once so many Vienna films. One generation later the First World War as well as its disastrous results seems to have disappeared from Austrians' collective memory, together with the Viennese songs and Austrian military marches. But these are the politics of remembrance: both remembrance and forgetting are processes in need of explanation. The shape of Austrian cultural memory of the First World War is neither fixed, nor entirely organic: fundamental societal forces, interests, conflicts and their connected emotions all influence memories.

We begin to see this reality in the growing academic attention to the war that accompanied the fading away of its actual participants, and new intellectual approaches emerging in the historical profession in the 1970s and 1980s. With the growing significance of the social–historical paradigm, we observe an increase in academic publications on the First World War. In the 1980s, the 'Dokumentationsarchiv lebensgeschichtlicher Aufzeichnungen' at the Institut für Wirtschafts-und Sozialgeschichte of the University of Vienna started collecting autobiographical texts, most of which had been written by older people. Many of them have been published in the series 'Damit es nicht verloren geht … (Lest it is lost …)', the 68th volume of which has just been released. One volume is dedicated to the topic of childhood during the First World War, another to being a prisoner of war of the Russians, and yet another to the military from the point of view of recruits.[54]

A further increase in academic publications occurred in the 1990s in the course of the cultural turn – new questions were raised: the common man's war at the front or that of the women in the hinterland, as well as the topic of remembrance, increasingly came to the fore in historical investigations. As underlined by Werner Suppanz, however, both the cultural–scientific approach and the theoretical–methodological debate on the 'modern war experience' in Austria came belatedly. There are hardly any examples, Suppanz states, of cooperation and debate with former war enemies.[55] Among the public more generally, knowledge of the war and contestation over its meanings remains undervalued, despite the fact that the war had very broad effects on civilians and servicemen alike. Food shortages and internment brought the war directly to civilians, while servicemen fought not only in trenches, but in a war against civilians, most of all in Galicia and at the Serbian front.[56] Together with the fate of the many suffering from psychological trauma, all offered fertile grounds for powerful collective memories of the war, which nevertheless failed to achieve a strong foothold in collective remembrance.[57] The trends towards erasure have been much more compelling.

The commemorative year 2014

In 2014 the European states commemorate the centenary of the outbreak of the First World War in quite different ways. Whereas in Great Britain and France the First World War has its place within a strong remembrance culture, in Austria it does not count among the 'essential places of memory', as Heidemarie Uhl underlines.[58] Accordingly, in Austria planning for the centenary has been low-key. There will be no official commemoration in the form of state occasions but, as the historian Siegfried Mattl has critically observed, 'Austria will approach the topic rather in a scientific–cultural way – or as "nostalgia".'[59] Numerous exhibitions with different foci in the federal capital of Vienna and the federal states, scientific congresses in Austria and abroad, as well as a number of recent academic publications pay homage to the significance of the outbreak of the First World War for the history of the twentieth century, even if in Austria there will be no 'really big commemorative events' as in France or even 'victory celebrations' as in Great Britain.[60]

The closest thing to an official line might be found in the document produced by the Federal Ministry for European and International Affairs, entitled 'Das Grundlagenpapier österreichischer Wissenschaftlerinnen und Wissenschaftler aus Anlass des Gedenkens des Ausbruch des Ersten Weltkriegs'. This document provides politicians, diplomatic representatives abroad and the individual ministries with 'a concise information aid concerning crucial topics' as they are 'discussed by most recent research in the context of World War I' – and which 'is embedded into the general historical background from an Austrian point of view and a European perspective'.[61] This document is mature in its coverage and content, dealing broadly with the European alliances; the issue of war guilt; the role of Emperor Franz Joseph, who is said to have wanted the war and not have considered an 'armistice' as an option until his death; the 'social militarization' of society in the Habsburg Monarchy during the final decades before the war; the ambivalent relation to Germany as an alliance partner; and the meaning of the Paris Treaties naming Austria, Hungary, Germany, Bulgaria and Turkey collectively as the culprits of the war; as far as all this is considered relevant for the longer history of the twentieth century. It also moves beyond the macro-perspective of war to the actors' micro-perspective: that of the intellectuals who in their overwhelming majority supported the war in 1914, and indeed sometimes welcomed it as a cathartic liberation from the sterility and decadence of the pre-war period; of the soldiers at the front; of the women, children and refugees in the hinterland. The narratives developed by those who themselves endured the war have largely disappeared. The war memorials remain, though they too are re-inscribed with the even longer lists of the dead of the Second World War, and the even more difficult politics of remembering and forgetting that followed 1945.

Today the First World War is returning to view in Austria. The publishing houses flood the book market with literature – expert books, popular-scientific presentations, photo books and fiction books – on the First World War. Just a few months ago Edwin Baumgartner called them 'latecomer war profiteers'.[62] But there are still reasons for this late return. For Düffler the current 'media hype' around the First World War reflects also 'the current feeling of crisis in Europe'.[63] If we look at the closer scientific discourse in Austria, currently we may observe – as Christa Hämmerle notes – that 'World War I ... is moving from a marginalized position which it had occupied compared to the dense remembrance culture on World War II back to the centre of the collective memory of the "age of catastrophe" of the twentieth century.'[64] Or, as Heidemarie Uhl argues, we may after all be seeing the extension of our knowledge of the First World War as a 'place of remembrance', not only in respect of Austria but also of other central European states.[65] In this context, the 'Peace Path' in the Carnic Alps,[66] and the school project 'Europe lost and found in war and peace', with students from seven countries (Austria, Bosnia-Herzegovina, Turkey, France, Germany, Serbia and Slovenia) contributing, seek to foster common memories of the war across the former European belligerents.[67] They deal with the consequences of the First World War and relate them to current challenges when it comes to international understanding and peace in Europe. Currently it cannot be estimated just how regional, national, trans-national or even global the remembrance culture will become in the years of the anniversary 2014–18. Still, in Austria we see that the difficult and neglected histories of Austrian remembering have again been reformulated.

Notes

1 This article was translated from German into English for the most part by Mirko Wittwar, to whom I would like to say sincerely 'thank you'.
2 Recently Jost Düffler has given a very informative overview of the 'historians' boom' in regard to the First World War: see J. Düffler, 'Die geplante Erinnerung. Der Historikerboom um den Ersten Weltkrieg', *Osteuropa* 64: 2–4 (2014), 351–68.
3 See among others 'Schwerpunkt', *Der Standard*, 30 November/1 December 2013, and '1914 Der Erste Weltkrieg 1918. Spezial', *Kleine Zeitung*, 10 May 2014.
4 See for example '14 Diaries of the First World War' on Arte TV. Online. Available HTTP: <www.14-tagebuecher.de/page/de/about/1/> (accessed 14 May 2014). The ORF-documentary film 'Menschen & Mächte: Der Weg in den Untergang'. Online. Available HTTP: <www.ots.at/presseaussendung/OTS_20140423_OTS0103/100-jahre-erster-weltkrieg-menschen-maechte-dokumentiert-den-weg-in-den-untergang> (accessed 14 May 2014). Also 'Das Attentat Sarajevo 1914' (Assassination at Sarajevo), directed by the famous Andreas Prochaska. Online. Available: <https://presseportal.zdf.de/pm/das-attentat-sarajevo-1914> (accessed 14 May 2014).
5 S. A. Haring and H. Kuzmics, 'Einleitung', in H. Kuzmics and S. A. Haring, *Emotion, Habitus und Erster Weltkrieg. Soziologische Studien zum militärischen Untergang der Habsburger Monarchie* (Göttingen: V & R. unipress, 2013), 15–16.
6 A. Assmann, 'Speichern oder Erinnern? Das kulturelle Gedächtnis zwischen Archiv und Kanon', in *Speicher des Gedächtnisses. Bibliotheken, Museen, Archive, vol. 2: Die Erfindung des Ursprungs; die Systematisierung der Zeit*, eds M. Csáky and P. Stachel (Wien: Passagen, 2001), 15.
7 See J. Assmann, 'Kollektives Gedächtnis und kulturelle Identität', in *Kultur und Gedächtnis*, eds J. Assmann and T. Hölscher (Frankfurt am Main: Suhrkamp, 1988), 9–19.
8 For example, according to data from Germany, many of those born between 1905 and 1920 grew up fatherless, or within 'damaged family structures'; see H. Radebold, W. Bohleber and J. Zinnecker, 'Einleitung', in *Transgenerationale Weitergabe kriegsbelasteter Kindheiten. Interdisziplinäre Studien zur Nachhaltigkeit historischer Erfahrungen über vier Generationen*, 2nd edn, eds H. Radebold, W. Bohleber and J. Zinnecker (Weinheim/München: Juventa, 2009), 7–8.
9 B. Völter, 'Generationenforschung und "transgenerationale Weitergabe" aus biografietheoretischer Perspektive', in *Transgenerationale Weitergabe kriegsbelasteter Kindheiten. Interdisziplinäre Studien zur Nachhaltigkeit historischer Erfahrungen über vier Generationen*, 2nd edn, eds H. Radebold, W. Bohleber and J. Zinnecker (Weinheim/München: Juventa, 2009), 105.
10 H. Welzer, 'Die Nachhaltigkeit historischer Erfahrungen. Eine sozialpsychologische Perspektive', in *Transgenerationale Weitergabe kriegsbelasteter Kindheiten. Interdisziplinäre Studien zur Nachhaltigkeit historischer Erfahrungen über vier Generationen*, 2nd edn, eds H. Radebold, W. Bohleber and J. Zinnecker (Weinheim/München: Juventa, 2009), 76.
11 See J. Assmann. The cultural memory preserves that which the respective society is able to reconstruct as its specific stocks of values and meanings (see E. M. Hois, P. Karoshi, V. Munz, P. Stachel, W. Suppanz, and H. Uhl, 'Gedächtnis/Erinnerung und Identität – Konstruktionen kollektiver Identität in einer pluriethnischen Region', in *Kultur – Identität – Differenz. Wien und Zentraleuropa in der Moderne, vol. 4: Gedächtnis – Erinnerung – Identität*,

eds M. Csáky, A. Kury and U. Tragatschnig (Innsbruck/Wien/Bozen: Studienverlag, 2004), 218).

12 C. Wassmann, *Die Macht der Emotionen. Wie Gefühle unser Denken und Handeln beeinflussen* (Darmstadt: Wissenschaftliche Buchgesellschaft, 2002), 14.

13 J. Winter, *Remembering War. The Great War between Memory and History in the Twentieth Century* (New Haven: Yale University Press, 2006), 4.

14 See M. Csáky and P. Stachel, 'Vorwort', in *Speicher des Gedächtnisses. Bibliotheken, Museen, Archive*, vol. 2: *Die Erfindung des Ursprungs; die Systematisierung der Zeit*, eds M. Csáky and P. Stachel (Wien: Passagen, 2001), 11–12.

15 See A. Assmann, 21–2.

16 See ibid., 22–6, reference number 26.

17 J. Assmann, 14.

18 Hois, Karoshi, Munz, Stachel, Suppanz and Uhl, 218.

19 See Haring and Kuzmics.

20 Haring and Kuzmics, 20–2.

21 Ibid., 20.

22 W. Suppanz, 'Der "überschriebene" Krieg. Der Erste Weltkrieg in der österreichischen Zeitgeschichte', in *Update! Perspektiven der Zeitgeschichte. Zeitgeschichtetag 2010*, eds L. Erker, A. Salzmann, L. Dreidemy and K. Sabo (Innsbruck/Wien/Bozen: Studienverlag, 2012), 208–9.

23 On contrasting Jünger to Remarque, see among others S. A. Haring, 'Ernst Jünger, Erich Maria Remarque und der Erste Weltkrieg. Eine literatursoziologische Betrachtung', in *Krieg, Medizin und Politik. Der Erste Weltkrieg und die österreichische Moderne*, ed. K. Helmut (Wien: Passagen, 2000), 351–71.

24 N. Elias, *Studien über die Deutschen. Machtkämpfe und Habitusentwicklung im 19. und 20. Jahrhundert*, ed. M. Schröter (Frankfurt am Main: Suhrkamp, 1989), 240.

25 Haring and Kuzmics, 20–1.

26 L. Cole, 'Der Habsburg Mythos', in *Memoria Austria I. Menschen, Mythen und Zeiten*, eds E. Brix, E. Bruckmüller and H. Steckl (Wien: Verlag für Geschichte und Politik, 2004), 476.

27 Soon after the war, and partly already during the war, thousands of war memorials were erected in all parts of shrunken post-war Austria.

28 V. Moritz, 'Nachwirkungen der "Fronterfahrung" des Ersten Weltkriegs auf die Entwicklung Österreichs in der Zwischenkriegszeit', in *19/2014: Gedenken 1. Weltkrieg*, eds Helmut Konrad, Verena Moritz and Manfried Rauchensteiner (Wien: Bundesministerium für europäische und internationale Angelegenheiten, Kulturpolitische Sektion, 2013), 33–6. Online. Available HTTP: <www.bmeia.gv.at/fileadmin/user_upload/bmeia/media/3-Kulturpolitische_Sektion_-_pdf/Themen_Dateien/Grundlagenpapier_1914_-_2014.pdf> (accessed 19 May 2014).

29 S. Reiß (ed), *Ehrenbuch der Heßer: Geschichte des altösterreichischen Infanterie-Regimentes Freiherr von Heß Br. 49, 1715–1918*, vol. 2: Der Weltkrieg 1914–1918 (Wien: Schöler, 1926); J. Waldstätten-Zipperer and J. Seifert, *Die Deutschmeister. Taten und Schicksale der Infanterieregiments Hoch-und Deutschmeister Nr. 4 insbesondere im Weltkriege* (Wien: Österreichische Staatsdruckerei, 1928).

30 See among others L. Freiherr von Vogelsang, *Das steirische Infanterieregiment Nr. 47 im Weltkrieg. Zum 250. Errichtungsjahr des Regiments*, vol. 1 and 2 (Graz: Leykam, 1932); E. Straßmayr, *Das Hessenregiment: aus der Geschichte des Infanterie-Regimentes Nr. 14; mit 61 Bildern* (Linz: Preßverein, 1933); R. Assam, *Des Kärntner Infanterieregiment Graf von Khevenhüller Nr. 7 letztes Ringen und Ende* (Graz: Assam, 1935); M. Klement, W. Weyrich and H. Wilhelm, *Die k. u. k. reitende Artillerie-Division Nr. 5 (2) im Weltkriege 1914–1918: geschrieben nach offiziellen Unterlagen und Tagebuchnotizen* (Wien: Selbstverlag, 1934); H. Sauer, *Linzer Hessen 1733–1936* (Linz: Hessen Offiziersbund, 1936); H. Fröhlich, *Geschichte des steirischen k.u.k. Infanterie-Regimentes Nr. 27 für den Zeitraum des Weltkrieges 1914–1918*, vol. 1 and 2 (Innsbruck: Wagner'sche Universitäts-Buchdruckerei, 1937).

31 H. Strohschneider, *Das Schützenregiment Graz Nr. 3 und der steirische Landsturm im Weltkrieg 1914–1918*, vol. 1 (Graz: Selbstverlag, 1931), 52.
32 Haring and Kuzmics, 23.
33 H. Fröhlich, *Geschichte des steirischen k.u.k. Infanterie-Regimentes Nr. 27 für den Zeitraum des Weltkrieges 1914–1918*, vol. 1 (Innsbruck: Wagner'sche Universitäts-Buchdruckerei, 1937), 45.
34 R. Andraschek-Holzer, 'Österreichische Prosa zum Ersten Weltkrieg im Vergleich', in *Frontwechsel. Österreich-Ungarns 'Großer Krieg' im Vergleich*, eds W. Dornik, J. Walleczek-Fritz and S. Wedrac (Wien/Köln/Weimar: Böhlau, 2013), 188.
35 In the 1930s Weber wrote 'Das Ende der Armee', 'Menschenmauer am Isonzo', 'Sturm an der Piave', 'Granaten und Lawinen', 'Isonzo 1915', 'Isonzo 1916', 'Isonzo 1917', 'Alpenkrieg' and 'Frontkameraden'. See C. Hämmerle, 'Es ist immer der Mann, der den Kampf entscheidet, und nicht die Waffe ... ', in *Der Erste Weltkrieg im Alpenraum. Erfahrung, Deutung, Erinnerung. La Grande Guerra nell'arco alpino. Esperienze e memoria*, eds H. J. W. Kuprian and O. Überegger (Innsbruck: Universitätsverlag Wagner, 2006), 36.
36 S. Andexlinger and J. Ebner, '"Friedlich leuchtet die Sonne auf Tod und Leben". Die Erfahrungen des Ersten Weltkrieges in literarischen und nicht-literarischen Quellen', in *Das Gesicht des Krieges: Militär aus emotionssoziologischer Perspektive*, eds S. A. Haring and H. Kuzmics (Wien: ReproZ Wien/Akademiedruckerei LVAk, 2008), 59–113.
37 Hämmerle, 'Es ist immer der Mann', 48.
38 Ibid., 54.
39 F. M. Hartinger, *Die Kriegstagebücher des Franz Matthias Hartinger, Offizierstellvertreter im k. k. Landsturm-Infanterie-Regiment Laibach No. 27, 1915–1918*, ed. Volker Rutte (Graz: Eigenverlag, 2012), 78.
40 Ibid., 107.
41 See George Mosse, *Fallen Soldiers: Reshaping the Memory of the World Wars* (New York: Oxford University Press, 1990).
42 Haring and Kuzmics, 24.
43 F. Heer, *Der Kampf um die österreichische Identität* (Wien/Köln/Weimar: Böhlau, 1981).
44 H. Kuzmics and S. A. Haring, *Emotion, Habitus und Erster Weltkrieg. Soziologische Studien zum militärischen Untergang der Habsburger Monarchie* (Göttingen: V & R. unipress, 2013).
45 Suppanz, 210.
46 Düffler, 351.
47 Cole, 484.
48 See, among others, the following films: 'Kaisermanöver' (1954), directed by Franz Antel; 'Die Deutschmeister' (1955), directed by Ernst Marischka; and 'Kaiserjäger' (1956), directed by Willi Forst.
49 D. A. Binder, 'Die Erzählung der Landschaft. Aspekte zur österreichischen Geschichte des 20. Jahrhunderts', in *Geschichte und Identität. Festschrift für Robert Kriechbaumer zum 60. Geburtstag*, ed F. Schausberger (Wien: Böhlau, 2008), 223–4.
50 Cole, 489.
51 Ibid., 491.
52 Letter to the editor, *Kronen-Zeitung*, 22 April 1965. See Haring and Kuzmics, 25–6.
53 Haring and Kuzmics, 26.
54 C. Hämmerle (ed.), *Kindheit im Ersten Weltkrieg (Damit es nicht verloren geht ... 24)* (Wien/Köln/Weimar: Böhlau, 1993); H. Leidinger and V. Moritz (eds), *In russischer Gefangenschaft. Erlebnisse österreichischer Soldaten im Ersten Weltkrieg. Damit es nicht verloren geht ...* vol. 56 (Wien/Köln/Weimar: Böhlau, 2008); C. Hämmerle (ed.), *Des Kaisers Knechte. Erinnerungen an die Rekrutenzeit im k.(u.)k. Heer 1868 bis 1914* (Wien/Köln/Weimar: Böhlau, 2012).
55 Suppanz, 211.
56 A. Holzer, *Das Lächeln der Henker. Der unbekannte Krieg gegen die Zivilbevölkerung 1914–1918*. (Darmstadt: Primus Verlag, 2008); G. Hoffmann, N.-M. Goll, and P. Lesiak, *Thalerhof 1914–1918–1936. Die Geschichte eines vergessenen Lagers und seiner Opfer*.

Mitteleuropäische Studien IV, eds D. A. Binder, G. Kastner and A. Suppan (Herne: Gabriele Schäfer Verlag, 2010).
57 H.-G. Hofer, 'Was waren "Kriegsneurosen"? Zur Kulturgeschichte psychischer Erkrankungen im Ersten Weltkrieg', in *Der Erste Weltkrieg im Alpenraum. Erfahrung, Deutung, Erinnerung. La Grande Guerra nell'arco alpino. Esperienze e memoria*, eds H. J. W. Kuprian and O. Überegger (Innsbruck: Universitätsverlag Wagner, 2006), 309–21.
58 H. Uhl, 'Der Erste Weltkrieg im Gedächtnis Österreichs und (Zentral-)Europas – Gedächtnistraditionen in (trans)nationaler Perspektive', in *19/2014: Gedenken 1. Weltkrieg*, eds Helmut Konrad, Verena Moritz and Manfried Rauchensteiner (Wien: Bundesministerium für europäische und internationale Angelegenheiten, Kulturpolitische Sektion, 2013), 37–9. Online. Available HTTP: <www.bmeia.gv.at/fileadmin/user_upload/bmeia/media/3-Kulturpolitische_Sektion_-_pdf/Themen_Dateien/Grundlagenpapier_1914_-_2014.pdf> (accessed 19 May 2014).
59 'Die Welt gedenkt 1914 – jeder auf seine Art', *Wiener Zeitung*, 4/5 January 2014, 1.
60 M. Schmölzer and W. Zaunbauer, 'Das große Gedenken', *Wiener Zeitung*, 4/5 January 2014, 10–11.
61 *19/2014: Gedenken 1. Weltkrieg*, eds Helmut Konrad, Verena Moritz and Manfried Rauchensteiner (Wien: Bundesministerium für europäische und internationale Angelegenheiten, Kulturpolitische Sektion, 2013). Online. Available HTTP: <www.bmeia.gv.at/fileadmin/user_upload/bmeia/media/3-Kulturpolitische_Sektion_-_pdf/Themen_Dateien/Grundlagenpapier_1914_-_2014.pdf> (accessed 19 May 2014).
62 E. Baumgartner, 'Späte Kriegsgewinnler', *Wiener Zeitung*, 23 May 2014, 25.
63 Düffler, 351.
64 C. Hämmerle, *Heimat/Front. Geschlechtergeschichte/n des Ersten Weltkriegs in Österreich-Ungarn* (Wien/Köln/Weimar: Böhlau, 2014), 9.
65 Uhl, 38.
66 P. Ernst, S. A. Haring and W. Suppanz, 'Der Erste Weltkrieg – Zeitenbruch und Kontinuität. Einleitende Bemerkungen', in *Aggression und Katharsis. Der Erste Weltkrieg im Diskurs der Moderne*. Studien zur Moderne 20, eds P. Ernst, S. A. Haring and W. Suppanz (Wien: Passagen, 2004), 27.
67 L. Hagen, 'Europa im Klassenzimmer wiederfinden', *Der Standard*, 30 November/1 December 2013, 16. These students communicate via internet platforms.

Afterword
Remembering the First World War
An international perspective

David Reynolds

This chapter offers an international perspective on remembering the First World War. It assesses some of the differing national contexts in which remembrance has been shaped and investigates the impact of the two global events that have prompted intensive efforts at re-conceiving the First World War for contemporary purposes: the Second World War and the dénouement of the Cold War. The last quarter-century since 1989 has seen an international surge of interest in the Great War and those who fought in it, and this requires explanation. While persistent, the processes of remembrance have not been uniform either in intensity or trajectory. The afterlife of the Great War over the course of the twentieth century has been a tale of continued reshaping, in light of the preoccupations of those who returned to 1914–18, to find meaning in and for their own time and place.

In this chapter, I want to reflect on how a series of nations have remembered the two world wars, seeking to give meaning to the slaughter. The narratives that they constructed about these two appalling conflicts, only a quarter of a century apart, have had a profound effect on how these countries have seen themselves and how they came to understand the twentieth century. I shall look in turn at France, Germany, Russia, America, Britain and Australia – examining how the two world wars have been interpreted in very different ways to create distinctive national narratives, not only in terms of their domestic contexts, but in light of new patterns of international relations. The two world wars have existed in a symbiotic relationship, each giving meaning to the other and to the twentieth century as a whole. The end of the Cold War offered space for seeing the First World War afresh in its own terms, though still refracted through the politics and preoccupations of the moment.

In the first part of the chapter, I will examine the process of constructing the First World War through the experience of the Second World War. In the latter part I want to reflect on some of the more recent developments in the process of remembrance.

* * *

The First World War has been seen in large part through the lens of its successor a quarter-century later. One might even say that, conceptually if not chronologically, the First World War was a consequence of the Second.

In Britain and across the British Empire and Commonwealth the conflict of 1914–18 was known at the time as the Great War – a verbal echo of the epic struggle against Napoleon a century before. Germans and Americans, for different reasons, tended to refer to it as a world war (*Weltkrieg*), while French terminology oscillated between *grande guerre* and *guerre mondiale*. It was only after a second, indisputably global conflict that the discourse of 'world war' caught on in the British Commonwealth: indeed the British Government took a formal decision on its terminology in 1948. And so the Second World War begat the First. This is not merely a *jeu d'esprit* on my part: the serious point is that, in all the countries I want to examine, the conflict of 1914–18 took on a different colour and significance in the light of the war of 1939–45. The crucial issue, as we shall see, is whether the two wars became linked in a sequential and progressive narrative, or whether one seemed at odds with the other – creating dissonance, bitterness or denial.[1]

Let me begin with the two central belligerents of 1914–18, France and Germany. For the French *la grande guerre* was remembered as a story of tragic simplicity, a fight to save the national territory from German invasion and occupation. The struggle was appalling, costing over 1.3 million dead or 13 per cent of the male population between the ages of fifteen and forty-nine.[2] But it ended in victory, with the Germans driven out of north-eastern France and also from Alsace and Lorraine – ceded to Germany after France's defeat by Prussia in 1870. The dead of the Great War were commemorated in vast cemeteries, notably at Verdun, the epic killing field of 1916, under plaques stating that the soldier had died for France (*mort pour la France*). Here was a narrative of grim but meaningful sacrifice, consecrated by victory. Even after Hitler set out along the road to a new war in the 1930s, the French – unlike the British, as we shall see – did not question the war of 1914–18. For them the issue became why France had won the war but lost the peace.

The German narrative was very different. Germany's losses were among the highest of all belligerents – over two million dead or 12.5 per cent of males aged fifteen to forty-nine – but its war ended in defeat. Except that most Germans did not recognize 1918 as a defeat. In the spring of 1918, having knocked Russia out of the war, their all-out offensive in the west came close to breaking the British and French front. But the assault cost nearly a million casualties and eventually ran out of steam. In October 1918, with British, French and American armies now pushing eastward and Germany's allies collapsing, the High Command asked the Allies for an armistice – a cessation of hostilities preparatory to an eventual peace conference. Yet German troops remained on French and Belgian soil, with official propaganda still promising imminent victory. The news that Germany was seeking peace therefore came as a traumatic shock. It took five weeks to negotiate the armistice, during which time the armed forces mutinied, the Kaiser's regime collapsed in revolution and a new socialist-led democracy was installed. The chaos left Germany in no condition to resist the harsh peace terms imposed on it by the Allies – what became known to Germans as the *Diktat* of Versailles. The wrenching disjunction between the heady optimism of March 1918 and Germany's total collapse in November encouraged many Germans to accept the claims of Hitler and the right that a near-victorious army had been 'stabbed in the back' by revolutionaries and pacifists at home. This *Dolchstosslegende* became a staple of German politics and helped make the revision of the Versailles settlement a broad national goal. Millions of Germans simply did not accept that they had been defeated; memorials such as the great stone circle at Tannenberg, where the Germans had routed the Russians in 1914, became shrines to a lost victory that had to be redeemed.[3]

The war of 1939–45 turned out very differently from that of 1914–18 and that, in turn, cast new light for both French and Germans on the earlier conflict. In 1914–18 France had held out for four years; in 1940 it collapsed in little more than four weeks. To some extent the Germans were lucky: by risking nearly all their armour (a mere ten Panzer divisions) in an attack through the Ardennes rather than a head-to-head encounter with the French and British in Belgium they surprised the French army whose command and control system fell apart. But, at a deeper level, France was a nation that lacked the stomach for another fight barely two decades after the last blood sacrifice. This time only 92,000 soldiers 'died for France' whereas 1.8 million were taken prisoner.[4] Compounding this bitter irony, the fascist-style government in Vichy that collaborated with the Germans was led by Marshal Philippe Pétain, hero of Verdun in 1916. This was not just defeat but humiliation. France was eventually liberated in 1944 by British and American armies, installing in power their prickly client, General Charles de Gaulle, who had spent the intervening years in exile in London. His Free French forces, together with communist-led partisans within France, became symbols of France's resistance to Nazism, and the Gaullist historiography of the conflict depicted a polarized struggle between the majority who resisted Nazism and a minority who collaborated – *résistants* versus *collabos*. Yet, however hard the French tried, nothing could expunge the pain and humiliation of 1940 and this became an open sore from the 1960s as the extent of collaboration was exposed – most famously in the film *The Sorrow and the Pity* (*Le Chagrin et la Pitié*). All this served to cast an even nobler and yet more tragic light on 1914–18.[5]

After 1945 Germans, too, could not deny the reality of defeat and this was a major contrast with their collective remembrance of 1918. Yet the stance of Konrad Adenauer's post-war government was one of 'public penance' but 'strictly limited liability'.[6] Responsibility for the war was laid on Hitler and his evil clique, rather than on the German nation as a whole: veteran historian Friedrich Meinecke, writing in 1946, ascribed what he called the 'German catastrophe' to a 'singular' personality and 'singular' circumstances which in combination succeeded in 'compelling the German people for a limited period to follow a false path' at odds with their cultural and religious traditions.[7]

It was not until the 1960s that attitudes began to change, as the enormity of the Holocaust was exposed and as West Germany lurched to the left. Student radicals exposed the complicity of their elders, the 'Silent Generation', in Nazi crimes.

Historian Fritz Fischer also attacked the conventional wisdom, rooted in the myths of 1918, that Germany bore no special responsibility for the outbreak of war in 1914. Instead, he argued, the Kaiser's inner circle had not only started the war but had done so for imperialist goals akin to Hitler's in the 1930s, including the dream of living space in the east. In other words Germany bore a 'double guilt' – for the Kaiser's war as well as Hitler's war. During the 1960s and 1970s leftist social historians of the so-called Bielefeld School, taking up criticisms already current outside Germany, brought the German people into the circle of guilt rather than, like Meinecke, blaming a criminal few. These scholars developed the thesis that modern German history had evolved differently from that of western Europe along a special path (*Sonderweg*) characterized by the weakness of liberal democracy and the persistence of autocracy and militarism.[8]

For the French, then, despite the humiliations and awkward history of 1939–45, the war of 1914–18 retained its sacred status; for Germans, on the other hand, both wars became tainted – indeed the country effectively renounced war and big armaments, with consequences for international peacekeeping that extend right up to the present day. Yet for both France and Germany the common experience of 1939–45 as defeat and disaster prompted a remarkable change of heart and policy that defied the trend of recent history. Having fought three epoch-changing wars between 1870 and 1945, France and West Germany cooperated as pioneers of western European integration in the 1950s. This process started in 1950 with the Schuman Plan for a Coal and Steel Community, realized in 1952, under which France, Germany, Italy and the Benelux countries surrendered sovereign control over the industries that had been central to war-making in the first half of the twentieth century. Robert Schuman embodied the integration process within his own life. Growing up in Lorraine under German occupation, he had been educated at German universities and was only spared on health grounds from having to fight in the German army in the Great War. But after 1918 Lorraine was handed back to France and Schuman climbed the ladder of French politics. In 1950 this reject from the Kaiser's army was France's Foreign Minister.

Building on the success of the Coal and Steel Community, the Six signed the Treaty of Rome in 1957, establishing the European Economic Community. This was, in effect, a peace-treaty for the Second World War, established on the principle 'if you can't beat them, join them'. Concluded only twelve years after 1945, it marked an astonishing rapprochement after three-quarters of a century of bitter Franco-German conflict and it also served to put the two world wars into a completely different perspective. One of the most evocative symbols of the new entente was the image in 1962 of Adenauer and de Gaulle on their knees taking Mass before the High Altar of Reims Cathedral, ancient coronation site of French kings, whose great Gothic nave had been ravaged by German shells in 1914. De Gaulle spoke about how the endless Franco-German rivalry 'conducted by the elite on both sides' had led only to 'a series of victories and defeats and countless graves' but now, he told Adenauer, their two countries were finally able to realize 'the dream of unity that has haunted the souls of our Continent for twenty centuries' back through Charlemagne and the Holy Roman Empire to Imperial Rome itself.[9] And so emerged a progressive narrative about the era of the two world wars – a saga of ruinous nationalism eventually transcended in internationalism as the bloody first half of the twentieth century gave way to a second half characterized by peace and prosperity. This has been the basis of the Franco-German relationship ever since.

The Soviet Union also developed a sequential and meaningful account of the two world wars, albeit very different in character. For Russians the Great War lasted from 1914 to 1917 – the year when the Tsarist regime collapsed in defeat on the battlefield and in revolution at home. Soviet historiography represented 1914–17 as an imperialist struggle, worth remembering merely as the catalyst for revolution. Russia's total death toll in 1914–17 will never be known exactly but it was probably around two million, which is at least equivalent to Germany's losses. Yet, as historian Catherine Merridale has noted, there were no Soviet memorials to the dead of the First World War – a staggering contrast with western Europe and the countries of the British Empire, especially Australia where perhaps 1,500 public memorials were erected. Unlike the Australians, for whom the war was physically distant, for the Russians, 1914–17 was a brutal conflict fought on or close to home soil and also displacing millions of civilian refugees. Yet for the bereaved, the grief was as 'distant' as for Australians – perhaps more so given the chilling official silence.[10]

It was not inevitable that Russia's war should be entombed in silence. In 1915–16 the government developed elaborate plans for a national war museum, church and cemetery on the outskirts of Moscow, under the patronage of the Tsarina's sister, but this grand project was overwhelmed by the revolution. Although the All-Russian War Cemetery did survive, it fell into disrepair, becoming a convenient dumping ground for the victims of Stalin's purges until the site was cleared in the 1950s to build a movie theatre. The cinema's name was 'Leningrad' which underlines the point that, although the communist regime blotted out any memory of 1914–17, it later built up the war of 1941–5 as a central myth of the Soviet state. This was especially true in the 1960s, after Nikita Khrushchev's partial but shocking revelations about the iniquities of Stalin had raised questions about the credibility of the regime. So, after Khrushchev's fall in 1964, Leonid Brezhnev and his colleagues created a new justification for party rule in the cult of the 'Great Patriotic War'. This trumpeted the heroism of the people and the resilience of their leaders in the face of Hitler's dastardly surprise attack of June 1941, and asserted that the regime had built on its far-sighted policies of collectivization and industrialization of the 1930s. The epics of hero cities, notably Leningrad which survived a brutal siege of nearly 900 days, became a feature of this master narrative.[11]

The year 1917 also helped to define American narratives of the century but for totally different reasons. The year that Russia left the war was also the year when America entered the conflict, with President Woodrow Wilson's ringing call to 'make the world safe for democracy'. For the United States the First

228 *David Reynolds*

World War was brief – little more than a year and a half from April 1917 until the Armistice of November 1918. Because of this and also because of America's geographical remoteness compared with the other great powers, the United States was much less affected by the conflict. Although four million soldiers were mobilized and two million served 'over there', the death toll was only 114,000 (0.4 per cent of males aged fifteen to forty-nine), with more than half of these being troops who died not in combat but from the influenza pandemic. Moreover, Wilson's Great Crusade for peace and democracy quickly turned sour. In 1919 Wilson tried to railroad his version of a League of Nations through the US Senate on the back of ratification of the Treaty of Versailles. A majority of Senators would probably have accepted a loose international league, even a limited guarantee of France against future German aggression, but they would not accept the President's grandiose vision which implied worldwide American commitments to international peace-keeping. In the 1930s a mood of deep popular disenchantment about the Great War set in, amid sensational claims about how the country had been seduced into war in 1917 by cunning British propagandists and America's own 'merchants of death' – the bankers and arms manufacturers in league with the Allies. As Europe slid towards another great war, the dominant mood in America was distinctly isolationist. 'Of the hell broth that is now brewing in Europe we have no need to drink', declared novelist Ernest Hemingway. 'We were fools to be sucked in once in a European war, and we should never be sucked in again.'[12]

This widespread conviction that 1917–18 had been a foolish aberration from America's historic tradition of 'no entangling alliances' shaped US foreign policy from the mid-1930s right up to Pearl Harbor. But Japan's surprise attack, and Hitler's concurrent declaration of war on the United States, transformed American attitudes. Although isolationism remained a powerful undercurrent, the dominant mood in 1942–5 was supportive of the war and, increasingly, of a new internationalism. The State Department mounted a big domestic publicity campaign to sell the United Nations organization as America's 'second chance' to redeem the missed opportunity of 1919 and establish a new American-led international order. The folly of the European powers in starting two suicidal wars in a generation added weight to this new American sense of mission. The war ended in August 1945 with two mushroom clouds over Japan: these became defining images of America's new status as a 'superpower' in the 'atomic age'. The conflict's moral cachet as 'The Good War' (in journalist Studs Terkel's celebrated phrase)[13] was confirmed by the 1960s revelations of the Holocaust and the 1970s disenchantment with America's disastrous war in Vietnam. On this reading of history, therefore, 1917 began America's rise to twentieth-century hegemony. As tension with the Soviet Union deepened, many US historians also depicted that year as the opening of the Cold War, pitting Wilson's vision against that of Lenin, thereby setting the parameters of debate about the meaning of America's First World War.[14]

In Soviet and American national narratives, therefore, 1917 was seen as marking a first step to global leadership – a position finally gained by blood and treasure in 1941–5. For both countries the two world wars became key points on a rising arc of power and prosperity from which they dominated global politics after 1945, at least until the USSR collapsed in 1991.

* * *

I have suggested that in all the four countries discussed so far the First and Second World Wars were gradually linked up into sequential narratives that helped give meaning to the second half of the twentieth century. The British experience is, I think, significantly different: in 1914–18 the country was neither invaded nor did it suffer extensive bombing, or revolutionary or paramilitary violence. And, unlike the countries discussed so far, the British failed to construct a positive sequential narrative of the two world wars and their aftermath. This failure has coloured the now predominant British interpretation of 1914–18 as tragic folly.

The cliché about Britain going to war in 1914 in a state of naïve patriotic fervour has now been overtaken – as for the other belligerents – by a more nuanced account of public attitudes. To some degree the Great War was, even for the British, a 'distant' war since national territory was not directly threatened. The Liberal Cabinet's reluctance to go to war was overcome both for politicians and the public at large by Germany's invasion of Belgium – whose neutrality Britain was pledged by treaty to protect. Germany's unprovoked and brutal assault on 'little Belgium', following the attack by Berlin's ally, Austria-Hungary, on 'little Serbia', gave the struggle a sharp and simple moral edge for the majority of the British people. The war was widely supported as a struggle for the principles of 'liberty' and 'civilization' against Prussian autocracy, 'militarism' and 'barbarism'. Even after the horrors of the Somme and Passchendaele, most of the British people, soldiers and civilians alike, still felt that they had been fighting a necessary war to prevent German domination of Europe. And, to quote historian Adrian Gregory, 'many would continue to believe it for their entire lives'.[15]

The immediate exception to this narrative was Ireland, but even here the story is more complex than Irish nationalist mythology suggests. On the eve of war in 1914 the British government conceded the principle of Irish Home Rule, bitterly contested for half a century, and this historic gesture had a profound effect on Irish opinion. Even fervent Irish nationalists were ready to volunteer for the British army, convinced like Thomas Kettle that Britain, despite its past iniquities, was now standing up for the rights of small nations such as Belgium and Serbia against 'the Blood-and-Ironmongers' of Prussia who had 'entered into possession of the soul of humanity'.[16] Fervour cooled when the British government failed to implement the Home Rule decision but Irish support for the war remained reasonably solid throughout 1915. When the 1916 Easter Rising broke out, most mainstream nationalists condemned it as a quixotic and suicidal act by a few hotheads, but opinion changed dramatically after the British military acted with heavy-handed brutality in executing the ring-leaders, thereby turning them into national martyrs. For Protestant opinion, however, the key month of 1916 was not April but July, when the 36th (Ulster) Division lost a third of its 15,000 men in the opening days of the battle of the Somme. Protestants contrasted the 'blood sacrifice' of these soldiers, mostly Belfast boys, with the 'back-stabbing treachery' of the Easter Rising. In Ireland, therefore, the events of 1916 served to deepen communal divisions – igniting the Catholic bid for independence from Britain but also hardening Protestant determination not to live in a Papist-run Ireland. Their rival ideologies, respectively justifying nationalism and partition, were rooted in interpretations of 1916 and they helped to sustain Ulster's open sectarian conflicts from the 1960s to the 1990s.

Despite the power of the war in producing these competing national narratives in Ireland, the theme of justified sacrifice for the values of civilization held sway in Britain into the 1930s. In mainland Britain, indeed, the conflict helped defuse pre-war Home Rule demands from Wales and especially Scotland, replacing separatist passions with a shared sense of solemn pride in Britain's war. And whereas it has now become almost axiomatic in Britain that a generation of innocent young men, pumped up with grand abstractions such as Honour, Glory and England, were sacrificed pointlessly by their elders in stupid battles conducted by stupid generals, such a narrative was hardly 'fixed' in popular memory at the time. In Britain, as elsewhere, the tenth anniversary of the Armistice in 1928 did produce a rash of reflective writing, much of it critical of the war and often emulating the success of Erich Maria Remarque's *All Quiet on the Western Front*. But this revisionist writing did not undermine the dominant British sense of justified sacrifice. R.C. Sherriff's play *Journey's End*, today celebrated for an unequivocally anti-war message, was regarded very differently by its author. 'I have not written this play as a piece of propaganda. And certainly not as propaganda for peace', Sherriff declared, 'nor to point any kind of moral. I wanted to perpetuate the memory of these men.'[17] Like Sherriff, historians also struggled to draw morally compelling and easily digestible narratives about the war. As Hitler broke free of the Treaty of Versailles and a new conflict loomed, therefore, the hope that 1914–18 had been a 'war to end all wars' looked increasingly ludicrous. The outbreak of a new conflict in September 1939 cast doubt on the efficacy of what had been achieved at such cost in 1914–18. A British nurse, E.M. Selby, had ended her First World War diary with words of passion: 'one could hardly keep from crying – and when one thought of all the boys who would never be coming home'. But she began her Second World War diary in June 1940, just after the evacuation from Dunkirk, with the leaden entry: 'Another war. Same enemy.'[18]

Except that, eventually, this second war gained a very different meaning. In 1940–1 Britain was heavily bombed and threatened with invasion so that, unlike 1914–18, the struggle clearly became a war for national survival. Yet victory was achieved at half the human cost of 1914–18. Moreover revelations of the death camps confirmed the bestiality of the enemy, while the categorical nature of Germany's defeat was expressed in unconditional surrender and Allied occupation. So the Second World War was seen as less costly and more meaningful than the First; it resolved the unfinished business left over from 1918 – this was a knock-out victory not the prelude to another round.

The British have remained committed to a heroic, positive view of the war of 1939–45, in the process distorting the nature of their war effort. The empire – meaning the so-called White Dominions, India and the British Crown colonies – was essential to Britain in this world war as in 1914–18, enabling a small island of forty-eight million people to punch way above its weight in the international arena. Secure imports of raw materials and food allowed Britain to concentrate on war production, while manpower from its empire was essential to waging global war, on the battlefields and beyond them. After 1945, however, the contribution of the Commonwealth and Empire to British victory was gradually marginalized in popular memory, in official accounts and in many histories as the Churchillian interpretation of the war as Britain's 'finest hour' took hold. This process of 'nationalization' was accelerated by a succession of war films in the 1950s that highlighted Britain's armed forces standing alone against Hitler's Europe and displaying stereotypical British male attributes such as gritty courage and a stiff upper lip – movies such as *Angels One Five*, *The Cruel Sea* and *The Dam Busters*.[19]

In the 1960s, however, a series of developments raised questions about what the war had achieved for Britain, as the country's global power diminished. First, Britain's colonial empire crumbled very rapidly. Between 1948 and 1960 only three British colonies had gained independence; over the next four years the figure was seventeen – many of them African territories previously judged incapable of standing on their own for several more generations.[20] As the Sterling Area disintegrated, Harold Wilson's Labour government also decided to withdraw British troops from east of Suez (apart from Hong Kong). And the British, having ignored European integration in its early days, were forced to come to terms with the existence and success of the European Community. 'If we try to remain aloof', a Cabinet committee warned in 1960, 'bearing in mind that this will be happening simultaneously with the contraction of our overseas possessions, we shall run the risk of losing political influence and of ceasing to be able to exercise any real claim to be a world Power.'[21] In December 1962 Dean Acheson, the former US Secretary of State, observed that 'Great Britain has lost an empire and has not yet found a role.' The outcry that this remark provoked in London indicated that Acheson had struck a raw nerve. But his stark depiction of 1960s Britain marooned between empire and Europe was apposite and the sense of drift left a question mark hanging over the larger meaning of the Second World War. Perhaps it had been a pyrrhic victory? Heroic, yes, but unable to arrest the decline in British power and influence? Maybe even accelerating that slide from international predominance? For Britain, the saga of the two world wars lacked an overarching positive meaning comparable to the narratives that have been constructed in France, Germany and the United States. The country prized an epic struggle against Hitler but wrestled with the challenges of losing an empire and seeking a role.

All this encouraged renewed mining of the past, beyond the most recent war, in an effort to understand how the two world wars informed the direction of modern British history. The advent of the fiftieth anniversaries of the war in the 1960s offered opportunities to reconstruct Britons' relationship with the First World War, in ways that reflected contemporary social ideas and attitudes. What emerged was a relentlessly negative view of 1914–18, the narrative of which spoke to lost innocence and satirized both the military elite and the rhetoric that had fuelled the war, to the point of rendering the conflict either a poignant tragedy or a pointless farce. These conceptions of the war were expressed most notoriously in Joan Littlewood's musical *Oh, What a Lovely War!* (1963) and Alan Clark's book *The Donkeys* (1961) which popularized the cliché about British Tommies of 1914–18 as 'lions led by donkeys'. The BBC's multi-part *The Great War* (1964) helped to evoke mud and destruction as the central characteristics of the war experience; it is significant, too, that the installation of Sassoon and Owen as the canonical figures of British war poetry also dates from this period, rather than from the 1930s.[22] It was now, rather than three decades earlier, that an ironic mode of remembering the war emerged as the primary mode of remembrance in Britain.

* * *

In Australia, the linking of the two world wars was initially rather more consistent than the divergence I have sketched in other contexts. Australians exhibit an obsession with Gallipoli that belies its material consequences: of some 60,000 Australian war deaths only 8,000 occurred during this ill-fated campaign. But, as historian Joan Beaumont has noted, 'Gallipoli was Australia's first mass experience of modern war', little more than a decade after the Federation had been formed in 1901.[23] It therefore became a critical, defining test of national fibre, to which a clear sense of national identity was harnessed, even as the war was still in progress. Here, the avowed superiority of the Australian soldier was rooted in supposedly unique digger traits of toughness and mateship, a myth built on its nineteenth-century antecedents and set in the Australian bush.[24] During the Great War and the interwar era the Anzac story was not aggressively anti-British. There was a more specific anti-English animus among Australian soldiers, especially towards stereotypically upper-class English officers, but this was compatible with what was known as 'British race patriotism' – rather in the same way that Scots (with whom the diggers got on very well) could detest the English while being proud of the British Empire. The Australian contingent's title, the 'Australian Imperial Force', was therefore entirely apt. As 25 April became established during the 1920s as Australia's national day, commemoration still emphasized what celebrants called the 'crimson thread of kinship' with the 'British race'. When Australia went to war a second time in 1939, in a war again declared by the King on behalf of the Empire, its soldiers took on the mantle of their revered predecessors, cultivating their 'digger' image as the '2nd AIF'.

In other ways, however, Australia's Second World War offered sharp contrasts with the First. Combat deaths were less than half the figure for 1914–18, and they were spread around numerous theatres of action. The conflict seemed largely a story of defeats or surrender – Greece, Crete, Singapore, Ambon, Timor and Rabaul. Victories such as Alamein were rare exceptions and thirty per cent of Australian war deaths occurred in captivity.[25] The tendency to blame the disasters on London's military and political ineptitude was strong, especially in the shocking months of early 1942 when Singapore surrendered and the Japanese bombed Darwin. Prime Minister Paul Keating, on the fiftieth anniversary of the end of the Second World War in 1995, used that occasion to argue that the Second World War was when Australia's modern image was formed as an independent, Pacific power. And yet it is a considerable simplification to suggest that during the Second World War Australia suddenly turned away from Britain towards the United States or to a policy of independent self-assertion. 'First and foremost, Australia is a Pacific power', declared Percy Spender in 1944. But, he insisted, that did not 'in the slightest degree lessen her ties of kinship with Great Britain' – a sentiment shared across the major political alignments.[26]

The catalyst for clear-cut policy change – and ultimately the kind of sensibility Keating promoted in the 1990s – was not so much burgeoning Australian nationalism as declining British imperialism. The British decision in 1961 to apply for membership of the European Community pointed up in stark symbolic terms a fundamental shift of British focus from Empire to Europe. As Stuart Ward has argued, this forced Australians, at both the governmental and popular levels, to address explicitly the readjustments in Australia's position that had been going on gradually for some years. Although the British may have jumped first by turning their backs on Empire, Australians did then move rapidly to assert much greater independence. It was during this latter phase that the Anzac saga developed a more pronounced anti-British sting, evident for instance in Peter Weir's 1981 movie *Gallipoli*. The film's publicity poster – 'From a place you have never heard of ... A story you'll never forget' – said a lot about where the Anzac saga was coming from in the 1970s and equally where it would be going. Some had predicted its ultimate demise but *Gallipoli* did an enormous amount to revive popular interest in 1915, providing as it did a new conception of the First World War in light of the Second, and in light of Britain's own response to the two world wars in the 1960s. As the country's imperial origins faded, observes historian Mark McKenna, 'the legend could now be refashioned as the Bastille Day or Fourth of July Australia never had, the day which cut Australia adrift from its Imperial past'.[27]

* * *

The surge of interest internationally in the Great War since the end of the 1980s – uneven but persistent at both public and private levels – cuts across some of the major contrasts detailed above. Apart from anything else, the fall of the Berlin Wall and the revolutions of 1989, together with the collapse of the

Soviet Union in 1991, changed the terms in which the war could be remembered, recalling as they did the chaotic circumstances of 1917–19, and allowing the First World War to emerge again from the shadow of 1939–45. One trajectory of remembrance over the last quarter-century has been factious and sometimes violent conflict. Elsewhere, however, we see efforts to construct a more eirenic story of internecine nationalist conflict giving way to European reconciliation.

The most radical shifts naturally occurred in Russia and the former Soviet states. With greater academic freedoms, historians took up the challenge to start examining the war itself, and its place in the series of crises concluding with the end of Russia's civil war in 1921. There was room in public, too, to address the commemoration of the war and its losses – a process that had barely begun during the war before it was halted and denied. Russians could now remember in public, through public symbols and sites – though remembrance of this war, the revolution and the civil war, remains contentious, in terms of who can and should be remembered, and whether the revolution itself might now be regarded as a disaster. How to talk about all this will be a major challenge in 2017.

In several states formerly under Soviet hegemony, such questions were even more powerfully loaded. The dissolution of Yugoslavia in particular, but also the post-communist transition in the Baltic states, saw a resumption of ethnic violence comparable to eastern Europe after the First World War. The violence was fuelled by nationalist narratives, often anchored around the First World War, that were invoked to critique the present and shape the future. In a broader sense, eastern Europeans brought to the table of European integration demands that their legacies of the First World War – Soviet communism and Stalinist repression – should be recognised as part of a full sense of European identity. The attendant concepts of 'double occupation' and even 'double genocide' challenged the existing foundational narrative about building a democratic Europe, which to date had been built pre-eminently around recognition of the Holocaust and the end of Nazism.

In eastern Europe as in Russia, therefore, the end of Soviet repression had finally unleashed real historical debate. And this was a region with many skeletons in the closet – relics from being the prime battlefield in two world wars, from the double Nazi–Soviet occupation and from the Holocaust, right back to the bloody tangle of nationalism and revolution in 1917–18. After 1989 the closet was ransacked and its contents appropriated selectively by rival political and ethnic groups. The bitter, chaotic 'memory wars' that ensued were a far cry from the steady, layered process of reflection and then refraction that had characterized Great War remembrance in Britain since 1918.

Beyond eastern Europe, where remembrance was not so violently contentious, there were opportunities to re-examine the history of the war in terms of reconciliation between former enemies and the fostering of greater understanding among former allies. In 1990, a reunified Germany might have posed the same problems that it had done in 1914. It did not, and its even deeper commitment to European integration led to the production of conciliatory narratives of a shared trauma of 1914–18. As with public recognition of the Holocaust, museums have played a key role in this process. The First World War museum at Kobarid (Caporetto), in Slovenia, is presented in four different languages: Italian, Slovenian, German and English. The site in 1917 of a disastrous Italian defeat by the Habsburg and German armies, it now articulates a narrative of common suffering among all the soldiers who are evoked to exclaim 'Damn all war!' More sophisticated is the Historial de la Grande Guerre at Péronne, at the heart of the Somme battlefield, which opened in 1992. This was underpinned by the commitment of key academics from Britain, France and Germany and helped to initiate a transnational approach that challenges the national paradigms through which the war has been understood. Again, the impression strongly conveyed is of indescribable human tragedy, reflecting the theme that the war was the foundational catastrophe that shaped the modern world. In the case of Australia and Turkey – enemies at Gallipoli – reconciliation of another kind has proceeded, in which two stories of nationalist origins anchored in the events of 1915 increasingly come into contact. In Australia, Turks now march in major parades on 25 April, while at Gallipoli, services at the officially named 'Anzac Cove' are jointly organized and conducted – all signs of a new approach to national remembrance as international reconciliation.

In the United Kingdom and Ireland one can also see an erosion of the structures that the war had helped put in place. For Scotland and Wales, whose own home rule agenda had faded with the war's reinforcement of a British identity, the economic decline that commenced in the 1960s encouraged nationalist politics, while the end of the Cold War loosened the bonds forged by a strong external foe. The processes of devolution accelerated to the point – in Scotland – of a national referendum on independence in 2014. In Ireland, the longer perspective on the violent twentieth century afforded by the collapse of the Soviet Union prompted closer and more eclectic examination of Ireland's part in that experience. The Good Friday agreement between London, Dublin and the main Northern Ireland political parties, and the concomitant removal of British troops from the streets of Ulster, made discussion of Irish involvement in British wars less contentious and difficult. The Western Front itself became a place in which sectarian divides might be bridged to construct a more common history. Not until the end of the so-called 'Troubles' was it possible officially to acknowledge the sacrifice of Irishmen, both Catholics and Protestants, in Britain's army during the Great War. The Island of Ireland Peace Tower at Messines, unveiled by Queen Elizabeth II and Irish President Mary McAleese on 11 November 1998, was a hugely symbolic act as the Irish tried to move on from their traumatic twentieth century.[28]

Shifting international relationships have therefore played a significant part in changing modes of remembrance of the First World War, but other factors have been at work as well. These include a boom in family history that connects with much greater interest in individual experiences of war and its traumatic legacies for many survivors. Paradoxically, as 1914–18 has become more remote in time, it seems closer emotionally. A fascination with individual experiences of the war, growing in strength since the 1960s and 1970s, was reflected in the so-called new military history that attracted very large popular audiences. In the 1990s, popular literature increased the currency of the repertoire of images that had become central to British war memory since the 1960s: the novels of Sebastian Faulks and Pat Barker encapsulated the British identification of the Great War with the experience of the Tommies. Internationally, the passing of the last veterans of the war drew common expressions of awe at their longevity, but more importantly promoted their elevation beyond the particularities of their own lives to become 'heroes', or at least representatives of a heroic generation. Such public narratives, and the public ceremonies that carried them, could also be met with the increasing resources of family history to vindicate – and sometimes challenge – narratives of heroism, endurance and suffering. Here, in the fusion of state funerals of the last veterans, the ceremonies of armistice anniversaries, and the quiet corners of family history, one finds much of the emotional power that drives the processes of remembrance in the twenty-first century.

* * *

The global story of remembering the First World War is rooted in the international search for meaning that attended the war in its own time. But our ways of seeing it also reflect multifarious responses to the major events of the twentieth century through which the war has been refracted. These events are, of course, only a framework: there is no easy formula for making a global history of remembrance. As ever, national histories are insistent, and vital to understanding and explaining the most recent formulations of the war and its meanings. Our task is to understand the processes of remembering, and the shaping of the narratives surrounding the war, rather than simply to partake in 'remembrance'. In this sense, the most significant effect of the end of the Cold War in many countries has been the decoupling of the two world wars, so that for all their similarities, there is potential now for the First World War to be understood as distinct from its successor. From this flows the opportunity for fresh reflections on the conflict's meaning and significance. Will the greater capacities for accessing and sharing information across borders in our internet age encourage broader, perhaps novel, conceptions of the war? Or will the mass of information now available, on ever more intimate levels, reinforce engagement with the war within national cultures of remembrance? The challenge is now not to wait and see, but to understand those potentialities and to see what vistas they open up as twenty-first century historians look back on 1914–18.

Notes

1 For a fuller discussion see my essay 'The Origins of "The Second World War": Historical Discourse and International Politics' in David Reynolds, *From World War to Cold War: Churchill, Roosevelt and the International History of the 1940s* (Oxford: Oxford University Press, 2006), 9–22. On a larger canvas, themes in this chapter are developed in David Reynolds, *The Long Shadow: The Great War and the Twentieth Century* (London: Simon & Schuster, 2013).

An international perspective 237

2 These and other casualty figures are taken from the international table in J.M. Winter, *The Great War and the British People* (London: Macmillan, 1985), 75.
3 On the myth of the war and Hitler's own war service, see Thomas Weber, *Hitler's First World War: Adolf Hitler, the Men of the List Regiment, and the First World War* (Oxford: Oxford University Press, 2010).
4 Figures from Sarah Fishman, *We Will Wait: Wives of French Prisoners of War, 1940–1945* (New Haven: Yale University Press, 1991), 27.
5 The classic study remains Henri Rousso, *The Vichy Syndrome: History and Memory in France since 1944*, translated by Arthur Goldhammer (Cambridge, MA: Harvard University Press, 1991).
6 Mary Fulbrook, *German National Identity after the Holocaust* (Cambridge: Polity Press, 1999), 59.
7 Friedrich Meinecke, *The German Catastrophe*, translated by Sidney B. Fay (Boston: Beacon Press, 1950), 96.
8 Patrick Finney, *Remembering the Road to World War Two: International History, National Identity, Collective Memory* (London: Routledge, 2011), 74–84; on the Fischer controversy see for example David Stevenson, *The Outbreak of the First World War: 1914 in Perspective* (London: Macmillan, 1997), 10–12.
9 Quoted in Hans-Peter Schwarz, *Adenauer: Der Staatsmann, 1952–1967* (Stuttgart: Deutsche Verlags-Anstalt, 1991), 760.
10 Catherine Merridale, *Night of Stone: Death and Memory in Russia* (London: Granta, 2000), 122–4, 452; Ken Inglis, *Sacred Places: War Memorials in the Australian Landscape*, 3rd ed. (Melbourne: Melbourne University Publishing, 2008), 471.
11 Melissa Stockdale, 'United in Gratitude: Honoring Soldiers and Defining the Nation in Russia's Great War', *Kritika* 7 (2006), 465–8, 482; Daniel Orlovsky, 'Velikaia voina i rossiiskaia pamiat', in *Rossiia i pervaia mirovaia voina: Materialy mezhdunarodnogo nauchnogo kollokviuma*, ed. N.N. Smirnov (St Petersburg: D. Bulanin, 1999), especially 50. On the 1960s see Nina Tumarkin, *The Living and the Dead: The Rise and Fall of the Cult of World War Two in Russia* (New York: Basic Books, 1994), ch. 6.
12 Cushing Strout, *The American Image of the Old World* (New York: Harper and Row, 1963), 205.
13 Terkel placed his title in quotation marks 'because the adjective "good" mated to the noun "war" is so incongruous' but, for most Americans, the phrase has lost its irony and become almost descriptive. Studs Terkel, *'The Good War': An Oral History of World War Two* (London: Hamilton, 1985), vi; see also the discussion in John W. Jeffries, *Wartime America: The World War Two Home Front* (Chicago: I.R. Dee, 1996), 8–11.
14 Arno Meyer, *Political Origins of the New Diplomacy, 1917–18: Wilson versus Lenin* (New Haven: Yale University Press, 1959); N. Gordon Levin Jr, *Woodrow Wilson and World Politics: America's Response to War and Revolution* (New York: Oxford University Press, 1968).
15 Adrian Gregory, *The Last Great War: British Society and the First World War* (Cambridge: Cambridge University Press, 2008), 1–3.
16 T.M. Kettle, *The Ways of War* (London: Constable, 1917), 57.
17 Samuel Hynes, *A War Imagined: The First World War and English Culture* (London: Pimlico, 1990), x–xii; Rosa Maria Bracco, *Merchants of Hope: Middlebrow Writers and the First World War, 1919–1939* (Oxford: Berg, 1993), 178.
18 Gregory, 275.
19 David Edgerton, *Britain's War Machine: Weapons, Resources and Experts in the Second World War* (London: Allen Lane, 2011), 47, 272–3; Malcolm Smith, *Britain and 1940: History, Myth and Popular Memory* (London: Routledge, 2000), 120–3.
20 David Reynolds, *Britannia Overruled: British Policy and World Power in the Twentieth Century*, 2nd ed. (London: Longman, 2000), 208.
21 N. Piers Ludlow, *Dealing with Britain: The Six and the First UK Application to the EEC* (Cambridge: Cambridge University Press, 1997), 32.

22 Dan Todman, *The Great War: Myth and Memory* (London: Hambledon Continuum, 2005), 99–111.
23 Joan Beaumont, ed., *Australia's War, 1914–18* (Sydney: Allen and Unwin, 1995), xx, 1, 13.
24 Alistair Thomson, *Anzac Memories: Living with the Legend* (Melbourne: Oxford University Press, 1994); Graham Seal, *Inventing Anzac: The Digger and National Mythology* (St Lucia: Queensland University Press, 2004).
25 Joan Beaumont ed., *Australia's War, 1914–1918*, 1, 174; see also Joan Beaumont, ed., *Australia's War, 1939–1945* (Sydney: Allen and Unwin, 1996), xx, 47–8. Counting deaths of service personnel from accidents, illness and training brings the total to about 40,000.
26 David Lowe, *Australian Between Empires: The Life of Percy Spender* (London: Pickering and Chatto, 2010), 97; Stuart Ward, *Australia and the British Embrace: The Demise of the Imperial Ideal* (Melbourne: Melbourne University Press, 2001), 21.
27 Mark McKenna, 'Anzac Day: How did it become Australia's national day?' in *What's Wrong with Anzac?: The Militarization of Australian History*, eds Marilyn Lake and Henry Reynolds (Sydney: New South, 2010), 122.
28 For a brief and effective overview see Keith Jeffery, *Ireland and the Great War* (Cambridge: Cambridge University Press, 2000).

Index

References to figures are shown in *italics*. References to notes consist of the page number followed by the letter 'n' followed by the number of the note, e.g. 36n32 refers to note no. 32 on page 36.

14–18, It's Our History! (exhibition, Brussels) 11
36th (Ulster) Division 166, 171, 180, *181*, 230
'1916 – myth, fact and mystery' (F. X. Martin) 167, 168

Acheson, Dean 231
Adam-Smith, Patsy, *The Anzacs* 41
Adamson, Ian 175
Adenauer, Konrad 225, 226
Admiral (film about Aleksandr Kolchak) 138
African soldiers 95–96
Agos (newspaper), Armenians and Çanakkale 160
Ahern, Bertie 171
AHRC (Arts and Humanities Research Council, UK) 75
AKP (Justice and Development Party, Turkey) 147–48, 155–57, 159–61
Albert I, King of the Belgians 187–88, 190, 191–92, 194
Albert II, King of the Belgians 171
Alexander, J. 72n52
Allen, Jim 178
All Quiet on the Western Front (Erich Maria Remarque) 209–10, 230
All-Russian War Cemetery 227
All Together Now (The Farm) 121
amateur family history phenomenon: digitization of archival records 27; 'Heirlooms 4 Heroes' leaflet 10, 21–23, *22*; 'Lives of the First World War' project 21, 31–34; media/fictional representations of the war (novels (1990s) 26–27; oral histories (1970s) 26; satirical portrayals of the war (1960s) 26; TV BBC series *The Great War* 26); motives of amateur family historians 28–29; narrowing gap between historians and public 23–24; passing of the last 'Tommy' (Harry Patch) 24–25; photographic tribute on Western Front *31*; post 'living memory' generations 25–26; professional research/advisory services 30; resources for research 36n32; tailored battlefield tours 30–31; *see also* family history and Great War in Australia
Amazing Grace 120
Anderson, B. 148
Angels One Five (film) 231
Anthems in Eden (Shirley Collins) 119
Anzac: Anzac and Çanakkale (Gallipoli) commemorations 150, 153; Anzac biscuits (Kingsley Baird's 'Tomb') 106, *107*; 'Anzac centenary' 51; Anzac Cove joint Australian-Turkish services 235; Anzac Day, Australia 2, 41–42, 48, 51; Anzac Day, Turkey (2013) 157; Anzac Day, Villers-Bretonneux, France 100; Anzac legend 39, 40, 45–46; Anzac spirit 42; Anzac story and anti-British sentiments 233; Anzac story and 'British race patriotism' 232; Families and Friends of the First A.I.F. 50; 'Mapping Our Anzacs' website (National Archives of Australia) 47–48, 49, 50; Victorian Anzac Centenary Committee 51–52
Anzacs, The (Patsy Adam-Smith) 41
Apollinaire, Guillaume, *Le poète assassiné* 103, 107

240 Index

Archive of Serbia, exhibition 11
archives: Australian soldiers' repatriation files archive 39–40, 50; digital archives 89n32; digitization of wartime records 9–10, 27, 30; digitized newspapers 49; 'Mapping Our Anzacs' website (National Archives of Australia) 47–48, 49, 50
Aristov, Mikhail 135
Armenians: Armenian genocide 11, 160–61; and Çanakkale 160
Armistice Nights (Britain) 113, 114, 115, 116
Army Museum, Les Invalides (Paris, France) 96
art *see* memorial art and museums (Western Front)
Arthur – or the Decline and Fall of the British Empire (The Kinks) 120
Arts and Humanities Research Council (AHRC, UK) 75
Ashe, Thomas 175
Ashplant, T. G. 5, 10, 38n67
Assmann, Aleida 207
Assmann, Jan 4, 208
Association of Turkish Travel Agencies (TÜRSAB) 153–54
Astor, John Jacob, 3rd Baron Astor of Hever 64–65
Atatürkism 147, 149
Atatürk, Mustafa Kemal: Atatürk memorial on Çanakkale battlefields *152*; and Çanakkale Epic Promotion Centre 158, 159; and Çanakkale myth 147, 148–52; personality cult 163n31
Attenborough, Richard, *Oh! What a Lovely War!* 118, 119
At the Abbey Gate (Charles Villiers Stanford) 112
'At the war memorial' (Chris de Burgh) 169
Attia, Kader 107–8
Audoin-Rouzeau, Stéphane 6
Australia: Australian soldiers' repatriation files archive 39–40, 50; 'Cobbers' (Peter Corlett), Australian Memorial Park, Fromelles, France 100, *101*, *102*; last Gallipoli veteran's state funeral 42; number of public WWI memorials 227; public's knowledge of war history 2, 3; war narratives (First World War, Anzac story 232; Second World War 233); *see also* Anzac; family history and Great War in Australia
Austria and memory of First World War: context, time and memory 207–9; first two decades (defeat and war narratives 209–10; Habsburg mythos 210; protest and pacifism 213–14; regimental histories 211–12; sadness and fight for Austrian identity 214; war memoirs 212–13); The 'forgotten war' (academic research (1945–48) 214–15; academic research (1970s-) 216–17; cinema and nostalgia for Habsburg past 215; controversy re. TV version of *Radetzkymarsch* (Josef Roth) 215–16); planning for 2014 centenary (official line 217–18; publishing and media hype 218–19)
Austrian National Library exhibition 11
AVV–VVK 189, 190, 196, 199

Baillieu, Ted 51–52
Baird, Kingsley, 'Tomb' 106–7, *107*
Baker, Chris 30, 31
Baker, Tilly 88n17
'Ballads of the Great War, The' (BBC commission) 124
Baltic states, post-communist transition and re-examination of First World War 234
Barber, Samuel, *Adagio for Strings* 120–21
Barbusse, Henri 210
Barker, Pat 77, 87n12, 236; *Regeneration* 60, 65–66
Barnwell, Ashley 44
Barr, Glenn 171
Barthes, Roland 110
Basu, P. 36n36
battlefield sites: battlefield tours/visits 30–31, 74, 84, 89n36; Landscapes and Sites of Memory of the Great War (UNESCO) 91
Baumgartner, Edwin 218
Bax, Arnold 114
Baxter, James Keir 77
BBC (British Broadcasting Corporation): Armistice Nights 116; 'The Ballads of the Great War,' commissioning of 124; *Blackadder Goes Forth* 59, 60, 62–63, 69, 70; *Britain's Great War* (Jeremy Paxman) 74; *The Great War* series 26, 232; 'People's War' website 32; Remembrance Day broadcasts 126n35; 'World War One At Home' series 74
Beatles, The 119
Beaumont-Hamel Newfoundland Memorial (France) 100
Beaumont, Joan 232
Becker, Annette 6, 12
Behr, R. 71n26
Belder, Paul De 202

Belfast: Belfast Cenotaph 173; 'Belfast nationalists and WW1' (Heritage Lottery project) 180
Belfast Telegraph (newspaper): reference to *Downton Abbey* 64; Ulster unionists 166–67
Belgian politics and the Great War: Belgian vs Flemish memory of the war 186; *flamingant* and Flemish soldiers 186, 187–89, 190, 193, 194, 195, 197–98; Flemish Movement 188, 189, 198, 201, 202, 205; Front Movement (Frontbeweging) 188–89, 190, 194, 195, 196, 198, 202; *heldenhuldezerken* (hero's tombstones) 186–87, *187*, 189–91, *191*, 194–96, 202, *203*; IJzertoren (first tower 192–93, *193*, 194, 195–98, *197*; second tower 198–200, *199*, 202–3, 204); IJzerwake pilgrimage 191, 200–205, *203*; Infantry Memorial of Brussels 193; military cemeteries and cultural affiliations 194–95; *see also* IJzer
Belgische Standaard (newspaper), *heldenhuldezerken* (hero's tombstones) 190
Belgium: *14–18, It's Our History!* (exhibition, Brussels) 11; commissioning of memorial art 90–91; *see also* Belgian politics and the Great War
Beyen, Marnix 204
Bielefeld School of historians 226
Binyon, Laurence: *For the Fallen* (set to music) 112; Remembrance Day broadcasts 126n35
Birdsong (Sebastian Faulks) 59, 63–64, 66, 70, 236
Bishop, R. 28, 38n73 to 74
Blackadder Goes Forth (BBC series) 59, 60, 62–63, 69, 70
Bliss, Arthur 114, 123; *Morning Heroes* 112, 116–18
Bolt Thrower 121–23, *122*; *Those Once Loyal* 122–23; *For Victory* 122
Bond, B. 60
Bottero, W. 29
Boult, Adrian 114
Bourke, Joanna 4
Bozdoğan, S. 151, 159
Bradford, Andrew 81
Branagh, Kenneth, *Forester's House* (Simon Patterson) 106
Brassens, Georges 119
Brennan, Miranda 38n72
Breuer, J. 69
Brezhnev, Leonid 139, 227

Britain: Armistice Nights (Britain) 113, 114, 115, 116; Arts and Humanities Research Council (AHRC) 75; British military cemeteries 100; First World War terminology 224; pardons for executed soldiers 65; post-1989 re-examination of First World War 235–36; public's knowledge of war history 2; war memory and family history 8, 9; war narratives (First World War 229–30, 232; Second World War 230–31); *see also* amateur family history phenomenon; BBC (British Broadcasting Corporation); British Legion; media representations of the Great War (Britain); music and Britain's remembrance of First World War; teaching of First World War (English secondary schools)
Britain's Great War (Jeremy Paxman) 74
British Legion: and John Foulds's *World Requiem* 114–16; and Wexford Great War memorial (Ireland) 178–79
British Library, 'First World War' portal 89n32
Brittain, Vera 77
Britten, Benjamin, *War Requiem* 112, 118–19, 120, 123, 124
Broken Years, The (Bill Gammage) 41
Brooke, Rupert 77, 126n35
Brusilov, General Aleksei, 1916 Offensive 136
Buff Medways, The, *Merry Christmas Fritz* 121
Butcher's Tale – Western Front 1914 (The Zombies) 119
Butterworth, George 113
Byrne, Gay 167–68

Cahir Great War memorial (Ireland) 171
'Call, The' (Jessie Pope) 77
Cameron, Charles 49, 50
Cameron, David 176
Campbell, Alec 42
Canada: Beaumont-Hamel Newfoundland Memorial (France) 100; Canadian National Vimy Memorial (France) 100; public's knowledge of war history 2
Çanakkale 162n1; *see also* Turkey and Çanakkale War (Gallipoli Campaign)
Çanakkale Epic Promotion Centre 158–59
Çanakkale martyrs' memorial (Turkey) 151–52
Canetti, Christine 104
Carion, Christian, *Joyeux Noël* 121
Carrington, Charles 115

Index

Casement, Roger 165–66
Cavatina (Ennio Morricone) 120
Caverne du Dragon (museum, Chemin des Dames, France) 95–96
Chagrin et la Pitié, Le/The Sorrow and the Pity (film) 225
Chemin des Dames (France), Caverne du Dragon museum 95–96
Chevallier, Gabriel 210
Childish, Billy 120, 121
China, Cimetière chinois de Nolette, Noyelles-sur-Mer, France 100
Chirac, Jacques 91–92
CHP (Republican People's Party, Turkey) 147, 151–52
Christmas Truce (1914) 96, 121
Chubar'ian, Aleksandr 132
Churchill, Winston 135, 231
church sermons, references to Great War and fiction/poetry 66
Cimetière chinois de Nolette, Noyelles-sur-Mer (France) 100
Clark, Alan, *The Donkeys* 26, 232
Clercq, Staf De 201
'Cobbers' (Peter Corlett), Australian Memorial Park, Fromelles (France) 100, *101, 102*
Cohen, Aaron 138
Çölaşan, Emin 153
Cold War 223, 228, 235, 236
Cole, Laurence 210
Cole, Margaret 77
Coles, Cecil 113
collective memory 4, 110; *see also* memory
Collins, Shirley, *Anthems in Eden* 119
commemorations: and historians 182; political tensions 11
Confino, Alon 4
Cork City war memorial (Ireland) 177, *177*
Corlett, Peter, 'Cobbers,' Australian Memorial Park, Fromelles (France) 100, *101, 102*
Cornish, P. 27
Corrigall, J. 72n39
counter-memory 194, 204; *see also* memory
Craonne, France 92, 95
Cruel Sea, The (film) 231
cultural institutions, and family history 9–10
cultural memory 4–5, 60–61, 207–8; *see also* memory
cultural trauma concept 68–69
Cumberbatch, Benedict 67
Cumhurriyet (newspaper), Atatürk and Çanakkale War 150

Daily Express (newspaper): Armistice Day celebrations 115, 116; reference to *Blackadder Goes Forth* 62
Daily Mail (newspaper): Armistice Day celebrations 115; wartime family history 25
Dam Busters, The (film) 231
Damousi, Joy 41
Dardanelles *see* Gallipoli
Davison, Graeme 7, 44, 45
Davutoğlu, Ahmet 156, 161
Dawson, Graham 5, 10, 38n67
DC Thompson Family History, 'Lives of the First World War' project 31–34
de Burgh, Chris, 'At the war memorial' 169
'Decade of Centenaries' programmes (Ireland): Irish Department of Arts, Heritage and Gaeltacht 180–82; Northern Ireland Community Relations Council/ Heritage Lottery Fund guidance 180
de Gaulle, Charles 225, 226–27
Delius, Frederick, *Requiem* 112
Demoen, Hendrik 196
Demurie, Dirk 202
Denyn, Bart 201
Deprez, Firmin 200, 201
De Rudder, Renaat 190
De Student (Flemish journal), AVV–VVK 189
De Valera, Eamon 168
digital archives 9–10, 27, 30, 89n32; *see also* archives; 'Lives of the First World War' project (Imperial War Museum)
digitized newspapers 49
Disorder, *Perdition* 121
Dix, Otto 98
Dobell, Eva 77
Dokumentationsarchiv lebensgeschichtlicher Aufzeichnungen (Institut für Wirtschafts- und Sozialgeschichte, University of Vienna) 217
Dolchstosslegende 225
Donkeys, The (Alan Clark) 26, 232
Douaumont (France): 1984 commemoration (Mitterrand and Kohl) 95; German remains controversy 102
'double genocide' concept 234
'double occupation' concept 234
Downton Abbey (TV historical drama) 64–65
Dream of Gerontius (Edward Elgar) 112
Drijvers, Frans 189
Drogheda First World War memorial (Ireland) 169
Duffell, John 43
Düffler, Jost 215, 218

'Dulce Et Decorum Est' (Wilfred Owen) 77, 81, 106, 121
Dundonald (Northern Ireland), 'The forgotten men of Dundonald cemetery' (Heritage Lottery Fund project) 180
Dunne, Tom 182
'Dur yolcu!' verses (Necmettin Halil Onan) 146–47, *146*
Dylan, Bob 119

Eastern Europe, post-communist transition and re-examination of First World War 234
Easter Rising (Ireland, 1916) 165–66, 229, 230
Economist, The (magazine), reference to Barker's *Regeneration* trilogy 65
education *see* teaching of First World War (English secondary schools)
Einhaus, Ann-Marie 11–12
Elgar, Edward: *Dream of Gerontius* 112; *Fringes of the Fleet* 112; *The Spirit of England* 112
Elias, Norbert 209, 210, 214
Elizabeth II, Queen of the United Kingdom 171, 176–77, 178, 235
Elmslie, Margery 42, 43–44, 45
Emmanuel, Paul, 'Lost Men' 108
England 1914 (Ralph McTell) 119
English, Joe 189, 196, 197, 200
Englund, Peter 97
Enniskillen 'Poppy Day bombing' (Northern Ireland) 169
Entertainment Weekly (magazine), *Harry Patch – In Memory of* (Radiohead) 120–21
Erdoğan, Recep Tayyip 147, 157–58, 159
Eroica (Charles Villiers Stanford) 112
Ersoy, Mehmet Akif 151, 159
Ertanı, E. 163n47
Esbroeck, Jan Van 201
Europeana 14–18 (database project) 9–10, 37n64, 89n32
European Commission, and First World War commemorations 11
'Europe lost and found in war and peace' project 218
Evans, Tanya 24, 40
exhibitions: *14–18, It's Our History!* (Brussels) 11; Austrian National Library 11; joint French/German exhibition 11

Families and Friends of the First A.I.F. 50
family history: and First World War remembrance 9–10, 235–36; and postmemory 8; *see also* amateur family history phenomenon; family history and Great War in Australia
family history and Great War in Australia: commemoration day (Anzac Day 2, 41–42, 48, 51; Anzac legend 39, 40, 45–46; Anzac spirit 42; Victorian Anzac Centenary Committee 51–52); Families and Friends of the First A.I.F. 50; family histories and national narratives 39–41, 52–53; 'Mapping Our Anzacs' website (National Archives of Australia) 47–48, 49, 50; renewed interest in Great War (1980s-) 41–43; role of government agencies 50–52; role of politicians 41–42; self-examination and national narratives 44–45; soldiers' repatriation files archive 39–40, 50; soldiers' suffering and the Anzac legend 45–46; strength of public myths 47; understanding of context and of impact on families 48–50, 51; *see also* amateur family history phenomenon; Anzac
Farm, The, *All Together Now* 121
Faulks, Sebastian, *Birdsong* 59, 63–64, 66, 70, 236
Fauré, Gabriel, *Requiem* 120
Ferdinand, Archduke Franz 11
First A.I.F., Families and Friends of 50
First World War, diversity of terminology 224
First World War centenary: politics of 1–2; public receptiveness 2–3
'First World War Poetry Digital Archive, The' (University of Oxford) 89n32
'First World War' portal (British Library) 89n32
First World War, The – An Illustrated History (A.J.P. Taylor) 26
Fischer, Fritz 226
Fitzpatrick, David 182
Flanders: Raad van Vlaanderen (Council of Flanders) 188; *see also* Belgian politics and the Great War; In Flanders Fields museum, Ypres (Belgium)
Flanders and Swann: *Twenty Tons of TNT* 119; *The War of 14–18* 119
Flanders, Michael *see* Flanders and Swann
Fleischer, Alain 104, 109n23
Flemish Interest (Vlaams Belang) 191, 201, 204
Flemish Movement 188, 189, 198, 201, 202, 205; *see also* Belgian politics and the Great War

244 Index

Flowers of the Forest (song) 120
Ford Maddox Ford, Parade's End 67
Forester's House (Simon Patterson) 106
For the Fallen (Laurence Binyon set to music) 112
Forthomme, Pierre 194
For Victory (Bolt Thrower) 122
Foucault, Michel 110
Foulds, John 118, 123; World Requiem 113–16
Fourteeneighteen – Soldier research (company) 30, 31, 34
frame analysis 61
France: commissioning of memorial art 90–92; First World War terminology 224; joint French/German exhibition 11; war narratives (First World War 224; Franco-German rapprochement and European integration 226–27; Second World War 225)
Franz Joseph, Emperor 216, 218
Freud, S. 69
Fringes of the Fleet (Edward Elgar) 112
Fröhlich, Hermann 212
Fromelles (France), 'Cobbers' (Peter Corlett), Australian Memorial Park 100, 101, 102
Front Movement/Frontbeweging (Belgian) 188–89, 190, 194, 195, 196, 198, 202
Fussell, Paul 117; The Great War and Modern Memory 80
futility of war 66, 78, 79, 80, 81, 110, 123–24

Gallipoli: Anzac Day service (2015) 51; Australian public's knowledge of 2; Bob Hawke's 'pilgrimage' to 41; Green Hill cemetery war memorial 175; last Gallipoli veteran's state funeral (Australia) 42; significance of campaign for Australia 232; see also Anzac; Turkey and Çanakkale War (Gallipoli Campaign)
Gallipoli (Peter Weir) 41, 43, 46, 233
Gammage, Bill, The Broken Years 41
Geertz, Clifford 110–11
Gelibolu (Tolga Örnek) 155
Gellner, E. 148
'genealogical imaginary' concept 28
genealogy, and First World War 9
Genteur, Noël 95
Germany: Douaumont ossuary German remains controversy 102; First World War terminology 224; joint French/German exhibition 11; low-key approach to commemoration 11; public's knowledge of war history 2, 3; Tannenberg Memorial 225; war narratives (First World War narrative 224–25; First World War narrative and German reunification 234–35; Franco-German rapprochement and European integration 226–27; Second World War narrative 225–26); Western Front military cemeteries 101–3
Gezi Park protests (Turkey) 161
Giannangeli, M. 71n24
Gifted and Talented initiatives 84
Golden, Michael 178
Good-bye to All That (Robert Graves) 60
'Good War, The' (Studs Terkel) 228
Gorbachev, Mikhail 129
Gove, Michael 74, 81
Granatstein, Jack 2
Grandfather wasn't Nazi (Opa war kein Nazi) study 208
Grant, Peter 12
Graves, Robert 77, 210; Good-bye to All That 60; Remembrance Day broadcasts 126n35
Grayson, Richard 173
Great War and Modern Memory, The (Paul Fussell) 80
'Great War Archive, The' project (University of Oxford) 32
Great War, The (BBC series) 26, 232
Green Hill cemetery war memorial (Gallipoli) 175
Gregory, Adrian 229
Grey, Edward 119
Gül, Abdullah 159

Haig, Douglas 114–15
Halbwachs, Maurice, On Collective Memory 110
Hämmerle, Christa 212–13, 218
Hanioğlu, S. M. 149
Hanks, R. 72n37
Hanna, Emma 12, 26
Hardy, Thomas 77
Haring, Sabine A. 14; Emotion, Habitus und Erster Weltkrieg (Kuzmics and Haring) 214
Harp Mecmuası (war magazine), Çanakkale and Mustafa Kemal 148
Harte, Paddy 171
Hartinger, Franz Matthias 213
Hartley, Tom 173
Harvey, P. J., Let England Shake 123–24
Hasan, H. 71n27
Hawke, Bob 41

Heer, Friedrich 214
'Heirlooms 4 Heroes' leaflets 21–23, *22*
heldenhuldezerken (hero's tombstones) 186–87, *187*, 189–91, *191*, 194–96, 202, *203*; *see also* Belgian politics and the Great War
Hellebaut, Albert 195
Hemingway, Ernest 228
Heritage Lottery Fund: 'Belfast nationalists and WW1' project 180; 'Decade of Centenaries' guidance 180; 'The forgotten men of Dundonald cemetery' project 180
Her Privates We (Frederic Manning) 77
Hill, Susan 77
Hirsch, Marianne 8, 28–29
Historial de la Grande Guerre museum, Péronne (France) 98, 101–2, 106, 235
historians: Bielefeld School 226; and commemoration 182; narrowing gap between historians and public 23–24; revisionist historians 23, 59, 60, 63, 68, 124
historical remembrance 7, 10, 14
Hitler, Adolf 224, 225, 226, 227, 228, 230
Hoffman, E. 37n48
Holbrook, Carolyn 10
Hollande, François 91–92, 96, 97
Holocaust: and building of democratic Europe 234; and 'era of the witness' 40; impact of 1960s revelations 225, 228; and memory boom 7; and National Curriculum (UK) 82; and postmemory/prosthetic memory 29
Holst, Gustav: *Ode to Death* 113; *Planet Suite* 120
Homer, *The Iliad* (in Arthur Bliss's *Morning Heroes*) 117
Hooper, Linley 42
'Hosties noires' (Léopold Sédar Senghor) 96
Howard, John 42
Howlin, Brendan 179
Hungary, fragmentation of 209
Hürriyet (newspaper), Anzac and Çanakkale commemorations 153

IJzer: IJzer, Battle of (1914) 188; IJzer Pilgrimage 190, *197*; IJzer Pilgrimage Committee 195, 196, 198, 199, 200, 202, 204; IJzer symbols 190, 196; IJzertoren (first tower 192–93, *193*, 194, 195–98, *197*; second tower 198–200, *199*, 202–3, 204); IJzerwake pilgrimage 191, 200–205; *see also* Belgian politics and the Great War
Iles, J. 37n58, 37n61

Iliad, The (Homer), in Arthur Bliss's *Morning Heroes* 117
Imperial War Museum, London, 'Lives of the First World War' project 10, 21, 31–34
Independent, The (newspaper): reference to Barker's *Regeneration* trilogy and Faulks' *Birdsong* novel 66; reference to *Blackadder Goes Forth* 62
Infantry Memorial of Brussels 193
In Flanders Fields museum, Ypres (Belgium) 98–99, 101
Institute of Education (University of London) 75
international perspective 223–24; Australian war narratives (First World War 232; Second World War 233); British narratives (First World War 229–30, 232; Second World War 230–31); France and Germany (French First World War narrative 224; French Second World War narrative 225; German First World War narrative 224–25; German Second World War narrative 225–26; rapprochement and European integration 226–27); Soviet Union and United States (Soviet First and Second World War narratives 227; US First World War narrative 227–28; US Second World War narrative 228; from world wars to global leadership 228–29); war remembrance since late 1980s (Britain 235–36; former Soviet states and Russia 234; reunified Germany 234–35; Turkey and Australia (Gallipoli) 235)
internet: and digitization of wartime records 27; and national memory 34
Interreg 14–18 Mémoire 91
Invalides, Les (Paris), Army Museum 96
'invention of tradition' concept 60, 70
Ipswich Unitarian Meeting House 66
Ireland: 36th (Ulster) Division 166, 171, 180, *181*, 230; Easter Rising (1916) 165–66, 229, 230; First World War narrative 229–30; post-1989 re-examination of First World War 235; Republican Sinn Féin 176; Sinn Féin 166, 173–74, 178, 179; Ulster unionists 166–67; *see also* Ireland and First World War commemorations; Northern Ireland
Ireland and First World War commemorations: commemoration and politics (1916 Rising and First World War 165–67; emergence of Northern

Ireland 167; narrative of healing 167; 'national amnesia' and 'Great Oblivion' 167–68); commemorations from 1920s to the Troubles 168; 'Decade of Centenaries' (Irish Department of Arts, Heritage and Gaeltacht programme 180–82; Northern Ireland Community Relations Council/Heritage Lottery Fund guidance 180); Heritage Lottery Fund projects ('Belfast nationalists and WW1' 180; 'The forgotten men of Dundonald cemetery' 180); historians and commemoration 182; memorials (Belfast Cenotaph 173; Cahir Great War memorial 171; Cork City war memorial 177, *177*; Irish National War Memorial, Islandbridge 168, 171, 173, 176; Killarney First World War memorial 174–75, *174*, 176; Wexford Great War memorial 177–80); memorial vandalism (Drogheda First World War memorial 169; Enniskillen 'Poppy Day bombing' 169; Limerick war memorial 169; Moy war memorial 169; South African War memorial, Cork 169); revival of interest in the war (family history and new 'Irishness' 169–70; Island of Ireland Peace Tower 171–72, *172*, 175, 176; joint Irish-British/nationalist-unionist commemorations 175–77; new memorials 174–75; Newry initiative 172–73; refurbishing of war memorials 171; Royal Dublin Fusiliers Association 170; Sinn Féin's engagement with commemorations 173–74; 'Somme Association' (Northern Ireland) 170, 175); Ulster (36th) Division 166, 171, 180, *181*

Ireland and the Great War (Keith Jeffery) 171
Irish Independent (newspaper), 'Moment of Healing' 176
Irish National War Memorial (Islandbridge, Dublin) 168, 171, 173, 176
Irish News (newspaper), Elizabeth II at Islandbridge 176
Irish Times (newspaper), Elizabeth II at Islandbridge 176
Islamism: Turkey 147, 155–56, 157, 159, 160; *see also* neo-Ottomanism
Island of Ireland Peace Tower (Mesen, Belgium) 171–72, *172*, 175, 176, 235
Isonzo Front 214
Italy, Vittorio Veneto victory and memorials 209

Jack, Michael 63–64
James, William 67
Jeffery, Keith 13; *Ireland and the Great War* 171
Jenkins, Simon 2
Jones, Adrian 151
Jones, H. 34n6
Jospin, Lionel 92, 95
Journey's End (R. C. Sherriff) 87n10, 230
Joyeux Noël (Christian Carion) 121
Jünger, Ernst, *Storm of Steel* 209
Justice and Development Party (AKP, Turkey) 147–48, 155–57, 159–61

Kahn-Harris, Keith 126n48
Kant, Vedica 13
Kastalsky, Alexander, *Requiem for the Fallen Heroes of the Allied Armies* 112
Keating, Paul 233
Kelly, Anthony 178, 179–80
Kemalism 147, 149
Kemal, Mustafa *see* Atatürk, Mustafa Kemal
Kenny, Enda 176
Kenyon, D. 25
Kern, Haïm, 'Ils n'ont pas choisi leur sépulture' (They did not choose their tomb) 92–95, *93*, *94*
Kettle, Thomas 229
Khrushchev, Nikita 227
Killarney First World War memorial (Ireland) 174–75, *174*, 176
King, Anthony 25, 33–34
Kinks, The, *Arthur (or the Decline and Fall of the British Empire)* 120
Kipling, Rudyard 77, 112
Knopfler, Mark, *Remembrance Day* 120
Kobarid (Caporetto, Slovenia) First World War Museum 235
Kolchak, Admiral Aleksandr 138
Kolh, Helmut 95
Kollwitz, Käthe, *The Grieving Parents*, Vladslo German war cemetery, Belgium 101
Koval'chuk, Andrei, Victory Park monument to the First World 132, 140–42, *141*
Krainova, Natalya 133
Kramer, A. 28
Kraus, Karl, *The Last Days of Mankind* 213–14
Kriuchkov, Koz'ma 136–37, 138
Kurds, and Turkey 156
Kusters, Frans 197
Kuzmics, Helmut 209; *Emotion, Habitus und Erster Weltkrieg* (Kuzmics and Haring) 214

Lacan, Jacques 110
Laidler, Eunice 44
Lambert, Constant 113
Landsberg, A. 28–29
Landscapes and Sites of Memory of the Great War (UNESCO) 91
Lapie, Christian, 'The constellation of grief' 95–96
Last Days of Mankind, The (Karl Kraus) 213–14
leaflets, 'Heirlooms 4 Heroes' leaflets 21–23, *22*
Ledward, Gilbert 123
Le Monde (newspaper), Haïm Kern's sculpture 92
Lenin, Vladimir 130, 228
Lernet-Holenia, *Die Standarte (The Standard)* 214
Let England Shake (P J Harvey) 123–24
Lewie, Jona, *Stop the Cavalry* 121
Lewis, Luke 121
Lieux de Mémoire (Pierre Nora) 110
Limerick war memorial (Ireland) 169
Li-tai-Po, in Arthur Bliss's *Morning Heroes* 117
Littlewood, Joan, *Oh! What a Lovely War!* 232
'Lives of the First World War' project (Imperial War Museum) 10, 21, 31–34
London Cenotaph 172
Longueval (France), South African Memorial and Museum, Cemetery and Visitor Centre 100
Lorette *see* Notre Dame de Lorette (France)
'Lost Men' (Paul Emmanuel) 108
Lourie, Marilyn 48, 49, 50
Lutyens, Edwin: Irish National War Memorial (Islandbridge, Dublin) 168, 171; London Cenotaph 172
Lynskey, Dorian 123

McAleese, Mary 171, 174–75, 176, 235
MacCarthy, Maud, and John Foulds's *World Requiem* 113–16
McCartney, Paul, 'Pipes of Peace' 121
Macdonald, Lyn 26
McGuinness, Martin 178
McKenna, Mark 41–42, 233
MacLeod, D. 71n23
McTell, Ralph, *England 1914* 119
Maes, Steven 202
Maison Forestière, La (Simon Patterson) 106
Mandela, Nelson 100
Mangin, General Charles 96
Mango, Andrew 162n5

Manning, Frederic, *Her Privates We* 77
'Mapping Our Anzacs' website (National Archives of Australia) 47–48, 49, 50
Marinetti, Filippo Tommaso 90
Marischka, Ernst, Sissi trilogy 215
Martin, F. X., '1916 – myth, fact and mystery' 167, 168
Maskey, Alex 173
Mattl, Siegfried 217
Meaux (France), Musée de la Grande Guerre du Pays de Meaux, France 98, 99
media representations of the Great War (Britain): cultural memory and frame analysis 60–61; framework of reference vs framework of memory 59; framing present with past (*Blackadder Goes Forth* TV series 59, 60, 62–63, 69, 70; *Downton Abbey* TV series 64–65; Faulks's *Birdsong* novel 59, 63–64, 66, 70); framing sense of trauma (Barker's *Regeneration* novel 60, 65–66; Ford Maddox Ford's *Parade's End* (TV adaptation by T. Stoppard) 67; *Oh! What a Lovely War!* 67–68, 69; popular memory and cultural trauma concept 68–70); 'invention of tradition' concept 60, 70
Medinskii, Vladimir 133, 134, 141
Medvedev, Dmitrii 132
Mehmet Akif *see* Ersoy, Mehmet Akif
Meinecke, Friedrich 225, 226
memorial art and museums (Western Front): art, museums and sites of memory 90–91; art vs museums and memorials 103–4; Beaumont-Hamel Newfoundland Memorial 100; Canadian National Vimy Memorial 100; Chemin des Dames (Caverne du Dragon museum 95–96; Haïm Kern's sculpture 92–95, *93*, *94*); Cimetière chinois de Nolette, Noyelles-sur-Mer 100; contemporary artists (Alain Fleischer 104; Christine Canetti 104; Ernest Pignon-Ernest 105, *105*; Kader Attia 107–8; Kingsley Baird 106–7, *107*; Paul Emmanuel 108; Simon Patterson 106); Douaumont military cemetery, Verdun 95, 102; In Flanders Fields museum, Ypres 98–99, 101; Fromelles Australian Memorial Park (Peter Corlett's 'Cobbers') 100, *101*, *102*; Historial de la Grande Guerre museum, Péronne 98, 101–2, 106; Käthe Kollwitz's sculpture, Vladslo German war cemetery 101; Longueval South African Memorial and Cemetery 100; military cemeteries (British, American and German)

100–103; Musée de la Grande Guerre du Pays de Meaux 98, 99; Notre Dame de Lorette 2014 memorial 96–97; *Plugstreet 14–18 Experience* 97; Thiepval Memorial to the Missing of the Somme 108; Villers-Bretonneux military cemetery 100
Memorial Park Complex of the Heroes of the First World War (Moscow) 138, 139–40
memory: collective memory 4, 110; contested memory 130; counter-memory 194, 204; cultural memory 4–5, 60–61, 207–8; family memory 8; framework of reference vs framework of memory 59; inner vs outer memory 204; postmemory theory 8, 28–29; prosthetic memory 28–29; vs remembrance 4, 5; *see also* remembrance
memory booms 7–8
memory studies 3–4, 83–84
Menin (Menen) Gate, Ypres (Belgium) 98, 113, 176, 192
Merridale, Catherine 130, 227
Merry Christmas Fritz (The Buff Medways) 121
Middlebrook, Martin 26
military cemeteries: Belgian cemeteries and cultural affiliations 194–95; Western Front cemeteries 100–103
Miller, Gary 120
Milliyet (newspaper), Çanakkale martyrs' memorial fundraising campaign 152
Mitterrand, François 91–92, 95
Moffett, Colin 173
Moritz, Verena 211
Morning Heroes (Arthur Bliss) 112, 116–18
Morpurgo, Michael 77; *Private Peaceful* 66, 80; *War Horse* 66, 80, 81
Morricone, Ennio, *Cavatina* 120
Morton, H. V. 116
Moscow: Memorial Park Complex of the Heroes of the First World War 138, 139–40; Victory Park monument to the First World (Poklonnaia Gora) 132, 140–42, *141*
Moscow Times (newspaper), new history curriculum in Russia 133
Mosse, George 214
Moy war memorial (County Tyrone, Northern Ireland) 169
'mud, blood and poppycock' image 84; *see also* 'rats, gas, mud and blood' image
Mullen, John 112, 125n8
Murphy, B. 37n49

Murphy, Conor 173
Murphy, John A. 182
Murrison, Andrew 89n35
Musée de la Grande Guerre du Pays de Meaux (France) 98, 99
museo al aperto (open museum) concept 90
museums *see* memorial art and museums (Western Front)
music and Britain's remembrance of First World War: memory and music 110–11; music during the war 111–13; music in the inter-war years 113–18; post-1945 music 118–24
Mussolini, Benito 209
mutineers: Army Museum, Les Invalides 96; Caverne du Dragon (Chemin des Dames museum) 95; Haïm Kern's sculpture 92–95, *93*, *94*
'Mutineers' monument, The' 93
Myers, Kevin 170, 171

Naryshkin, Sergei 132
Nash, Paul 105
National Archives of Australia: and Anzac Day service (Gallipoli, 2015) 51; 'Mapping Our Anzacs' website 47–48, 49, 50
nationalism: Russia 134–37, 142–43; Turkey 148–49, 159
neo-Ottomanism 156, 159
New Flemish Alliance (Nieuw-Vlaamse Alliantie) 191, 201
New Musical Express (publication), *Harry Patch – In Memory of* (Radiohead) 121
Newry, County Down (Northern Ireland), war memorial 172–73
New Zealand, Kingsley Baird's 'Tomb' 106–7, *107*
Nice, David 126n55
Nichols, Robert, in Arthur Bliss's *Morning Heroes* 117
Nietzsche, Friedrich 112
Nieuw-Vlaamse Alliantie (New Flemish Alliance) 191, 201
Nikonov, Viacheslav 133, 134, 135, 137
Noakes, L. 32
Nora, Pierre, *Lieux de Mémoire* 110
Northern Ireland: Belfast Cenotaph 173; 'Belfast nationalists and WW1' (Heritage Lottery project) 180; creation of 167; Enniskillen 'Poppy Day bombing' 169; 'The forgotten men of Dundonald cemetery' (Heritage Lottery Fund project) 180; Somme Association 170,

175; war commemoration community initiatives 172–73; *see also* Ireland; Ireland and First World War commemorations
Northern Ireland Community Relations Council, 'Decade of Centenaries' guidance 180
Notre Dame de Lorette (France), new memorial (2014) 96–97
Nott, David 42, 44, 48–49
novels, and representation of the war 26–27
Novick, P. 69
Noyelles-sur-Mer (France), Cimetière chinois de Nolette 100

Observer, The (newspaper), teaching of First World War (teacher's letter) 81
Ode to Death (Gustav Holst) 113
Oh! What a Lovely War! 26, 59, 60, 66, 67–68, 118, 119, 232
O'Morchoe, Major General David, The 179
O Muilleoir, Mairtin 174
Onan, Necmettin Halil, 'Dur yolcu!' verses 146–47, *146*
Ons Vaderland (publication), *heldenhuldezerken* (hero's tombstones) 190
Ons Volk (publication), *heldenhuldezerken* (hero's tombstones) 190
Opa war kein Nazi (Grandfather wasn't Nazi) study 208
open museum (*museo al aperto*) concept 90
oral histories 26
Örnek, Tolga, *Gelibolu* 155
Osovets Fortress, defence of (1914–15) 135–36
Overmeire, Karim Van 201
Owen, Wilfred: and BBC Remembrance Day broadcasts 126n35; in Benjamin Britten's *War Requiem* 118; 'Dulce Et Decorum Est' 77, 81, 106, 121; *Forester's House* (Simon Patterson) 106; and futility of war perspective 66, 123; installation of as canonical figure 232; and revisionist historians 60; 'Spring Offensive' (in Bliss's *Morning Heroes*) 116–17; and teaching of First World War 77, 82, 87n12

Parade's End (Ford Maddox Ford) 67
pardons for executed soldiers (Britain) 65
Parish Church of St John-at-Hampstead (London) 66
Parker, P. 34
Parmaksız, P. M. Y. 148–49, 160, 161
Paşa, Enver 148
Passchendaele Experience, The (museum) 97

Pastoral Symphony, A (Ralph Vaughan Williams) 113, 117
Patch, Private Harry 24–25; *Harry Patch – In Memory of* (Radiohead) 120–21
Patterson, Simon, *Forester's House* 106
Paxman, Jeremy 74, 75
Peace Path (Carnic Alps) 218
Peace Tower *see* Island of Ireland Peace Tower (Mesen, Belgium)
Pennell, Catriona 11–12, 24, 89n37
'People's War' BBC website 32
Perdition (Disorder) 121
Péronne (France), Historial de la Grande Guerre museum 98, 101–2, 106, 235
Pétain, Marshal Philippe 225
Petrone, Karen 13
photographs, photographic tribute on Western Front *31*
Pickerd, Jeff 42, 49
Pignon-Ernest, Ernest, *Bois de Soyécourt, Somme* 105, *105*
Pillecyn, Filip De 196
'Pipes of Peace' (Paul McCartney) 121
Planet Suite (Gustav Holst) 120
Platoon (Oliver Stone) 121
Ploegsteert (Belgium), *Plugstreet 14–18 Experience* (interpretation centre) 97
Plowman, Max 21
Poète assassiné, Le (Guillaume Appolinaire) 103, 107
Ponticelli, Lazare 95
Pope, Jessie: 'The Call' 77; 'War Girls' 77
postmemory theory 8, 28–29
post-traumatic stress, and public perception of war 46
Pretty Things, The, *S.F. Sorrow* 119
Princip, Gavrilo 11
Private Peaceful (Michael Morpurgo) 66, 80
prosthetic memory 28–29; *see also* memory
Putin, Vladimir 129, 133, 137–38
Puts, Kenneth, *Silent Night* 121

Raad van Vlaanderen (Council of Flanders) 188
Radetzkymarsch (Josef Roth) 215–16
Radiohead, *Harry Patch (In Memory of)* 120–21
Raemdonck, Edward Van 200, 201
Raemdonck, Frans Van 200, 201
'rats, gas, mud and blood' image 60, 69; *see also* 'mud, blood and poppycock' image
Ravel, Maurice, *Le Tombeau de Couperin* 112
Read, Peter 42
Redmond, John 176, 177, 178

Redmond, William 176, 178
Regeneration (Pat Barker) 60, 65–66
Remarque, Erich Maria, *All Quiet on the Western Front* 209–10, 230
remembrance: beyond living memory 5–9; historical remembrance 7, 10, 14; vs memory 4, 5; *see also* memory
Remembrance Day (Leon Rosselson) 121
Remembrance Day (Mark Knopfler) 120
Remembrance sermons, references to Great War and fiction/poetry 66
Rentoul, J. 71n25
Republican People's Party (CHP, Turkey) 147, 151–52
Republican Sinn Féin (Ireland) 176
Requiem for the Fallen Heroes of the Allied Armies (Alexander Kastalsky) 112
Requiem (Frederick Delius) 112
Requiem (Gabriel Fauré) 120
revisionist historians 23, 59, 60, 63, 68, 124
Reynolds, David 3, 23, 24, 34
Richardson, Marc 120–21
Rieff, David 182
Robertshaw, A. 25
Robinson, Mary 170–71
Rodenbach, Albert 189
Romanov monarchy, nostalgia for 138
Rootham, Cyril, *For the Fallen* (Laurence Binyon) 112
Roots (TV series) 26
Roper, Michael 5, 10, 38n67
Rosenberg, Isaac 66, 77
Rosoux, V. 192, 206n17
Rosselson, Leon, *Remembrance Day* 121
Roth, Josef, *Radetzkymarsch* 215–16
Royal Dublin Fusiliers Association 170
Rushton, Jan 66
Russia: All-Russian War Cemetery 227; post-1991 re-examination of First World War 234; *see also* Russia and centenary of First World War; Soviet Union
Russia and centenary of First World War: focus on official narratives 130–31; historical perspective (from 'glasnost' to Putin era) 129–30; international component of commemoration 134; Memorial Park Complex of the Heroes of the First World War (Moscow) 138, 139–40; nationalism and reinterpretation of the war as 'heroic' 134–37, 142–43; nostalgia for Romanov monarchy 138; relationship between First World War and Russian Revolution 137–38; relationship between First World War and Second World War 139–40; Remembrance Day (1 August), designation of 132; Russian Historical Society and new history curriculum 132–33; Russian Military History Society 133, 135–36, 138, 140–42; Tsarskoe Selo Museum of the First World War 132, 138–39; Victory Park monument to the First World (Poklonnaia Gora, Moscow) 132, 140–42, *141*; Women's Battalion of Death, production of film on 132
Russian Historical Society 132–33
Russian Military History Society 133, 135–36, 138, 140–42

Saar, M. 28
Sach, Carole 47–48
Sands, Bobby 178, 179
Santos, C. 33
Sarkozy, Nicolas 91–92, 95
Sassoon, Siegfried: and BBC Remembrance Day broadcasts 126n35; and futility of war perspective 66, 123; installation of as canonical figure 232; and pacific propaganda 210; poems set to music 112; and pro-war Anglican clergymen 119; and revisionist historians 60; and teaching of First World War 77, 82, 87n12
satire, and representation of the war 26
Satter, David 145n30
Saunders, N. 27
Savage, Kirk 204
Scates, Bruce 40, 45, 50
Schmidt-Dengler, Wendelin 215
Schofield, J. 27
schools *see* teaching of First World War (English secondary schools)
Schopenhauer, Arthur 112
Scotland, Home Rule agenda and First World War 230, 235
Second World War: combined commemoration of First and Second World War (Russia) 139–40; memory boom 7; 'People's War' BBC website 32; *see also* international perspective
Selby, E. M. 230
Senghor, Léopold Sédar, 'Hosties noires' 96
Seraji-Bozorgzada, Nasrine 95
Serbia, and First World War commemorations 11
sermons, references to Great War and fiction/poetry 66
S.F. Sorrow (The Pretty Things) 119
Sheehy, John 176

Sheffield, Gary 34n5
Shelby, Karen 13–14
Sherriff, R. C. 87n12; *Journey's End* 87n10, 230
Silent Night (Kenneth Puts) 121
Simon, Heinrich 112
Sinclair, Monica 43, 44
Sinn Féin party (Ireland) 166, 173–74, 178, 179; *see also* Republican Sinn Féin (Ireland)
Sissi trilogy (Ernst Marischka) 215
Sloboda, John 110
Smith, A. 159
'social commemoration' concept 27
soldiers: family historians' view of 29; photographic tribute on Western Front 31; rise of the 'traumatised soldier' 40–41; soldiers' songs 111–12, 116, 118; soldier's story, the 7
Somme Association (Northern Ireland) 170, 175
Sorrow and the Pity, The/Le Chagrin et la Pitié (film) 225
South African Memorial and Museum, Cemetery and Visitor Centre (Longueval, France) 100
South African War memorial (Cork, Ireland) 169
Soviet Union: first and second world war narratives 227; war narratives and global leadership 228–29; *see also* Russia; Russia and centenary of First World War
Spender, Percy 233
Spirit of England, The (Edward Elgar) 112
'Spring Offensive' (Wilfred Owen) 116–17
Stalin, Josef 227
Standarte, Die (Alexander Lernet-Holenia) 214
Stanford, Charles Villiers: *At the Abbey Gate* 112; *Eroica* 112
Stone, Oliver, *Platoon* 121
Stoppard, Tom, *Parade's End: Adapted for Television* 72n43
Stop the Cavalry (Jona Lewie) 121
Storm of Steel (Ernst Jünger) 209
Strachan, Hew 2
Sunday Sun (newspaper), reference to Faulks's *Birdsong* 64
Sun, The (newspaper), reference to *Blackadder Goes Forth* 62
Suppanz, Werner 209, 214–15, 217
Swann, Donald *see* Flanders and Swann

Tannenberg Memorial (Germany) 225
Tardi, Jacques 99

Taylor, A.J.P., *The First World War – An Illustrated History* 26
teaching of First World War (English secondary schools): details of AHRC study and issues 74–75; English literature texts and history topics taught 75–77; goals and motivations of teachers 77–82; obstacles to wide-ranging/nuanced teaching 82–83, 84–85; opportunities for more innovative teaching 83–86
television series: *Blackadder Goes Forth* (comedy) 59, 60, 62–63, 69, 70; *Britain's Great War* (history) 74; *Downton Abbey* (drama) 64–65; *The Great War* (history) 26, 232; *Roots* (drama) 26; *Who Do You Think You Are?* (family history) 28; World War One At Home (history) 74
Terkel, Studs, 'The Good War' 228
Thiepval Memorial to the Missing of the Somme (France) 108; 'Ulster Tower' 166
Thomas, Edward 77, 87n12
Thomson, Alistair 39–40, 50
Thomson, P. 71n29
Those Once Loyal (Bolt Thrower) 122–23
Times, The (newspaper), John Foulds's *World Requiem* review 115
Todman, Dan: attraction of rediscovering the war 35n10; British public's knowledge of war history 15n8; cultural representations of the war 110; remembrance and experienced vs unexperienced past 5–6; war memory and family history 8; war's cultural baggage 29
Tombeau de Couperin, Le (Maurice Ravel) 112
trauma: cultural trauma concept 68–69; as a mode of analysis 69
Treaty of Brest-Litovsk (1918), Vladimir Putin on 137–38
Treaty of Rome (1957) 226
Treaty of Trianon (1920) 209
Treaty of Versailles (1919) 224, 225, 228, 230
Trenker, Luis 212
Tsarskoe Selo Museum of the First World War 132, 138–39
Turkey: AKP (Justice and Development Party) 147–48, 155–57, 159–61; Anzac Cove joint Australian-Turkish services 235; Armenian genocide issue 11, 160–61; Association of Turkish Travel Agencies (TÜRSAB) 153–54; CHP (Republican People's Party) 147, 151–52; Gezi Park protests 161; Islamism 147,

155–56, 157, 159, 160; *see also* Turkey and Çanakkale War (Gallipoli Campaign)
Turkey and Çanakkale War (Gallipoli Campaign): 'Dur yolcu!' verses and historical background 146–48, *146*; Kemalist state and Çanakkale myth 148–52 (Atatürk memorial on Çanakkale battlefields *152*; Çanakkale martyrs' memorial 151–52); public re-engagement with Çanakkale (1990s-) 152–55 (institution of Martyrs' Day 153–54, 160; ordinary soldiers' statues 154–55, *154*; television shows, films and documentaries 155); Turkish identity and AKP's reinterpretation of Çanakkale 155–61 (Çanakkale Epic Promotion Centre 158–59; symbolic cemetery 157–58, *158*)
TÜRSAB (Association of Turkish Travel Agencies) 153–54
Twenty Tons of TNT (Flanders and Swann) 119
Twomey, Christina 40–41
Tyne Cot Commonwealth war cemetery (Belgium) 176

Uhl, Heidemarie 217, 218
Ulster, 36th (Ulster) Division 166, 171, 180, *181*, 230
'Ulster Tower' (Thiepval) 166
Ulster unionists 166–67; *see also* Ireland; Ireland and First World War commemorations; Northern Ireland
UNESCO, Landscapes and Sites of Memory of the Great War 91
United Kingdom *see* Britain
United States: First World War terminology 224; war narratives (First World War 227–28; Second World War 228); war narratives and global leadership 228–29; Western Front cemeteries 100
University of London, Institute of Education 75
University of Oxford: 'The First World War Poetry Digital Archive' 89n32; 'The Great War Archive' project 32
University of Vienna, Institut für Wirtschafts-und Sozialgeschichte, Dokumentationsarchiv lebensgeschichtlicher Aufzeichnungen 217
University of Wolverhampton, First World War Research Group 89n31

Vanslambrouck, Johan 201–2
Vaughan Williams, Richard, *A Pastoral Symphony* 113, 117

Verdery, Katherine 205
Verdun (France): 1984 commemoration (Mitterrand and Kohl) 95; Douaumont ossuary, France 95, 102
Verplancke, Peter 202
Verschaeve, Cyriel 188, 190, 195, 199, 201
victimhood 69, 94–95
Victorian Anzac Centenary Committee (Australia) 51–52
Victory Park monument to the First World War (Poklonnaia Gora, Moscow) 132, 140–42, *141*
Vietnam War 41, 46, 119, 228
Villers-Bretonneux (France), military cemetery 100
Vimy (France), Canadian National Vimy Memorial 100
Vimy Ridge, battle of (1917), Canadian public's knowledge of 2
Vines, Margaret 46
Vittorio Veneto, battle of (1918) 209
Vlaams Belang (Flemish Interest) 191, 201, 204
Vladslo, Belgium, *The Grieving Parents* (Käthe Kollwitz), Vladslo German war cemetery 101
Völter, B. 208
Vozick-Levinson, Simon 121

w2k (weltkrieg2Kindheiten – world war2childhoods) research group 208
Wales, Home Rule agenda and First World War 230, 235
Wallis, James 10
Ward, Stuart 233
'War Girls' (Jessie Pope) 77
War Horse (Michael Morpurgo) 66, 80, 81
War of 14–18, The (Flanders and Swann) 119
war poetry: and BBC Remembrance Day broadcasts 126n35; 'The First World War Poetry Digital Archive' (University of Oxford) 89n32; set to music 112, 124; and teaching of First World War 79–80, 81–82; *see also* Owen, Wilfred; Sassoon, Siegfried
War Requiem (Benjamin Britten) 112, 118–19, 120, 123, 124
Watkins, Glenn 112, 124n6
Watson, J. 26
Weber, Fritz 212
Weir, Peter, *Gallipoli* 41, 43, 46, 233
Wertsch, J. V. 61
Western Front *see* memorial art and museums (Western Front)

Wexford Great War memorial (Ireland) 177–80
Wharton, Edith, *Fighting France, from Dunquerque to Belfort* 105–6
White, Jenny 155, 156
Whiteside, Elizabeth 43–44, 45–46
Whitman, Walt, in Arthur Bliss's *Morning Heroes* 117
Who Do You Think You Are? (TV series) 28
Wieviorka, Annette 40
'Willing Experts' 89n31
Wilson, Gordon and Marie 169
Wilson, Harold 231
Wilson, Ross 11, 35n17, 35n25 to 27, 36n45, 38n69
Wilson, Woodrow 227, 228
Winter, Jay: drama of and fascination with war 161; historical remembrance 7, 10, 14; memory booms and witnesses 7–8; memory reconstruction process 208; memory vs remembrance 3, 4; remembrance and family life 9, 10, 29; remembrance and multiplicity of groups 149
witnesses: 'era of the witness' 40; and remembrance 7

Wit, Wim de 202
Women's Battalion of Death (Russia, 1917) 132
Wood, Henry 112
World Requiem (John Foulds) 113–16
'World War One At Home' BBC series 74
Wydra, Harald 6

Yan, G. 33
Yeltsin, Boris 129
Yeni Mecmua (The New Review), Çanakkale and Mustafa Kemal 148
Young Men's Christian Association (YMCA), Music Department's motto 113
Ypersele, L. van 192, 206n17
Ypres (Belgium), In Flanders Fields museum 98–99, 101
Yugoslavia, dissolution of and re-examination of First World War 234

Ziino, Bart 10
Žižek, S. 68
Zombies, The, *Butcher's Tale (Western Front 1914)* 119
Zürcher, E. J. 149, 163n31